CONSUMER HEALTH AND PRODUCT HAZARDS - COSMETICS
AND DRUGS, PESTICIDES, FOOD ADDITIVES

The MIT Press
Cambridge, Massachusetts, and London, England

CONSUMER HEALTH AND PRODUCT HAZARDS - COSMETICS
AND DRUGS, PESTICIDES, FOOD ADDITIVES


VOL. 2 OF THE LEGISLATION OF PRODUCT SAFETY


Samuel S. Epstein and Richard D. Grundy, editors

Dedicated by Samuel S. Epstein to his children:
Mark, Julian, and Emily

This book was typed by Kathy Lane.
It was printed by Clark-Franklin-Kingston Press
and bound by the Colonial Press, Inc.
in the United States of America.

Library of Congress Cataloging in Publication Data

Epstein, Samuel S.
Consumer Health and Product Hazards - Cosmetics and Drugs,
Pesticides, Food Additives.


[The Legislation of Product Safety, v. 2]

CONTENTS: v. 2.  Regulatory aspects.
1.  Hazardous substances.  2.  Product safety.
I.  Grundy, Richard D., joint author.  II.  Title.
T55.3.H3E67        604'.7        74-995
ISBN 0-262-05015-3

# CONTENTS

"Consumerism" is a word much in the air today, and there are many opinions as to the import of the "new consumerism." Yet, at base, consumerism is a reflection of the old fashioned sense of fair play.

[Consumerism is the product of frustration:

- about shoddy goods and empty promises of satisfaction;
- at unanswered complaints and faceless sellers;]
- above all, at the endless shrinking of the consumer dollar - an inflated dollar for deflated values.

And consumerism is anger:

- at slippery Madison Avenue tricks of deception and confusion;
- at polished techniques for turning our children into programmed buying agents for toys that don't work and food that won't nourish.

At the heart of consumerism lies an overriding sense of injustice and of betrayal of our faith in the integrity of our society and its institutions, particularly business and government.

The American people have become an angry, alienated people. A constant source of consumer outrage has been the nagging gap between the promise of an abundant, affluent consumer economy and the frustrating reality which the consumer faces in the daily, dreary round of confrontations. In effect, the marketplace has become a remote government without any apparent humanity and accountability.

Here is how biologist Barry Commoner describes the post-World War II American revolution:

"In general, what has happened is that old production technologies have been displaced by new ones. Soap has been displaced by synthetic detergent; natural fibers - cotton and wool - have been displaced by synthetic ones; steel and lumber have been displaced by aluminum, plastics and concrete; railroad freight has been displaced by truck freight; returnable bottles have been displaced by non-returnable ones. On the road the low powered automobile engines of the 20s and 30s have been displaced by high powered ones. On the farm, where per capita production has remained about constant, the amount of harvested acreage has decreased; in effect fertilizer has displaced land. Older methods of insect control have been displaced by synthetic insecticides, such as DDT; for

controlling weeds, the cultivator has been displaced by the
herbicide spray.  Grange feeding of livestock has been
displaced by feedlots.  In each of these cases, what has
changed drastically is the technology of production rather
than overall output of the economic good."

    While this technology has been one of the most formative
agents in our country - it has lengthened our lives, improved
our health, increased our physical comfort, fed, clothed, and
sheltered us - it has also been the source of frustration and
outrage.
    What must we do to help our nation maintain our
technological excellence, the benefits of which have fueled
the dreams, hopes and talents of countless citizens?  How can
we steer and manage this potent force for change so as to be
sure that our technologies do not create unexpected, unwanted
consequences or develop a mindless, self-renewing momentum
that might threaten the treasured human and humane qualities
of our society?  How can we assess the implications of planned
technological developments and the possible influences on
social goals and values, on the health and safety of our
citizens, and on the quality of our environment?
    Increasingly, business is cast as the villain.  Unfair?
Yes, it's unfair.  For decades business has done precisely
what the country has asked it to do - exploit the abundant
natural resources of this country; create jobs and secure the
fruits of technology; and provide the highest standard of
living in the world.  Yet instead of being grateful, the
American public seems hell-bent on making business a scapegoat
for every evil, real or imagined, which plagues our country.
    The failures that have occurred have started brewing a
dangerous and senseless confrontation between technology and
society which imperils our future.  The cry:  "Turn technology
off" keeps rising.  But the cry should be for us to "turn
technology on" - on to the fulfillment of the promise.  [In
the area of product safety there must be technology:
technological innovation leading to refined quality control
procedures, to sophisticated risk-based analysis which will
result in sound commercial policies, and to sound government
regulatory actions and reactions.] The safety- and quality-
oriented disciplines which have traditionally been used
extensively in, say, the aerospace industry must now be used
with increasing frequency in consumer-product industries.
    An example of self-interest rather than public interest and
of the advantages of self-regulation to an industry is the
cigarette controversy.  Cigarette smoking, formerly regarded

as an innocent habit, now stands condemned by the medical and
scientific community as a lethal health hazard.  But the
cigarette industry, in its desire to maintain sales and
profits by attracting women, if not children, to the habit,
now uses seductive advertising messages in magazines, in
newspapers, and at points of sale.

In 1964, the health community and several of us in the
Congress called for a warning on the hazards of cigarettes on
packages and in advertisements, for labeling of cigarettes as
to tar and nicotine content, and for the elimination of
advertising directed towards the young people, primarily on
television and radio.

After many years of what may have been the most bitter
battle in the Congress on a health matter, the industry
volunteered to place a warning in cigarette advertisements, it
volunteered to remove cigarette advertising from the broadcast
media, and it volunteered to place its tar and nicotine
information in cigarette advertising.  But it took years of
prodding, shouting, charges, and counter-charges to tear down
the man-the-barricades attitude prevalent in much of the
industry.  During those years what faith people may have had
in the integrity of the tobacco industry gradually eroded.
The only ones who profited by this battle were the law firms
handling the industry's case in the Congress and the
regulatory agencies.

Our challenge in the Congress is to protect consumers, and
through appropriate legislation, to reform and strengthen
existing institutions, both public and private, and enhance
their capabilities of responding adequately to consumer needs.
Beyond consumer education programs and the monitoring of
business practices, we must give the consumer the legal
weapons for self-help in the courts.  For example, we must
institute procedural reforms in consumer class actions.  Only
through self-help in the marketplace can the citizen remain
independent and escape the vagaries of corporate and
governmental indifference.

This volume discusses regulatory policies and practices in
a variety of areas of consumer concern:  cosmetics and drugs,
pesticides, and food additives.  Just as the legislator must
determine policy based upon the evidence which has already
been generated and is available to him, it is necessary for
any regulatory scheme to create a balance between premarket
assessments and post-marketing regulation.

Unfortunately, due to the sophistication of manufacturing
processes it is often impossible for the consumer to have an
input into either the premarket assessment of consumer

products or the regulatory judgments involving them.  Such
opportunities are critical in our consumer culture.

In reviewing the subject matter of the chapters in this
volume, it is interesting to note that significant legislation
has passed in some of the areas mentioned, while a dearth of
adequate regulation exists in other areas.

We must remember that even the best of laws, if not
enforced evenhandedly, are meaningless.  What we have come to
know as "Watergate" is an important challenge to both the
business and the government community.  Decision making
processes must be based upon facts, must be administered
fairly, and must above all be conducted under policies in the
best interest of the American people.  If any one of these
three criteria is not adhered to, then more fuel will be
tossed upon the fires of alienation.

Frank E. Moss

JOHN E. BLODGETT, Ph.D.
Analyst in Environmental Policy, Environmental Policy
Division, Congressional Research Division, Library of
Congress, Washington, D.C.

RICHARD D. GRUNDY, M.P.H., E.I.T.
Professional Staff, Senate Committee on Public Works;
Executive Secretary, National Fuels and Energy Policy Study,
Senate Committee on Interior and Insular Affairs, Washington,
D.C.

ROBERTA G. MARKS
Executive Editor, Product Management Magazine, Medical
Economics Co., Oradell, N.J.

RALPH NADER
Consumer Advocate, Washington, D.C.

JAMES TURNER, J.D.
Co-director, Consumer Action for Improved Food and Drugs,
Washington, D.C.

HARRISON WELLFORD
Chief Legislative Assistant to Senator Philip A. Hart (D.-
Mich.), United States Senate, Washington, D.C.

CONSUMER HEALTH AND PRODUCT HAZARDS - COSMETICS
AND DRUGS, PESTICIDES, FOOD ADDITIVES

# 1

## THE CONCEPTS OF NEW CONSUMERISM

Richard D. Grundy

CONTENTS

## Introduction

Western culture is aptly characterized as one primed by
population growth and driven by an unprecedented capacity for
technological innovation.  Moreover, our capability for
innovation has become generally equated with progress to such
a degree that society's prevailing attitude is to accept such
innovations as inherently "good."

Yet all change originates from creative human efforts,
whether technological innovation or reform of social policy.
Thus the problems of environmental degradation and
unanticipated consumer product hazards can also be attributed
to the actions of man himself.

Consequently, in recent years there has emerged a school of
thought that technologic innovations can be directed and, in
particular, prejudged as to their economic, societal, and
environmental implications.  This concept has come to be known
as "technology assessment."

Examples of our previous failure to perceive or prejudge
the adverse consequences of technological innovations abound.
Witness the presence of DDT in animals whose life cycles are
confined to the Antarctic; the health effects of cigarettes,
LSD, the PCB's or the various contraceptive pills.  A long
list of similar examples attests to the wisdom of adopting a
skeptical view of our capacity for appraising and preassessing
the benefits and, particularly, the social costs of change or
innovation.  Stemming from a realization of this apparent
failure, the consumer and environmental advocate has emerged
as a significant force for social reform.

Nevertheless, innovation has been an essential ingredient
to the achievement of our standard of living and a principal
characteristic of our social structure.  At issue is whether
what has come to be accepted as progress, from a short-term
perspective, is always beneficial for our society over the
long term.

In the last two hundred years, the U.S. population has
increased 50 times over, and spread across an entire
continent.  In the process, the American consumer has become
accustomed to an abundance of material goods and energy.  This
cultural expansion has also been accompanied by a relentless
and often poorly understood transformation of natural
ecosystems.  The not so small social cost is the highest per
capita consumption, or depletion, of nonrenewable as well as
renewable resources in the world.

In a very real sense the risks of adverse environmental and
societal effects are the full price society must assume for
progress.  The challenge is how to keep such adverse consumer

and environmental risks to a minimum.  A principal feature of
technology assessment is a concern for finding ways to include
or reflect these risks in business cost accounting.  The
objective is to internalize these costs so that the market
place reflects the full social costs of progress or growth.

The public debate that has followed over the social costs
of growth reflects an increased awareness that the way growth
is incurred and the uses to which growth is put by society
requires a continuing re-examination.  The social costs of
growth or the adverse consequences of the processes of
production, plus the side effects of individual technologic
innovations - a responsibility for which private entrepreneurs
are not easily held accountable.

Once such social accounting becomes a matter of general
business practice, the composition of the gross national
product (GNP) will be altered in the direction of increased
quality.  This internalization of social costs also would aid
in redirecting growth toward a more socially desirable mix.

Unfortunately our present legacy is a crescendo of concern
for technology's adverse consumer, environmental, and public
health effects that have become almost synonymous, in the
public's eye, with any new technological innovations.  Yet the
problems that arise are characteristic of much broader social
concerns:  the historical contradiction and conflict between
man's natural desire and quest to improve his material
standard of living - which requires an ever increasing
consumption of natural resources - and man's concurrent desire
to conserve these resources and the environment for the use of
future generations.  For Western man and his governmental and
economic institutions, this inherent conflict in social values
represents an unprecedented challenge.

Also, new political forces have come upon the scene,
testing the responsiveness of our society's institutions.
Consumer and environmental imperatives alike are the symptoms
of a social movement which, generally, seeks to augment the
rights and powers of the consumer in relation to the sellers.

## The Prologue

The American Consumer  Today the American consumer is more
concerned about the products he purchases than at any other
time in history.  His fixation not only encompasses price but
it extends to issues of the safety, the quality, and the
utility of products from the perspective of meeting his
personal needs as well as desires.

As a protest movement, the new consumerism must be viewed

as a signal from the body politic that something is seriously wrong. Were such signs of deep societal problems and strains to be ignored, an explosive situation would result. At issue is the incorporation of intellectually refined concepts of the common good into today's corporate and government practices.

Thus, the principal feature of the "new consumerism" is the addition of a requirement for social efficacy as a condition of human use. The challenge is to foresee and take the necessary steps to forestall the adverse effects and risks of actions by government, business, and society alike.

Achievement of this objective will require the adoption of a new perspective by business - a concern not only for the immediate or short-term benefits of one's labors, but also a concern for the ultimate consequences of one's actions or decisions over the longer term for the consumer, for the environment, and for society. This concept reflects the difference between serving consumer desires efficiently, for today, and serving their long-run interests, which includes protection against any adverse implication of technological innovation (for example, protection against innovations that may carry with them the possibility of adverse chronic health effects).

The essential ingredient of the new consumerism is a national perspective in which, quite properly, technology as well as our social institutions are our servants, not masters. For, inherently, technology has no ideology, no morality, no sense of social purpose or the common good. In truth, as citizens, we must ultimately provide technology with a sense of moral direction and human purpose. This is the essence of the "new consumerism."

Consumerism There is a growing awareness by business that today's consumer is quite different from his predecessors. "Consumerism" is usually dated from President John Kennedy's March 15, 1962, address to the Congress on consumer affairs.

However, the first recognition by the Congress of the need for consumer protection actually occurred with passage in 1872 of the Criminal Fraud Statute. Charges against the railroads, in 1887, also led to establishment of the Interstate Commerce Commission. Today, the movement is more appropriately termed "new consumerism," since this is the third wave in this century.

Phase I: 1901 to 1916 The 20th century's first major consumer movement came in the early 1900s, and resulted in enactment of the Sherman Antitrust Act in the United States and the Combines Act in Canada.

In retrospect, we can see that this first consumer movement was fueled by such factors as rising prices, the conditions of the meat packing plants that were attacked by Upton Sinclair in his novel The Jungle, and "ethical" drug scandals that resulted in death and illness (1).

This period saw the establishment of the Food and Drug Administration (FDA) in 1906 and the Federal Trade Commission (FTC) in 1915. Statutes included the Pure Food and Drug Act, and the Meat Inspection Act, both enacted in 1906.

Phase II: 1930s A second phase during the late 1920s and early 1930s stimulated establishment of such bodies as Consumer's Union. This movement was fanned by a number of factors, including an upturn in consumer prices in the midst of the depression, the sulfanilamide scandal, and the widely imitated Detroit housewife strike (1). This phase culminated in the strengthening of the Pure Food and Drug Act, in enlarging the FTC's powers, and establishment of the Federal Securities and Exchange Commission in 1934 to regulate "Wall Street."

Phase III: 1960 to Date The third phase of consumerism was born in the middle 1960s from a complex combination of circumstances, not the least of which was increasingly strained relations between standard business practices and long-run consumer interests (1). However, as far back as May 1934 Franklin D. Roosevelt, then Governor of New York, had predicted this eventual change when he said, "In the future we are going to think less about the producer and more about the consumer." (2)

New Consumerism During the early 1960s the new consumerism was sweeping through many countries. In the United Kingdom this third phase actually started almost two years before President Kennedy's 1962 address, when that nation's Board of Trade appointed a Royal Commission, the Malony Commission, which subsequently recommended a vigorous program of consumer protection. About this same time Sweden enacted comprehensive consumer protection statutes and regulations.

In the United States, consumerism was reborn in the mid-1960s because all of the conditions that normally combine to produce a successful social movement were present (1). Among the broad social factors present were an institutional conduciveness, structural strain, growth of a generalized belief, precipitating events, mobilization for action, and social control (3). When the climate was right this total situation then was fanned by Ralph Nader and other consumer advocates, the thalidomide tradegy, rising prices, the mass

media, and Presidential consumer messages to the Congress
beginning with the March 15, 1962, message of President
Kennedy, in which he declared four basic consumer rights:  the
right to be informed, the right to safety, the right to
choose, and the right to be heard.  Accompanied by a strong
legislative program to protect these rights, the "New
Frontier" was committed to a comprehensive consumer protection
program based on executive and legislative action.  However,
only one element of this program was realized during
President Kennedy's lifetime:  the first Consumer Advisory
Council, formed in 1962.

Under President Johnson the concept of a Consumer Advisory
Council was embraced and expanded.  In 1964, President Johnson
appointed the first Special Assistant to the President for
Consumer Affairs.  This period also saw enactment of such
legislation as the Truth-in-Lending and the Wholesale Meats
Acts (Table 1).

Previously identified with liberal Democrats, consumer
protection achieved a new scope when, in October 1969,
President Nixon asked the Congress to pass a "Buyer's Bill of
Rights," that stated,

"Consumerism in the America of the Seventies means that we
have adopted the concept of 'buyers rights.'  The buyer has
the right to expect that his health and safety are taken into
account by those who seek his patronage."  The buyer has a
right to register his dissatisfaction, and have his complaint
heard and weighed, when his interests are badly served." (4)

Although the President's message was viewed as inadequate
by some consumer advocates and public officials, it was the
first such message to emphasize the need for permanent
institutions to give the consumer representation.  The
proposals included provisions for a statutory Office of
Consumer Affairs within the Executive Office of the President;
a new Division of Consumer Protection in the Justice
Department; legislation to give private citizens the right --
upon successful termination of a government suit -- to bring
action in a federal court either individually or collectively
to recover damages; and legislation in the field of food and
drug safety (4).

Later (in 1971), President Nixon created by Executive
Order the Office of Consumer Affairs in the Executive Office
of the President.  At the time, he said:

"The increasing complexity and sophistication of many of our

Table 1 Major Consumer Protection Laws Enacted Between 1962
and 1973 (2)

| Year Enacted | Statute | Major Provisions |
| --- | --- | --- |
| 86th Congress 1962 | Kefauver-Harris Drug Amendments | Requires drug manufacturers to file all new drugs with the FDA and to label all drugs by generic name. All drugs must be pretested for safety and efficacy |
| 89th Congress 1966 | Fair Packaging and Labeling Act | Regulates the packaging and labeling of consumer goods. Provides that voluntary uniform packaging standards be established by industry |
| | National Traffic and Motor Vehicle Safety Act | Authorizes the Department of Transportation to establish compulsory safety standards for new and used tires and automobiles |
| | Child Protection Act | Strengthens Hazardous Substances Act of 1960 and prevents the marketing of potentially harmful toys. Permits FDA to remove inherently dangerous products from the market |
| | Drug Abuse Amendments | Regulates the sale of amphetamines, barbiturates |

Table 1 (cont.)

| Year Enacted | Statute | Major Provisions |
| --- | --- | --- |
| 1966 | Cigarette Labeling Act | Requires cigarette manufacturers to label cigarettes: "Caution: Cigarette smoking may be hazardous to your health" |
| 90th Congress 1967 | Wholesome Meat Act | Requires states to upgrade their meat inspection systems to federal standards and clean up unsanitary meat plants |
| | National Commission on Product Safety | Establishes a seven-member commission to review household products that represent hazards to public health and safety and file recommendations for necessary legislation |
| | Flammable Fabrics Act Amendments | Extends scope of 1953 Flammable Fabrics Act to allow the Secretary of Commerce to establish regulatory standards for clothing, bedding, draperies and other interior furnishings |
| | Clinical Laboratories Act | Requires all clinical laboratories operating in interstate commerce to be licensed by the Federal Government |
| 1968 | Fire Research and Safety Act | Provides funds to collect, analyze and disseminate |

Table 1 (cont.)

| Year Enacted | Statute | Major Provisions |
| --- | --- | --- |
| 1968 | Fire Research and Safety Act | information on fire safety, to conduct fire prevention education programs and conduct projects to improve fire-fighting efficiency |
| | Truth-in-Lending Act | Requires full disclosure of annual interest rates and other finance charges on consumer loans and credit buying, including revolving charge accounts |
| | Automobile Insurance Study | A two-year comprehensive study and investigation by the Department of Transportation to focus on the adequacy of state regulation of auto insurance and to evaluate industry rates, compensation, sales and policy discrimination practices |
| | Natural Gas Pipeline Safety | Authorizes the Secretary of Transportation to develop minimum safety standards for the design, installation, operation and maintenance of gas pipeline transmission facilities |
| | Poultry Inspection | Requires states to develop inspection |

Table 1 (cont.)

| Year Enacted | Statute | Major Provisions |
| --- | --- | --- |
| 1968 | Poultry Inspection | systems which meet federal standards for poultry and poultry products |
| | Fraudulent Land Sales | Requires federal registration of all land offered for sale through the mail to protect consumers against sharp and unscrupulous practices |
| | Radiation Control for Health and Safety | Directs Secretary of DHEW to set and enforce standards to control hazardous radiation from television sets, X-ray equipment, and other electronic devices. Establishes a committee to advise him on performance standards for electronic products capable of emitting radiation |
| 91st Congress 1969 | Child Protection and Toy Safety Act of 1969 | Amends the Federal Hazardous Substances Act to protect children from toys and other articles which contain thermal, electrical or mechanical hazards |
| | National Commission on Product Safety | Extends the life of the National Commission on Product Safety until June 1970 |

Table 1 (cont.)

| Year Enacted | Statute | Major Provisions |
|---|---|---|
| 1970 | Public Health Smoking Act | Bans cigarette commercials on radio and television effective Jan. 2, 1971.  Requires all cigarette packages to be labeled:  "Warning: The Surgeon General Has Determined That Cigarette Smoking Is Dangerous To Your Health" |
| | Egg Products Inspection Act | Provides for a Federal program of inspection of certain egg products |
| | Amendment to the Federal Deposit Insurance Act (Fair Credit Reporting Act) | Requires insured banks to maintain certain records, requires that certain transactions in U.S. currency be reported to the Department of the Treasury.  Also bans unsolicited credit cards and regulates credit bureaus |
| | Poison Prevention Packaging Act | Requires special packaging of potentially dangerous household goods to protect children from serious injury or illness resulting from handling, using, or ingesting such substances |
| | Occupational Safety and Health Act | Empowers the Federal Government to set and enforce health and |

Table 1 (cont.)

| Year Enacted | Statute | Major Provisions |
| --- | --- | --- |
| 1970 | Occupational Safety and Health Act | safety standards for all companies in interstate commerce. Creates a three-member commission to enforce the regulations |
| | Extension of the National Traffic and Motor Vehicle Safety Act of 1966 for three years | Authorizes funds to carry out the auto and tire safety provisions of the original act. Requires tire manufacturers to notify purchasers of defective tires and manufacturers of motor vehicles to notify purchasers and potential purchasers of performance and technical data at all dealer locations. Directs the Secretary of Transportation to set minimum standards for manufacture or sale of equipment intended exclusively to safeguard motor vehicles and their passengers |
| 92nd Congress 1971 | Lead-Based Paint Elimination Act of 1970 | Calls for financial assistance to help cities and communities develop and carry out intensive local programs to detect and treat incidents of such poisionings |

Table 1 (cont.)

| Year Enacted | Statute | Major Provisions |
|---|---|---|
| 1972 | Consumer Product Safety Act of 1972 | Creates an independent agency to protect consumers from unreasonable risk of injury from hazardous products. The Agency, to be headed by a five-member commission commission, would have the authority to set safety standards |
|  | Motor Vehicle Information and Cost Savings Act | Amends the National Traffic and Motor Vehicle Safety Act of 1966 in order to promote competition among motor vehicle manufacturers in the design and production of safe motor vehicles having greater resistance to damage. Requires the Secretary of Transportation to set front and rear bumper standards for passenger motor vehicles to eliminate or reduce the amount of damage sustained by autos in low-speed collisions and to reduce auto repair costs |
| 93rd Congress 1973 | Little Cigar Advertising Act | Amends the Federal Cigarette and Labeling Advertising Act to redefine the term "cigarette" so that |

Table 1 (cont.)

| Year Enacted | Statute | Major Provisions |
|---|---|---|
| 1973 | Little Cigar Advertising Act | cigars will be restricted in their advertising and promotion in the same manner as other cigarettes |

consumer goods are sometimes accompanied by the increasing possibility of product failure, malfunction, or inadvertent misuse resulting in physical danger to the consumer." (5)

Throughout this period, the political response of the business community only served to strengthen the cause of new consumerism. While an affirmative response to this movement from the business community was unlikely, many members, rather than remaining neutral, went so far as to attack, resist, or ignore the issues being raised by consumer advocates. Initially, legislative bodies also were slow to respond with positive programs, adding more fuel to allegations that the political system was unresponsive to consumer needs. This only served to foster the view on the part of consumer spokesmen that more direct action was needed. A number of organizations arose in defense of the consumer, including labor unions, consumer co-operatives, credit unions, product testing organizations, senior citizen groups, public interest law firms, and certain government agencies.

Their common concern--a general consumer dissatisfaction-- was manifested in such issues as packaging proliferation, truth-in-lending, or disposable bottles. All these manifestations reflected the consumer's belief that he has solutions to his own disaffection.

Although the social conditions and consumer concerns which led to the new consumerism most likely could have been accomodated by business, due to the political character of the response by business the issues were stimulated into a major social movement. As such it is safe to assume this new form of consumerism is here to stay. Its mainstay is a better educated and more affluent consumer than during earlier consumer movements.

The protest phase of the new consumerism movement may end soon replaced by various continuing watchdog activities;

however there already is a legacy of policies attempting to
augment the rights and powers of buyers in relation to
sellers.  New institutions and strengthened laws have been
created, as Table 1 illustrates.

## Congressional Initiatives

Beginning in 1966 with enactment of Sen. Phillip A. Hart's
Truth in Packaging bill (The Fair Packaging and Labeling Act),
the Congress also established standards for automobile tire
safety and provided for highway safety research under the
National Traffic and Motor Vehicle Safety Act; hazardous
substances and toys were regulated under the Child Protection
Act; and under the Cigarette Labeling Act cigarette packages
were required to carry the warning:  "Caution:  Cigarette
smoking may be hazardous to your health."

90th Congress, 1967 and 1968 (2) The tempo accelerated
following President Johnson's January 1967 legislative message
to the Congress; several consumer protection laws were
enacted, perhaps the most significant being that extending
federal standards to all meat-packing and processing plants in
the United States.  Federal regulation also was extended to
the licensing of clinical laboratories and strengthening of
the regulation of flammable fabrics to include clothing,
draperies, bedding, and other interior furnishings.

However, the greatest impact on industry was eventually to
be felt from establishment in 1967 of a temporary National
Commission on Product Safety, discussed subsequently.  Some
two and one-half years later a permanent Consumer Product
Safety Commission was created by law.

The second session of the 90th Congress was even more
responsive to the issues of new consumerism, with significant
support from President Johnson, who devoted a special section
of his 1968 State of the Union Message to "The Consumer
Cause."  A special message to the Congress immediately
followed on February 6, 1968, setting forth an eight-point
consumer protection program:

- new powers for the Federal Trade Commission to end
fraudulent practices;

- new powers to insure the quality of fish and poultry;

- new powers regarding the safety of community water supplies;

- protection against hazardous radiation from television sets
and other electronic products;

- a proposal for a study of the automobile insurance industry;

- a proposal for regulation of auto repairs, warranties, and guarantees; and

- establishment of a consumer counsel in the Department of Justice.

Three of these proposals actually were enacted - appointment of a consumer counsel, the study of auto insurance, and inspection of poultry products. The second session of the 90th Congress also enacted a comprehensive truth-in-lending measure to assure consumers accurate information on interest rates and other finance charges on loans, credits, and revolving charge account.

Under the Wholesome Poultry Products Act of 1968, the States were given two years to establish poultry product inspection systems comparable to the federal system. Poultry processors are now subject to either federal inspection (93 percent) or State programs of at least equal structure.

91st Congress, 1969 and 1970 (2) During the 91st Congress no less than 25 measured were enacted to deal with some form of consumer protection.

Stemming from the efforts of the National Commission on Product Safety, the Child Protection and Toy Safety Act was enacted in November, 1969. This amendment to the earlier Federal Hazardous Substances Act authorizes the DHEW Secretary to ban the sale of toys and other articles that present electrical, mechanical, or thermal hazards.

During the second session (1970) of the 91st Congress the issue of cigarettes and health was again active, leading to enactment of the Public Health Cigarette Smoking Act which banned all cigarette commercials from radio and television as of January 2, 1971. The Act also required the updated warning statement on all cigarette packages and in all printed ads: "Warning: The Surgeon General Has Determined That Cigarette Smoking Is Dangerous to Your Health."

Another major law to be enacted in 1970 was the Poison Prevention Packaging Act which requires special packaging of potentially dangerous household goods to protect children from serious injury or illness resulting from handling, using or ingesting poisonous substances. Other legislation prohibited the distribution and use of unwholesome eggs in intrastate and interstate commerce and providing for continuous inspection by the Department of Agriculture of egg-product processing plants; banned the distribution of unsolicited credit cards and calling for fair credit reporting; and, in order to safeguard motor vehicles and their passengers, required tire

manufacturers to notify purchasers of defective tires and
directing the Secretary of Transportation to set minimum
automobile safety standards for the manufacture or sale of
equipment.

Finally, 1971 saw enactment of the comprehensive
Occupational Health and Safety Act, empowering the Federal
Government to set and enforce safety standards and programs
for about 55 million industrial, farm, and construction
workers employed by all companies in interstate commerce.
The Act also established a three-member commission to enforce
the regulations, a National Institute for Occupational Health
and Safety in the DHEW, and an Occupational Safety and Health
Administration within the Department of Labor.

The 92nd Congress, 1971 to 1972 (2) The 92nd Congress saw
enactment of eleven pieces of consumer-related legislation,
the most important being the Consumer Product Safety Act of
1972.  Creation of a new Consumer Product Safety Commission
(CPSC) to protect consumers from unreasonable risk of injury
from hazardous products stemmed directly from the 1971
recommendations by the National Commission on Product Safety
(NCPS).

The 93rd Congress, 1973 (2) Although the last 10 years have
witnessed a number of congressional actions in response to the
new consumerism movement, they actually represent but a small
fraction of what is being sought.  Perhaps the most active
issue, as discussed subsequently, is the proposed
establishment of a new Consumer Protection Agency (CPA).

An area commanding increasing attention is the consumer's
desire to be more informed so that he can more intelligently
and economically exercise his buying power.  Legislation has
been introduced in such areas as (a) authorization for the FTC
to establish standards for waranties; (b) requirements for
truth in food labeling, nutritional labeling, open dating,
unit prices, and pure foods; and (c) the requiring of
documentation of advertising claims concerning safety,
performance, efficiency, efficacy, characteristics, and
comparative prices of products and services.

Consumer credit remains a major political issue.  In
January 1973, the National Commission on Consumer Finance,
established by the Truth-in-Lending Act of 1968, submitted its
final report to the President, stressing the importance of
competition within the consumer credit industry.  The
Commission also stated their belief that greater competition
could be achieved only by repealing State laws which restrict

potential lenders' access to the industry.

Another area of continuing interest is the automobile, with enactment of federal no-fault automobile insurance legislation appearing imminent.  A uniform system would be established nationwide to pay the basic economic losses to persons injured in automobile accidents regardless of who was "at fault."  It also would reserve rights to sue in court. While administered by the Secretary of Transportation, each State would be required to adopt the federal minimum standards or institute a State program providing payment of certain basic benefits, including medical expenses and reimbursement for work loss and replacement service loss.

In addition legislation to amend the National Traffic and Motor Vehicle Safety Act of 1966 would require remedies of defects in all recalled automobiles without charge.

This review only highlights some of the major consumer proposals which cover a wide range of areas including advertising, cigarettes, consumer education, consumer protection, cosmetics, drugs, franchises, packaging and labeling, sales promotion games and public and private utilities, among others (Table 2).

Many of these issues carry-over from one Congress to the next; nevertheless, as a social movement, new consumerism must be viewed as a success.  Many social reforms have been accomplished, new federal statutes enacted, and new institutions created.  Precisely because of these social reforms and congressional actions the protest phase can be expected to decline, while experience is gained in the implementation of consumer protection laws and policies.

Table 2 Consumer Bills Considered in the 93rd Congress
December 1973

| Bills | Major Provisions | Status |
| --- | --- | --- |
| Consumer Protection Agency Act | To establish an independent consumer protection agency | Pending before Senate and House Govt. Operations Committees and Senate Commerce Committee |
| No-Fault Auto Insurance | To establish an adequate and uniform motor vehicle accident reparation system nationwide and require no-fault motor vehicle insurance as a condition precedent to using a motor vehicle on public highways | Pending before House Interstate and Foreign Commerce Committee; in Senate, referred to Judiciary Committee until February 1974, following action by Commerce Committee |
| FTC-Warranties Bill | To provide disclosure standards for written consumer product warranties against defect or malfunction; to define federal content standards for such warranties; to amend the FTC act in order to improve its consumer protection activities | Passed the Senate and pending before House Interstate and Foreign Commerce Committee |
| Fair Credit Billing Act/ Truth-in-Lending Act Amendments | To prohibit interest charges on monthly bill items already paid and require creditors to correct billing errors promptly | Passed the Senate and pending before House Banking and Currency Committee |
| Class Actions | To protect against fraudulent and deceptive practices through civil action | Referred to Senate Commerce Committee |

Table 2 (cont.)

| Bills | Major Provisions | Status |
|-------|------------------|--------|
| Class Actions | suits, permit groups of consumers to file single suit in federal court for actions involving consumer fraud | |
| Auto Safety Repair | To amend National Traffic and Motor Vehicle Safety Act of 1966 to provide for remedies of defects in all recalled autos without charge | Passed the Senate and pending before House Interstate and Foreign Commerce Committee |
| Truth in Food Labeling | To require food makers to show on their labels all ingredients by percentage, including all additives and preservatives, and by their common or usual names | Referred to House Interstate and Foreign Commerce Committee and Senate Commerce Committee.  FDA voluntary regulation published January 1973 on ingredient and nutritional labeling |
| Nutritional Labeling Act | Requires packaged consumer food products be labeled by the producer to show net and drained weight, percentage weight and nutritional content | As above |
| Open Dating Perishable Food Act | To require that all packaged perishable and semi-perishable foods be prominently labeled to show clearly the date beyond which they should not be sold and optimum storage conditions at home | Referred to House Interstate and Foreign Commerce Committee |

Table 2 (cont.)

| Bills | Major Provisions | Status |
|-------|------------------|--------|
| Consumer Food Grading Act | Requires a uniform system of retail quality grade designations for consumer food products based upon quality, condition, and nutritional value | Referred to House Interstate and Foreign Commerce Committee |
| Honest Label Act | Requires labels on foods, drugs, and cosmetics to contain the name and place of business of the true manufacturer, packer and distributor | Referred to House Interstate and Foreign Commerce Committee |
| Unit Pricing Act | Requires disclosure by retailers of the unit price of packaged consumer commodities | Referred to Senate Commerce Committee and House Interstate and Foreign Commerce Committee |
| Pure Food Act | Increases the powers of the Food and Drug Administration to upgrade sanitation and hygiene practices in the U.S. food processing industry | Referred to House Interstate and Foreign Commerce Committee |
| Utility Consumers Council | To establish an independent agency known as the U.S. Office of Utility Consumers Council to represent consumers before federal and State regulatory agencies with respect to matters pertaining to certain electric, | Referred to House Interstate and Foreign Commerce Committee and Senate Govt. Operations Committee |

Table 2 (cont.)

| Bills | Major Provisions | Status |
|-------|------------------|--------|
| Utility Consumers Council | gas, telephone, and telegraph utilities | |
| Truth in Advertising Act | Requires documentation of claims concerning safety, performance, efficacy, characteristics, and comparative price of advertised products and services | Referred to Senate Commerce Committee and House Interstate and Foreign Commerce Committee |
| National Institute of Advertising Act | To establish within the Federal Trade Commission an agency to be known as the National Institute of Advertising, Marketing and Society, and to direct the Institute to undertake research concerning the impact of advertising and marketing upon society, particularly the psychological and social effects of advertising and marketing techniques upon the consumer | Referred to Senate Commerce Committee |
| School Bus Safety | To require the Department of Transportation to set minimum standards for school bus construction regarding crash worthiness and structural integrity | Referred to Senate Commerce Committee |

## From a National Perspective

Overview  Over the years the various activities by consumer
advocates and groups have demanded new federal agencies to
represent the consumer in disputes at the national level
between "big business" and "John Q. Public."  The byproduct is
some 938 consumer programs being administered by some 438
federal agencies (2).  In addition, there are many more State
and local government bodies performing similar consumer
protection functions.

Among the federal agencies directly concerned with consumer
affairs (Table 3) are the Federal Trade Commission (FTC),
Consumer and Marketing Service (Department of Agriculture),
Federal Communications Commission, Federal Housing
Administration, Federal Power Commission, Food and Drug
Administration (FDA), Interstate Commerce Commission, National
Bureau of Standards, National Commission on Consumer Finance,
National Highway Safety Bureau, Consumer Product Safety
Commission (CPSC), National Transportation and Safety Board,
Office of Consumer Services, the President's Committee on
Consumer Interests, and the Securities and Exchange Commission
Commission.

There has emerged a large State and federal bureaucy to
administer all these agencies.  With all these "watchdog"
agencies, it cannot be said that a laissez-faire policy has
left the consumer at the mercy of malevolent manufacturers.
These same agencies now are being asked to preassess the full
social implications of technological innovation with
sufficient foresight to keep our total social structure in
balance.

Historically, social structures and institutions have
eventually accomodated to social change.  However, there now
is considerable evidence that suggests that traditional
institutions often are no longer receptive to or capable of
change.  Many of the Federal Government's efforts to aid the
American consumer still are geared to the issues of past
decades, which were often restricted to classical economic
concerns.

There exists a clear need for a comprehensive national
consumer protection policy.  Meanwhile, as exemplified by
discussions in the other chapters, current federal policies
and practices stem from a body of separate and discrete
statutes; each new policy reflects an ad hoc response by the
Congress to a specific, immediate problem, with laws enacted
at different times and under varying circumstances.

While a comprehensive and cohesive national consumer

Table 3 Major Federal Government Agencies with Consumer-
Related Responsibilities (2)

| Name | Year Founded | Function |
|------|--------------|----------|
| Office of Consumer Affairs, Office of the Secretary, DHEW | Established by executive order, 1971. Reorganized and transferred to DHEW, 1973 | Coordinates activities of federal agencies, facilitates communications on consumer affairs between government, business, and the consumer, and provides consumer education |
| Consumer and Marketing Service, USDA | Established by the Secretary of USDA, 1965 | Protects consumers by assuring that farm products are safe, wholesome and efficiently marketed through food inspection and grading; advises consumers of available, plentiful foods and best buys |
| Consumer Product Safety Commission | Established by law, 1972 | Sets safety standards for consumer products, bans hazardous products, conducts safety studies and tests |
| National Highway Safety Bureau, Department of Transportation | Established by law, 1966 | Administers national program to make roads and highways safer for motorists and pedestrians. Sets national standards of tests and regulations for drivers and manufacturers |
| Department of Transportation | Established by law, 1966 | Responsible for transportation promotion, safety and policy. Enforces gas pipeline safety and public safety regulations involving transportation |
| Department of Justice | Established by law, 1870 | Provides means for the enforcement of federal laws, furnishes legal counsel in federal cases and interprets laws under which other departments act. Enforces federal laws for consumer |

Table 3 (cont.)

| Name | Year Founded | Function |
| --- | --- | --- |
| Department of Justice | | protection through cases referred to it by other government agencies |
| Federal Power Commission | Established by law, 1920 | Independent agency regulating interstate aspects of the electric power and natural gas industries, including the issuance of licenses for construction and operation of non-federal hydroelectric power projects on government lands or on navigable waters of the U.S., the regulation of rate and other aspects of interstate wholesale transactions in electric power and natural gas, and the issuance of certificates for state pipelines and construction and operation of pipeline facilities |
| Federal Trade Commission | Established by law, 1915 | An independent agency with five commissioners that regulates commerce between states; identifies and takes action on false and deceptive advertising; controls unfair business practices, policies and product labeling and prevents sale of dangerous flammable fabrics |
| Food and Drug Administration | Established by law, 1906 | Regulatory division of DHEW that controls the marketing of drugs, food, cosmetics, medical devices and potentially hazardous consumer products |

Table 3 (cont.)

| Name | Year Founded | Function |
| --- | --- | --- |
| Consumer Product Information Coordinating Center, General Services Administration | Established by executive order, 1970 | Responsible for encouraging the development of relevant and meaningful consumer product information as a by-product of government's research, development and procurement activities |

protection policy would be preferable, the consumer must depend on a composite of statutes which are replete with incongruities.  For example, while a new drug must be pretested and receive advance approval from the Food and Drug Administration before marketing (21 U.S.C. 355), other new products such as laundry detergents may be freely marketed unless and until they are affirmatively found to be unsafe or unduly hazardous (15 U.S.C. 1261) even though they represent a risk to virtually every consumer.  This is the case even though the government may believe substantial and unresolved questions exist as to consumer hazards of these products.  Some products such as cyclamates are virtually barred from the marketplace if there is evidence that they induce cancer in animals (21 U.S.C. 348).  Nevertheless cigarettes, which have been found to cause cancer in humans, not only are freely sold but prior to 1966 government agencies were forbidden to require that advertisements promoting their sale should also disclose the attendant consumer hazards (15 U.S.C. 1331).

A few products and services, however, are subject to stringent regulations, including criminal sanctions and requirements for affirmative disclosure of information.  These statutes include:  Wool Products Labeling Act (15 U.S.C. 66); Fur Products Labeling Act (15 U.S.C. 69); Textile Fiber Products Identification Act (15 U.S.C. 70); Cigarette Labeling Act (15 U.S.C. 1331); Flammable Fabrics Act (15 U.S.C. 1193); and the Truth-in-Lending Act (15 U.S.C. 601).

Inconsistencies exist between statutes.  For instance, criminal penalties exist for failure to disclose on an imported fur or textile product its country of origin (15 U.S.C. 69). At the same time, it is not a criminal offense to violate the Automobile Safety Act, no matter how aggravated the offense or how much the public is endangered (15 U.S.C. 1391).

Similarly, while violations of the Automobile Safety Act can
be significantly deterred by imposition of substantial civil
penalties, no civil penalties may be assessed unless the
defendant has previously been enjoined for past violations
under any of the labeling acts or the Flammable Fabrics Act.

Food And Drug Administration Among the various consumer
protection functions scattered through the Federal Government,
no agency is more closely identified with issues of consumer
interest than is the Food and Drug Administration (FDA),
housed within the Department of Health, Education, and Welfare
(DHEW).  Originally the Bureau of Chemistry in the Department
of Agriculture, the FDA is principally concerned with the
regulation of consumer hazards from foods; drugs, including
serums and blood fractions; cosmetics; household chemicals;
and some sources of radiation.

The magnitude of the FDA's task is exemplified by the fact
that, in 1970, personal consumer expenditures reached an
estimated $610 billion (6).  Some $230 billion of these
consumer dollars, or 38 percent, were expended on FDA
regulated products (6).

In the areas where the FDA operates there are still several
specific instances where stronger statutes appear to be
needed, despite existence of adequate broad authority.  One
major problem is the lack of knowledge on what drugs are
actually being manufactured (7).  (Consequently, in the 93rd
Congress (1973-1974), there is pending a Drug Listing bill).
Another area requiring stronger authority is the FDA's
regulation of medical devices.

As presented elsewhere, there also is considerable
disparity between the emphasis given by the FDA to the
regulation of different classes of consumer products.  For
example, prescription drugs are vigorously regulated by
comparison with cosmetics.  Yet, the use of such drugs is
usually under the immediate supervision of a physician where
at least the immediate side-effects to the population at risk
may be observed almost at once.  On the other hand, new
cosmetics are less vigorously controlled, although the
population at risk is considerably greater, and the element of
supervision is absent.

It must be recognized, however, that the FDA will never be
able to assure the safety of every consumer product.  Although
considerable reduction of consumer risks can be achieved from
the FDA's effective implementation of existing or even
strengthened authorities, in the final analysis absolute
consumer safety is unrealistic or impossible.  While it is

possible to preassess and frequently avoid some of the
potential short-term and even long-term consumer hazards
there still remains the possibility for unknown adverse
consequences of scientific innovation, let alone products
already in commerce.

Thus an effort also must be undertaken to educate the
consumer about how to safely use products whether foods,
drugs, or household chemicals.  Almost any product, no matter
how well designed, can be dangerous if improperly used:  for
example, microwave ovens.  Nevertheless, consumer education is
no substitute for consumer protection.  Former FDA Deputy
Commissioner James D. Grant suggested that comprehensive
consumer protection can be achieved in two ways only:

"First, the wishes and intent of consumers as conveyed to
their legislative representatives.  Second, by the creation of
a higher priority among consumers to take the time and make
the effort to educate themselves concerning the use, safety,
and utility of foods and drugs.  A poorly informed consumer is
divested of protection.  A consumer who responds to
information placed before him can be helped." (6)

While there is considerable justification for an improved
and even an enhanced program of consumer education, more
information cannot substitute for a preventive approach to
consumer protection.  Responsible public health programs
cannot be predicated solely upon voluntary consumer action to
avoid unreasonable risks.  This presumes sufficient
sophistication on the part of the consumer to enable him to
understand the attendant risks as well as the actions to be
followed to reduce his risks.  For example, it seems
unrealistic to expect even an informed consumer to either
understand or appreciate the risks from a chemical carcinogen.
Even when a physician, who is supposedly informed, prescribes
radiologic services he very seldom takes the necessary
precautions to reduce consumer-patient risks.  Rather, it
takes an expert, such as a radiologist or certified radiologic
technologist, to fully appreciate the implications of the
physician's actions for the consumer-patient.

Likewise, the hazards of many consumer products are beyond
the capability of consumers to assess.  Two examples are
radiation emitted by faulty television sets and
electromagnetic radiation leakage from microwave ovens.  Even
in areas with which the consumer is familiar, such as foods
and cosmetics, by no means is there professional agreement on
the hazards.

For instance there are six categories of hazards associated
with foods alone:  foodborne disease, malnutrition,
environmental contaminants, natural toxins, pesticide
residues, and deliberate food additives.  An unaided or even
worse, an uninformed consumer cannot easily protect himself
against many of these potential hazards (8).

In the final analysis, government must operate in the
consumer's interest.  It is the responsibility of the FDA to
assure the safety of consumer products, both prior to
marketing and afterwards, based on a continuing surveillance
with the best and latest in scientific knowledge and
technology (7).  The FDA continues to bear the statutory
responsibility of assuring consumer product safety.  Moreover,
these actions often must be accomplished in the midst of
disarray and confusion and frequently with less than adequate
scientific data and sometimes with fundamental scientific
disagreement on technical data (9).

A particularly illustrative example of the issues with
which the FDA must deal is in the area of food additives
previously "Generally Regarded as Safe (GRAS)."  In 1958, some
533 food additives were officially designated as on the GRAS
list.  Since then, these GRAS listed ingredients have been
exempted from pre-market safety clearance as food additives.
Other food additives have been exempted from the clearance
regulations through "prior sanctions."

In August 1973, the FDA announced a federal review of the
GRAS listed ingredients.  Now the FDA, at the taxpayers'
expense, has had to assume the task of assuring the American
people that the hundreds of ingredients long added to food
are, in fact, safe for that purpose.

Meanwhile, the behemoth food industry continues to gross
some $128 billion annually crowding the shelves of American
supermarkets with at least 32,000 different kinds of food
items (10).  Over half of this massive market consists of
manufactured or prepared items, which contain more than a
billion pounds of chemical food additives - five pounds per
person per year.  Overseeing this vast industry and others is
the FDA, whose previous concern for unadulterated and
uncontaminated foods has now shifted to questions of safety
and chronic health hazards.

Yet even when the FDA renders a decision, the matter again
may emerge.  Public disagreement on the policy issues often
exists.  Not infrequently, new scientific evidence also will
come to light reactivating an issue.  For example, the 1959
cranberry episode, the 1962 thalidomide tradegy, the 1970
cyclamate ban, the 1970 withdrawal of NTA as a detergent

phosphate substitute, the 1972 ban of DES as an animal growth promotant, and the issues surrounding saccharin can be expected to receive continuing debate for years.

In spite of the very difficult obstacles facing the FDA, it has ostensibly undertaken to respond to the spirit of the new consumerism. Their goal is to fully articulate policy decisions and the reasoning behind them (9).

However, issues of public access to certain types of information still require resolution - particularly where trade secrets may be involved. In response to consumer pressure and to the Freedom of Information Act, the FDA modified its policy regarding disclosure of information and data. Their new rules apply to much FDA data on the safety and alleged hazards of food additives and antibiotic drugs, reports of unsanitary conditions in the food processing industry, and communications between FDA officials and industry. Nevertheless, with respect to drug data the FDA's new rules remain a matter of dispute between the FDA and consumer advocates.

Federal Trade Commission With respect to most products and services offered to the public, the principal protection for the consumer has been the Federal Trade Commission (FTC). Created by statute in 1915, the FTC's principal function continues to be the stopping of misleading advertising and deceptive sales practices. Long considered ineffective the FTC recently shed its reputation as "The Little Old Lady of Pennsylvania Avenue," by becoming both activist and controversial in consumer affairs.

Over the years the FTC's powers to prohibit unfair and deceptive practices have been limited solely to the issuance of orders to cease and desist present practices, which only affects future conduct.

Until recently the FTC was handicapped even further because action on past violations was required before criminal or civil penalties could be imposed for more recent practices that violate the law (11). This was true no matter how flagrant and harmful to the public these practices may be. Even where respondents were under order, they were subject to civil penalties only if violations of the order could be proved in a new, separate proceeding brought by the Attorney General in a federal court (11).

Finally, while injured consumers are given a private right of action under a few statutes such as the Truth-in-Lending Act, recovery of damages is not possible under the FTC Act even when they result from unfair and deceptive practices which violate an outstanding order to cease and desist (11).

Nevertheless, the FTC has exercised admirable ingenuity in
fashioning cease and desist orders that have served to reduce
deceptive practices and render the marketplace safer for
consumers (12).  Additonal authority empowering the FTC to
seek preliminary court injunctions in consumer cases has been
under active congressional consideration since 1961.  In fact,
in 1970, the Senate Commerce Committee reported a bill that
would have given the FTC broad remedial authority in consumer
cases, but the measure did not receive full Senate action.
The very existence of this authority might obviate the need
for its use (12).

There remains a need to increase the FTC's general consumer
protection authority to provide injunctive authority as well
as the regulation of warranties.

In the eyes of many consumer spokesmen, the FTC's
regulatory effort in connection with consumer fraud is seen as
ineffectual because existing statutes do not provide the FTC
with clear authority to bring about an immediate halt to
deceptive consumer practices or to require that a consumer's
money be refunded.

In addition to the refusal on the part of some merchants
and manufacturers to respond to what consumers feel are
reasonable complaints, there is the feeling on the part of
many consumers that they have no effective recourse if a
seller refuses to repair a product or make amends for a
misrepresentation (13).  Consumer advocates also regard court
action as too expensive for many consumer grievances since
they do not involve serious bodily injury (13).  Thus consumer
protection is for the most part left to the FTC.

The FTC itself is cognizant of the need to increase such
protection of the public.  Speaking of the need for a
Consumer Bill of Rights, in 1969, FTC Commissioner Philip
Elmar stated:

"The time has come for Congress to wrap up all the bits and
pieces of existing and proposed consumer protection
legislation into a single, comprehensive Consumer Bill of
Rights.  Implicit in the whole panoply of Congressional and
Executive actions in this area has been a recognition of
certain basic rights of consumers, and of the obligation of
government to declare and secure those rights.  Without having
said so explicitly in legislation, Congress has junked the old
concept of caveat emptor.  In its stead has come gradual and
increasing acceptance of the fundamental rights of a consumer
buying products in today's markets:  the right to receive a

product which is safe, which will perform as represented, and
is free from defects in materials or manufacture; the right to
be sufficiently informed of the material characteristics of a
product, so that he will have a basis for making a choice
among competing products offered for sale; and the right to be
free from unfair, unconscionable, or dishonest sales
practices.

"A Consumer Bill of Rights could provide explicit statutory
recognition of these rights, and affirm their application to
all, not merely some, products.  It would have the legal
effect of making these rights derive from Act of Congress, and
thus not depend on the action of sellers.  In effect, all
sellers of all products would be furnishing a statutory
warranty to their customers that the product is safe, free
from defects of manufacture or materials, and will perform as
represented.  The protections to the consumer afforded by such
a statutory warranty could not be reduced by an 'express
warranty,' such as is now commonly used by manufacturers of
automobiles and household appliances, containing conditions
and restrictions which have the practical effect of cutting
down the consumer's rights.

"The law should also make a new allocation of the
responsibilities of government, Federal and State, in carrying
out effective vindication of those rights." (14)

   Perhaps the most serious limitation to the FTC's authority
is its inability (a) to prevent unsafe products from reaching
the market-place and (b) to regulate the degree of hazards to
which consumers may be exposed.  Nevertheless, the FTC's
recent new stance has produced several advances in consumer
protection that offer considerable promise for the future, for
the FTC has perhaps the broadest powers of any federal agency
for protecting the consuming public.  The extent to which
these powers can be realized will be determined by their
initiative and the outcome of future litigation.

## Citizen Enforcement

Overview In recent times, many people have begun to ask who is
to regulate the regulators.  Administrative procedures of
government unquestionably have become complex and doctrinaire.
There now are allegations of bias and recalcitrance.
   Yet these same administrative agencies collectively must
exercise the tripartite powers of the legislative, executive,

and judicial branches of government.  A product of necessity,
these agencies are now faced with administering and regulating
the affairs of a complex government in a time of technological
and industrial expansion.  Once considered the focus of
expertise directed at protecting the public's interest,
recently these agencies have been subjected to criticism by
consumer advocates and by industry alike.

Since the early 1930s the courts have restricted the scope
of their review of administrative decisions.  Initially, the
courts were concerned with the test of "substantial evidence."
Following enactment of the Administrative Procedures Act of
1946, the test has become whether the challenged decision is
"arbitrary, capricious, unreasonable, or supported by the
facts."  Furthermore, judicial review has relied on the record
developed in the administrative proceedings; in other words,
litigants are not entitled to a trial de novo.  The courts
usually will not overturn the decisions of administrative
agencies unless there is a clear abuse of discretion.

Issues of administrative procedure and questions of law
arise frequently in the implementation of federal policies
governing consumer hazards.  The environmental and consumer
movements have raised the most poignant conflicts in public
administration.  Environmental law suits, particularly, have
challenged agency decisions, have tested the boundaries of
judicial review, and have even tested the concept of standing
to sue.  What is clear from these consumer actions is that the
litigation surrounding environmental issues is a manifestation
of the desire for public participation in the decision
processes of government.

Nevertheless, a major policy issue exists as to whether the
courts should, or are equipped to, render decisions involving
consideration of the total economic, societal, and
environmental benefits and costs attendant to technological
developments.  The more classical modes of public
administration consider such litigation to be unnecessary,
counterproductive, and an affront to the professional and
ethical qualifications of an administrative agency's
personnel.

Traditionally the courts have been reticent to make value
judgments on important matters of public policy - particularly
judgments involving the weighing of social benefits and costs
arising from new environmental and consumer imperatives.
Rather, our judiciary has insisted that such issues are more
appropriately those for the legislature, reasoning that only
in the public exposure of the legislative process are all the
parties affected able to plan for the future with any degree

of certainty.  However, the courts can serve significant
functions in social reform, as in cases such as consumer class
action lawsuits, citizen suits against administrative
agencies, and product liability suits.

Product Liability Concern for consumer protection against
deceptive marketing practices and consumer product hazards
always has been considered an inherent element of responsible
business practice and government regulation, even before the
rise of the "new consumerism."  The key element is a better
educated consumer who also has a greater purchasing power,
more discretionary income, and more sophisticated tastes.
This is coupled with not only more discerning judgement but
also the necessary knowledge, skills, and willingness to speak
out and seek redress when, in the consumer's judgement, he has
been treated poorly in the marketplace.

    For this purpose, the courts have always been available for
consumer redress against sellers and the "tort action" has
been available to those individuals or groups of individuals.
who can show direct or proximate injury under various theories
of negligence, breach of warranty, and strict liability (15).

    Prior to 1916 the manufacturer, as distinguished from the
seller, of most products had absolutely no legal
responsibility or liability for them, except to those
customers to whom direct sales were made.  With the landmark
case of MacPherson vs. Buick Motor Company in 1916 this
changed (16).  The consumer was provided the right to sue the
manufacturer or distributor, or both, for damages from faulty
products.

    Nevertheless, tort actions suffer from several deficiencies
(17):

First, because the harm must already have been incurred,
preventive actions are not possible;

Second, a consumer interest group must seek out those
individuals actually harmed in order to have standing in
court; and

Third, tort claims allow for affirmative defenses such as
contributory negligence.

    Lately, a new dimension has been added to product liability
as a result of several recent court actions that have evoked
comments to the effect that the burden for payment of claims
against a product should be shifted to those who can best bear
the cost - frequently the manufacturer.  In effect, everyone
in a production-marketing chain now can be held liable for a

product's shortcomings (18).

Thus, a new ingredient has been added to a manufacturer's considerations in product development. Failure to take issues of product liability into account could have a catastrophic effect upon a firm's financial security. The age-old phrase "let the buyer beware" has evolved to "let the manufacturer and the seller be sued."

Recent liberal interpretations by the courts of strict liability in tort have created the situation, for the most part, where a consumer-plaintiff need only prove that a product is indeed defective or reasonably dangerous to collect damages. Nevertheless, issues of product liability arise from individual dissatisfactions with the marketing system, after the fact. In each instance, the validity of a complaint is subject to the court's interpretation, and it often is not even heard if the complaint stems from a matter of principle rather than alleged damages.

Where issues of public policy are involved, a more desirable approach would be to provide specific statutory authority for consumer groups and citizens to enforce and protect their interests. Such provisions could be tailored to the specific situation (ie., environmental class actions). As it now stands, private rights of action frequently are not provided for by statute, such as in the Federal Food, Drug, and Cosmetic Act (17).

Class Action Lawsuits Private citizens as consumers are no longer content to rely on existing regulatory institutions to be their sole agent in the protection or enforcement of their rights. While the causes for this change in attitude are many, two important factors are the formation of consumer interest groups and class action suits.

Class action lawsuits traditionally have provided a broad avenue for redress of all sorts of social wrongs. Used with varying degrees of success, they have served as a broad tool for the modification of social policies, being employed by groups fighting for minority rights, women's rights, and prisoners' rights; for fair apportionment of electoral districts; for removal of objectionable television programming; for more equitable financing of schools; for redress of consumer grievances; and for protection of the environment.

Originally, the class action technique was employed when the question before the court was one of common or general interest to many persons constituting a class so numerous as to make it impractical to bring them all before the court.

One or more were permitted to sue or defend for the whole.  An
example of this process in action is shown in the
environmental case of <u>Sierra</u> <u>Club</u> <u>vs.</u> <u>Rogers</u> C. B. <u>Morton</u>
wherein plaintiffs, an environmental interest group, brought a
class action suit against a federal official (19).
Declaratory and injunctive relief was sought against the
issuance of permits for the commercial exploitation of a
national game refuge.

With the new consumerism there has emerged a concern to
provide effective relief for consumers who are harmed or
victimized by fraud.  There are endless variations on old
themes in the marketplace and even, from time to time, new
efforts are made to separate the consumer from his dollar
without a fair return.

In light of the success of some of these class action
efforts, it is not surprising that consumer groups now are
using this same tactic of class action in the case of such
consumer products as food, drugs, and cosmetics.  To this end
of opening up the federal courts to class action, several
bills have been introduced in the Congress during recent
years.  Yet, the legal profession remains divided over the
issue of citizen enforcement and administrative
accountability.  The pros and cons of this issue are
summarized by a leading proponent of citizen suit legislation,
Professor Joseph L. Sax of The Univeristy of Michigan, who
stated that

"To a degree that has not yet been fully recognized, Congress
has begun to narrow the traditional sweeping discretion given
to federal agencies and to substitute explicit, if broad,
legal standards for the express purpose of imposing greater,
and legally enforceable, restraints on those agencies.

The implications of this legislative transformation are
very far reaching.  Where once the potential for the assertion
of legal rights by members of the public against federal
agencies was averted by the congressional grant of exceedingly
broad discretion, the Congress has now begun to say that the
balance...is not simply to be set by the unchallengeable
determination of an administrator.

The essential point here, as far as the federal courts are
concerned, is an emerging congressional desire to reduce the
scope of administrative discretion and to subject the
environmental decisions of administrative agencies to greater
scrutiny than had previously been the case." (20)

The opposite opinion is expressed by Roger C. Cramton, then

Chairman of the Administrative Conference of the United
States, and now Dean of the Cornell University Law School:

"Litigation in the courts brought by private citizens plays an
important role in our governmental scheme, but it is not an
all-purpose remedy that can cure every ill in our society.  It
is a disservice to the federal courts, whose resources are
already strained to the breaking point, to ask them to perform
tasks for which they are relatively ill-equipped.  This is
particularly the case when they are given no guidance other
than a vague mandate to balance the public interest in
protection 'the air, land, water, or public trust of the
United States from pollution, impairment, or destruction'
against the social and economic benefits of the polluting
activity." (20)

   Thus the issue returns again to whether the courts can or
should render decisions on the substance of scientific and
technical matters with broad implications for society.  If the
courts cannot successfully judge such questions, the
alternative ultimately may be to return many of these decision
decisions to the Congress for final resolution.
   Another major concern of the courts regarding class actions
is their manageability, became a lawsuit that is unmanageable
will not provide effective relief even if it gets into court.
And if in the judge's opinion a class action is not
manageable, he may dismiss the case; again, there will be no
relief for consumers.
   Ultimately, if class actions are going to be an effective
consumer remedy, consideration must be given to the ability of
the courts to process such actions.  Currently the federal
courts have limited jurisdiction, with a limited number of
judges.  Our federal district courts are ill-equipped to
withstand their very substantial workloads.  It has become
necessary to provide a mechanism to distinguish between the
types of consumer class actions that are appropriately brought
in the federal courts.
   At present, consumer class actions are difficult to pursue
in either State or federal courts.  Nevertheless, many
consumer advocates view class action lawsuits as the public's
first line of defense against fraud and deception.  Thus,
liberalization of the rules is viewed as a major goal.  For
enactment of class action legislation would place in the
consumers' hands a new capability to defend his own rights in
the marketplace.  The difficult role for the Congress will be
to minimize the drawbacks and strengthen the benefits of any

federal class action legislation.

Citizen Suits Statutory provision for citizen suits is new to
federal environmental policies and has yet to be reflected in
federal consumer policies. Such authority generally is
limited to providing for citizen suits against an
administrator (e.g., of the EPA) to enforce mandatory duties
and/or against a manufacturer or processor to enforce
adherence to regulations.

Initial provisions authorizing citizen civil actions are
contained in the Clean Air Amendments of 1970 (P.L.91-604),
the Federal Water Pollution Control Act of 1972 (P.L.92-500),
and the Noise Control Act of 1972 (P.L.92-574). Similar
provisions were endorsed by the Council on Environmental
Quality (CEQ) and the Environmental Protection Agency (EPA)
for inclusion in the Toxic Substances Control Act of 1973.
Another major statute containing even more far-reaching
provisions authorizing citizen suits is the Consumer Product
Safety Act of 1972 (P.L.92-513). This Act permits citizen
suits to bring to the attention of the Consumer Product
Safety Commission (CPSC) and the courts failures to comply
with the law or to perform duties imposed by the Congress.

Opponents of citizen suits on environmental and consumer
matters are quick to argue that they impede an administrator's
effectiveness and result in delays while he is required to
defend many unfounded actions in court. This contention is
refuted by the history of citizen actions under the Clean Air
Amendments of 1970. Out of some 12 law-suits brought in the
first three and one-half years since inception of the law,
eleven were against the EPA Administrator. In most cases the
plaintiff has prevailed and the courts have directed a
modification of procedures or decisions to comply with the
requirements of the Act. Officials of the EPA have at no time
suggested that the effect of the Act has been other than
therapeutic.

A 1973 survey by the Consumer Interests Foundation also
refutes the contention that citizen suits on environmental
matters unduly burden the courts or administrative agencies
(21). In the seven States surveyed which have laws
authorizing citizen suits on environmental matters, in no case
did any State official assert that such provisions were
either burdensome or unfair (21).

Citizen suits currently are authorized on environmental
matters; however, where consumer product hazards are involved,
comparable authority does not exist.

In authorizing civil action the Congress would, in effect,

be demonstrating its confidence in public participation in
government.  This would be a vote for government of, by, and
for the people.

## Institutional Reform

Alternative Structures Riding crest of the new consumerism
movement, the 91st Congress saw introduction in 1969 into both
Houses legislation (S. 860, H.R. 6037) to create a Cabinet-
level Department of Consumer Affairs.  Similar proposals were
introduced in the 92nd and 93rd Congresses.  In addition the
new department's proposed regulatory responsibilities in food
and drugs and other areas, it also would have authority to act
as an advocate before other agencies.

The proposal actually stemmed from a faction of New Deal
consumerists, being revived in 1969 by the late Senator Estes
Kefauver and kept alive by him, and later Rep. Benjamin S.
Rosenthal (D.-N.Y.), for a decade (22).  Prior to 1969, "many
Congressmen were personally convinced that such a Department
would soon be legislated into existence." (23)

Several events then ensued which eventually led to separate
congressional consideration of a federal consumer advocate and
issues associated with the federal regulation of consumer
products.  The new department proposal was viewed as a
Democratic initiative, the Executive Branch preferring a White
House Office of Consumer Affairs similar to proposals by then
Rep. Florence P. Dwyer (R.-N.J.) and Sen. Charles H. Percy
(R.-Ill.).  This concept also was supported by Republicans on
both the Senate and House Government Operations Committees
(22).

However, on October 30, 1969, President Nixon, in his first
Consumer Message to the Congress, provided another
alternative.  Endorsing statutory status for his Office of
Consumer Affairs, he suggested that federal consumer advocacy
functions more appropriately should be placed in the
Department of Justice.

About this time, the National Commission on Product Safety
was completing its recommendations, initiating a new phase of
Congressional deliberations which later led to establishment
of a Federal Consumer Product Safety Commission and a
proposed complementary Consumer Protection Agency to serve as
a federal consumer advocate.

National Commission On Product Safety A major landmark for
consumerism was President Johnson's 1967 request that the
Congress authorize a National Commission on Product Safety

(NCPS).  When congressionally chartered in 1968 (P.L. 90-146) the NCPS was charged with investigating whether consumers were adequately protected against unreasonable risks of injury associated with the use of hazardous household products.

Concern was for the hazards associated with the 10,000 or so different consumer products around the home, in schools, or on the recreation field associated with about 20 million personal injuries each year by such items, including 110,000 cripplings and 30,000 deaths.  The annual costs of the carnage are an estimated $5.5 billion (24).

The full scope of the injuries caused by consumer products is unknown.  However, statistics on injuries treated in emergency rooms are available which indicate that (24):

- The most frequent accidents were associated with stairs, ramps and landings; glass; bikes; nails, carpet tacks and screws; football, baseball and basketball activities; folding, track and panel doors; playground equipment, including swings, climbing devices, slides and seesaws.

- The most frequent injuries in the kitchen were related to cutlery, ranges, refrigerators, irons and ovens.

- The most frequent workshop accidents involved hammers and other manual tools, power saws and automotive tools.

- The most frequent accidents with toys involved skates, tricycles, toy cars, trucks, airplanes and boats.

- The most severe home injuries are associated with propane gas tanks and fittings; portable LP gas heating devices, portable gasoline stoves and grills; clothing, including nightwear; home internal combustion engines; meat grinders; boilers and oil furnaces; electric rug cleaners and shampooers.

To combat the problem, the NCPS after two years study recommended in June 1970 that the Congress enact product safety legislation modeled after their draft product safety bill (25).  In summary the NCPS's recommendations provide:

1.  That the Congress enact an omnibus Consumer Product Safety Act committing the authority and resources of the Federal Government to the elimination of unreasonable product hazards.

2.  That an independent Consumer Product Safety Commission be established as a federal agency concerned exclusively with the safety of consumer products.

3.  That the Consumer Product Safety Commission be directed to secure voluntary cooperation of consumers and industry in advancing its programs and that, when necessary to protect consumers from unreasonable risks of death or injury, the Commission be empowered to

- Develop and set mandatory consumer product safety standards;

- Enforce compliance with consumer product safety standards through a broad range of civil and criminal sanctions;

- Enjoin distribution or sale of consumer products which violate federal safety standards or which are unreasonably hazardous;

- Require notice to consumers of substantially defective products, and recall of products which violate consumer product safety standards or which are unreasonably dangerous;

- Make reasonable inspections of manufacturing facilities to implement compliance with safety standards and regulations; and

- Conduct public hearings and subpoena witnesses and documents.

4.  That the Consumer Product Safety Commission be given the further responsibility to

- Establish an Injury Information Clearinghouse to collect and analyze data on deaths and injuries associated with consumer products;

- Disseminate information to the public about hazardous consumer products and practicable means of reducing hazards; and

- Cooperate with and assist States and localities in programs germane to consumer product safety.

5.  That a Consumer Safety Advocate to the Commission be appointed by the President, with specific responsibility to represent consumer interests before the Commission.

6.  That the Consumer Product Safety Commission, in cooperation with the Secretary of Commerce, be authorized to accredit private testing laboratories which are qualified to test and certify compliance with specific product safety standards, and that the Commission be empowered to require independent testing of consumer products which may present an unreasonable risk.

7.   That the Federal Trade Commission promulgate trade regulation rules for those who certify or endorse the safety of consumer products.

8.   That federal agencies provide industry and standards-setting groups with relevant technological information which may be utilized to reduce product hazards and that, where proprietary, such information be ruled in the public domain with provision for adequate compensation.

9.   That upon enactment of a comprehensive Consumer Product Safety Act a method be developed to permit federal technical experts other than those with responsibility for evaluating the adequacy of industry standards and testing programs to participate in voluntary safety standard activities.

10.   That the Consumer Product Safety Commission be authorized and afforded funds for the construction and operation of a facility suitable for research, development of test methods, and analysis of consumer products for safety considerations.

11.   That existing programs of the Small Business Administration be expanded to authorize low interest loans to assist small businesses in meeting requirements of product safety standards.

12.   That the Federal Government, through its purchasing and insuring agents, look to established safety standards and, wherever practicable, new safety designs in selecting products for use, and that federal agencies publicize acquired information about hazards in consumer products.

13.   That injured consumers be permitted to file claims for treble damages in the District Courts of the United States against manufacturers who intentionally violate federal safety standards; that federal class action procedures be made applicable; and that the principles of strict tort liability be adopted by State and federal courts to assure fair compensation for injury to consumers in suits at common law.

14.   That consumer products for import into the United States be denied entry if they violate federal safety standards and that export of consumer products which do not meet federal safety standards be prohibited unless waiver is obtained from a responsible official of the country of destination.

15.  That the United States support the development of
international consumer product safety standards, and assure
fair representation of consumer interests in such proceedings.

These remedial actions were deemed essential to reduce the
chronic disability, the mental anguish, the burden of medical
costs, and the economic waste associated with unreasonable
consumer product hazards.

Two fundamental changes were proposed in the Federal
Government's approach to product safety.  First, the NCPS
recommended that a single agency be given the basic
responsibility within the Federal Government for regulation
intended to promote the safety of consumer products.  Second,
the NCPS recommended that this new agency have authority over
the safety characteristics of a broad range of consumer
products.

On February 25, 1971, the NCPS's bill was introduced into
the 92nd Congress as S. 983 by Senators Warren G. Magnuson
(D.-Wash.) and Frank E. Moss (D.-Utah).  On the preceeding
day President Nixon, in his message to the Congress on
Consumer Affairs, had proposed that DHEW be given authority to
set minimum safety standards for a wide variety of consumer
products.  In addition, the President proposed that DHEW be
authorized to ban products from the market, after public
hearings, where safety standards would be inadequate to avoid
the risk of consumer injury.

Later, the Administration's bill, S. 1797, was introduced
in the Senate by Senators Magnuson and Norris Cotton (R.-N.H.)
and in the House as H.R. 8110 by Representatives Harley O.
Staggers (D.-W.Va.) and William L. Springer (R.-Ill.).  In
May, 1971, H.R. 8157 was introduced by Rep. John E. Moss
(D.-Calif.), Chairman of the House Commerce Committee's
Subcommittee on Commerce and Finance.  Although based upon the
NCPS's bill, it contained several significant changes.

At this same time, President Nixon created an Office of
Consumer Affairs in the Executive Office of the President
(26).  Mrs. Virginia H. Knauer, the President's Special
Assistant for Consumer Affairs, was appointed Director of this
new office, thus expanding the area of her activities.

The principal feature of the President's message which was
to influence congressional deliberations was postponement of
any deliberations on the controversial issue of the manner in
which consumers should be represented before federal agencies.
In the final analysis, congressional debates distinguished
between a Consumer Product Safety Commission and a Consumer
Protection Agency.  The latter agency was conceptualized as

being for the purpose of representing consumer interests in
regulatory actions.

Consumer Product Safety Commission On October 27, 1972, the
Consumer Product Safety Act was signed into law (P.L. 92-573).
In establishing a Consumer Product Safety Commission (CPSC),
the Act represents a dramatic step forward in the Federal
Government's efforts to protect the consumer against
unreasonable injuries associated with consumer products.

The CPSC will be responsible for regulating a wide variety
of consumer products.  The purposes of the Act are:

- to protect the public against unreasonable risks of injury
associated with consumer products;

- to assist consumers in evaluating the comparative safety of
consumer products;

- to develop uniform safety standards for consumer products
and to minimize conflicting state and local regulations; and

- to promote research and investigation into the causes and
prevention of product-related deaths, illnesses, and injuries.

Authorities transferred to CPSC were principally those
administered by the FDA's Bureau of Product Safety.  These
statutes include:

- the Federal Hazardous Substances Labeling Act of 1960
(74 Stat. 372);

- the Child Protection Act of 1966 (80 Stat. 1303);

- the Child Protection and Toy Safety Act of 1969 (83 Stat.
187);

- the Poison Prevention Packaging Act of 1970 (84 Stat. 1670);
and

- the Flammable Fabrics Act (67 Stat. 111, 81 Stat. 568).

At the same time, the CPSC was specifically prohibited from
regulating food, drugs, and cosmetics.  The Commission also
was forbidden from issuing regulations under the Occupational
Health and Safety Act of 1970, the Atomic Energy Act of 1954,
the Clean Air Act of 1963, or certain products emitting
radiation.  It was also forbidden to regulate tobacco
products, firearms, motor vehicles, pesticides, aircraft, and
boats covered by the provisions of the Federal Boat Safety Act
of 1971.  The regulation of these items is left to other
agencies.  The regulation of foods, human and veterinary

medicines, cosmetics, medical devices, biologicals, and
radiation remains with the FDA.

The Commission consists of five Commissioners appointed by
the President, who must be confirmed by the Senate. In turn,
the Commissioners are advised by a 15-member Product Safety
Advisory Council. The Council's members are selected for
their expertise in various areas of product safety from
governmental agencies, industry, small business, state and
local governments, and consumer interests.

The primary function of the CPSC, of course, is to protect
the consumer from injuries associated with consumer products.
A variety of legal mechanisms are available to the CPSC:

- to require industry to maintain specific records, make
reports, and provide needed information;

- to conduct hearings and inquiries;

- to develop standards for products to eliminate or reduce the
risk or injuries to consumers; and

- to ban a product entirely if it decides that no standard
could significantly reduce a hazard.

The CPSC's jurisdiction covers all consumer products sold
in the United States or at federal overseas installations.
Companies and individuals who violate the Commission's rules
can be fined up to $500,000 under a civil suit; under a
criminal action, a company executive or other individual can
be fined up to $50,000 or spend a year in jail, or both. The
CPSC also can seek court action to seize products found to be
particularly hazardous. Through federal court action the
CPSC can require the recall, repair, or replacement of items;
it can require that refunds be made. If necessary, a board
chairman, corporate president, or other company official can
be sought out to assure corporate compliance with CPSC
regulations.

During its first year, the CPSC took action against several
consumer products. For example, several adhesive sprays and a
plug-in TV antenna were banned (24). The Commission seized
illegal fireworks in Mississippi, announced a defect in certa
certain built-in gas ovens, and also ruled that products must
resist being ignited by cigarettes.

Spurred on by public pressure, the CPSC has declared war on
dangerous toys. Some 1,500 toys out of the 150,000 now
marketed in the United States are now labelled "hazardous."
Such toys have been banned and ordered off store shelves (27).

This emphasis on toys stems from estimates that in 1972

alone 700,000 children were injured by unsafe toys; some
132,000 of the injuries were serious enough to require
hospital treatment.  However, toys are only one of the over
100,000 different types of consumer products.  In turn, these
are sold in over one million stores (27).

In the years ahead the CPSC faces a challenging future as
well as a very real opportunity to provide maximum protection
to the public with minimum disruption of the supposed "free-
market" system.

A Consumer Advocate  Accompanying the new consumerism movement
has been the concept of a consumer representative or
"advocate."  Several proposals regarding such an advocate have
been set forth:

- a Cabinet-level Department of Consumer Affairs with
authority to act as an advocate before other agencies;

- a White House Office of Consumer Affairs to serve this
function and others;

- satisfaction of this function by the Department of Justice;

- an Independent Consumer Council as proposed (S. 2959,
91st Congress) by Sen. Philip A. Hart (D.-Mich.);

- an independent Bureau of Consumer Protection as proposed
(S. 3165, 91st Congress) by Sen. Joseph M. Montoya (D.-N.M.);
and

- federally assisted State consumer protection programs as
proposed (S. 861, 91st Congress) by Sen. Jacob K. Javits
(R.-N.Y.).

The premise behind the concept of a consumer advocate is
that every citizen has consumer interests and rights isolated
from his or her ordinary citizenship interests and rights as a
worker, employer, investor, taxpayer, elector, parent, etc.
(28).  The critical feature is institutionalization within the
federal establishment of the consumer movement; up to now this
has been a strictly voluntary movement on the American scene.

Although it is undetermined where such an advocate should
be lodged, it is clear that there is a consensus among both
Democrats, Republicans, and the Administration in favor of
some new form of federal consumer advocacy (22).  In theory,
such a consumer advocate would not only represent consumer
interests before regulatory bodies but also would be in a
position to support or oppose any policy, rule, regulation,
decision or order of the Federal Government.

Leaving aside any debate whether the consumer is subjected to unwarranted hazards in the marketplace, there still remains the basic policy issue of whether "consumer interests" can or should be separated or substituted for the "public interest" as a basis for law and administrative policies.  There is a significant difference between consumer interest and the traditional public interest responsibilities of all established government bodies.

For example, the Federal Trade Commission (FTC) and the Food and Drug Administration (FDA) are structured to protect citizens from marketing practices and risks that are specifically prohibited by statute.  Their historical function regarding consumer transactions has involved fraud and public health and safety (28).  Yet, such agencies do not exist to reflect the specific values of new consumerism.  Their powers are predicated on the overall role of government to regulate government for the protection of the total public interest (28).

In contrast, the proposal for a consumer advocate intends to interpose a new agent of the consumer on the total commerce and trade of our country (28).  Although the consumer advocate would not be empowered to regulate any particular legal misconduct, he nevertheless could touch every form of social and business conduct within the economy.  The justification is representation and protection of the consumer's interests.

This discussion would not be complete without recognizing that the entire case for creation of an independent consumer protection agency "to represent the interests of consumers" rests on the proposition that public regulatory agencies have failed to fulfill their responsibilities in this regard.  In many ways, the debate over statutory provision for a consumer advocate is an astonishing admission of the egregious failure of consumer protection regulation.

In view of this potential conflict, the National Commission on Product Safety in its final report recommended that a Consumer Safety Advocate be appointed with specific responsibility to represent consumer interests before the then proposed CPSC (25).  However, when CPSC was created by Congress this position on the Commission was omitted. Instead, the Congress was locked in debate over establishment of a Consumer Protection Agency (CPA) to fill this role.  As proposed the CPA would serve as an independent, non-regulatory agency to represent consumer interests before other federal agencies and the courts.

The legal concept on which the CPA concept is based is that of amicus curiae, or friend of the court.  Proponents contend

that the amicus concept would effectively place consumer
concerns before the proper administrative and judicial bodies
without slowing down administrative processes, tying up the
courts, and setting federal agencies against each other.

However, the proposed CPA is not limited to
that of amicus curiae but rather is empowered as the advocate
of the consumer's interest. As such, the agency would have
the additional powers to intervene, introduce evidence, cross-
examine witnesses, and present arguments on all aspects of a
case. Needless to say, even CPA supporters express concern
that it could assume an advocate role that would disrupt the
orderly processes of government and unduly interfere with
responsible business practices.

Since they were first proposed, the merits and demerits of
a federal consumer advocate and the CPA have been the subject
of vigorous debate in both Houses of the Congress.
Nevertheless the Senate passed the legislation S. 4459, in
1970 by an overwhelming vote of 74 to 4. Although this event
often is cited as substantiation of the validity of the bill
later introduced in the Senate in 1972, it is now undisputed
that we are fortunate that this 1970 measure was not enacted
(22). Subsequently, due to a tie vote in the House Rules
Committee a companion measure to S. 4459, H.R. 18214 was
unable to obtain a rule authorizing floor action and thus died
in the closing days of the 91st Congress.

This 1970 bill serves as a monument to the dangers inherent
in a popular, complex, and far-reaching bill that is promoted,
sold, and perceived on the basis of its goals. Although
hearings were held on several bills, S. 4459, as reported by
the Senate Government Operations Committee, actually was a
product of intensive work after the hearings were terminated.
In fact the measure created an independent CPA which was not
contained in any of the bills considered during the Senate
hearings (22). After being reported on October 12, 1970, the
bill was referred to the Senate Commerce Committee where
several amendments were added as of November 25, 1970.

Five days later the bill was called up in the
Senate although the Commerce Committee's report was not
available (22). Concern over the extensive consumer advocacy
powers was voiced by an unlikely pair, Sen. Philip A. Hart,
who had more problems with the language and structure than the
concepts, and Sen. Samuel J. Ervin (D.-N.C.), who had problems
with both (22). Nevertheless, the measure receive Senate
approval on the second day of debate, December 1, 1970.

During this period the Nixon Administration was opposed to
such an independent advocate. In fact, President Nixon in his

February 24, 1971, consumer message to the Congress requested
postponement of action on CPA until completion of a study
being performed by the Advisory Council on Executive
Reorganization.  At the same time, he urged the CPA be made
part of the FTC if the Congress felt that immediate action was
necessary.

Nevertheless, the first session of the 92nd Congress saw
House passage of H.R. 10835 by a vote of 345 to 44 (29),
providing for a Consumer Protection Agency with authority to
intervene as a party in certain as a party in certain formal
agency proceedings.  However, the CPA's participation in
informal activities and court proceedings was strictly
limited.

In sharp contrast to President Nixon's earlier statement,
the Administration threw its support behind the House
Government Operations Committee's bill, with the President's
special assistant for consumer affairs supporting the measure
as "a balanced and responsible proposal which will go far
towards guaranteeing the consumer a strong new voice in
government activities affecting consumer interests." (29)
However, a possible Presidential veto was implied by then Rep.
Gerald Ford (R.-Mich.), should either of the two House floor
amendments then pending be adopted (22).

An amendment sponsored by Representatives Benjamin S.
Rosenthal (D.-N.Y.), William Moorhead (D.-Pa.), and others
would have expanded the CPA's authority to intervene in
adjudications involving fines, penalties, and forfeitures as
well as its investigatory role in areas involving potential
informal activities by other federal agencies.  The amendment
was defeated (22).

The other amendment was sponsored by Representatives Don
Fuqua (D.-Fla.), Clarence J. Brown Jr. (R.-Ohio), and others.
It would have expanded the CPA's authority to virtually any
formal or informal federal proceeding or activity, but it
would have denied CPA legal party status and standing to seek
judicial review (22).  This so-called "amicus" as
distinguished from "amicus curiae" amendment also was
defeated.

Meanwhile the Senate Government Operations Committee was
proceeding cautiously on what had turned into a very
controversial proposal.  When the bill reached the Senate
floor in late September 1972, it was faced with 77 proposed
floor amendments and a mini-filibuster (22).

The only amendment to result in a roll-call vote, offered
by Senators Samuel J. Ervin, James Allen (D.-Ala.), and
Edward J. Gurney (R.-Fla.), was written to restrict the CPA's

authority to that of amicus curiae.  However, it was tabled
early in the Senate debate by a 49 to 31 vote.

The bill's opponents then mounted a successful filibuster
that supporters were unable to break despite three
unsuccessful attempts to invoke cloture (29).  The Senate's
action reflected a sustained lobbying effort for over three
months by a coalition of more than 150 business groups
representing thousands of companies (29).

As the 93rd Congress began its work, so did the debate over
the need for a CPA.  At least six stipulations or points of
agreement can be identified (22):

- The major intended purpose of the CPA bill should be to
improve that part of the federal administrative agency process
that affects substantially the interests of consumers.

- The intent behind the CPA bill should be to achieve this
improvement of the administrative process through the granting
of procedural rights for CPA involvement in the process, not
through granting the CPA substantive regulatory powers.

- The intent should be for the CPA to use its procedural
rights before federal agencies and courts to assist them in
exercising their statutory responsibilities in a manner
consistent with the public interest and with effective,
efficient, fair and responsive government.

- Too often, administrative agencies fail to give due
consideration to the interests of consumers when making
decisions that might affect substantially those interests.

- As far as structured proceedings in general are concerned,
those of a rule-making nature are far more significant to the
interests of consumers than are those in the nature of an
adjudication.

- No one has an accurate conception of the numbers, types and
locations of the structured and unstructured proceedings and
activities of federal agencies that may result in a
substantial effect on the interests of consumers.

There are four crucial questions which may very well
determine the ultimate success of CPA's establishment; these
are (22):

- Should the CPA be granted, as a matter of unchallengeable
right, authority to represent the interests of consumers at
all levels of federal administrative agency activity?

- Should the suggested CPA advocacy powers for informal

activities serve as the model for CPA advocacy in the more
formalized proceedings of federal agencies, or is there reason
to require the CPA to assume the status of an adversary before
some of these agencies?

- Should the CPA be given the right to seek to overturn the
decisions of other federal agencies by appealing these
decisions to the courts?

- What advocacy rights should be granted to the CPA for
representation of the interests of consumers in civil court
cases involving the review or enforcement of federal agency
action?

Despite these unsettled issues, the overriding question is
the propriety of the CPA's proposed ability to oppose another
federal agency on a government vs. government basis.  Such
federalization of consumerism obviously represents something
quite different than the function now being performed without
inhibition (or even objection) by voluntary organizations and
national publications (29).  These outlets are presently
exercising their rights of free speech, free assembly, and
free press.  A statutory transfer of this function to
government would represent a significant change in the
character of this consumer interest function.

The proposed CPA is in no way analogous to consumer
representation by legal counsel.  The agency alone would
decide when and for what reasons to intervene in the
proceedings of other agencies.  In the final analysis, the
decision would rest on CPA's assessment of what is in the
consumer's interest.

## Technology Assessment

Throughout this discussion the common theme is a requirement
for preassessment of the social and environmental implications
of man's activities.  Practically speaking, this new
imperative requires scientific application of the art of
prophecy.

In moving from an art to a science the purpose of prophecy
has shifted:  the art sought to predict changes in the human
environment; the science, however, tends to focus on
alternative actions.  An attempt is made to predict their
consequences on a rational basis in order to render decisions
in areas of managerial or political sensitivity (18).

As a society we are no longer allowed the luxury of
assuming that technological innovation is inherently
beneficial.  The principals of new consumerism insist on

social efficacy, or the incorporation into decisions of people
and their human needs as a condition of human use.

The application of this concept has come to be known as
"technology assessment"; i.e., a concern for determining in
advance the full consequences from some public action or
technologic innovation. The overriding objective is to
evaluate the nature of alternative actions relative to
society's immediate and long-term goals. However, such
evaluations are complicated because (a) social goals are, in
fact, intangible, (b) the reality that resources can only be
used for tangible programs, (c) the output of such programs
are not always exactly what was anticipated, and (d) there are
undesired and often unanticipated side effects (30).

The Congress in recent years has taken two significant
actions to formalize and incorporate technology assessment
into the Legislative process with enactment of the National
Environmental Policy Act of 1969 (P.L. 90-190), and the
creation of a Congressional Office of Technology (P.L. 92-484).
Both these statutes reflect, rightly or wrongly, the
prevailing attitude that we do not have the ability or
foresight to predict the technological innovations which will
be derived from applied science for the next few decades.
Yet, application of this same capability for innovation is the
essential ingredient in mankind's struggle to rise above
natural limitations. In the words of Richard A. Carpenter,

"Technology is limited intrinsically by the intelligence and
resources of civilized man; but more so by our attitude,
spirit, or nerve...the availability and application of the
tools needed for survival and progress are being artificially
limited by wrong attitudes toward science and technology.
These wrong attitudes are generated and sustained by innocent,
uninformed misunderstanding, and by willful resistance to
change and anti-intellectualism. Dangerous and damaging
public attitudes can be corrected by a forthright effort from
the technical community combined with a receptivity on the
part of progressive leaders in the political process." (31)

Such full disclosure in matters of technological innovation
is essential to restoring public confidence. The National
Academy of Engineering, in 1969, concluded that

"The social impact of technological development has become so
great that it affects many fundamental aspects of national
policy and national life. Unless dependable means are
developed to identify, study, and forecast the varying impacts

that these technological developments might have on sectors of our society, the nation will be subjected to increasing stress in a time of social turbulence and will not benefit fully from technological opportunities." (32)

Unfortunately, technology assessment is viewed by many as technology arrestment or harassment. In 1969, the National Academy of Sciences observed that, "we can now, for the first time in human history, realistically aspire to have it both ways: to maximize our gains while minimizing our losses. The challenge is to discipline technological progress in order to make the most of this vast new opportunity." (33)

The NAS panel also doubted that technology assessment would retard the total quantity of innovation and concluded rather that "there will simply be a change in the quality of innovation - a change that will quite properly reflect the broader concerns that have heretofore been given too little weight." (33)

Consumer attitudes reflect a concern for the quality of consumer goods. Stress is placed not only on the intrinsic quality of products but also on the means whereby the user can better judge this quality in making more reasoned buying decisions. Yet, a consumer's perception of risks and benefits is affected by many factors, not the least of which is an acceptance of the general practices of society. A consumer may actually be more aware of the risks of unfamiliar activities than those accompanying "normal" habit patterns.

Another factor often shaping a consumer's choice is his perception of the uncertainty of the benefits and risks. In the final analysis, an individual's "quality of life" decisions are made as a consumer, alone, or for the benefit of society.

A recurrent debate is over the balancing of benefits and risks from an individual's own decisions versus class decisions made for society by regulatory agency. The consumer is constantly taking voluntary risks in smoking, sports, flying, or in choosing whether or not to use seat belts and a shoulder harness when using an automobile.

On the other hand, many other benefit-risk decisions are performed by individuals under limitations imposed by social action decisions; the use of drugs in medicine is a case in point. Under such circumstances, the actual decision represents a compromise between a consumer's freedom of choice and a decision by government to limit that choice in the name of greater benefit or safety to society. Similar questions apply to other innovations, such as pharmaceuticals, cosmetics, and even building codes.

A third category are those pervasive consumer hazards over which the consumer can exercise little choice regarding his own exposure, such as air pollution and food additives. Another example is the Federal Government's requirement that consumers purchase safety devices on automobiles, including padded instrument panels, seat belts, energy absorbing steering columns, and dual braking systems. Under such circumstances acceptable risks are actually determined by public policy decisions rather than individual choice. Moreover, from the perspective of a consumer, regulator, or businessman issues of risk and benefit ultimately are a matter of human judgement, whether seen individually or collectively.

National Environmental Policy Act The National Environmental Policy Act of 1969 (NEDA) represents a response to an increasing congressional awareness of the consequences of environmental degradation. This statute establishes a national policy was set forth to encourage productive and enjoyable harmony between man and his environment; to promote efforst which will prevent or eliminate damage to the environment and biosphere and stimulate the health and welfare of man; to enrich the understanding of the ecological systems and natural resources important to the nation; and to establish a Council on Environmental Quality (CEQ). Although the Congress had previously enacted environmental policies concerned with pollution control, NEPA represented the first comprehensive policy advocating environmental quality management, through the prevention and avoidance of environmental damage.

Achievement of these environmental goals is to be realized through the imposition of substantive procedural duties on federal officials and agencies. Stemming from NEPA's implementation, a substantial body of case-law has developed that adds considerable gloss to the statutory language - expanding NEPA's scope, thrust, and significance.

The most notable applications of NEPA are seen at the energy-environmental interface in the federal licensing of nuclear power plants, the federal leasing of resource development rights on the outer continental shelf, and the construction of a trans-Alaska pipeline. Perhaps more significant, however, was the July 1972 publication by the Food and Drug Administration (FDA) of proposed procedures for the preparation of environmental impact statements. These FDA regulations propose to extend NEPA requirements for an environmental impact statement to the following thirteen FDA actions (34):

1.  Recommendations or reports made to the Congress on proposals for legislation in instances where the agency has primary responsibility for the subject matter involved;

2.  Destruction of articles condemned after seizure or enjoined;

3.  Destruction of articles following detention or recall at agency request;

4.  Destruction of articles banned by regulation;

5.  Disposition of Food and Drug Administration laboratory waste materials;

6.  Establishment by regulation of labeling or other requirements for marketing articles;

7.  Establishment by regulation of standards for articles (except food standards);

8.  Approval of new drug and abbreviated new drug applications and oil drug monographs;

9.  Approval of new animal drug and abbreviated new animal drug applications and oil animal drug monographs;

10.  Approval of antibiotic drug monographs;

11.  Approval of food additive petitions;

12.  Approval of color additive petitions; and

13.  Policy, regulations, and procedure-making which significantly affect the quality of the human environment.

In addition, any person requesting any of these actions will be required to include with their application or petition an environmental impact analysis of the requested action on the quality of the human environment.  An environmental impact analysis report also is required whenever a manufacturer, distributor, or dealer proposes to destroy materials (food, drug, cosmetic, medical device, electronic product, or hazardous substance) which have been condemned, enjoined, detained, or banned by regulation.  The emphasis of the report is to be a rigorous assessment of alternative actions, sufficient to avoid premature commitments which might have greater environmental effects than other options.

The lesson here is that traditional corporate management decisions do not reflect today's overall social priorities, which are based upon an increased concern for protection

against adverse public health, environmental, and consumer
product side-effects of technologic growth.  In part, this
stems from a failure of our business and industrial
institutions to provide the consumer and governmental bodies
with the requisite information to make judgements which are
valid from the perspective of the new consumerism movement.
   The major influence on any decision makers who controls
technological development includes information on (a) resource
availability, (b) technical and economic feasibility, (c)
actual and potential side-effects, and (d) operational-
institutional values.  Such values are comprised of the common
law, legislation, economic and social policy, institutional
management policies, and other "given" values that are
recognized and accepted at the time of a decision (35).
Dealing with unquantifiable benefits and consts always remains
a problem and the assignment of values and weights to
environmental and social amenities may be either intentionally
or unintentionally designed to bias decisions in favor of
predetermined outcomes (35).
   Even considering these difficulties, the NEPA is slowly
stimulating wiser environmental practices, more sensitive
agency bureaucracies, and more effective roles for citizens
(35).  Nevertheless, information manipulation still must be
faced as an inevitable problem.  Secrecy is still a common
practice on the part of public agencies and the Executive
Branch to protect decision makers from public criticism,
despite the 1967 Freedom of Information Act (35).  However,
public pressures and recent enactment of the Federal Advisory
Committee Act may lead to a further diminution of secrecy in
the public sector (35).

Freedom Of Information
Information is essential to making informed judgements, no less
for a regulatory agency than for a consumer, and the common
law of trade secrets is frequently invoked to protect
corporate information - presumably from competition (the
common law basis for the concept), but increasingly from the
public and government) (35).  This the corporate veil normally
cloaked by trade secrecy has been pierced by the Federal Clean
Air Amendments of 1970 and the 1972 Water Pollution Control
Act, which grant the EPA access to formerly secret information
on air and water pollutant emissions.  Likewise in the area of
corporate advertising for new products and technological
processes,(the rapid evolution of the "Fairness Doctrine" now
means that radio and television broadcast licensees must make
reasonable and fair presentations of the contrasting sides of

a controversial issue)(35).  This doctrine has been applied by
federal courts to advertising for products such as cigarettes,
large-engine automobiles, and high-test gasolines, where it
was felt that only one side of the effects of such products on
health and safety was being presented (35).  Thus, the idea
that broadcast licensees should present balanced advertising
information on what are viewed as controversial issues is now
a reality.

The issue of public access to information which serves as
the basis for government decisions still remains.  This is
particularly significant where factual information is being
withheld from the public on federal scientific programs whose
future is the center of debate (e.g., supersonic transport
development).  Government officials are reluctant to reveal
their records of agency activities to anyone who requests
access.  Yet, as cogently stated by Ramsey Clark,

"Nothing so diminishes democracy as secrecy.  Self-government,
the maximum participation of the citizenry in affairs of
State, is meaningful only with an informed public." (36)

Federal agencies have historically withheld information
from the public or have limited the availability of records to
the public.  Since 1789, when the Congress enacted the
so-called "Housekeeping" law authorizing federal agencies to
regulate their internal operations and to establish records
and filing systems, this statute has been relied on to
withhold certain types of information from the public (37).
However, this 1789 statute was amended in 1958 by the first
"freedom of information" legislation, prohibiting "withholding
information from the public or limiting the availability of
records to the public (5 U.S.C. 301)."

During the early 1960s it became apparent that federal
agencies were still withholding information from the public,
notwithstanding enactment of Rep. John E. Moss' 1958 measure.
Not to be deterred, Rep. Moss (D.-Cal.) sponsored the Freedom
of Information Act (FOIA) which was enacted on July 4, 1967
(5 U.S.C. 552) as an amendment to the Administrative
Procedures Act of 1946.  The measure provided the ground rules
by which federal agencies must perform their functions.

The 1967 Freedom of Information Act required all federal
agencies to make "identifiable" records available "to any
person" who requests them in accordance with prescribed
procedures.  Guidance was furnished by the Attorney General to
Executive agencies in June 1967 emphasizing that:

"Disclosure is the general rule, not the exception.  All
individuals have equal rights of access and the burden is upon
government to justify the withholding of the document, not
upon the person who requests it." (37)

Because of difficulties encountered by some federal
agencies in adhering to the 1967 Act, the Department of
Justice established a Freedom of Information Committee on
December 8, 1969.  The Committee is in the unique position
where it could act as arbiter of the Federal Government's
decisions to disclose or withhold information.  In fact it
potentially could assume the role of ombudsman, or protector
of the public, against arbitrary handling of sensitive
information; however, this committee has not assumed a
progressive stance - at best its position has been neutral.
Perhaps the most important function of the Committee is
"to extract the real reasons for a denial, to penetrate the
bureaucrats' blind recitations of regulations and cases." (36)
The Freedom of Information Committee has the option of
refusing to defend an agency's decisions if brought to court.
With enactment of FOIA, its rigorous application became a
matter of concern to not only public interest groups but
major corporations, the American Bar Association, and the
Congress.  On the other hand, the Act has received little
judicial attention and the case law surrounding it to date has
fallen far short of shaping it into an effective instrument of
public information (38).  In fact John Shattuck, staff counsel
for the American Civil Liberties Union, claims that
conflicting legislative history, as well as bureaucratic
hostility and inertia, coupled with a general reluctance on
the part of the judiciary to give it broad effect, has
converted the statute into a "Freedom from Information Act."
(36)
The FOIA's author, Rep. Moss, intended that it represent
"an in-between solution which will guarantee the right of
every citizen to know the facts of his government while
protecting that information which is necessary to the
functioning of government." (26)  Consistent with this
objective, nine categories of information are protected by
statutory exemption:  matters concerning national defense;
internal agency rules; statutory exemptions; trade secrets and
confidential information; inter- and intra-agency memoranda;
personnel and medical files; investigatory files; financial
institution reports; and geological and geophysical
information concerning petroleum wells.
The issue now centers on the question of free and

reasonable exchange of both nontechnical and scientific
information - fundamental tenet of a "free society."
While under the Justice Department's tutelage, the Act's
exemptions have been interpreted broadly.  The courts,
however, have often construed the exemptions more narrowly,
and thus the threat of being taken to court has had a
moderating influence on the natural impulse to secrecy of
government officials (38).

Differences in agency policies are reflected in a varied
application of the FOIA.  For example, while the FDA has
alleged that "toxicological and other information is valuable
commercial property that is regarded as confidential
information," the EPA has ruled that data on the toxicity and
efficacy of registered pesticides, as supplied by their
manufacturers, should be made available to the public under
FOIA because such data are not trade secrets or confidential
information (38).  The FDA is moving to amend its regulations
relating to confidentiality, and the outcome of the case
Morgan vs. The Food and Drug Administration et. al. could have
critical consequences.  The complaint filed by Carolyn Morgan
on June 29, 1970 was based upon denial of her request for
access to safety and efficacy data relating to eight birth
control pills (27).  As of December 1973, this case was
pending before the U.S. Court of Appeals for the District of
Columbia.

Although the Department of Health, Education, and Welfare
also has promulgated proposed regulations (29) which are more
consistent with the purposes and scope of FOIA, the
regulations do not affect the FDA's proposed regulations (37).
Whether the FDA's final regulations are inconsistent with
DHEW's regulations remains to be seen.

Despite its setbacks, the FOIA does represent a modern-day
reaffirmation of America's commitment to open government.  The
issue now is to stimulate firm commitments by federal agencies
to the principles embodied in the Freedom of Information Act.

## Business Response To Consumerism
Without question, the new consumerism movement came as quite a
shock to many businessmen who believed they were serving the
consumer extraordinarily well.

Over the year a marketing concept had evolved which was
structured around the meshing of the actions of business with
the perceived interests of consumers (1).  This total
marketing concept was focused on a customer orientation backed
by integrated marketing aimed at generating customer
satisfaction as the key to attaining long-run profitable

volume.  The assumption that followed was that the consumer
therefore was being served well (1).

In retrospect, the weak link in this concept was in its
mode of implementation, for all too frequently consumer
satisfaction was equated with consumer desires as the focus
for product and market planning.  However, although a
consumer's desires may be efficiently served, at the same
time it is possible to hurt his long-run interests (1).

Now the advocates of new consumerism are calling upon
business to employ a societal marketing concept aimed at
generating consumer satisfaction and long-run consumer
welfare, including social and environmental considerations.
The challenge and problem is how to reconcile company profits,
consumer desires, and long-run consumer interests.  Moreover,
the scope of long-run consumer interests in the development
and marketing of consumer products.  New consumerism is
setting the stage for the evolution of a societal marketing
concept (1).

An effective response to this concept will require removal
of the battle line which is often present between the consumer
and manufacturers.  To do so will require a restructuring of
administrative and corporate decision-making to explicitly
reflect social and environmental benefits and costs in
management decisions and accounting systems.

Whether termed "social auditing," "environmental
accounting," "social-economic accounting," or "social
accounting," in practice the concept must ultimately reflect:

- extended and revised definitions of economic or business
costs and benefits which include direct social costs and
benefits as well as second and higher (or lower) order
consequences of business activities;

- new concepts and techniques for quantifying these costs and
benefits which traditionally have not been reflected in
corporate accounting systems but rather as externalities;

- new approaches to government and/or corporate institutions
capable of balancing divergent perceptions of social costs and
benefits in a manner that can be reflected in corporate
accounts;

- techniques for monitoring the evolution of our understanding
of the social costs and benefits of man's activities and
expanded concepts of social and environmental accounting.

A 1973 survey of business responses to new consumerism
supports the following conclusions (40):

- planned and coordinated programs are the exception, not the rule;

- most industrial manufacturers seem to regard consumerism erroneously as something that does not influence them;

- there is a widespread ignorance of the basic nature of new consumerism;

- a disturbing number of businessmen view consumerism in "us" versus "them" terms, as something to be resisted and openly attacked.

While the response of business often has been passive and confused or reactive and misguided (41), noticeable change is occuring as companies and trade associations accept the reality of the new consumerism movement and gain experience with positive programs. The question is no longer whether a response should be made by business, but how to make the effort effective. Even with good faith and no overt attempt to mislead the consumer, the manufacturer still conceivably could find himself frustrated and in court. The issue is how to evaluate a product as a total concept, including packaging, labeling, and advertising.

Several possible steps can be taken to achieve this goal (41):

First, it is necessary to focus on underlying consumer problems instead of chasing their symptoms, thus requiring new information and measures of consumer attitudes, values, and life-styles;

Second, it is useful to establish an independent consumer interest organization, provided it is properly supported with funds and staff;   .

Third, attention must be given to the design and implementation of programs, including measurable indications of performance; and

Fourth, a new orientation for design and marketing concepts to emphasize utility and long-term consumer welfare.

The new consumerism movement advocates the concept of "societal marketing" under which it is envisioned that an enlightened businessman or marketer would attempt to satisfy the consumer and enhance his total wellbeing on the theory that what is good in the long run for consumers is good for business (1).

## The Epilogue

The lesson that emerges from the new consumerism movement is that economic growth and technological innovation no longer can expect to receive the almost unquestioning popular support and acclaim that it did in the past. While the Congress and State legislatures can define by statute criteria and general constraints for governmental and corporate behavior, a need for institutional reform is also indicated.

An insight into anticipated institutional reform is provided from a review of the public's recent disaffection with technology. The former president of Stanford, Kenneth Pitzer (42), and others, including this author (43), have suggested that technologists need to review their relationships with society in general, as well as their relationship with the Congress, which is almost non-existent.

Frequently, the posture of the technologists is characterized as pursuit of individual scientific excellence. Many others view this ambition as a preoccupation with furnishing information acceptable to one's professional peers (or stockholders) - not society (the consumer) - thereby securing their (the stockholders') respect and attention - not society's. All too often, only that which has value in the intellectual marketplace or the quarterly statement survives (43). Consequently, "peer groups" have emerged among the innovators' elite which exclude not only the layman but other scientific and engineering disciplines from both their intellectual and social company (44). The extreme is reflected in the technologist who considers his research worthy of preferential federal support by virtue of his membership in the "peer group." There is no concomitant recognition of social accountability in the sense that men of public affairs understand this phrase.

Yet, the new criterion is social efficacy or a concern for the side-effects of our scientific and engineering labors at technology's interface with the public, the environment, and the social priorities of our times. Application of this concept will require a far greater flow of information across the interface between scientific, engineering, and business communities and society, than has occurred in the past. At least three changes can reasonably be expected (45): (a) a breakdown in the traditional isolationism which is characteristic of these communities; (b) a movement of corporate and technical concerns closer to society's total problems; and (c) the development of technical centers of unimpeachable quality to which all can turn for reliable appraisals, with identified biases, of alternative technical and corporate decisions.

If the public's present disaffection with science is to be overturned, there must be a greater transfer of scientific information to decision makers. Toward this end, the role of the scientific advisory system must be strengthened. When properly structured, the scientific advisory system can serve a unique and vital means of communication between our society's technical communities and the generalists who are faced with making decisions from their positions in government, government, in industry, and in public interest groups. Where the advice being sought is evaluation, there is an obvious requirement to balance experience against possible conflict of interest. Although no one is without bias, society rightly deserves and should demand the most competent expert judgement which is available. Anything less would increase the chance of not reaching an optimum decision (31).

Yet scientists and engineers historically have shown an ambivalence toward participation in the public domain - on occasion even pronouncing politics as corrupting. When participating in public affairs (e.g., the legislative process) their performance judged in political terms is usually ineffective, leaving much to be desired (43). Their usual approach, as the experts, is to depend upon the powers of persuasion rather than the use of logic (46). Dominated by peer group selectivity, they do not fully understand the meaning of public accountability and are unwilling to accept the risks inherent in expressing opinions in the gray area where matters of science end and the "trans-scientific" decisions (47) involved in politics begin. As Dr. Alvin Weinberg commented:

"We scientists value our republic of science with its rigorous peer group review. The uninformed public is excluded from participation in the affairs of the republic of science rather as a matter of course. But when what we do transcends science and impinges on the public, we have no choice but to welcome public participation. Such participation by the uninitiated in matters that have both scientific and trans-scientific elements may pose some threat to the integrity of the republic of science. To my mind, however, this is a lesser threat than is the threat to our democratic processes that would be posed by excluding the public from participation in trans-scientific debate." (47)

Moreover, we live in an age of "participatory democracy," where the public demands accountability from all segments of society - scientists, engineers, and corporate interests are not exempt.

Under our federal form of government, matters of national policy are the responsibility of the Congress and, indirectly, State legislatures. These bodies and their associated legislative and investigatory committees are uniquely constituted for the formulation of social policies and priorities - serving as a forum for the presentation and resolution of divergent and often controversial viewpoints. The function of such committees is to appraise alternatives and formulate criteria for judging administrative decisions which statutorily reside in the Executive agencies (43).

The principal objective of public participants in this forum should be to provide assistance in the form of information which defines alternatives and assesses their merits, a service for which the scientist and the engineer are uniquely qualified. They likewise should be concerned with expressing opinions on the specific language of legislation - the reverse of current attitudes and practices which verge on the touting of pet ideas and projects (43).

The role of the technologist as the assessor of options may seem limited, if not demeaning, but this is a significant service not routinely provided to the Congress and State legislatures on matters of technology. This led to the recent creation of an Office of Technology Assessment to aid the Congress. The resolution of social policies in such areas as public health, the environment, land use, transportation, housing, and energy policy represent unprecedented challenges for the Congress, for scientists and engineers, and, indeed, for the world. Resolution of these policy issues will require crossing the "trans-scientific" interface where matters of science end and political decisions involving social priorities begin (43).

Trans-scientific decisions must ultimately rest upon basic questions of personal beliefs and human values. While rigorous scientific analysis often may facilitate quantification of risks associated with a product's usage or alternative products, the moral and ethical issues involved in finally deciding whether a risk is acceptable do not require a degree in science. By their very nature, these types of policy issues require intense public scrutiny and debate where scientific credentials are no more impressive nor pertinent than those of any other discipline.

Nevertheless, controversy is an essential ingredient for ventilation of these issues and optimization of the necessary decisions. Yet, to be beneficial in the formulation of social

priorities, controversy should never require battle to the
death. Frequently differences of opinion on the part of all
parties are often differences of perception or interpretation
where there is incomplete information rather than factual
differences. Crisis, like beauty, is largely in the eyes of
the beholder. For the mayor of Calcutta, where a million
people sleep every night on the street, drink water from the
gutters and find their food in garbage pails, the concepts of
"new consumerism" and "environmental crisis" represent quite
different priorities than they do for the mayor of New York
City. As stated by Arnold Toynbee,

"Our greatest challenge today is the morality gap between our
cumulative accelerating advance in science technology and our
appalling failure in our relations with each other." (48)

# References

1.   Kotler, Philip, "What Consumerism Means for Marketers." Harvard Business Review 50:48-57 (May-June 1972).

2.   Burson-Marsteller, "Consumerism: A Growing Force in the Marketplace." Fourth Edition (August 1973), Washington, D.C.

3.   Smelser, Neil J., "Theory of Collective Behavior." The Free Press, New York (1963).

4.   Nixon, R. M., Message to the Congress on Consumer Protection, October 30, 1969.

5.   -----, Message to the Congress, February 24, 1971.

6.   Grant, James D., "New Issues in Consumerism." FDA Papers, December 1970 - January 1971, pp. 15-24

7.   Edwards, Commissioner Charles C., "FDA Today: An Interview with the Commissioner." FDA Consumer 6:8-13 (December 1972 - January 1973).

8.   Wodicka, Virgil O., "The Government Agency's Response to Consumerism." Food Drug Cosmetic Law Journal 28:308-316 (May 1973).

9.   Hutt, Peter Barton, "Safety Regulation in the Real World." Food Drug Cosmetic Law Journal 28:460-462 (July 1973).

10.  -----, "Food Additives: Health Questions Awaiting An Answer." Medical World News 14:73-80 (Sept. 7, 1973).

11.  Elman, Commissioner Philip, Hearings on Consumer Protection, Consumer Subcommittee of the Committee on Commerce, U.S. Senate, December 16, 1969, pp. 57-58.

12.  Acheson, Eleanor D., and Tauber, Mark, "The Limits of FTC Power to Issue Consumer Protection Orders." Georgetown Law Review 4:496-526 (March 1972).

13.  American Enterprise Institute, "Proposals to Regulate Consumer Warranties and Expand the Powers of the FTC." Legislative Analysis No. 9, 93rd Congress (ISBN 0-8447-0156-4), July 17, 1973.

14.  Elman, Commissioner Philip, Federal Trade Commission
Annual Report, 1968, pp. 60-61.

15.  Woods, E., "Effect of the Federal Food, Drug, and
Cosmetic Act on Private Litigation." Food Drug and Cosmetic
Law Journal 8:511 (1953).

16.  MacPherson vs. Buick Motor Company, 217 N.Y. 382, 11 N.E.
1050 (1916).

17.  Sales, B. D., "Does the FDC Act Creat a Private Right of
Action?" Food Drug Cosmetic Law Journal 28:501-511 (August
1973).

18.  Berenson, Conrad, "The Product Liability Revolution."
Business Horizons 12:10, 71-80 (October 1972).

19.  92 S. Ct. 1361 (1972).

20.  U.S. Congress, House of Representatives. Committee on
Merchant Marine and Fisheries, Subcommittee on Fisheries and
Wildlife Conservation.  Hearings on H.R. 59.  92nd Congress,
2nd Session (1972).

21.  Consumer Interests Foundation, "Do Citizen Suits
Overburden Our Courts?" Washington, D.C. (1973).

22.  Leighton, Richard J., "The Consumer Protection Agency
Bill - Ghosts of Consumerists Past, Present and Future." Food
Drug Cosmetic Law Journal 28:21-50 (January 1973).

23.  House of Representatives.  U.S. Congress.  Report of
Committee on Government Operations on H.R. 10835, H. Rept. No.
92-542.

24.  ------, "Coming:  Crackdown on Dangerous Products."
Changing Times:  The Kiplinger Magazine November 1973, p. 44.

25.  National Commission on Product Safety, Final Report,
Washington, D.C. (June 1970).

26.  Executive Order No. 11583.

27.  Morse, Ralph, "Consumer Watch:  Dangerous Toys." Parade
December 9, 1973, p. 16.

28.   Stuart, John A., "Consumerism Within Government."
Consumer Credit Leader April 1972, pp. 8, 27-32.

29.   -----, "Consumer Protection Agency -- How Much Power?"
Congressional Quarterly 31:719-723 (March 31, 1973).

30.   Enzer, Selwyn, "Cross-Impact Techniques in Technology
Assessment." Futures 4:30-51 (March 1972).

31.   Carpenter, Richard A., "Limits to Technology." Paper
presented before the American Association for the Advancement
of Science, Washington, D.C., December 30, 1972.

32.   NAE, "Study of Technology Assessment." 1969.

33.   NAS, "Technology:  Process of Assessment and Choice."
1969.

34.   DHEW, FDA, Environmental Impact Statements, Proposed
Preparation Procedures. Federal Register, Vol. 137, No. 134
(Wednesday, July 12, 1972), pp. 13636-13640.

35.   Baram, Michael S., "Technology Assessment and Social
Control." Science, 180:465-473 (May 4, 1973).

36.   Eleccion, Marce, "Science, Secrecy, and the Law." IEEE
Spectrum 10:11, pp. 65-70 (November 1973).

37.   Rodwin, Roger M., "The Freedom of Information Act:
Public Probing into (and) Private Production." Food Drug
Cosmetic Law Journal 28:533-544 (August 1973).

38.   Wade, Nicholas, "Freedom of Information:  Officials
Thwart Public Right to Know." Science 175:498-502, (February
4, 1972).

39.   DHEW, 38 FR 8274 (March 30, 1973).

40.   Webster, Jr., Frederick E., "Does Business Misunderstand
Consumerism?" Harvard Business Review 51:89-97, (Sept. - Oct.
1973).

41.   Aaker, David A., and Day, George S., "Corporate Response
to Consumerism Pressure." Harvard Business Review 50:114-124
(Nov. - Dec. 1972).

42.  Pitzer, K. S., "Science and Society:  Some Policy Changes are Needed." Science April 16, 1971.

43.  Grundy, Richard D., "Environmental Policies as a Congressional Requirement for Social Efficacy." Environmental Affairs 4:639-652 (Spring 1973).

44.  Bevan, William, "The Welfare of Science in an Era of Change." Science 176:990-996 (June 2, 1972).

45.  Wilmotte, Raymond W., "Technology and the Social System Spectral Lines." IEEE Spectrum April 1971.

46.  Clarke, Lieut. Gen. F. J., "Engineers in a Dynamic Society." Professional Engineer 40:24-26 (July 1970).

47.  Weinberg, Alvin M., "Science and Trans-Science." Science July 21, 1972.

48.  Toynbee, Arnold, "Toynbee at Eighty." Saturday Review April, 1969.

# 2

THE REGULATION OF THE SAFETY OF COSMETICS

Ralph Nader

CONTENTS

Cosmetics:   The Nature of the Problem

Introduction Cosmetics, a $7 billion business, is a glamour
industry in ways other than that depicted by corporate
advertisements.  The soap and cosmetics industry ranks third
in the Fortune list of top growth sectors of our economy, with
15.7 and 15.1 percent increases in 1970 and in 1971,
respectively (1).  By 1980, $15 billion will be spent annually
on cosmetics (2).  Some thirty-one companies control about 83
percent of this market; amongst these are Avon, Gillette,
Bristol-Myers, Revlon, Max Factor, Alberto-Culver and Faberge
(3).  In their aggregate, these companies achieve a return on
sales of about 7.7 percent, making the cosmetics and toiletry
industry the fourth most profitable sector of the U.S. economy
by this measure (1).  A star performer of the industry is the
very successful Avon Company, the world's largest cosmetic
manufacturer, with 1971 sales of $871 million and a return of
34.4 percent on its stockholders equity (1).

   With cosmetics, creative advertising and the hard sell can
generate new markets almost overnight.  An example is the now
controversial class of feminine hygiene sprays, which were
first introduced in late 1966; sales in 1967 were $3.8 million
and had grown to $41 million by 1971 (4).  Women are by no
means the exclusive consumers of cosmetics; in 1971 the
American male spent over $700 million in a fast-growing market
for masculine cosmetics (5).

   The image of cosmetics is all pervasive in our mass-media-
dominated society.  Cosmetics promise beauty, charm, softness,
gentleness, sparkle, color, vivacity, excitement and, above
all, love.  From the medieval love potion to the nut brown
hair dye, from the priceless oriental perfume to the one
dollar, 24-hour, stay-with-it roll-on deodorant, it is what
the product claims to do that counts, and not what the product
is,  or what it actually does.

   Because of this illusory image, cosmetics are not taken as
seriously as they should be by health professionals and
toxicologists.  This attitude persists even though cosmetics
represent a major source of intimate and prolonged human
exposure to mixtures of chemical ingredients.  One consequence
of cosmetics' public image is reflected in the 1938 Federal
Food, Drug and Cosmetic Act (FFDC Act), the principal existing
basis for the Federal Government's regulation of cosmetics.
This Act defines a "cosmetic" in terms of its intended
purpose, rather than in terms of the ingredients with which it
is formulated.

"An article intended to be rubbed, poured, sprinkled, sprayed on, introduced into or otherwise applied to the human body for cleansing, beautifying, promoting attractiveness or altering the appearance." (6)

Cosmetics, however, are not always the innocuous products that they are often assumed to be. Allergic sensitization, photosensitization, microbial infection, skin and mucous membrane irritation, caustic burns, and systemic poisoning are among the recently documented immediate injuries which may accompany the use of beauty products. In addition, there is growing concern that there also may be chronic toxic effects, such as neurotoxicity and carcinogenicity, associated with the use of some cosmetic ingredients. This has focused belated attention on the critical need for a proper pre-evaluation of the safety of each cosmetic ingredient that may be inhaled, ingested, or absorbed through the skin during the use of a cosmetic product.

Under the current FFDC Act, cosmetics manufacturers are not required to fully evaluate the safety of a new cosmetic or ingredient prior to its marketing or use, nor does the Food and Drug Administration (FDA) have the regulatory authority to pre-clear each new product for safety prior to its being marketed. Only after a marketed cosmetic has been shown to be harmful by the FDA can the Federal Government act to remove the product from the market. In such an action, the burden of proof of potential harm or lack of safety is on the FDA. In addition, FDA action is restricted by not having rights of access to whatever test data the cosmetic manufacturer may have collected on potential hazards. However, where a cosmetic can also be classified as a drug, the FDA can, under the drug provisions of the FFDC Act, require the manufacturer to carry the burden of proof regarding consumer safety. (This issue is discussed in more detail later in this chapter).

The first section of this chapter describes some of the major classes of chemical ingredients found in cosmetics. A summary is provided on what is known about the potential risks that have been associated with the use of cosmetics along with details on some illustrative cases of toxic cosmetics ingredients that have been revealed in recent years. This is followed by a survey of the history and framework of the present statutory or regulatory controls governing the marketing of cosmetics. Next there is a review of the operation of the present regulatory system, through early 1973; and the changes and reforms presently under way.

This chapter focuses primarily on the regulation of

cosmetics by the FDA, through the end of the 92nd Congress
(December 1972).  The Federal Trade Commission (FTC), which
has to ensure the accuracy of cosmetics advertising claims, is
discussed elsewhere in this book (See Chapter 6).

<u>Cosmetics Ingredients</u> Currently, cosmetic formulators and
manufacturers are not required to list ingredients on their
products; consequently, very few do.  Presently, however,
there are moves under way by the FDA to require full
ingredient labeling under the provisions of the Fair Packaging
and Labeling Act.  Nevertheless, enough general information is
available to permit the following survey of the major classes
of cosmetics ingredients - two recent books are recommended
for a more detailed description of the formulation of these
consumer products (7, 8).
<u>The Form of the Cosmetic</u> Cosmetics are dispensed in a variety
of forms, including powders, creams, gels, lotions, aerosols,
and solid "sticks."

   <u>Powdered</u> forms of cosmetics, in general, are formulated
from talcum powder, zinc and magnesium salts of the long chain
fatty acids, aluminum hydrosilicate, powdered silk, kaolin,
zinc oxide, titanium dioxide, bentonite, calcium and magnesium
carbonate, and starch.  Softness, slip, covering power, skin
adhesion, and absorbency are some of the qualifying
characteristics of cosmetic powders.

   <u>Lotions</u> frequently employ water or low molecular weight
alcohols, such as ethanol.  Rapidity of evaporation, solvent
properties, and cooling effects are among the qualifying
characteristics.

   The base of anhydrous <u>creams</u> is usually composed of some
combination of mineral oils and waxes, petrolatum, animal and
vegetable oils, fats and waxes (lanolin), hydrogenated oils
and fats, synthetic waxes, silicone oils and waxes, and fatty
alcohols.  Melting characteristics, lack of odor, feel,
solvent properties, color, interaction with skin and natural
skin oils and fats, and stability with regard to light, heat,
and air are the key characteristics.  For creams that are
<u>water-in-oil</u>, or <u>oil-in-water emulsions</u>, easily emulsified
oils and waxes and suitable emulsifying agents must be chosen.
Examples include the lanolins, long chain alcohols, sterols,
beeswax and fatty acid esters of polyalcohols.

   In the case of aerosols, the key is choice of suitable
mixtures of propellants, and design of a container that will
allow proper ingredients mixing and dispensing.  The major
propellants are the halogenated hydrocarbons, such as
dichlorodifluoromethane (Freon 12) and

trichloromonofluoromethane (Freon 11). Hydrocarbons, such as n-butane, are also used.

Functional Ingredients Most cosmetic products also can be expected to contain some of the following ingredients that are chosen to fulfill specific functional needs.

Surfactants are added as detergents, emulsifiers, foaming agents, and as agents to disperse insoluble solids in fats and waxes. Examples of the various classes of surfactants include

- Anionics:  soaps, alkali metal salts of fatty alcohol and polyalcohol sulphates, phosphates, and carboxylates.
- Cationics:  quaternary salts of long chain amines, morpholinium and pyridinium salts.
- Amphoterics:  imidazol derivatives.
- Nonionics:  polyalcohol and polyglycerol esters and ethers (Tweens).

Preservatives are added to prevent bacterial growth and spoilage of cosmetics in storage and in use. Examples include phenol derivatives, such as hexachlorophene, p-chloro-m-xylenol, 5-chloro-2-(2,4-dichlorophenoxy)phenol; anilides, such as tribromosalicylanilide and trichlorocarbanilide; cationic surfactants, especially the quaternary ammonium salts; iodine complexes, such as polyvinylpyrrolidone iodine, sulphur compounds, such as Captan, N-trichloromethyl-thio-4-cyclohexene-1 and 2-dicarboximide; phenylmercuric salts; ethyl and propyl alcohols; and organic and inorganic acids, such as lactate and borate.

Antioxidants are important in any preparation compounded from fats and waxes susceptible to autoxidation. Butylated hydroxytoluene (BHT) and butylated hydroxyanisole (BHA) are commonly used.

Humectants and emollients are hygroscopic ingredients designed to slow evaporation of water from emulsions and to smooth skin by holding or increasing its water content. Glycerol is the most commonly used; propylene glycol, sorbitol, polyethylene glycols, and polypropylene glycols are also used.

Colors include "aniline" or "coal-tar" dyes (chiefly aromatic azo derivatives), natural pigments (yellow ochre), synthetic pigments (e.g., synthetic iron oxides), and natural and synthetic lakes, formed by the co-precipitation of water soluble dyes onto insoluble substrates such as alumina or zinc oxide.

Perfumes and fragrances are blends of essential oils, flower oils, natural resins, animal oils, and synthetic oils. Major constituents are medium molecular weight alcohols,

esters, ketones, and ethers.  Highly complex mixtures of many
organic molecules are the general rule.
Specialized Ingredients Many ingredients are specific to
particular types of cosmetic products.  These ingredients are
described on a product-by-product basis in Table 1.
Benefit-Efficacy-Risk
Benefit The precise social and personal benefit derived from
the use of a given cosmetic is usually an elusive factor to
determine.  The art of painting and perfuming the body has
been practices since earliest civilization, and although
cosmetics may not be a necessity, they are certainly, and
traditionally, a much desired luxury.  Social mores and social
norms play an important role in determining which cosmetics
and which cosmetic treatments are acceptable, and which are
not.  In this regard, fashions change from year to year.
Whether or not most cosmetics achieve their aim to beautify or
to promote attractiveness, this almost certainly is an
entirely subjective matter.  A touch of silvery gray in the
hair or deeper shadows around the eye may be actively sought
to create either a more alluring face, or feverishly avoided
as signs of advancing old age.  Thus, questions of personal
benefit become relative to individual tast, and prevailing
social totems, idiosyncracies, and fads.

An example of changing tast is the now passé swarmed-down,
Brylcream look in hair styling for men, which has given way to
the "natural" look.  The social benefits of using a heavily
gelatinous hair cream are certainly less today than they were
fifteen years ago!

The United States is a society where human cleanliness is
of paramount social concern and where human body odor (b.o.)
is generally fought by every available means:  soaps,
deodorants, antiperspirants, perfumes and fragrances.  This
fight to achieve an odorless norm (perhaps, more correctly, a
perfumed norm) is a powerful motivating force on today's
consumer.  Objectively, the phobia of human b.o. may be
challenged as an unnatural and perhaps even a decadent
manifestation of the superfluity of our civilization.
However, within the cultural context and assumptions that most
people operate in, the subjective benefits of controlling b.o.
cannot be casually dismissed.

In the above contexts, it is well to remember that the
consumer's demand for cosmetics, and many of the "benefits"
associated with their use, is strongly influenced by
advertising.  Cosmetics advertising forms a major part of the
daily bombardment from the media to which we are all
subjected.  As so many other consumer goods, a synergistic

Table 1  Types of Ingredients in Specific Cosmetic Products
(7, 8)

| Cosmetic Products | Ingredients |
| --- | --- |
| Cleansing Creams | Detergents, oils and waxes, emollients, skin softeners (such as cocoa butter) |
| Antiperspirants | Aluminum chlorhydroxide, and related aluminum and zirconium salts |
| Deodorants | Antiperspirant ingredients and antibacterial agents.  Since the use of hexachlorophene was restricted, the chief antibacterials in common use are: 3,4'5-tribromosalicylanilide (TBS); 3,4,4'-trichlorocarbanilide (TCC); 3,4-dichloro-4-trifluoromethyl-carbanilide (TFC); and 5-chloro-2-(2,4-dichloro-phenoxy)phenol (Irgasan) |
| Lipsticks | Indelible dyes (such as fluorescein or eosin), and color additives approved for ingestion.  "Pearlessence" is supplied by crystals of guanine or bismuth oxychloride, or mica coated with titanium dioxide |
| Eye Cosmetics | Coal tar colors are excluded from eye cosmetics by law.  The allowed colors are insoluble colors such as carbon black, iron oxide black and prussian blue |
| Dentrifrices | Surfactants, humectants, binders (hydrophilic colloids such as starch), abrasives (calcium carbonate, calcium phosphates and sodium metaphosphate), flavors and fluoride compounds (stannous fluoride) |
| Mouthwashes | Water, alcohol (to solubilize other ingredients and as a mild astringent), antibacterials, surfactants and sweeteners |
| Shampoos | Surfactants, protein extracts, oils and waxes, humectants |
| Hair lacquers, hair sprays | Shellac, polyvinylpyrrolidone, and similar resins in an organic solvent such as methylene chloride |

Table 1 (cont.)

| Cosmetic Products | Ingredients |
| --- | --- |
| Hair dyes | Temporary and semi-permanent hair dyes are water-soluble coal tar colors.  Permanent (oxidation) hair dyes are mixtures of aromatic amines, phenols and nitroamines which are oxidized in situ with hydrogen peroxide to produce polymeric azo dyes. Vegetable dyes (such as henna) and metal salt dyes (lead acetate) are also used |
| Hair bleaches | Hydrogen peroxide, or alkaline earth metal salts of persulphate or perborate |
| Permanent waves | Heat waves use metal sulphites, ammonia, alkylamines, while cold waves use thioglycollates; hydrogen peroxide is used to neutralize.  Hair straighteners are essentially similar, being chiefly formulated from calcium thioglycollate and sodium or potassium hydroxide |
| Depilatories | Thioglycollates or metal sulphides |
| Nail lacquers | Nitrocellulose, natural and synthetic resins, plasticisers (alkyl phthalates), dissolved in organic solvents (ethyl acetate) with suitable colors |
| Nail elongators | A vinyl monomer (methyl methacrylate) benzoly peroxide and a catalyst to initiate the free radical polymerization process |
| Sun tan products | UV light screening agents (p-aminobenzoates, benzophenones) and artificial tanners such as hydroxyacetone |
| Skin lighteners, bleaches | Covering agents (zinc oxide, talc, titanium dioxide), or bleaches such as hydrogen peroxide, sodium hypochlorite, ammoniated mercury or hydroquinone |
| Shaving creams | Detergents, emmolients, styptic agents (alum, to prevent bleeding from minor cuts); preshave preparations include talc (as a lubricant), detergents (to soften the beard) and alcohol (as an astringent |

Table 1 (cont.)

| Cosmetic Products | Ingredients |
| --- | --- |
| Shaving creams | to tighten and dry the skin); postshave preparations include alcohol, menthol (for its cooling effect), emollients, fragrances, and mild antibacterials |

flow of new ideas and aspirations continually reshapes the advertising message and reshapes social tastes and the popular culture.

Ever alert to new opportunities, the advertising imperative launches musk as the latest, wildest fragrance that will set all pulses, if not just the opposite sex's pulse, racing, and touts the mauve fingernails of Liza Minelli into a wave of zany colored cutical varnishes and polishes. Paradoxically, to the extent that a person feels more attractive as a result of using an advertised cosmetic, he or she may actually believe that he or she is more attractive. But the success of the advertising may very well simply reinforce the user's confidence in the advertised product rather than in herself or himself, thus creating a compelling psychological dependency on cosmetics. The benefit is the message, and so the product is sold. As the FDA notes,

"...with confidence that a new shade of nail enamel and intoxicating scent, or 'covering up the grey' may lead to romance, social acceptability, job advancement or other elusive goals, Americans spend billions of dollars every year on cosmetic products." (9)

The cosmetic industry spends very heavily on advertising. Alberto Culver, one of the industry leaders, spent $55 million on advertising between September 1970 and September 1971 out of a total sales income for that period of $171 million (10). Multi-million dollar advertising budgets for single products are not unusual. Noxell Corporation spent over $5 million advertising their Noxzema skin cream; the Mennen Company budgeted $12 million to launch their new "Mennen E" deodorant and Alberto-Culver invested $5 million in a year-long TV campaign to press their new "FDS Dry Comfort" anti-perspirant (10).

Efficacy As with the question of benefit, the efficacy of many cosmetics will sometimes be an issue of subjective rather than

objective judgment. How else can the essence of Chanel No. 5
be evaluated? Nonetheless, there are many questions of
efficacy that can be settled by objective means. Many
cosmetic ingredients are added for specific functional
purposes; e.g., the preservatives, antioxidants, emollients,
humectants and detergents. The efficacy of such ingredients
in their appointed tasks are consequently objectively
measurable, independent of any consideration of ultimate
aesthetic benefits.

Cosmetics that make any "active" claim (whether a drug
claim or not) also can be judged for efficacy by objective
criteria. A hair straightener must straighten curled hair, an
anti-perspirant must cut perspiration, a masking cream must
hide the natural blemishes of the skin. If by any reasonably
objective criteria such products are non-efficacious in their
chosen roles, then the question of any benefit associated with
their use clearly becomes moot!

The present FTC Advertising Substantiation Program requires
manufacturers to provide detailed evidence to back advertising
claims. Essentially the FTC is demanding objective proof for
advertising claims of efficacy (and relative efficacy).
Dentrifice manufacturers were requested by the FTC to
substantiate various claims of whitening, breath freshening,
and lack of abrasion in an order at the end of 1971 (11). The
agency released the results on July 25, 1972 (12). More
recently, the agency has requested soap manufacturers to
provide objective proof of their efficacy claims (13).
Risk A priori, the consumer might reasonably expect a cosmetic
to be free of risk and to be safe in use. In the words of
former FDA Commissioner Charles Edwards,

"...cosmetics, unlike foods and drugs...are not essential to
human welfare. They do not enjoy a benefit-to-risk
consideration as do drugs. In a word, cosmetics must be
safe." (14)

Nonetheless, as the ensuing discussion will show, cosmetics
are not, in the fullest sense of the word, all safe.

In some cases, the safety of particular ingredients has
been recently challenged as a result of new toxicological
data. In other cases, the lack of safety in use of particular
cosmetics has long been recognized. For example, the FFDA Act
grants a specific protection for coal tar hair dyes from any
application of the adulteration provision of the Act. Yet
this is the chief legal weapon against unsafe cosmetics.
These dyes are recognized potent allergens, and also can cause

blindness if they contact the eye.  The FFDC Act requires such
products to carry labels warning the potential user to patch
test before use, and to not use the product around the eye.
Nevertheless, use of such products on the hair must inevitably
carry the risk of accidental splashing into the eye.

Depilatories are usually formulated from various alkaline
keratolytic agents that will dissolve hair, but which can also
attack skin (which also contains keratin).  Thus, their use,
especially on sensitive skin, can lead to soreness and burns.
Benefit-Risk Considerations Where the objective efficacy of a
cosmetic product can be proven, then traditional benefit-risk
considerations can be applied whenever a question as to the
product's safety is raised.  The fully informed consumer may
still wish to accept certain limited risks, such as soreness
and other skin reactions in order to be able to use the
product.  As precautionary actions, the government may require
a specific warning label on the product, or the manufacturer
may limit use of the product to trained, professional
beauticians.  Cosmetics such as depilatories, hair bleaches
and hair straighteners are some examples of products which
fall into this group.  However, even with the efficacy of a
product objectively proven, the need for the product may well
be challenged if the risk associated with its use is at all
serious.  Thus, where any risk of chronic toxicity exists, a
prudent public policy should almost certainly dictate the
banning of the product.

Where efficacy claims for a product cannot be objectively
demonstrated, it is difficult to justify any risks of adverse
effects that may be associated with the product.  While strong
claims may be made for the product's popularity or value,
based on subjective criteria, the fact is that subjective
judgments are so influenced by external factors, such as
advertising, as to be inappropriate to balance against the
general health of the public.

One industry spokesman recently told of a series of panel
tests of consumers to evaluate their relative preference for
Arpege and Chanel fragrances.  (The Chanel fragrances are, of
course, the more expensive of the two.)  In the absence of any
labels, Arpege was favored over Chanel, even by regular users
of Chanel.  This finding was reversed when the panels were
offered samples with all the packaging and promotional
materials intact (15).

## Cosmetic Health Hazards

The Human Experience There is a general paucity of hard data

on the extent of the risk to health posed by various
cosmetics.  At the outset, however, a distinction must be made
between injuries related to the normal use of a cosmetic, and
those injuries associated with the accidental or deliberate
misuse of a cosmetic.  Cosmetics are part of the array of
potential household hazards - the infant can drink a hair
lotion out of curiosity, or a serious cut can be caused by the
broken glass of a shampoo bottle dropped in the shower.
Deliberate misuse of cosmetics can be a serious problem.  For
example, the "sniffing" of aerosol propellants by teenagers
seeking a "high" can be fatal (16).  The cure for many of
these problems must be sought in labeling and packaging
requirements, and in the design of suitable deterrents.
Nevertheless, an injury arising from the accidental misuse of
a cosmetic product is no less serious for having been
accidental.

The National Commission on Product Safety (NCPS) estimated
that each year there are 60,000 injuries associated with
cosmetics and serious enough to result in the loss of a day's
work or the need to see a physician (17).  However, the NCPS's
description of the nature of its published estimate is
incorrect.  The figure of 60,000 is in reality an estimate of
the number of accidental ingestions of cosmetics in 1967 (18).
As such it excludes other types of injuries associated with
the use of cosmetics.

The National Clearinghouse of Poison Control Centers
(NCPCC) monitors cases of the accidental ingestion of
household products.  The Center estimates that between
one-eighth and one-tenth of all cases of ingestion of
household products are reported to it (19).  In 1970, some
5,112 cases of ingestion of cosmetics by children under five
years of age were reported to the NPCC, indicating about
40,000 cases nationally:  another 675 cases were reported for
consumers older than five years (which can be extrapolated to
another 5,000 cases nationally).  Four fatalities were
reported (20).  This NCPCC estimate (about 45,000 cases of
accidental ingestion of cosmetics each year) agrees quite
closely with the NCPS's figure (17).

The National Electronic Injury Survey System (NEISS) is a
new system which monitors cases of consumer product-associated
injuries which are treated in the national hospital emergency
rooms (21).  It is of interest to note that an estimate
prepared for the NCPS indicated that somewhat over one third
of all injuries associated with the use of consumer products
are treated in hospital emergency rooms.  Preliminary NEISS
estimates are that some 14,500 cosmetics-associated injuries

(95 percent confidence limits are ± 7,700) are treated
annually in hospital emergency rooms.  No breakdown of this
figure exists, however, so that it is not known how many
injuries are associated with the product packaging and how
many with the product itself.  Further the words "cosmetic-
associated" are used because causality has not necessarily
been established (22).

The FDA relies very heavily on the letters of complaint
that it receives from affected consumers to monitor consumer
experience with cosmetics.  The FDA does not actively solicit
them, however, and the numbers it receives (227 in 1970, 314
in 1971) are recognized by the agency to represent "only a
small fraction of the total reactions." (23)  In turn, the
cosmetics industry maintains its own files of complaint
letters from consumers, but these are not currently made
public or made available to the FDA.  (A proposal that a
digest of the industry files be made available to the FDA is
described later.)

Analysis of FDA data on letters of complaint from consumers
shows that hair products are responsible for about one-third
of the complaints.  The major problems are associated with
shampoos, principally eye irritation, and with dyes and color
rinses, mostly allergic reactions.  Deodorants and
antiperspirants are associated with skin and allergic
reactions, and eye preparations are another important category
of complaint (23).

Industry reports that it receives complaints at rates
between 1 and 50 per 1,000,000 units of a cosmetic product
sold.  Such a figure can be somewhat misleading, since it
lumps together those who suffer some untoward experience (who
are likely therefore to only use the product once) with those
who have only a good experience with the product (and who may
buy many units).  Further, there is no knowledge of how many
consumers do not go to the length of writing a formal letter
of complaint.  In a recent law suit, one company was required
to divulge details of consumer complaints about its feminine
hygiene sprays.  A complaint rate of 6 per million units sold
was claimed, meaning that the company had knowledge of over
100 cases of women suffering complications from use of the
product (24).

The chief category of known untoward consumer experience
with cosmetics appears to be allergic reactions to particular
ingredients.  Tests done on patients at dermatological clinics
suggest that 2 to 4 percent of this select population is
sensitive to cosmetics in some form.  Estimates for the
frequency in the normal population are less than 1 percent

(25).  However, no statistically reasonable estimates have
been made of the extent of the problem.

Besides consumer complaint letters, the cosmetics industry
is, or should be, alerted to injury problems by the results of
controlled human testing, and by monitoring the health of
company employees who manufacture and handle the cosmetics
products.  These data are not presently public knowledge,
however.  The FDA also does not have any formal follow-through
procedure on cases of cosmetics-associated injury treated in
hospitals, or any survey or reporting system designed to
monitor the physicians's experience in treating cosmetics-
associated problems.

In conclusion, there is a serious lack of both hard data,
and the ability to collect hard data, on adverse consumer
experience with cosmetics.  The data from the NCPCC point up a
serious problem of accidental ingestion of cosmetics by
children under five years of age.

## Direct Health Problems

Irritancy In early 1971, the FDA persuaded several
manufacturers of bubble baths to reformulate their products
(26).  The agency had received a number of consumer complaints
of severe genital irritation in young children using these
products.  The agency concluded that the detergents in the
products, alkylaryl sulphonates, were to blame.  However,
whether the detergents were the direct cause of the
irritation, or whether they were lowering the resistance of
the genital tract to secondary infections that were causing
the irritation was not established.

In a similar action, the FDA sought reformulation of
dentrifices containing chloroform after complaints of swelling
and severe irritation of the mucous membranes of the mouth had
been traced to that ingredient (29).

Feminine hygiene sprays have been responsible for a number
of complaints of severe genital burning, irritation, swelling
and other problems (27, 28).  It is still unclear whether the
antimicrobial (generally hexachlorophene), perfume, or
aerosol ingredients in the products are to blame.  Since
mid-1971, the FDA has been considering issuing a regulation
requiring such products to carry warning labeling.

Eye irritation and eye damage caused by shampoos is another
major source of consumer complaint.  The FDA has taken a
seizure action against one shampoo forumlated with a synthetic
detergent (Neutronyx 600) and potassium oleate (29).  In 1972,
the agency also awarded a contract for the evaluation of the
potential of various shampoo constituents to cause corneal
damage (30).

Systemic Toxicity Bleaching creams containing up to 3 percent
ammoniated mercury are still available commercially.  Several
complexion creams containing ammoniated mercury are also on
the market, which avoid making the bleaching claim that could
lead to their being classified as drugs.  No controlled study
of the efficacy of ammoniated mercury as a skin bleach has
ever been published - and, in the opinion of the American
Medical Association's handbook on cosmetics,

"...it is questionable whether age spots or freckles are
significantly lightened by these preparations even
temporarily." (31)

Ammoniated mercury creams have been used by some
dermatologists for the treatment of such skin diseases as
psoriasis.  However, the most recent AMA Drug Evaluations
lists such treatments as "not recommended" because of the risk
of mercury poisoning if absorbed through the skin (32).
    A 1972 study has shown that the inorganic mercury salts can
penetrate the human skin, at a sufficiently high rate that the
daily uptake of mercury by a woman using the cream could
exceed the total daily uptake of mercury through her food by a
factor of over 20 times (33).  The study also describes case
histories of six women, all users of bleach creams, suffering
from seriously elevated blood and urine mercury levels, and
showing the symptoms of mercury poisoning.  In January 1973
the FDA published final regulations banning the use of
ammoniated mercury in cosmetics (34).
    In 1972 there also was reported that potentially hazardous
amounts of lead were detected in three major national brands
of toothpaste (35).  The lead was apparently being leached
from the walls of the flexible alloy tube by the acidity of
the paste packed in the tubes.  The FDA accepted at face value
the manufacturer's assurance that the leaded tubes were being
phased out of use and, as of December, 1972, had taken no
further action.
Local Toxicity A number of hair products contain ingredients
that present a serious caustic risk to the skin and to the eye
if at all misused.  These include hair waving and depilatory
preparations (alkali metal thioglycollates), hair
straighteners (thioglycollates, caustic soda) and hair
bleaches (hydrogen peroxide).  All of these products can cause
damage to hair (weakness, brittleness) and hair breakage under
some conditions.  Traditionally, these products have been
restricted to use by professional beauticians only.  However,
in recent years an increasing number of these products have

been marketed directly to the consumer.

Allergy (Contact Dermatitis) The most frequent cause of untoward consumer experiences with cosmetics are allergic reactions to ingredients in the cosmetic. One of the most pressing reasons for full ingredient labeling of cosmetics is the need to provide the allergic consumer with the opportunity to avoid the cause of the allergic reaction, once the allergen is established. The topic of allergic reaction to cosmetics has been reviewed in detail (36).

Para-phenylenediamine, a major constituent of oxidative hair dyes, is a strong allergic sensitizer. For this reason, such hair dyes are required, by law, to carry a warning label that the consumer should perform a preliminary patch test for possible allergic sensitivity before extensive use.

The formaldehyde resins of nail hardeners and nail lacquers, the indelible dyes in lipsticks (i.e., tetrabromofluorescein), the aluminum salts in anti-perspirants, the antibacterial ingredients in deodorants, and a number of essential oil ingredients in perfumes have all been recorded as major causes of consumer allergy to cosmetics (36). As noted earlier, the frequency of allergic reaction to cosmetics among consumers is not known at present because of the lack of an adequate monitoring system.

Human "patch testing" methods exist that allow some estimate to be made of the potential degree of allergic hazard posed by a cosmetic ingredient; the methodology of these tests has been reviewed in detail (37). However, even the largest feasible test panels, consisting of approximately two hundred volunteers, can provide data that are really of little value as a guide to the likely experiences for a market of tens of millions of consumers. Consequently the present lack of an operational consumer experience monitoring system is all the more unfortunate.

For several decades, a number of the smaller cosmetics companies, most notably Ar-Ex of Chicago and Almay of New York, have marketed "hypoallergenic" cosmetics. These cosmetics are formulated with especial attention to avoid potential sensitizing ingredients. At their best, these cosmetics should result in a much reduced rate of incidence of allergic reactions. They also have had the added advantage that the manufacturing companies have frequently been the most open and cooperative with physicians in solving consumer allergy problems where they have arisen. Unfortunately, the term "hypoallergenic" has now come to be used very widely in cosmetics advertising (along with the claim of "dermatologist tested"). Since no accepted definition of the term presently

exists, it is ripe for such exploitation.  The former FDA
Commissioner, Dr. Charles Edwards, has called the term
"meaningless" (38), but the FDA has yet to move to say so
formally, or to provide a definition of the term sufficient to
control its use.  The FTC, in turn, has reported that it
cannot take action against the advertising industry's
definition of the term (38).

In essence, all marketed cosmetics should be as free as
possible of potential allergens.  Careful premarket testing
with large panels of volunteers can serve to screen out the
more potent allergens; but only a very careful monitoring of
consumer experience with cosmetics can screen for the weaker
allergens.  Recent federal regulatory developments have
focused both on improving this monitoring and on providing
the consumer with ingredient labeling.

Photosensitization This is a form of allergic reaction in
which a cosmetic ingredient sensitizes the victim to sunlight
(36).  The causative agents are chiefly aromatic and
polyaromatic molecules capable of absorbing sunlight.  Thus,
various antibacterial agents (e.g., tribromosalicylanilide),
sunscreening agents (e.g., p-aminobenzoates) and dyes in
lipsticks (e.g., fluorescein) have been shown to be
photosensitizers.  The presence of bergamot oil in perfumes
and toilet waters have been shown to be the cause of
photosensitization of the users of such products (39), and
the specific photosensitizers in the natural oil have been
tentatively identified (40).

The FDA banned the use of the antimicrobial bithionol in
cosmetics, because of the high frequency of photosensitization
reported with products containing it (41).  An FDA panel,
presently reviewing data on the safety and efficacy of
antibacterials, has proposed in its summary minutes that
tribromosalicylanilide be similarly banned because of the
serious nature of the photosensitization it can induce in
certain individuals (42).

Microbial Contamination A 1969 study by the FDA showed that 33
of 169 samples of hand and body lotions were contaminated with
various types of microorganisms (43).  Earlier studies had
reported contamination of 62 of 250 samples of cosmetic
products (44).  Microbial contamination of cosmetics is
presently the major basis for FDA action to recall cosmetics
from the market shelf.  An analysis of 69 FDA recall actions
for the years 1969, 1970, and 1971 shows that 54 were for
reasons of bacterial or mould contamination (45).  In 1967,
there was a report of a serious outbreak of infection in a
hospital intensive care unit which was traced to bacterial

contamination of a hand lotion used by the nursing staff (46).

A twofold problem is faced. Good manufacturing practice and design of effective preservative systems can ensure that the manufactured product is free from contamination and will stay that way while unopened. Additionally, a cosmetic should be able to withstand repeated exposure to various common microorganisms once it is open and in use. Another study has shown that of 58 fresh eye cosmetics, only two gave bacterial isolates, while of 428 used eye cosmetics, 53 gave fungal isolates and 184 gave bacterial isolates (47). It also points out the risk of such cosmetics acting as culturing media of bacteria and fungi which may "seed" the eye with a massive dose of infection that the eye cannot resist (47). This point has been further illustrated in studies with Pseudomonas aeruginosa in rabbit eyes (48), which show a high sensitivity to infection following slight abrasion of the eye by a contact lens or irritation by a shampoo.

Insufficiency of existing preservative systems, and inadequate quality control are the chief causes of microbial contamination of marketed cosmetics. Since attention was focused on the issue in the late 1960s, the cosmetics industry has begun to act to establish guidelines for equipment design, raw materials standards, quality controls and preservative system design in an effort to combat the problem (49).

Hidden Hazards - Chronic Toxicity The consumer soon knows if a cosmetic causes personal skin irritation or strong allergic reactions, but he has no basis to judge those products whose deleterious effects are of a more subtle or longer term nature.

Suppose that some ingredient of a cosmetic were to be cancer-causing (carcinogenic). It is very unlikely that its hazards would be unmasked by a reading of mortality statistics and doctors reports, unless it were extremely potent and fast acting. The population that uses cosmetics is exposed to too many other products for cosmetics alone to produce epidemiologically obvious effects. Nonetheless, cosmetics are made from chemicals, and a very large number of people use them. While popular belief is that cosmetics are much safer than drugs or intentional food additives, the fact is that cosmetics ingredients can affect the body in various ways, including absorption through the skin, ingestion, and inhalation. Caution should therefore dictate that those marketing the product should be very aware of the various ways in which these chemicals may induce systemic and long term toxic effects.

Cosmetic safety testing to date has focused chiefly on identification of short term, more obvious adverse effects that the consumer is most likely to notice, such as acute oral toxicity, dermal toxicity, and allergic reactions.  The discovery, during the last few years, that a number of widely used cosmetics ingredients could have more subtle and dangerous deleterious effects has forced the industry and the FDA to reconsider the need for more comprehensive safety testing protocols.  It is therefore instructive to consider the following case histories of the discovery of the toxicity or potential toxicity of ingredients widely accepted as "safe" until recently.

Hexachlorophene During the 1950s and 1960s, hexachlorophene [bis-(3,5,6-trichloro-2-hydrozyphenyl) methane] or HCP became very widely used as a preservative in many cosmetics, and as an antibacterial agent in deodorants, soaps, cleansing and medicated lotions, and feminine hygiene sprays.  Soaps containing HCP also became widely established as surgical scrubs, and as an important weapon in the battle against Staphylococcal infections in hospital nurseries.  During this period, its human safety in use was never challenged.  A review of the existing literature on the toxicity of HCP by the scientist who originally patented it concluded in 1969 that

"The fairly high oral and systemic toxicity of hexachlorophene for animals presents no problems for its topical use by humans as long as misuses are avoided." (50)

In the late 1960s, however, a petition was filed with the FDA for the use of HCP as a fungicide on fruit.  The FDA's Pesticide Regulatory Division (PRD), since transferred to the Environmental Protection Administration (EPA), initiated its own animal feeding studies.  The key findings of these initial studies were that when rats were fed a diet including 100 ppm of HCP, half of the test animals developed a spongy degeneration of the brain tissue (51).  The blood levels of HCP in these animals ranged between 0.99 and 1.48 µg/ml, with a mean of 1.21 µg/ml (51).  These data, along with very similar data from experiments conducted by other PRD scientists (52), circulated within the FDA for two years before regulatory action was considered, and were not released for publication until 1971.

In 1971, further published studies on the blood levels of HCP in infants and adults exposed to products containing the antibacterial showed that the existing margin of safety was

almost non-existent (53).  Infants washed daily with a <u>diluted</u>
3 percent HCP detergent solution showed a median blood level
of 0.075 µg/ml, while infants bathed with a 3 percent HCP
solution showed a median blood level of 0.34 µg/ml, with a
range of 0.1 to 0.7 µg/ml (54, 55).  Adults who used a 3
percent HCP soap over their whole body showed median blood
levels of 0.68 µg/ml, with a range of 0.25 to 1.08 µg/ml.  Use
of a 75 percent HCP soap lead to mean blood levels of 0.52
µg/ml in men, 0.28 µg/ml for women (56).  Since HCP was in
such widespread use at the time, no real estimate could be
made of the total likely daily exposure of the average
consumer.

In the fall of 1971, the significance of these data was
strengthened by the results of tests with infant rhesus
monkeys which had been washed daily from birth with a 3
percent HCP emulsion for 90 days.  During this period, blood
levels of HCP ranged from 1.0 to 1.5 µg/ml.  At the end of the
90 day period, all the treated monkeys appeared externally
normal, except for possible blurred optic discs in two
animals.  Autopsies, however, showed that each treated monkey
had spongy degeneration of the cerebellum, brain stem and all
parts of the spinal cord (54).

In December 1971, the FDA issued a regulation requiring a
warning label on certain HCP containing products subject to
new drug applications (NDA's) and advising against the use of
these products in hospital nurseries on a routine basis (55).
Prior to this action, an in-house panel of FDA scientists has
reviewed the existing toxicity data on HCP and recommended
that it be declared unsafe for general use in cosmetics and
soaps.  Nonetheless, when the FDA finally issued a proposed
regulation for public comment in January, 1972, it instead
proposed a limit of 0.75 percent for non-prescription drugs,
and a limit of 0.1 percent for its use as a preservative in
cosmetics (56).  (In view of the data the FDA had had on
hand for at least two years and the strong recommendation for
immediate action by responsible FDA scientists, this lack of
action was very difficult to understand except in terms of
undue responsiveness to strong industry pressure.)

In the FDA's January 1972 notice, announcement was made
that an advisory panel would be set up to review the existing
data on the safety and efficacy of all antibacterials in over-
the-counter (OTC) drugs (56).  Action by this panel was
spurred by two events.  Firstly, a widely reported tragedy
occurred in the late summer of 1972, when approximately 40
babies died in France following treatment with a talcum powder
that had become contaminated with 6 percent HCP.  Secondly,

new data became available in August on 1972 showing a
correlation of the occurrence of brain lesions at autopsy in
premature babies who had died of HCP-unrelated causes with
prior washing with HCP lotions (57).  The panel recommended to
the FDA that the use of HCP be restricted to a few
prescription uses (57).

Almost one year after the FDA had been advised to take such
action by its own scientists, the agency banned the use of the
antibacterial in non-prescription products and initiated a
limited recall effort to remove products with more than 0.75
percent HCP from the open shelves of the retail store (58).

In retrospect, HCP had been used for 20 years with little
apparent human harm.  Only when basic toxicological questions
were asked, such as is HCP absorbed through the skin, what
levels are found in the blood, what is the apparent no-effect
level in test animals, and only once the proper animal tests
were subsequently conducted, was the nature and the degree of
the hazard uncovered.  As a result, the toxicity data now on
the public record clearly show that the very widespread use of
HCP in over the counter cosmetic products constitute a threat
to the health of the unwary consumer.  For twenty years, even
though the necessary toxicological techniques existed, neither
the FDA nor the industry had undertaken to seek answers to the
key questions of percutaneous absorption and the chronic
toxicity of the absorbed material.  Hexachlorophene had become
widely accepted as being safe with little real scientific
evidence or scientific challenge.

2,4-Toluenediamine (2,4-TDA) Permanent hair dyes are
formulated from mixtures of aromatic amines, nitroamines, and
aminophenols which are oxidized with hydrogen peroxide just
prior to the application of the dye mixture to the hair.
Although the individual aromatic amines in the hair dye
mixture undergo a rapid oxidative polymerization during this
process, studies with human volunteers have shown that small
quantities of the free amines are absorbed through the scalp
during the hair dyeing operation (59).  The general class of
aromatic amines includes a number of potent carcinogens such
as 2-naphthylamine and 4-aminobiphenyl (60).  In 1969,
Japanese researchers published a report that 2,4-TDA caused
cancer of the liver when fed to rats at levels of 0.1 percent
and 0.06 percent in their normal diets (61).  The following
year, after the significance of the Japanese results had been
given a public airing in the U.S. press (62, 63), the cosmetic
industry assured the FDA that use of 2,4-TDA in hair dyes
would cease while further tests were made.  The FDA then
initiated its own carcinogenicity tests for 2,4-TDA, by skin-

painting mice.  At the same time the National Cancer
Institute, as a part of its ongoing program to screen many
common chemicals for potential carcinogenicity, began testing
a number of other oxidative hair dye components by feeding
experiments with mice and rats (64, 65).  In the fall of 1971,
the cosmetic industry initiated its own testing protocol to
evaluate the safety-in-use of 2,4-TDA, and two other hair dye
components, using a mouse skin-painting assay.

Some forty different aromatic amines are currently used to
formulate hair dyes, although a more limited number
predominate in terms of the quantitative composition of the
dyes (66, 67).  Almost none of these amines have been
adequately tested for possible carcinogenicity (68).  Yet, as
noted above, they can be absorbed through the scalp during the
hair dyeing process.  As was the case with antimicrobials
(e.g., HCP), only once the safety of one member of the class
has been challenged has some action been taken by the FDA and
the industry to initiate chronic toxicity testing on other
members of the class of cosmetic hair dyes.

Asbestos in Talcum Powder  Talc, the mineral ore processed to
make talcum powder, is mineralogically related to various
asbestoform minerals such as the serpentine chrysotile, and
the amphibole crocidolite.  The same geological metamorphoses
that produce the one mineral can also produce the other.  Thus
it is not unusual to find talc ore mixed with, or geologically
proximate to, asbestos-rich ores (69).  Careful mining and
careful processing can produce a talcum powder that is
relatively asbestos free (<<1%).

The hazard presented by the presence of asbestoform
minerals in commercial talcs has been established since at
least the early 1940s (70, 71).  A 1968 study by Cralley and
his coworkers reported that each of 22 consumer talcum powders
tested by light microscopy contained fibrous materials that
could well be asbestoform (72).  More refined studies during
1972 and 1973 have identified the presence of asbestoform
fibers (>1 to 2%) in over one-third of 100 consumer talcums
tested, including one product with over 20 percent (73).

Asbestos fibers are potent human carcinogens.  Inhalation
of the fibers under occupational conditions of exposure can
cause a chronic fibrotic lung disease known as pulmonary
asbestosis (74).  Asbestos fibers can also induce an otherwise
rare form of cancer of the lining of the chest and abdominal
cavities called mesothelioma (75) and lung cancer and
gastrointestinal tract cancers.  Asbestos also markedly
potentiates the effects of cigarette smoking in causing lung
cancer (76).  Epidemiological studies have shown an increased

incidence of mesothelioma in populations only incidentally
exposed to asbestos fibers, such as those living near asbestos
mines, or living in the same house as an asbestos miner (77).
In a 1971 review of the toxicological properties of asbestos,
preparatory to setting guidelines for the control of asbestos
air pollution, the EPA concluded that a safe level of exposure
to asbestos has not been yet demonstrated and that community
exposure to asbestos in the ambient air "is a hazard to
health." (78)

     Talcum powder is easily inhaled during cosmetic use.  It is
the primary ingredient in face powder compacts, baby powders
and body and foot powders.  Recently, it also has become
available in aerosolized form in a number of deodorant sprays.
Any asbestos fibers present in a talc could easily be inhaled
during use.  This risk to the consumers' health is even more
unnecessary since an asbestos-free talcum powder can be
produced.

     The 1968 report by Cralley (72) initiated no apparent
interest within the FDA or the cosmetic industry.  In 1971,
the New York City Environmental Protection Administration
(NYC-EPA) became concerned about the problem after analyses at
the Mount Sinai Hospital in New York confirmed Cralley's
findings.  NYC-EPA Administrator Jerome Kretchmer wrote to
HEW Secretary Richardson requestion action.  In response, the
FDA assembled an advisory "symposium" in August 1971 to
discuss methods of analyzing for the presence of asbestoform
fibers in talcum powders (79).  Following the meeting, the
agency awarded a contract to develop a suitable method of
analysis, and to carry out a number of analyses.  Over one
year later, the final results of the analyses still had not
been made official because of industry challenges to some
aspects of the analytical methodology.

     The FDA's action on this issue was undoubtedly retarded by
its lack of scientific personnel qualified in the analytical
methodology involved.  In the wake of published reports that
rice had been treated with talc containing asbestos
fibers (80, 81), the FDA published a proposed regulation that
would set a zero tolerance on the presence of asbestos in talc
for use in food (82).  The proposed regulation, however, made
no mention whatever of a proposed analytical method (82).
Realistically, an _absolute_ zero tolerance is not a
possibility, especially in view of the ubiquity of asbestos as
an environmental pollutant.  At the same time, the industry
challenge to several aspects of the proposed analytical
methodology has apparently blocked the FDA's willingness to
take even interim action on the basis of the information it

already has.  Comments from the industry on the proposed
talc/food regulation indicate that most major talc producers
are only now initiating the necessary research and development
to provide them the means to handle the analytical and
production problems raised by this issue.

The problem has certainly been clearly defined since at
least 1968 and the technology to solve this has been on hand
for at least that time.  However, only after public attention
has been focused on the issue has remedial action been
belatedly initiated by the FDA.

The Color Additive FD&C Red 2 Under the 1968 Color Additive
Amendments to the Federal Food, Drug and Cosmetic Act, the
FDA is required to verify the safety of color additives for
their intended uses before permanently listing them as "safe"
under the provisions of the Act.  Contrary to the case for
most cosmetics ingredients, the burden of proof of safety is
on the manufacturer who would use a color additive in his
product.  Any color additive intended for ingestion must be
shown to be safe for that use, while any color additive
intended for purely external use must be shown to be safe in
that use.

During the decade following the passage of the 1968
amendments, color additives were listed on a provisional
basis by the FDA, pending the outcome of a long legal wrangle
with the cosmetic industry over the FDA's interpretation of
the intent of the amendments (see later in this chapter for a
fuller description).  In 1970, after the FDA had accepted the
ruling of a Federal District Court which favored, in the main,
the industry case, the cosmetic industry began completing its
petitions for the permanent listing of colors.

The industry petitions to the FDA included animal
carcinogenicity data, but did not deal with any other
potential long-term chronic toxic effects.  This was the case
despite recommendations by both an FAO/WHO Expert Committee,
and an FDA Advisory Committee on the safety evaluation of food
additives on the need for such broader testing (83).

In 1971, FD&C Red 2 was, by far, the most widely used color
additive in foods, drugs, and cosmetics, with a national
consumption of 1.5 million pounds a year (84).  It was widely
used in such ingestible cosmetics as mouthwashes and
lipsticks.

During 1970, two Russian studies on FD&C Red 2 were
published that suggested both carcinogenic and embryotoxic
effects in rats (85, 86).  By the following spring, the FDA
had become aware of these studies, and had initiated its own
testing program to verify the Russian studies, which had been

criticized as being inadequate in several ways.  In November
1971, an internal FDA panel reviewed the initial results of
these tests and concluded that

"In view of the evidence now available from both FDA and
Russian studies showing problems of reproductive interference,
the possible corroboration by the chick embryo system of the
questions raised by the Russians concerning carcinogenesis,
and the incompleteness of the multigeneration reproduction
study and other test systems, it was agreed that it would be
prudent to limit drastically the uses of FD&C Red 2 to
indirect or external applications..." (87)

During this period (in September 1971) the FDA had
requested that the food and cosmetic industries notify the
agency about the presnt levels of use of the color additive in
case the agency needed to limit its use (88).  However,
instead of accepting the advice of its own scientists at this
point, the agency prevailed upon the National Academy of
Sciences - National Research Council (NAS-NRC) to carry out a
further review of the existing data.  After an initial refusal
to do so, the NAS-NRC Committee on Food Protection established
a special review panel.  In its final report to the FDA,
submitted in June 1972, the Committee concluded that the
existing data did not warrant the conclusions that FD&C Red 2
was a hazard to human health or reproduction (89).  However,
an independent review of the data submitted to the NAS-NRC
Committee concluded that it had relied too heavily on data
summaries prepared by the industry which had failed to note
various significant reports on the toxicity of FD&C Red 2
(90).
    Following this, the FDA proposed limits on the use of FD&C
Red 2, developed by applying a 10 to 1 safety factor to the
15 mg/kg/day apparent "no effect" level for embryotoxicity
established from the test data.  This represented a departure
for the FDA's standard regulatory precedent of applying a 100
to 1 safety factor to animal toxicity data (91).  Use of this
lower safety factor was justified in the regulation by
reference to the conclusion of the NAS-NRC Committee that a
100 to 1 safety factor would have effectively prevented use of
the color additive.  The Director of the FDA Bureau of Foods
was quoted in April 1972 as saying, apropos of Red 2:

"...We're building in a large safety margin; we always do.  We
build in the 100 to 1 safety factor."

However, by the fall, his judgement had changed:

"We're stuck with Red 2 - if we went to a 0.15 mg limit, we would wipe out its use." (91)

Only as a consequence of the discovery of the embryotoxic effects of the FD&C Red 2 did the FDA insist on the industry submitting data on teratology and multigeneration reproductive studies as part of the petitions for the permanent listing of ingested colors. These studies are now in progress.

Conclusion No monitoring of consumer complaints or physicians reports is likely to pinpoint hazards faced by the consumer when the hazards are of this nature. The only way to avoid them is by the use of properly designed protocols of animal tests, carried out prior to the marketing of cosmetics containing these ingredients.

It is interesting that the consumer-interest case on the need for proper pre-market testing for the safety of cosmetics has, in the past, generally focused on those cosmetic injuries most easily detectable by the consumer - such as allergic reactions, infections, and serious local irritancy. Nonetheless, the most important consequence of a proper program of cosmetic ingredient safety testing would be the screening of those ingredients whose toxic effects would otherwise go unnoticed.

The Legal Basis

Cosmetics Regulation The Federal Food and Drug Act of 1906, which was the nation's first federal law seeking to regulate the safety of foods and drugs, made no mention of cosmetics. At that time, "the cosmetic industry of the USA was little more than a kitchen-pot and garage accomodation for 'painted ladies' on and off the stage." (92) However, as the use of cosmetics grew in social acceptability, so did the business of manufacturing and marketing cosmetics, and during the following decades reports of serious injuries associated with the use of cosmetics began to accumulate.

In 1932, in an effort to convince the Congress that some regulation of the safety of cosmetics was needed, the FDA created a display which the press referred to as the "chamber of horrors." Borrowing that name, Ruth de Forest Lamb published a book in 1936 entitled American Chamber of Horrors (95). One of her aims was to demonstrate that many cosmetics marketed at the time could not be regulated by the Federal Government under existing statutory authority even though they

contained dangerously potent drugs.  This was simply because
they made no medicinal claims.  The following are examples of
the cases which she discussed.

Othine Othine was a skin "whitener" and freckle remover which
contained sufficient mercury that long-term use could induce a
range of chronic toxic effects including renal damage,
inflammation and ulceration of the mouth and gums and necrosis
of the jawbone.  The extended interval between the application
of the cream and the appearance of the toxic symptoms made it
difficult to identify the cause of these effects (94).

Lash-lure Perhaps the most well known case was that of a young
woman who in 1933, as a result of having her eyelashes dyed
with a coal-tar product called "Lash-lure," which contained
p-phenylenediamine, suffered ulceration of the corneas of both
eyes, leaving her blind and disfigured.  The AMA documented 17
similar cases, some resulting in death.  However, this product
remained on the market for five more years before removal.
The Federal Government did not have authority to seize the
cosmetic under the 1906 Act because it made no medicinal claim
and therefore could not be considered a drug.  It took the
passage of the 1938 FFDC Act before "Lash-lure" could be
outlawed (95).

Koremlu Ruth Lamb's book also chronicles the history of
"Koremlu," a depilatory containing thallium acetate (which was
commonly used at that time as a rat poison.)  A woman
concocted this preparation with the help of her family doctor
and a pharmacist.  At the time she knew of its toxic effect
since a similar French product had been removed from the
market by its manufacturer.  She, nevertheless, formulated a
cream containing from 3 to 7 percent of the thallium salt.

In 1930 Koremlu entered the department store market, where
120,000 jars were sold that year despite warnings from the
Department of Agriculture and the AMA that the cream was
dangerous.  Doctors and hospitals all over the country were
reporting a new malady characterized by paralysis of the lower
limbs, intense abdominal pain, constant nausea, difficult
breathing, blindness, and the loss of all hair.  Many doctors
did not associate these effects with use of the cosmetic until
several suits were filed against its manufacturer.  In July
1932, the formulator of Koremlu was forced into bankruptcy by
unsettled claims for damages for more than $2,500,000.  No
effort was made, however, to recover jars of the cream already
in commerce; consequently it continued to poison women for
more than a year afterwards (96).

In 1933, because of the growing dissatisfaction with the
1906 Act, Senator Royal Copeland (D.-N.Y.) introduced a bill

which had been drafted by officials of the Solicitor's Office
of the Department of Agriculture, the enforcement agency for
the 1906 Act (97).  After five years of legislative hearings
and four major revisions it was enacted on June 25, 1938 as
the Federal Food, Drug and Cosmetics Act (FFDC Act) (98).

Provisions Of The Federal Food, Drug, And Cosmetic Act Of
1938 According to the FFDC Act of 1938, a cosmetic is any
article, except soap, "intended to be rubbed, poured,
sprinkled, sprayed on, introduced into or otherwise applied to
the human body for cleansing, beautifying, promoting
attractiveness, or altering the appearance." (99)
    Such an article must be neither adulterated nor misbranded.
That is to say it must be free of poisonous or deleterious
substances that make it injurious to the user; it must be
produced and held under sanitary conditions; it must be
packaged in a safe container which must also be non-deceptive.
The label of the package must contain information about the
manufacturer, packager or distributor and the quantity of its
contents, and it must contain no false or misleading
statements (100).
    A cosmetic which does not conform to these requirements may
be seized or criminal penalties may be imposed (101).  The
1938 FFDC Act, however, permits the sale of products
containing potentially poisonous or hazardous substances until
the FDA can prove them to be injurious to health.  In short,
the regulatory framework which the Congress chose does not
prevent harmful preparations from reaching the marketplace;
it simply makes their removal possible once hazards have been
reported.  Moreover, because there is no requirement that
cosmetic ingredients be disclosed, users of cosmetics are
unable to voluntarily protect themselves by avoiding cosmetics
which contain dangerous substances or ingredients to which
they may be allergic or sensitive.  This is because cosmetic
formulations are considered a trade secret; thus, even poison
control centers and doctors have no automatic right to such
information.
    Two kinds of products were given special treatment under
the 1938 FFDC Act.  Soap manufacturers prevailed upon the
Congress to exclude their products from regulation (99).
Their lobbyists argued that if soap were included in the
federal act then soap would soon be included in the cosmetics
tax laws of the various states, and "a tax on cleanliness is a
tax on health." (102)
    It is especially ironic that the Congress also created an
exception in the law for the coal-tar dyes responsible for the

Lashlure tragedy featured in the FDA's "chamber of horrors."
The 1938 FFDC Act simply requires that (a) a warning be
included on the label that blindness may result from the use
of the product on eyelashes and (b) a preliminary test should
be conducted to avoid allergic reactions.  Providing they are
thus labeled, coal-tar dyes cannot ever be considered
"adulterated" under the 1938 FFDC Act (103).

Attempts To Tighten The Regulation Of Cosmetics  In 1952,
hearings before the House Select Committee to Investigate the
Use of Chemicals in Food Products, chaired by Rep. James J.
Delaney, (D.-N.Y.), known as the "Delaney Committee," were
extended to receive testimony on cosmetics.  By that time,
there were a new series of toxic effects from such cosmetics
as deodorants, hair straighteners, depilatories, hair
lacquers, fingernail polishes, lipsticks, wave lotions and
shampoos.  Toni Stabile in her book Cosmetics:  Trick or
Treat? quotes from the record of these hearings the testimony
of the manufacturers of a dandruff shampoo containing a new
polyoxyethylene compound detergent which had caused semi-
permanent eye injuries.  The FDA had brought seizure actions
against the products which ended in decrees of product
condemnation and destruction.  One manufacturer testified that
his shampoo was the only cosmetic he made, and that he had not
tested his product for eye irritation before the FDA seized it
(104).

The Delaney Committee also learned that 1,000 "accidents"
occurring between 1947 and 1949 had involved damage to
fingernails caused by nail polish undercoats designed to
cause the polish to adhere more firmly.  These products
contained phenol formaldehyde resins which acted as sensitizer
and sometimes resulted in the loosening or loss of the nail.
These nail base formulae were withdrawn from the market, but
others with similar sensitizing agents replaced them; and even
after a $40,000 judgment was recovered against Revlon in 1963,
"nail strengtheners" containing up to 19 percent formaldehyde
were still on the market (104).

In 1952 the Delaney Committee reported:

"The evidence has convinced this committee that a number of
cosmetic companies are not adequately testing their
preparations; that the public is entitled to greater
protection with respect to products as widely used as
cosmetics; and that such protection is not afforded by
existing legislation, under which a manufacturer may be
punished and his product seized, after injury has occurred.

Your committee recommends, therefore, that the Federal Food,
Drug and Cosmetic Act be amended to require that cosmetics be
subjected to essentially the same safety requirements as now
apply to new drugs." (105)

Subsequently, in 1954, Rep. Leonor K. Sullivan (D.-Mo.)
introduced legislation requiring the listing of all
ingredients on the cosmetic product label and proper
pre-market safety testing.  The 83rd Congress, and each
successive one, has failed to act on such proposals.

At 1962 hearings on the proposed Drug Industry Act, held
before the House Committee on Interstate and Foreign Commerce,
and chaired by Rep. Oren Harris (D.-Ark.), Rep. Sullivan
testified on her proposals for better cosmetics regulation.
That year, and the following year, President Kennedy urged the
Congress to enact legislation requiring the pre-market testing
of all cosmetics.

In the 88th Congress, Rep. Harris introduced the
administration bill, H.R. 6788, as well as a similar proposal
drafted by the cosmetic industry, which were intended to
accomplish that goal.  The industry apparently had resigned
itself to the inevitability of pre-market testing.  However,
no hearings were held on either bill, and they died in
Committee.  No similar bills were introduced into the Senate.
Rep. Sullivan has continued to introduce her omnibus bill for
the overhaul of the FFDC Act in each subsequent Congress.

A new indication of interest in the increased regulation of
cosmetics surfaced during the 92nd Congress, when a proposal
was made to remove the FDA from the DHEW and to transfer its
regulatory responsibilities to a new and independent consumer
product agency.

The proposal for an independent consumer product agency,
with the responsibility of setting and enforcing safety
standards for all consumer goods, was made by the National
Commission on Product Safety in its final report (17).  Sen.
Warren G. Magnuson (D.-Wa.), Chairman of the Committee on
Commerce, introduced legislation embodying the principle into
the Senate (The Food and Drug and Consumer Product Safety Act
of 1972).  Under the bill, the FDA would have been trasferred
to the new, independent consumer agency.  Further, cosmetics
would have been redefined as consumer products, and as such
would have become subject to the provisions of the bill
calling for the setting, and enforcing, of consumer product
safety standards.  The Magnuson bill passed the Senate (106).
However, similar legislation, which was introduced in the
House (The Consumer Protection Agency Bill of 1972) by Rep.

John E. Moss (D.-Calif.), left the FDA intact within DHEW,
and did not touch the existing definition of a cosmetic under
the FFDC Act.  The final version of this measure that emerged
from the House/Senate conference, The Consumer Product Safety
Act (P.L. 92-573), was very similar to the House version.
Thus, cosmetics regulation is still left with the FDA.

During congressional debates on these two bills, cosmetics
regulation was not touched on, except for an attempt by Sen.
Thomas Eagleton (D.-Mo.) to carry through an amendment to the
FFDC Act to require cosmetic ingredient labeling.  Sen.
Magnuson, in collaboration with Sen. Frank E. Moss (D.-Utah),
did introduce separate legislation to overhaul the regulation
of cosmetics during the 92nd Congress (107).  The two Senators
also have proposed hearings on the issue of cosmetics
regulation on several occasions and have pressed the FDA for
more regulatory action to protect the consumer.  In the House,
Rep. Frank E. Evans (D.-Colo.), who sits on the House
Appropriations Subcommittee responsible for overseeing the FDA
budget, also has made cosmetics a special interest and
introduced legislation to amend the FFDC Act to increase FDA
control of cosmetics safety (108).

Impact Of Other New Legislation Although the Congress has
failed to address itself to the issue of the reform of
cosmetics regulation per se during the last thirty years, it
has passed other legislation that is relevant to the issue of
the safety of certain cosmetics ingredients.
The Color Additive Amendments of 1960 The Color Additive
Amendments of 1960 (P.L. 86-618) provide that foods, drugs and
cosmetics will be considered adulterated if they contain color
additives that have not been proved safe, to the satisfaction
of the FDA, for the particular use intended for the product.
A color additive is defined as a

"dye, pigment, or other substance, whether synthetic or
derived from a vegetable, animal, mineral or other source,
which imparts a color when added or applied to a food, drug or
cosmetic or the human body."

All color additives (including the coal tar colors covered
by the 1938 Act, but excluding the coal tar hair dyes) which
are not specifically exempted are required to be properly
tested for possible toxicity, and the burden of proof of
safety is placed on the industry, not on the FDA.  The
limitation that safety need only be proved for the intended
use of the color additive renders these Amendments more

permissive in their application that the original 1938 Act,
which required safety of the coal tar colors to be absolutely
established for all uses.

The FDA is required to issue regulations listing permitted
color additives and the conditions under which they may be
used, including the amounts that may be used when limitations
are judged to be necessary. Colors are grouped into a number
of categories, the chief being "FD&C" - for use in foods,
drugs and cosmetics; "D&C" - for drug and cosmetic use only;
and "Ext. D&C" - for use in externally applied drugs and
cosmetics only.  Most of the coal tar dyes and colors are
required to be certified for certain standards of purity.  The
analytical work involved is conducted by the FDA, and paid for
by the industry - each new batch of the manufactured color
additive has to be thus certified.

In the 1960 Amendments, the FDA was given the power to
provide a temporary listing of color additives for existing
uses while the industry conducted the necessary toxicological
studies.  The Amendments specified a period of two and one-
half years as the likely limit for such temporary listings.
Nonetheless, even though twelve years have passed since the
Amendments became law, most color additive listings are still
temporary.  A major cause of the delay has been a protracted
legal battle between the FDA and the industry as to the exact
scope of application of the 1960 Amendments.  (A more recent
cause of delay, briefly discussed earlier, has been the FDA's
belated recognition of the need to impose requirements for
more comprehensive long term toxicity tests.)

In 1963, the FDA proposed three regulations (109) under the
Act which

"...amplified the statutory definition of color additives by
including diluents; included certain cosmetics such as
lipstick, rouge and eye shadow within the scope of color
additives; and limited the exemption for hair dyes to those as
to which the 'patch test' was effective and excluded from the
exemption certain components other than the coloring
ingredient of the dye."

The cosmetics industry, considering that the Commissioner
had exceeded his rule-making authority under the 1960 Act,
immediately sought judicial review of the regulations.

Nine years later, the U.S. Supreme Court having meanwhile
decided the issue was ripe for review (110), Judge Friendly
of the Second Circuit ruled that the FDA had extended the
scope of the Statute beyond the point where the Congress

indicated it would "stop" by including finished cosmetic
product within the definition of color additives.  Likewise,
the attempt to remove the exemption for coal-tar hair dyes
which presented a danger for which patch testing provided no
safeguard was invalidated.  However, the FDA did succeed in
defending its ruling that the coal-tar hair dye exemption did
not apply to coloring ingredients in hair dyes not derived
from coal-tar or to poisonous or deleterious dilutents (111).
Federal Hazardous Substance Act and Poison Prevention
Packaging Act  In 1960, the Congress also passed what is now
entitled the Federal Hazardous Substances (FHS) Act (112), to
supercede the Federal Caustic Poison (FCP) Act of 1927, which
required warning labels with emergency antidotes on any
product, including cosmetics, which contained certain
enumerated poisons.  The new FHS Act, while requiring labeling
of virtually all hazardous materials, specifically exempts
foods, drugs, and cosmetics, leaving them to the outmoded
regulation of the 1927 FCP Act.

In hearings which preceded congressional passage of the
1960 FHS Act, the director of a Poison Control Center at a
Maryland hospital testified that 43 percent of all deaths
among children were caused by accidental poisoning.  The
following year the U.S. Public Health Service recorded more
than 1,700 cases of children who had been poisoned by
ingestion of cosmetics that year; the actual incidence of such
accidents at present is estimated at over 50,000 a year.

In 1963, President Kennedy, in a message to the Congress on
national health, urged protection of children from such
unnecessary hazards.  Nevertheless, it was not until December
30, 1970, that the Poison Prevention Packaging Act (P.L.
91-601) was enacted to provide for special packaging to
protect children from serious injury or illness from handling,
using, or ingesting household substances.  A year later,
standards for safety closures had been set only for hazardous
drugs, aspirins, wintergreen, and oil-based furniture polish.
As of December 1972 the Product Safety Division of the FDA had
not set standards for cosmetic containers.
Kefauver-Harris Amendments to the 1938 FFDC Act  In the wake of
the thalidomide tragedy, the Congress enacted in 1962 the
Kefauver-Harris Amendments (P.L. 87-871) to the new-drug
provisions of the 1938 FFDC Act, which amendments require
manufacturers to file an NDA containing substantial evidence
as to both the safety and efficacy of any newly developed drug
(113).  Consequently, the maker of a product classified as a
drug must present "substantial evidence" that it will have the
effect it claims under the conditions of use prescribed,

recommended, or suggested in the proposed labeling.
Substantial evidence consists of "well-controlled
investigations, including clinical investigation, by experts
qualified by scientific training and experience to evaluate
the effectiveness of the drug involved." (114)

Because some cosmetics may also be classified as drugs, the
1962 Amendments can seriously effect the way in which such
products are regulated.  Until the Congress enacts further
legislation to protect consumers of cosmetics, one way for the
FDA to keep harmful beauty preparations off the market would
be to classify them as drugs or "drug-cosmetics."

The Drug-Cosmetics The FFDC Act of 1938 broadened the
definition of "drug" so that it encompasses not only those
products which are offered "to prevent or cure an ailment" as
in the 1906 Act but also those offered "to affect the
structure or function of the body." (115)  Dandruff shampoos,
wrinkle removers, preparations to prevent baldness, and
anti-perspirants are among the examples of cosmetics which now
also are classified as drugs.

The effect of the expanded definition was to permit the FDA
to subject many more cosmetics products to drug regulation.
Manufacturers of "drug-cosmetics" have, of course, resisted
classification of their products as drugs to avoid these
testing obligations.

It should be emphasized that whether a cosmetic is also a
drug depends upon whether the manufacturer claims it prevents
or cures an ailment or affects the structure or function of
the body, and not upon whether or not it actually does so.
The crucial test for classification as a drug is the
representation of the product and not its actual performance
or effect.  For example, makers of soaps which contained HCP
were not required to test or label their products as
containing HCP until they decided to advertise their products
as "anti-bacterial" cleansers.

Another clear illustration of the regulatory weakness of
this situation is provided by the Purex Corporation's
simultaneous marketing of Sweetheart Deodorant Soap, a
cosmetic containing 0.6 percent tribromosalicylanilide (TBS)
as an antimicrobial ingredient, and Cuticura Medicated
Antibacterial Soap, an OTC drug containing 0.325 percent TBS.
The former product can be freely marketed unless the FDA can
prove hazard, while the latter is marketed under NDA status
(116).

The introduction of a protein lotion made from bovine
albumin which was offered as a wrinkle smoother gave rise to a

series of judicial decisions as to the difference between a
drug and a cosmetic.  In 1969, the U.S. Courts of Appeals for
both the Second and Third Circuits declared (117, 118) these
products drugs because they claimed to have therapeutic value
(i.e., "a face lift without surgery").  What the lotion did in
fact was to contract as it dried, forming a tightening film on
the face.  The effect was mechanical rather than
physiological, but the court in one case concluded that it
must consider how the unthinking or credulous consumer would
understand the representations made.  Both Courts declared the
wrinkle smoothers to be drugs and required that they be proved
safe and effective.

In 1971, however, the U.S. District Court for the District
of Maryland declared that a similar wrinkle-remover product,
"Caked Magic Secret," was not a drug because its promotional
claims that it was "pure protein" and caused "an astringent
sensation" would not lead even the "ignorant, unthinking and
credulous consumer" to think that it would alter the structure
of the skin (119).

It has been suggested that the sense of these three legal
cases (117-119) implies that cosmetics become drugs as well
when their claimed effect on the structure or function of the
body relates to health, rather than beauty, or if the labeling
is couched in medical or pharmaceutical phraseology (120).

The truth is, perhaps, that the words "intended to affect
the structure or any function of the body" are confusing to
the consumer and difficult for courts to interpret
consistently because they do not relate to biologic facts.
Dr. Naomi Kanof, of the AMA's Committee on Cutaneous Health,
has noted that virtually all cosmetics applied to the skin are
intended to, and do, affect the structure and function of the
skin in some way, just as a sudden change in temperature or a
drying wind will (121).  Thus, from this point of view, the
drug definition could easily be broadened to cover most of the
products now classified as cosmetics.  To avoid this result,
Dr. Kanof proposed, and the AMA Committee endorsed, amendments
to both the drug and the cosmetics definitions that would
narrow the scope of the former.  The proposals would revise
the drug definition to make clear that the phrase "intended to
affect the structure or any function..." had no biological
application to the term cosmetic.  The definition of a
cosmetic would be extended to include such articles "...as are
not intended to alter or interfere with the physiologic
competence", medical and scientific judgment would have to be
called upon to advise on the scope of its meaning and
application (121).

A benefit of Dr. Kanof's proposal, as phrased, would be to
provide a more scientific basis on which to judge the question
of whether or not a product is a drug-cosmetic.  However, it
still leaves the word intended as a key operating concept, and
its overall effect would be to restrict the ability of the FDA
to recategorize a cosmetic as a drug-cosmetic and so bring it
under tighter regulation.

Peter Barton Hutt, as the FDA General Counsel, has proposed
another means of reducing the number of cosmetics which can be
considered drugs (122).  This is to specifically exempt
cosmetics from the "structure and function" clause of the 1938
FFDC Act as food is presently exempted.  Counsel Hutt argues
that this would in no way exempt cosmetics from drug
classification if true medical or therapeutic claims were made
for them (122).  This argument implies that he believes that
purchasers of products for medicinal purposes should be
protected from injury and fraud, but that consumers who merely
wish to improve their appearance must abide by the common-law
rule of "caveat emptor."  Only a few cosmetics, such as
sunburn preventatives, are claimed to cure or prevent disease.
On the other hand, many manufacturers represent their products
as having some beneficial effect on the structure or function
of the skin or body.  Until 1967, the FDA published a periodic
list of "Cosmetics Subject to the Drug Provisions of the Act,"
the last of which showed 180 cosmetic products against which
the FDA had acted because they made drug claims; most of these
fell into the "structure or function" categories (122).

With the exception of the wrinkle-remover cases and the
color additives cases discussed above, the FDA has done little
to expand the category of drug-cosmetics.  For example, as
Counsel Hutt points out, the FDA does not consider hair and
nails as encompassed within the human body for purposes of the
drug definition, but does so consider them for purposes of the
cosmetic definition.  Thus, chemical compounds such as hair
straighteners, permanent waves, and cuticle removers, which
are intended to affect the structure of the hair or cuticle,
have been declared cosmetics, but not drugs (122).

Congressional Committees Presently, in the Senate, the Health
Subcommittee of the Committee on Labor and Public Welfare,
chaired by Sen. Edward Kennedy (D.-Mass.) has prime
responsibility for the oversight of the FFDC Act, and thus
also has responsibility for any proposals to amend the Act.
Similar responsibility in the House rests on the Health
Subcommittee of the Committee on Interstate and Foreign
Commerce; the present Subcommittee's Chairman is Rep. Paul G.

Rogers (D.-Fla.)

Significantly, the proposals for reform of cosmetics regulation advanced by Senators Warren G. Magnuson and Frank E. Moss have been offered as amendments to the Fair Packaging and Labeling Act.  This drafting step was undertaken so the legislation would be referred to the Senate Commerce Committee which has the oversight responsibility for that Act. In turn, Sen. Magnuson is Chairman of the Commerce Committee and Sen. Moss Chairman of its Subcommittee on Consumer Affairs.  Were the proposed bill to reform the regulation of cosmetics to have been cast chiefly as an amendment to the FFDC Act, under Senate rules it would have been referred to Sen. Kennedy's Subcommittee.  However, in the House, it is interesting to note that the Moss bill would be referred to Rep. Rodger's Health Subcommittee, which has legislative jurisdiction over both statutes.

Legislative responsibility is not the only basis for congressional committee interest or responsibility for this particular issue.  In the House, the Committee on Government Operations Subcommittee on Intergovernmental Relations maintains an investigative oversight of the operations of the FDA.  This Subcommittee is popularly known as the Fountain Committee after its chairman, Rep. L. H. Fountain (D.-N.C.). In the Senate, Sen. Abraham A. Ribicoff (D.-Conn.) chairs the Government Operations Subcommittee on Executive Reorganization, which plays a similar investigative oversight role.  In addition, Sen. Gaylord Nelson (D.-Wis.) chairs the Monopoly Subcommittee of the Senate Select Committee on Small Business.  From this position Sen. Nelson has conducted a five year series of hearings on the drug industry, and his findings, inter alia, have obvious relevance to the regulation of drug-cosmetics.

The annual congressional oversight of proposed government agency budgets by the Appropriations Committees also provides an important forum for the monitoring of the FDA's regulation of cosmetics.  In the House, the Appropriations Subcommittee on the Agriculture, Environmental and Consumer Protection is responsible for overseeing the FDA budget.  This subcommittee's chairman, Rep. Jamie L. Whitten (D.-Miss.), is primarily interested in agriculture.  Among the other members of this subcommittee is Rep. Frank E. Evans (D.-Colo.) whose interest in the regulation of cosmetics has already been noted.

In the Senate, Sen. Gale W. McGee (D.-Wyo.) is the chairman of the Appropriations Subcommittee on Agriculture, Environmental and Consumer Protection, which is responsible for the FDA.

## Regulation In Practice - The Parameters Of Change

Since 1970, there have been increasingly heavy pressures on
the FDA to act on many issues of cosmetics safety. Adding to
a prevalent feeling of the inadequacy of the FDA's action in
protecting the consumer in such fields as food and animal feed
additive safety, a number of cases of cosmetics ingredient
hazard have been brought to the public's attention by non-FDA
scientists, consumer groups, and newspaper reporters. One
consequence has been more active moves by consumer groups and
journalists to prove issues of cosmetics regulation. Another
consequence has been an increase in congressional interest in
cosmetics as part of a wider focus on consumer product issues
and, in turn, all aspects of FDA activity. The cosmetics
industry has carried through fairly substantial changes in the
policies and practices it has long followed in an effort to
protect itself from the possibility of tighter mandatory
government regulation. Measured on the scale of the public
interest, the pace of change and reform is most certainly
slow. Nonetheless, the present situation is a relatively
fluid one when compared to the more hardened status quo
positions of the 1960s.

Thus, this section summarizes the amalgam of regulatory
practice and reforming trends that presently exist, with a
view to establishing the essential parameters of the process.
In many ways, these reflect recent wider trends in consumer
policies, and relate closely to the possibility of more
fundamental reform of the principles underlying cosmetic
regulation.

## Enforcement - Procedures And Problems At The FDA Chief

enforcement responsibility for the 1938 FFDC Act within the
DHEW has been delegated to the FDA. In fiscal year 1972, the
FDA spent just over $1 million on the regulation of cosmetics,
inspecting 445 firms handling cosmetics products, analyzing
510 cosmetics samples, and reviewing 254 consumer injury
reports. In 1973, there was only a modest increase in this
activity, although an extra $200,000 was appropriated for the
implementation (vide infra) of the new voluntary agreements
with the cosmetics industry (123).

Organization Responsibility for the regulation of cosmetics
within the FDA lies chiefly in the Bureau of Foods. Thus,
curiously, regulatory association seems to be historically
based on the association of cosmetics with colors - the former
were initially regulated chiefly as food additives. Until

relatively recently, the chief research activity conducted
within the Bureau of Foods was the analysis of cosmetics.
Since cosmetic ingredient information was not generally
available to the FDA, the agency had to have the ability to
elucidate the composition of cosmetic products suspected of
being harmful.  Even today, the major laboratory manpower
devoted to cosmetics regulation consists of analytical
chemists and their support staff.  In the past, there has not
been a specific "cosmetics toxicology" laboratory.  Instead,
toxicological work and expertise was generally drawn from
other laboratories within the FDA's Bureau of Foods and Bureau
of Drugs.  However, one branch of the Bureau of Foods has
recently begun to devote most of its efforts to research on
cosmetics toxicology (see below).

The main lines of communication and responsibility for the
regulation of cosmetics within the FDA are indicated in
Figure 1.  The Division of Colors and Cosmetics Technology,
which falls within the Office of Product Technology, is
responsible for the development of analytical methodology, the
analysis of cosmetics, the review and analysis of consumer
complaints and, most recently, the organization of the new
registry of the cosmetic industry and cosmetic product
formulation data.  The Colors Branch of the Division is
responsible for the certification of batches of color
additives for purity:  this analytical work is paid for by the
colors industry on a fee basis.  The Office of Science of the
Bureau of Foods includes the Division of Toxicology, which is
responsible for reviewing the color additive safety petitions
and overseeing the process of color additive listing.  The
Dermal Toxicity Branch of this Division has, over the last
five years, come to devote much of its resources to issues of
cosmetics toxicology.  However, cosmetics that are legally
classifiable as drugs are the responsibility of the Bureau of
Drugs.

The field activities of the FDA, gathered into ten regional
offices, include factory inspections and product sampling in
the market place, as well as follow-through enquiries,
inspections, etc., in response to requests from the FDA
offices in Washington.  The Executive Director for Regional
Operations oversees the coordination of general policy between
the regional offices, while specific cases requiring federal
action (i.e., as the result of a factory inspection) are
handled by the Office of Compliance in the Bureau of Foods.
This office is responsible for the basic enforcement
activities of the FDA with respect to cosmetics.  However,
issues of any regulatory complexity are generally handled in

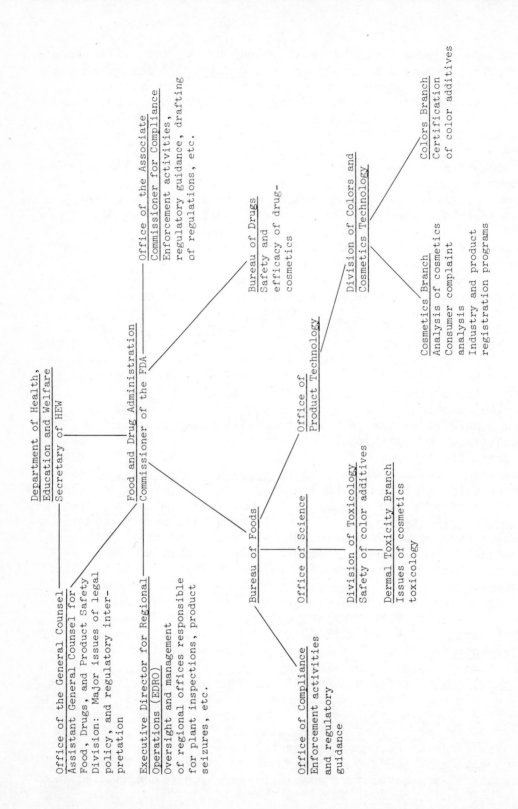

Figure 1 The regulation of cosmetics: a hierarchy of responsibiliti

the higher echelons of the FDA, by the Office of the Associate
Commissioner for Compliance, and by the FDA Commissioner's
Office in collaboration with the DHEW Assistant General
Counsel for Food, Drugs, and Product Safety.
FDA In-House Coordination Two features of this regulatory
hierarchy are of note.  Firstly, the basic responsibilities
for cosmetics regulation are rather scattered through a Bureau
whose main focus is the safety of food.  Secondly, there is no
single senior FDA official responsible for cosmetics
regulation.  Consequently, issues important enough to require
the attention of the upper level of FDA administration have to
be dealt with on an ad hoc basis by those senior officials
most likely to be interested.  Since the legal basis for
cosmetics regulation is limited, a substantial emphasis has to
be placed on creative policy making and creative enforcement
activities.  The absence of a single focus for cosmetics
regulation probably weakens the ability of the FDA to act as
effectively in this regard as it might otherwise.  Also,
because of the lack of a clear upper echelon responsibility,
policy issues can take a long time to be resolved - this
leaves junior staff without any clear basis for further action
in the meantime.
    Since 1971, the staff of the FDA's Division of Colors and
Cosmetics Technology has included an M.D. charged with
coordinating efforts relating to cosmetics safety, including
liaison with the Dermal Toxicity Branch.  Internal proposals
that a staff of suitable health professionals (i.e.,
toxicologists, dermatologists, microbiologists) be attached
to the Division of Colors and Cosmetics Technology have been
rejected by senior FDA administrators on the grounds that such
scientists and medical professionals work better if surrounded
by their professional peers.  Consequently, the Dermal
Toxicity Branch has remained within the Division of
Toxicology.  While this peer group argument has its strong
points, the fact remains that responsibility for cosmetics
regulation is presently so fractured as to be very inefficient
in practice.
Regulatory Practice The inputs into FDA regulatory oversight
of cosmetics can be broadly sketched as follows:

- Factory inspections which are limited in practice to
inspection for good manufacturing practices and possible
microbial contamination, because of trade secrecy strictures
on product formulation data;

- Analytical studies of cosmetics to detect particular
ingredients that are banned or controlled in some way, or on

which particular attention has been focused, such as HCP;

- In-house, and contracted, testing of particular cosmetics ingredients for toxicity; and

- Analysis of consumer complaint letters to establish problem areas, combined with analytical studies of the leading products to establish, where possible, the responsible ingredients.

The FFDC Act prohibits interstate commerce of cosmetics that are adulterated or misbranded.  The Act gives the FDA power to seize such products where necessary to prevent their consumption, to serve injunctions on violators of the law, and to criminally prosecute those who violate the law.
Injunctive Authority vs. Voluntary Recall In practice, the FDA has come to rely very heavily on voluntary action by the cosmetics industry to correct regulatory violations.  So much so, in fact, that any consideration of the utility of the present government regulation of cosmetics must evaluate the strengths and weaknesses of the voluntary approach.
When the FDA wishes to remove a product from the market, it relies heavily on a voluntary recall procedure, rather than the legally sanctioned process of seizure.  Although voluntary recall has no basis in law, it has become so common that it is fully formalized in FDA operational manuals.  There is, of course, the implicit underlying threat of seizure action by the FDA in the courts, but both the FDA and the affected company are aware that court action can be slow, and that it can provide opportunities for delaying action by a manufacturer.  Thus, the threat of legal action is a two-edged sword to the FDA.
The voluntary recall procedure, claims the FDA (124), gives the agency flexibility and speed of action.  However, in return, the affected company is often given the benefit of low "media profile" on the recall, and may end up being publicly praised for its cooperation with the FDA.  The key point is that it is the politics of the FDA-company relationship that dominates how the recall is handled.  The fundamental question of the broad public interest at stake may well become a secondary factor.  The whole issue of voluntary recall has been recently studied by the Fountain Committee (124).
Other Voluntary Actions Voluntary action also opens up the possibilities of other avenues of action to resolve violations of the FFDC Act.  The FDA may seek to have a product reformulated, a particular ingredient dropped, or the amount of some ingredient decreased.  The agency may pressure the

industry as a whole, or a particular company, to initiate
further toxicity testing of a particular ingredient.  Several
examples of such actions have already been described.  First,
after the hair dye ingredient 2,4-TDA was shown to be
carcinogenic when fed to rats, the FDA accepted industry
assurances that this ingredient was no longer used.  No
formal move, however, was made to ban the chemical, nor seize
existing stocks of products containing it.  Second, in the
case of the bubble baths that were apparently causing serious
urinary tract irritation in children, the FDA and the
companies concerned agreed on a reformulation of the products.
Third, when evidence was published in the scientific
literature that toxic quantities of lead were being leached
into toothpaste from toothpaste tubes, the FDA reported that
the manufacturers concerned had changed the packaging to a
safer plastic tube.  Once again, no move was made against
stocks of the older, possibly leaded, product still on the
market.

The FDA claims to see great advantages in such voluntary
actions - flexibility, speed, and low costs to the FDA.
However, there also are many negative factors.  For successful
voluntary action, a basic consensus must exist between
industry and the FDA.  This will usually reflect, in major
part, the industry judgment of the seriousness of the issue.
Thus, a company will not usually accept any proposed voluntary
action that runs counter to what it judges to be its real
interests.  The public and consumer interest is not a dominant
factor in arriving at this consensus.  Indeed, where industry
interests are really threatened, such as in the case of a
possible limitation on the use of FD&C Red 2, the removal from
the market of products containing more than 0.1 percent HCP,
or the proposed all-out ban on mercury skin bleaches, the FDA
always has to resort to formal regulatory action.

The cosmetics industry is well organized.  The Cosmetics,
Toiletry and Fragrance Association (CTFA) supports a network
of scientific committees, which regularly deal with the FDA on
the various issues raised.  An ad hoc FDA-CTFA liaison group
existed until a Presidential order opened its meetings to the
general public (125).  The FDA does not have the necessary
expertise to face such a barrage of scientific opinion on
every issue.  For example, in the development of a suitable
method of analysis for the determination of asbestos in talc,
the FDA was not represented by an interlocutor expert in use
of the key methodology, X-ray crystallography and electron
microscopy.  Industry challenges to the methodology, developed
by the FDA's contracted expert, who was a consultant to the

industry, could not be effectively evaluated by the FDA
itself.  Any final resolution of the issue runs the risk of
reflecting the industry position very strongly.

Further, a corollary of a heavy dependence on voluntary
procedures is a very close relationship between the regulators
and the regulated.  An illustrative example of the consequence
of this is the resolution of the issue of levels of HCP to be
allowed in aerosol products.  The FDA regulation, strongly
limiting the use of HCP in cosmetics, included a provision
that in the case of aerosol products, the amount of the
propellant should be <u>excluded</u> in calculating the allowable
percentage of HCP in a product (126); the propellant, after
all, evaporates very rapidly after use.  This part of the
regulation was deliberately written in by the responsible FDA
scientists, and reflected the judgment of the expert panel
that had reviewed the toxicity data on HCP (127).  However,
its implementation would have required removing from the
retailer shelves of millions of dollars worth of HCP-based
cosmetics.  A delegation of industry scientists, in a short
meeting with two FDA regulatory lawyers, was able to get this
provision changed, although none of the responsible FDA
scientists were consulted (128).  Only as a consequence of
action by a consumer group was the FDA decision even
challenged, both on procedural and scientific grounds.
However, despite continued scientific support within the FDA
for the original version of the regulations, the FDA
promulgated the industry-sought revision and (in what was
generally interpreted as a gesture to the consumer group),
also banned the use of HCP, even as a preservative, in
cosmetics likely to be used on mucous membranes (129).
However, such a move was of dubious value since the industry
was no longer using the antibacterial in new products in any
case.  The issue had always been existing stocks of products
manufactured before the HCP ban took effect.

The voluntary approach to cosmetics regulation pursued by
the FDA had recently become even more formalized with the
promulgation of the first two voluntary regulations for the
industry by the FDA.

Another limitation on the FDA's effective regulation of
cosmetics has been that cosmetics have long been a low
prestige field within the FDA.  In part, this is a reflection
of the low prestige of cosmetics as a branch of applied science
and medicine in the scientific community at large.
Consequently, it is not well funded, and it has not always
attracted its fair share of talented scientists.  Lack of
funding limits the ability of the agency scientists to develop

the scientific evidence necessary for confident regulatory
action.  It also encourages the FDA to seek voluntary industry
cooperation, since such a line of action is often the cheapest
in terms of time and manpower.

Even with the necessary data on hand, the FDA is slow to
act.  In some cases this reflects the usual bureaucratic
inertia and the agency's ordering of its priorities.  Issues
that are in the public eye, especially issues that are in the
congressional eye, have to be given high priority, and less
well publicized issues are thus frequently relegated to a
lesser priority.  In other cases, the agency acts as if it is
afraid of the consequence of threatening major industry
interests.

Proposals for action on the mercury bleaching creams took
over four years to gain the approval of the FDA.  As noted
earlier, internal panels of FDA scientists recommended urgent
action on HCP and on FD&C Red 2; in each case their advice was
ignored by the agency heads.  In the case of FD&C Red 2, the
subsequently proposed regulations apply a safety factor of 10
to 1 to animal test data, rather than the customary regulatory
factor of 100 to 1.  At the 100 to 1 level, too little color
would be allowed in a cosmetic for it to be of any value.

In such a case, the principle enunciated by FDA
Commissioner Edwards that "cosmetics must be safe" is not
really applied.  If there is any doubt as to the validity of
ingredient toxicity data, then the industry is often given the
benefit of the doubt, rather than the consuming public.

Pressure For Reform  As has been noted, for many years the FDA
has been under a steady and severe barrage of public
criticism.  One political consequence has been the determined
effort, made during 1972, to remove the agency from the DHEW,
and to transfer its regulatory responsibilities to a new and
independent agency.  The proposals for the reform of the
legislation regulating cosmetics, developed by Senators
Magnuson and Moss and Representatives Sullivan and Evans have
served to put the cosmetics industry on notice that an
overhaul of the existing basis of cosmetics regulation is a
likely possibility.

Pressure for change has come from other sources, also.  As
noted in the introduction to this section, there has been an
increase in general public interest in cosmetics in the wake
of a number of newspaper articles on various cosmetics issues.
Public attention has focused especially on the lack of FDA
power to require cosmetics to be tested for safety prior to
marketing, and the lack of ingredient labeling on the

cosmetics packaging.  Consumer groups and consumer
publications, such as <u>Consumer Reports</u>, have focused their
attention on cosmetics.  Virginia Knauer, President Nixon's
Advisor on Consumer Affairs, also has taken an active stand in
pressing for ingredient labeling on cosmetics (130).  Finally,
the FDA itself, partly in response to increasing congressional
and consumer pressure, and partly in response to its own inner
needs, also has been pressing the case for greater access to
industry information to improve its regulatory performance.
<u>Proposals for Self-Regulation</u>  Faced with this evidence of
mounting interest in legislative reform, the cosmetics
industry has sought to head off any serious restriction on its
freedom of action by proposing a series of voluntary
"self-regulation" proposals designed to satisfy at least a few
critics of the existing situation.

The prime mover in this effort has been the CTFA.  In the
formative stages of the effort, the CTFA also had the
important help of Peter Hutt, then a partner in the powerful
Washington law firm of Covington and Burling, and an expert in
the intricacies of the FFDC Act.  Having helped to shape the
key elements of the proposed program for the voluntary
self-regulation of the cosmetics industry, Hutt switched
sides, and in September 1971 became the FDA's General Counsel.
In making the move, Hutt gave assurances that he would not
involve himself in any decisions relating to the
then-published stages one and two of the voluntary regulations
(131).  In the following year, however, Counsel Hutt did
become active in FDA decision-making on the third stage of the
voluntary regulations, and on the issue of mandatory
ingredient labeling.  He had almost certainly dealt with these
same two issues while a Counsel to the CTFA.  The ins and outs
of Counsel Hutt's role in the FDA and of the conflict of
interest aspects of the situation have been described in an
article in <u>Science</u> (132).  The development of the program of
voluntary regulations for the cosmetics industry has had the
full blessing and encouragement of the FDA - it does, after
all, fit well into the now long established preference of the
FDA to rely on voluntary action in the regulation of
cosmetics.

During 1970 the industry began shaping its proposed
voluntary program.  On all evidence, the development of the
various proposals (vide infra) involved a very substantial
effort on the part of the CTFA, with industry counsel divided
between more conservative elements, who wished to maintain the
traditional patterns of extreme secrecy and industry
independence, and the more progressive elements, who were

anxious to shape proposals sufficiently complete to be able to
head off legislative threats.  The CTFA leadership has
apparently sided with the more progressive elements.

In a speech to the CTFA annual conference in February 1971,
FDA Commissioner Edwards outlined his agency's needs as

- Registration of the industry with the FDA;
- Disclosure of product ingredient formulation to the FDA; and
- Sharing of industry consumer complaint letter files with the
FDA.

He also raised the issue of requiring cosmetics to be
labeled with the names of potentially allergenic ingredients.
Touching on the question of requiring cosmetics to be fully
tested for safety prior to marketing, Commissioner Edwards
noted FDA's interest in the matter as reflecting the
"principle rather than the reality" at that stage (133).

In March 1971 the CTFA submitted two proposed regulations
to the FDA.  These dealt with the first two of Commissioner
Edward's demands.  After formal publication for public comment
in August 1971 (134), they were published in final form on
April 11, 1972 (135).

Manufacturer Registration Stage 1 of the voluntary regulation
calls for manufacturers to register themselves with the FDA.
By November 1971, some months after the official final date
for registration, 488 cosmetics manufacturing plants were
registered.  Almost all of the well-known names in the
industry registered.

A comparison between the companies who voluntarily
registered with the membership list of the CTFA, however,
showed that 50 out of CTFA's 131 member manufacturers had not
registered.  Most of these were the smaller cosmetics
companies.  Further, the FDA's Official Establishment
Inventory of manufacturers' establishments that it inspects,
lists over 1,300 cosmetics manufacturing establishments.  In
other words, only 488 such establishments registered under the
voluntary scheme, leaving about 800 establishments, chiefly
the smaller ones, who did not register.  Thus, grave doubt
exists regarding the ability of both the CTFA and the FDA to
communicate with these smaller members of the industry.  Since
the effectiveness of any voluntary scheme rests initially on
good communications, such a proven lack of communication is
dangerous.

Formula Registration Stage 2 of the voluntary regulations call
calls for the industry to register product formulation data

with the FDA in a semiquantitative format.*

The chief point at issue between the industry and the FDA
has been the confidentiality of this information.  The CTFA
sought summary protection of all submitted data on the
grounds of trade secrecy.  The FDA granted the industry the
right to petition for confidentiality protection for
particular ingredients, thus placing on the industry the onus
of establishing a reasonable claim to confidentiality on an
ingredient-by-ingredient basis.

A key document in this context is the FDA's regulations of
the interpretation of the 1967 Freedom of Information Act.
This has been published in proposed form, but not in its final
form as yet (136).  Under the proposed version of the
regulations, product-by-product ingredient data would be
public information except where specific confidentiality
protection is granted.  However, the registering industry
would have the opportunity to withdraw information not granted
the desired secrecy protection.

Consumer Complaint Files  The FDA has laid a heavy emphasis on
its desire to gain access to the manufacturer's consumer
complaint files.  As noted earlier, the FDA has relied heavily
on analysis of the several hundred letters it receives each
year to set priorities for action.  The industry has found
this request by the FDA the most difficult to handle.  For
example, although its proposals were first reported to be
ready in January 1972, they were some 10 months later than the
initial voluntary regulation proposals.  In turn, the CTFA did
not submit final proposals to the FDA until six months later.

These very restrictive proposals offered the FDA an annual
statistical analysis of "verified" consumer complaints, on a
complaint-per-unit-sales of each cosmetics product basis.
"Verified" consumer complaints were defined as those carrying
a physician's letter or those checked by a company agent.**
The FDA, clearly unhappy with the form of the proposals,
published both the industry proposals and its own counter
proposals side-by-side for public comment (137).  The FDA's

------------------------------------------------------------

*The quantitative details of the formulation are reported in
terms of various broad categories of use:  A=50% to 100%,
B=25% to 50%.

**The complaints-per-unit-sales figures are particularly
misleading since they dilute the experience of those who
suffer an injury from a product, who are likely to thus
consume one or two units of the product only, with the
experience of those who suffer no problem and who may buy many
units of the product.

counterproposals required industry to submit regular case-by-
case reports, including the name and address of the author of
each complaint letter.  The industry and FDA versions differ
also on the question of the confidentiality of the submitted
information.  The industry claims that all consumer complaint
letters are valid trade secrets.  The FDA contends that the
Freedom of Information Act regulations apply.  Such action
would place the details of the complaint on the public record,
but not the name of the affected consumer or cosmetics
company.

Ingredient Labeling The fourth issue that has been at the
focus of attention is ingredient labeling for cosmetics.
Consumer groups have long pressed the plight of the consumer
who is allergic to a certain cosmetic ingredient but who
cannot tell which cosmetics contain it.  Further, there is
strong feeling that the consumer has the right to know what is
contained in a product.

The cosmetics industry, however, has long traditionally
opposed ingredient labeling, arguing that trade secrets would
be at risk.  Thus, the various industry proposals for
voluntary regulation have not included a proposal for
voluntary ingredient labeling.

The Fair Labeling and Packaging (FLP) Act states that

"Whenever the promulgating authority determines that
regulations...are necessary to prevent the deception of
consumers or facilitate value comparisons as to any consumer
commodity, such authority shall promulgate...regulations
effective to...require that the label on each package of a
consumer commodity bear (A) the common or usual name of such
consumer commodity if any, and (B) in case such consumer
commodity consists of two or more ingredients, the common or
usual name of such ingredient listed in order of descending
predominance, but nothing in this paragraph shall be deemed to
require that any trade secret be divulged." (138)

The FDA has not been confident that the FLP Act gives the
agency the power to require ingredient labeling of cosmetics.
FDA Commissioner Edwards, first, in his spring 1971 address to
the CTFA annual meeting (133) and, later, at a press
conference in April 1972 (14) proposed that the FDA require
labeling only of sensitizing ingredients, as an aid to
allergic consumers.

This interpretation of the FLP Act was backed by Counsel
Hutt, but his deputy apparently disagreed, and argued that the
Act could be used to require full ingredient labeling (139).

The same conclusion was drawn by a Georgetown Law Center
student group headed by Professor Joseph Page, which
petitioned the FDA in May 1972 to issue regulations under the
FLP Act requiring full ingredient labeling of cosmetics (140).
Nevertheless, the FDA remained sufficiently uncertain that it
backed the independently initiated move by Sen. Thomas
Eagleton (D.-Mo.) to amend the FFDC Act so as to require
ingredient labeling.

Sen. Eagleton's proposal was adopted as a floor amendment
to the Consumer Product Safety Act on June 21, 1972 (141).
However, no move was made to add a similar amendment to the
House version of the bill, and the Senate provision was
dropped during the House-Senate Conference to reconcile the
two bills. Since then, the FDA has indicated its intention to
publish proposed labeling regulations under the provisions of
the FLP Act (140).

At the time that Sen. Eagleton's amendment and the Page
petition were both initiated, the CTFA indicated that the
cosmetics industry had no basic disagreement with either
proposed action, although it preferred the Page petition.
This sudden change in the traditional industry opposition to
ingredient labeling reflected a breakdown in industry
consensus on the issue.

In August 1971 Avon initiated a policy of providing
ingredient information to consumers on request. The move,
however, was not made public until 8 months later when
Virginia Knauer announced it at a press conference (141). In
May 1972 Mrs. Knauer started a campaign of letter writing,
first to the big retailing chains, and later to the cosmetic's
manufacturers, requesting that they take a firm positive
public stand on the question of ingredient labeling. However,
the initial replies from retailers and industry mostly avoided
or hedged the issue, or opposed ingredient labeling.
Nevertheless, by the early fall of 1972, Mrs. Knauer had begun
receiving replies indicating that a number of major cosmetics
companies, including Colgate-Palmolive, Mennen, Revlon,
Warner-Lambert, Max Factor, Shulton, Yardley, and Gillette,
were committed to ingredient labeling (143). By this time,
the CTFA had assembled and published a preliminary listing of
names suitable for ingredient labeling (144). Thus, it
appears that cosmetic ingredient labeling is an idea whose
time has come.

Reform Of Cosmetics Safety Testing The initial discussion in
this chapter has shown that various forms of consumer injury
accompanying the use of cosmetics still constitute a real

problem.  These include detectable consumer injury, such as
allergic reactions, or eye irritation, and less easily
causally related chronic toxicities such as neurotoxicity and
carcinogenicity.  The following discussion underlines a key
feature in the operation of the FFDC - the burden of proof of
lack of safety of a cosmetic or cosmetic ingredient lies on
the Federal Government.

   Nonetheless, one might hope that the responsible
manufacturer would fully evaluate the safety of any new
cosmetic product prior to marketing.  In the words of FDA
Commissioner Edwards,

"It is fundamental that no manufacturer of a consumer product
has the right to place that product on the market without
first substantiating its safety... In the case of a cosmetic
the Act [FFDC] does not require approval by the FDA prior to
marketing, but it necessarily contemplates that the
manufacturer has obtained all data and information necessary
and appropriate to substantiate the products safety prior to
marketing." (145)

Industry Testing Practices Industry practices vary widely.
Most major cosmetics companies maintain in-house testing
facilities.  Nevertheless, manufacturers will heavily contract
their safety testing to commercial testing houses.  Because
the present law does not require the industry to submit test
data to the FDA, there is insufficient material on the public
record to allow a detailed evaluation of existing practices.
Nonetheless, the situation described herein indicates that
there are considerable inadequacies in existing practice.

   On one hand, there do exist apparently well organized
safety evaluation programs that lay a heavy emphasis on the
scientific method, and which provide an active role for the
toxicologist in the decision-making process for new cosmetics
products.  The program described for the Gillette Medical
Evaluations Laboratory is representative, perhaps, of this
progressive wing of industry (146, 147).

   Attention is focused on determination of the $LD_{50}$ (the
median lethal dose), and on testing for acute oral toxicity,
ophthalmic irritancy, percutaneous toxicity, dermal irritancy,
and sensitization with animals.  Routine subacute and chronic
toxicity tests with animals also are undertaken.  The report
of the Gillette program stresses the need for monitoring a
full range of physiological parameters during these tests, for
histopathologic as well as gross examination of the test
animals, and for the determination of both apparent no-effect

and positive effect levels (146, 147).

While it mentions the need for teratogenicity testing in some cases, surprisingly the report does not raise the critical issue of long-term chronic toxicity tests, such as for carcinogenicity (146, 147). Human testing is carried out with volunteers for primary skin irritancy, contact sensitization, and contact photosensitization. The initial stages of product marketing are closely monitored. The Gillette Medical Evaluations Laboratory apparently has an effective veto in decisions on new product development. The scientific background and methodology of some of the safety tests mentioned here has been reviewed in papers given at a 1968 conference in Washington, D.C. (148). The point must be stressed, however, that such a relatively comprehensive program of safety evaluation is not the present norm for most cosmetics companies.

A typical example of a far more limited series of safety tests emerged as the result of a recent suit against the manufactuere of a feminine deodorant spray (149). The manufacturer, Alberto Culver, reported that it had conducted the following three tests for "efficiency, effectiveness and safety" prior to marketing the product, "according to an established protocol":

- To determine the vaginal irritation potential, the product was sprayed under controlled conditions onto the labia and vagina of 20 female albino rats. The procedure was repeated daily for three consecutive days, and the rats were examined daily. At the conclusion of a seven day observation period, the animals were wieghed, sacrificed and autopsied;

- Repeated insult patch testing procedure was carried out on 67 human subjects over a period of six weeks, on intact skin; and

- A gynecologist-supervised use test by 31 women over a period of 5 weeks, with the product being daily applied two to four times daily.

Quite obviously, the goal of the testing in this case was to predict the risk of potential untoward consumer experience, rather than to evaluate the toxicity parameters of the product in use.

Elements Of An Effective Testing Program The present industry judgement of what constitutes an adequate testing protocol is beginning to slowly change. Under the impact of greater FDA and public concern for product safety, the industry is attempting to raise its testing standards. The CTFA's

Pharmacology and Toxicology Committee has published a set of
suggested guidelines (150). These closely match the
procedures described for Gillette (146, 147). Judgement as to
the success of this effort cannot yet be made.

At the same time, the case histories of HCP, FD&C Red 2,
and 2,4-TDA, previously described, are providing a sharp
emphasis on the need for a detailed understanding of
physiological effects of cosmetics ingredients, and on the
need for long term chronic toxicity testing that is a novel
consideration for the industry. The 1968 conference on the
safety evaluation of cosmetics (148) included papers on
primary skin irritation, contact sensitization, and
photosensitization. There were only two papers, however, on
problems of carcinogenicity related to chronic toxicity, and
these were rather academic contributions that did not relate
as directly as the other papers to the experience of cosmetics
toxicologists. While methods for determining the percutaneous
absorption of cosmetics ingredients were described in some
detail in several papers, questions of the metabolic fate in
the body and of possible organ toxicity were not raised.

The gap between industry practice and toxicological need
has been well illustrated in the history to date of the FDA's
Antimicrobial Review Panel. This panel, established as part
of the now ongoing review of the safety and efficacy of all
OTC drugs, has been charged with evaluating the safety and
efficacy of antimicrobials used in various non-prescription
drug products such as medicated and antibacterial soaps,
medicated lotions, and first-aid creams. The panel was
responsible for the recommendations that finally persuaded the
FDA to withdraw its approval for the use of HCP in
non-prescription products.

At its August 1972 session, the panel set down a guide to
the evaluation of the safety and efficacy of these
ingredients. The section of the guide dealing with systemic
toxicity stressed the need for data on percutaneous
absorption, blood levels, metabolic fate and excretion, effect
on body organs, and possible mutagenicity, reproductive
effects, and carcinogenicity. The toxicity data submitted by
the industry, much of it the results of test methods
developed, and testing conducted, within the previous year,
and frequently underway, was seriously deficient. Data on
percutaneous absorption and blood levels were often not
available, and long term chronic toxicity data was rarely part
of the industry submissions. At its October meeting, it was
noted that

"The panel recognizes that the type of study required to answer the questions of percutaneous absorption, blood levels, organ toxicity and excretion are different from commonly run safety tests of the past. However, the answers from all these tests are required to declare a product generally recognized as safe." (151)

   Part of the blame for this situation can be shared by the FDA, which has had the opportunity in the past to pressure the industry to adopt more sophisticated and comprehensive testing programs. Many of these antimicrobials, including HCP, were approved by the FDA as safe and effective in various NDA's for OTC products during the 1960s. At that time, the FDA did not challenge the industry to produce the toxicity data that the review panel now finds the industry to lack. Similarly, it was only after the issues of the possible embryotoxicity of FD&C Red 2 had been raised that the FDA required multigenerational studies to be conducted for other ingested colors.

Legislation, Regulation, And The Safety Of Cosmetics The root causes of the present situation are various. A general belief that cosmetics, by their very nature, must be innocuous is partly to blame. Until recently, the FDA has not devoted the energy and attention to the issue that could have pressured industry into overhauling its inadequate testing programs. In placing the burden of proof for the lack of a cosmetic's safety on the FDA, the law has undoubtedly exerted a negative influence. The industry, with its scientific and other resources geared to profit in an advertising-dominated market place, has not been receptive to the rapid evolution of a modern cosmetics toxicology. The universities, and the medical and scientific professions generally, too often have failed to treat the hazards from cosmetics seriously, or have developed close consulting relationships with the industry.

   It was noted, in opening this chapter, that the underlying message of both cosmetics advertising and cosmetics regulatory law focuses on the intended use or action of the cosmetic product. If the real purpose of a regulatory scheme for cosmetics is to ensure the safety of cosmetics, then perhaps the underlying concept should be that cosmetics are mixtures of chemicals. For the average consumer, these products, which are intimately used and often for long periods of time, represent a significant addition to the environmental burden of chemicals to which he or she is daily exposed.

   Acceptance of such a conceptual approach to cosmetics safety leads to the necessity of asking questions about the

effect of these chemicals on the human physiology.  Given our
growing awareness of the complexity of our life system, and of
the varied number of ways that a chemical can interfere with
important life processes, a strong case can be made for the
very conservative approach that requires that each chemical
included in a cosmetic formulation should be assumed dangerous
until its safety is well established.  Such a dictum would be
the very reverse of present practice, which has tended to
assume the safety of an ingredient until hazard is shown.

Neither the FDA nor the CTFA has proposed new legislation
or regulations to tackle the issue of cosmetics safety.
Congressional Interest As discussed above, several legislative
proposals have been made to broaden the scope of cosmetics
safety regulation.  Bills proposed by Rep. Evans (D.-Colo.),
by Rep. Sullivan (D.-Mo.), and by Senators Magnuson (D.-Wa.)
and Moss (D.-Ut.) all seek to give the FDA the power to clear
a cosmetic for safety prior to marketing.  Several of the
bills (those of Rep. Evans and Senators Magnuson and Moss)
list safety tests, including carcinogenicity and mutagenicity,
skin irritancy, systemic toxicity, and preservative stability,
that each product would have to clear in order to gain FDA
approval.  These measured properly place the burden of proof
of safety on the cosmetic manufacturer.  However, none of the
bills change the existing legal definition of a cosmetic.

Any change in existing legislation that places the burden
of proof of safety of a cosmetic on its manufacturer is likely
to provide a strong impetus to the development of better
testing protocols in the industry.  However, the benefit to be
gained by requiring the FDA to pass judgement on each new
cosmetic's safety should be carefully evaluated.  If the FDA
were to be given access to all safety data and the power to
prosecute a cosmetic that had been marketed with insufficient
safety testing data, then essentially the same goal might be
achieved with a better use of limited resources.  Any new
legislation, realistically, should include a retroactive
provision to ensure that large numbers of cosmetics presently
on the market are adequately tested for safety.

In this context, or even in the absence of new legislation,
the FDA's expert review panels established for the OTC drug
review provide a possible model for action.  Senators Magnuson
and Moss, in an October 12, 1972, letter to FDA Commissioner
Edwards, proposed that panels similar to the OTC panels be
established to review the safety of cosmetics class by class
(152).  The same provision of the law that the FDA used to
establish the OTC panels can be applied to cosmetics, the two
Senators argue. The FDA's November 16, 1972, response does not

directly meet this challenge, but rather it argues the need to try the voluntary regulation approach before any fresh initiatives by the FDA are taken.

The advantage of such expert panels could be twofold. Besides assembling detailed monographs on the toxicity-in-use of most cosmetics ingredients, they might help to shape the new safety testing guidelines and protocols that the industry is going to have to use. In fact, in December 1972, the present FDA's Antimicrobial Review Panel was already doing just this.

In turn, the cosmetics industry, when faced with demands for more substantial toxicity data, is frequently pooling its resources and setting up joint industry testing programs. A number of these have been briefly mentioned earlier. The more rational use of testing resources that this represents is obvious. It also provides the opportunity for the smaller company to share the cost of safety testing procedures that, financially, it could not afford to pay for alone. The success of these joint efforts will have to be evaluated in time. Where the FDA has the regulatory authority to require new data, as with color additives, then test protocols have to be drawn in such a way as to satisfy the FDA. Where the FDA has less regulatory ability to demand further testing, as with aerosols or hair dyes, the risk exists that the testing protocols may be designed more to prove the safety of the ingredients than to evaluate their toxicity.

The issues met with here are the same as bedevil other areas of consumer product safety testing. The best safety and toxicity data are those which are subject to independent peer review and published in the open literature. However, the cosmetics industry still regards such data as important commerical information, and tries to keep them a trade secret. Since industry pays for the testing, the suspicion always exists that "he who pays the piper, calls the tune." Adverse test data can be suppressed or deemphasized, and test protocols can be shaped to favor the desired results. Ideally, what is needed is a buffer group which will collect samples of cosmetics ingredients for safety testing, collect payment for the testing, and then oversee the letting of test contracts. This could insure that the necessary toxicological tests are conducted by researchers unaware of the company origin of the samples being tested, or, at the very least, shielded from direct contact with the interested manufacturer. Ideally, the assembled data should be published or at least made widely available to interested researchers, to ensure a wide scientific peer review that will help maintain standards.

A comprehensive proposal similar to this, but focused on the
wider issue of insuring the safety of the wide variety of
chemicals in the human environment, has been recently detailed
(153).

The cosmetics industry does have an operation somewhat
similar to this, if more limited in concept.  The Research
Institute for Fragrance Materials (RIFM) is presently
submitting some 300 samples of fragrance oils a year to
various testing houses for contract safety testing.  The tests
conducted are limited - acute oral and dermal toxicity, skin
and eye irritancy, and phototoxicity.  Samples are submitted
to the RIFM by the Essential Oil Institute, so that the RIFM
does not know the corporate origin of the sample.  Samples are
then sent out for testing in coded bottles, with unidentified
duplicates as an additional check.  The final data are
reviewed by a panel of industrial and academic consultants.
The RIFM is supported by industry subscription.  The test data
are presently scheduled for regular publication in the
journal, Food and Cosmetics Toxicology.

Conclusion
The data and the case histories presented clearly establish
that there is in many cases a definite risk of hazard to
health associated with cosmetics.  While the type of injuries
involved may not lead to death or serious injuries, they are,
nonetheless, of sufficient severity and sufficient frequency
to merit real concern.  Further, they are associated with a
consumer product that is not essential to life, and which
clearly should be quite innocuous.  The discovery in recent
years of hazards such as the neurotoxicity of HCP and the
embryotoxicity of the color additive FD&C Red 2 underlines the
fact that the chemicals in cosmetics form a part of our
intimate, daily exposure to chemicals, and that we need to be
fully aware of the consequences of their exposure.

The legislative basis for the effective regulation of the
safety of cosmetics by the Federal Government is weak when
viewed in the perspective of today's understanding of the
hazards.  The law does not provide for the safety of a
cosmetic to be properly established by a full range of
toxicological tests conducted prior to marketing.  The burden
of proof of lack of safety of the marketed product continues
to lie on the FDA, which suffers under the additional
disadvantage of not being able to demand sufficient
information to determine what is in a cosmetic in the first
place.  Only in the case of cosmetics also classifiable as
drugs can the FDA demand of the manufacturer evidence of the

safety and efficacy of his product. Even in this case,
though, a simple change of the wording of advertising and
labeling claims can frequently absolve the manufacturer of the
legal burden to clear his product with the FDA prior to
marketing.

In practice, the FDA has relied heavily on voluntary action
by the cosmetics manufacturer to solve identified problems.
While the approach to cosmetics regulation has advantages in
providing flexibility of action, it is too often based on an
FDA-industry consensus that does not always reflect the
interests of the consumer. The voluntary approach is
presently being formalized in a series of industry-proposed,
voluntary regulations that should eventually provide the FDA
wtih details of the location of cosmetics manufacturing
plants, of the semiquantitative ingredient formulation of
cosmetics, and also access to some portions of the consumer
letters of complaint sent to the industry. It seems likely
that many cosmetics will soon be marketed with their
ingredients listed on the product label, and that the FDA may
move to make such ingredient labeling mandatory.

The key issue is that a marketed cosmetic should be safe in
use. The toxicology involved is routine and presents
relatively few major scientific challenges. The reason for
the present plethora of challenges to the safety of particular
cosmetics ingredients resides in an outmoded law, which has
failed to focus regulatory and industry attention of the
issues of cosmetics toxicology, and in the lack of general
scientific and medical interest in cosmetics, which has
insured that the traditional industry and FDA understanding of
the toxicology of cosmetics has lagged behind currently
accepted minimal standards of toxicological and regulatory
practice.

Acknowledgment I wish to thank Dr. Richard Sykes for his
steadfast assistance.

References

1.   "The Fortune 500." Fortune 86:5, 207 (May 1972).

2.   Aerosol Age 17:19, 56 (November 1972).

3.   Ibid. 18:2, 44 (February 1973).

4.   Drug Trade News February 21, 1972.

5.   Beauty Fashion April 1971.

6.   21 U.S.C. Sec. 201 (a)(2)(i).

7.   Jellinek, J.S., "Formulation and Function of Cosmetics."
Transl. G.L. Fenton, Wiley-Interscience, New York (1970).

8.   Balsam, M.S. and Sagarin, E., "Cosmetics: Science and
Technology," Second ed., vols. 1,2, Wiley-Interscience, New
York (1972).

9.   FDA Fact Sheet on Cosmetics, Washington, D.C., September
1971.

10.  Advertising Age August 28, 1972.

11.  Food, Drug and Cosmetic "Pink Sheets." January 3, 1972,
p. 26.

12.  Ibid. July 31, 1972, p. 7.

13.  Wall Street Journal 29 June, 1972.

14.  Edwards, FDA Commissioner, Press Conference, April 10,
1972, Washington, D.C.

15.  Drug and Cosmetic Industry 110:5, 56 (1972).

16.  Bass, M., J. Amer. Med. Assoc. 212:2075 (1970).

17.  National Commission on Product Safety, Final Report,
Washington, D.C. (June 1970).

18.  Morrison, Dr. Jack, Community Injury Control, USPHS,
Department of Health, Education and Welfare, private
communication.

19.  Verhulst, Dr. Robert, National Clearinghouse for Poison
Control Centers, USPHS, Department of Health, Education and
Welfare, private communication.

20.  NCPCC Bulletin, September-October 1971.

21.  National Electronic Injury Survey System, 5401 Westbard
Ave., Bethesda, Md. 20016.

22.  Verhalen, Dr. Robert, National Electronic Injury Survey
System, USPHS, Department of Health, Education and Welfare,
private communication.

23.  Schaffner, R., FDA Papers April 1972.

24.  Consumer Reports January 1972, p. 41.

25.  Spoor, H.J., Cutis 8:441 (1971).

26.  Food, Drug and Cosmetic "Pink Sheets" December 7, 1970,
T & G-1.

27.  Kaye, B.M., J. Amer. Med. Assoc. 212:2121 (1970).

28.  Gaudy, J.M., New Engl. J. Med. 287:203 (1972).

29.  Food, Drug and Cosmetic "Pink Sheets" February 22, 1971,
T & G-2.

30.  Marzulli, F.N., private communication

31.  Allen, Linda, Ed., "The Look You Like." American Medical
Association, Chicago, 1972.

32.  AMA Drug Evaluations 194 (1971).

33.  Marzulli, F.N. and Brown, B.D., J. Soc. Cosmet. Chem., to
be published.

34.  FDA, Federal Register 38:853 (Jan. 5, 1973).

35.  Berman, E., and McKiel, K., Arch. Environ. Health 25:64
(1972).

36.  Fisher, A.A., "Contact Dermatitis." Lea and Febiger,
Philadelphia, Pennsylvania, (1967).

37.  Kligman, J., J. Invest. Derm. 47:393 (1966).

38.  Appropriation Hearings before the Agriculture,
Environmental and Consumer Appropriation Subcommittee.
April 18-19, 1972, U.S. Government Printing Office,
Washington, D.C., 1972, p. 248.

39.  Burdick, K.H., Arch. Derm. 93:924 (1966).

40.  Marzulli, F.N., and Maibach, H.J., J. Soc. Cosmet. Chem.
21:695 (1970).

41.  FDA, Federal Register 3:60.

42.  Summary Minutes, F.D.A. Antimicrobial Review Panel.
Available from Public Information Office, FDA, Rockville, Md.
20852.

43.  Donnigan, A.P., and Evans, J.R., TGA Cosmetic Journal
2:4, 41 (1970).

44.  Wolven, A., and Leventsen, I., Ibid. 1:1, 34 (1969).

45.  Supra 38, pp. 240-255.

46.  Morse, L.J., Williams, H.L., Green, F.P., Eldridge, E.E.
and Rotta, J.R., New Eng. J. Med. 277:472 (1967).

47.  Wilson, L.A., Kuehne, J.W., Hall, S.W. and Abearn, D.G.,
Am. J. Ophthalmol. 71:1298 (1971).

48.  Marzulli, F.N., Evans, J.R., and Yoder, P.D., J. Soc.
Cosmet. Chem. 23:89 (1972).

49.  Cosmetic, Toiletry and Fragrance Association,
"Microbiological Limit Guidelines for Cosmetics and
Toileteries." Washington, D.C. (October 1972).

50.  Gump, W.S., J. Soc. Cosmet. Chem. 20:173 (1969).

51.  Curley, A. and Hawk, R.E., American Chemical Society,
161st Meeting, Los Angeles, California (March 28, 1971).

52.  Kimbrough, R.D. and Gains, T.B., Arch. Envir. Health
23:114 (1971).

53.  Curley, A., Hawk, R.E., Kimbrough, R.D., Natheson, G. and Finberg, L., _Lancet_ 2:296 (1971).

54.  Lockhart, J.D., _Pediatrics_ 50:229 (1972).

55.  FDA, _Federal Register_ 36:23330 (December 1971).

56.  FDA, _Federal Register_ 37:219 (January 1972).

57.  FDA, Press Conference on Hexachlorophene, Washington, D.C. (September 22, 1972).

58.  FDA, _Federal Register_ 37:20160 (Sept. 26, 1972).

59.  Kiese, M. and Rauscher, E., _Toxicol. Appl. Pharmacol._ 13:325 (1968).

60.  Hueper, W.C., and Conway, D., "Chemical Carcinogens and Cancers." Charles C Thomas, Springfield, Ill. (1964), pp. 258.

61.  Ito, N., Konishi, Y. and Masugami, M., _Cancer Research_ 29:1137 (1969).

62.  _National Observer_ September 14, 1970, pp. 1, 11.

63.  _Washington Post_ October 28, 1970, p. B4.

64.  Weisburger, E.K., _J. Soc. Cosmet. Chem._ 22:825 (1971).

65.  Weisburger, E.K., private communication.

66.  Kottman, J., _J. Assoc. Offic. Anal. Chem._ 49:1954 (1966).

67.  Wall, F.E., in "Cosmetics: Science and Technology." Vol. 3, Balsam, M.S., and Sagarin, E., eds., Wiley-Interscience (1972), p. 308.

68.  USPHS, "Survey of Compounds which have been tested for Carcinogenic Activity." GPO, Washington, D.C.

69.  Ross, M., Smith, W.L. and AShton, W.H., _Amer. Mineral_ 53:751 (1968).

70.  Weiss, B. and Boettner, E.A., _Arch. Envir. Health_ 14:304 (1967).

71.  Kleinfeld, M., Messie, J., Kooyman, O. and Zaki, M.,
Arch. Envir. Health 14:663 (1967).

72.  Cralley, L.T., Key, M.M., Groth, D.H., Lanhard, W.S. and
Lingo, R.M., J. Amer. Ind. Hyg. Assoc. 29:350 (1968).

73.  Weissler, A., FDA, private communication.

74.  Sayers, R.R. and Dreessmen, W.C., Am. J. Publ. Health
29:205 (1939).

75.  Wagner, J.C., J. Nat. Cancer Inst. 46:v (1971).

76.  Selikoff, I.J., Hammond, E.C. and Churg, J., J. Amer.
Med. Assoc. 204:106 (1968).

77.  Selikoff, I.J., Nicholson, W.J. and Langer, A.M., Arch.
Envir. Health 25:1 (1972).

78.  EPA, Office of Air Programs. "Background Information -
Proposed National Emission Standards for Hazardous Air
Pollutants - Asbestos-Beryllium-Mercury." OAP Publication
APTD-0753, December 1971.

79.  FDA, "Asbestos and Talc." Symposium held at FDA,
Washington, D.C., August 3, 1971.

80.  Merliss, R.R., J. Amer. Med. Assoc. 216:2144 (1971).

81.  Merliss, R.R., Science 173:1141 (1971).

82.  FDA, Federal Register 37:16407 (21 CFT Part 121).

83.  Food and Drug Administration, Advisory Committee on
Protocols for Safety Evaluations:  Panel on Reproduction,
Report on Reproductive Studies in the Safety Evaluation of
Food Additives and Pesticide Residues, Toxicol. Appl.
Pharmacol. 16:264 (1970).

84.  Food and Chemical News September 27, 1971.

85.  Shtenberg, A.I., and Gavrilenko, E.V., Vop. Pitan. 29:66
(1970):  C.A. 73, 44028b (1970).

86.  Shtenberg, A. and Gavrilenko, E.V., Ibid., 35:28 (1972).

87.    "Memorandum of a meeting on Red 2." November 18, 1971.

88.    FDA, Federal Register 36:18336.

89.    Ad Hoc Subcommittee on the Evaluation of FD&C Red 2, Committee on Food Protection, Food and Nutrition Board, NAS-NRC, Report to the FDA, June 13, 1972.

90.    "Report on Red 2."  Health Research Group, 2000 P St. N.W., Washington, D.C. 20036 (July 18, 1972).

91.    Medical World News September 8, 1972.

92.    Stabile, Toni, "Cosmetics:  Trick or Treat?" Houston Books, New York (1966), p. 16.

93.    Lamb, Ruth deForest, "American Chamber of Horrors." Farrar and Reinhart, New York (1936).

94.    Lamb, Ruth deForest, Ibid. pp. 26-27.

95.    Lamb, Ruth deForest, Ibid. pp. 15-17.

96.    Lamb, Ruth deForest, Ibid. pp. 29-37.

97.    Congressional Record 77:5721 (1933).

98.    Harvard Law Review 67:635 (1954).

99.    21 USC Sec. 321(i).

100.   21 USC Sec. 361, 362.

101.   21 USC Sec. 331(a), 332, 333, 334.

102.   Toulmin, S., "The Law of Food, Drugs and Cosmetics." W.H. Anderson, Cincinnati, Ohio (1963).

103.   21 USC Sec. 361(a).

104.   Supra 95, pp. 145-153.

105.   House of Representatives, 82nd Congress, House Report 82-2182.

106.   Senate, 92nd Congress, Senate Report 92-825 (June 1972).

107.  Congressional Record 118:S6583 (April 25, 1972).

108.  Congressional Record 118:E 2500 (March 15, 1972).

109.  Federal Register 28:19256.

110.  Gardner Vs. Toilet Goods Assn. 387 U.S. 167 (1966).

111.  Toilet Goods Assn. Vs. Finch 419 F2d 21 (1969).

112.  15 USC 1261-1273.

113.  21 USC Sec. 355.

114.  Toulmin, S., Ibid. p. 16.

115.  21 USC 321(g)(1)(c).

116.  Ingredient data provided by the Office of the Assistant
Commissioner for Public Affairs, December, 1972.

117.  U.S. Vs. An Article:  Sudden Change 409 F2d 734 (2nd
Cir. 1969).

118.  U.S. Vs. An Article:  Line Away 415 F2d 369 (3rd Cir.
1969).

119.  U.S. Vs. An Article:  Magic Secret 331 F. Supp. 914
(1971).

120.  DiParma, F.P., The Business Lawyer (November 1971) p.
49-60.

121.  Kanof, N.M., Cutis 6:527 (1970).

122.  Hutt, P.B., CTFA Cosmetic Journal Fall, 1971.

123.  Ibid. pp. 76, 238.

124.  U.S. Congress, House of Representatives, Committee on
Government Operations, "Recall Procedures of the Food and Drug
Administration," House Report 92-585, GPO, Washington, D.C.,
1971.

125.  FDA, Federal Register 37:11307 (June 7, 1972).

126.  FDA, Federal Register 37:20160 (September 27, 1972).

127.  Confidential Communication, member of FDA Antimicrobial
Panel (September 1972).

128.  FDA, Memorandum of a Meeting, "Determination of HCP in
Pressurized Containers." Food and Drug Administration
(September 27, 1972).

129.  FDA, Federal Register 37:23537 (November 1, 1972).

130.  Knauer, Virginia H., Speech to the Chemical Specialities
Manufacturers Association (December 5, 1972).

131.  Senate, Commerce Committee Hearings, 92-36:  Nomination
of Peter B. Hutt to be Assistant General Counsel for Food,
Drugs and Environmental Health, Department of Health,
Education and Welfare (September 17, 1971).

132.  Wade, N., Science 177:498 (1972).

133.  Food, Drug and Cosmetics "Pink Sheet" February 1971.

134.  FDA, Federal Register 36:16934 (August 26, 1971).

135.  FDA, Federal Register 37:7151 (April 11, 1972).

136.  FDA, Federal Register 37:9128 (May 5, 1972).

137.  FDA, Federal Register 37:23344 (November 2, 1972).

138.  Fair Labeling and Packaging Act, 15 USC Sec. 1454(c).

139.  Food, Drug and Cosmetics "Pink Sheet" May 29, 1972, p.
7.

140.  Page, Prof. Joseph, Georgetown Law Center, private
communication.

141.  _____, Debate on S.3419, Consumer Product Safety
Act of 1972, Congressional Record (June 21, 1972).

142.  Knauer, Virginia H., Special Assistant to the President
for Consumer Affairs, Press Conference, Washington, D.C.
(April 10, 1972).

143.  McLaughlin, Frank, Office of Consumer Affairs, White
House, private communication.

144.  Cosmetic, Toiletry and Fragrance Association, "CTFA
Dictionary of Cosmetics Ingredients." 1625 I St., N.W.,
Washington, D.C., (October, 1972).

145.  FDA, Federal Register 37:219 (January 7, 1972).

146.  Giovacchini, R.P., Toxicol. Appl. Pharm. Supplement 3,
13 (1969).

147.  -----, Toxicol. Appl. Pharm. Supplement 3, 13
(1969).

148.  "Evaluation of Safety of Cosmetics." Toxicol. Appl.
Pharm. Supplement 3, Academic Press, New York, 1969.

149.  Remington vs. Kresge, State of Michigan Circuit Court
for the County of Genesee, File 16151.

150.  Toilet Goods Association Cosmetic Journal Fall 1970.

151.  FDA Antimicrobial Review Panel, Summary Minutes, August-
October, 1972.  Available from the Public Information Office,
FDA, Rockville, Md. 20852.

152.  Letter from Senator Magnuson and Senator Moss to
Commissioner Edwards, FDA, October 12, 1970.

153.  Epstein, S.S., Am. J. Pathol. 66:352 (1972).

# 3

PHARMACEUTICALS

Roberta G. Marks

CONTENTS

## The Nature of the Problem

Introduction  In 1959, the Senate Judiciary Committee's
Antitrust and Monopoly Subcommittee, under the agressive and
persistent Sen. Estes Kefauver (D.-Tenn.), began a new
investigation of the pharmaceutical industry.

Expressing a profound dissatisfaction with all that he had
learned of the industry's workings, Sen. Kefauver probed into
drug prices, company profits, drug development, industry
advertising, drug patent laws, labeling, and more.  The
hearings, an almost three-year scourge to industry, ended in
1962.  As the hearings drew to a close, impatient observers,
both within and without industry, asked "when will it all
end?"

Following the Kefauver hearings, the 88th Congress
empowered a revision of the then existing Federal Food, Drug
and Cosmetic (FFDC) Act.  Nevertheless, the Kefauver-Harris
Drug Amendments of 1962 (P.L. 87-781) did not settle, to the
satisfaction of many, such questions as:  Who should test
pharmaceuticals before they are marketed?  How can unsafe
drugs be prevented from reaching the market?  How to ensure
that marketed drugs will perform as labeled?  How can quality
drugs be made available at low cost?  How to ensure that drug
company advertising and promotion are factual and help the
doctor to prescribe drugs wisely?  How to prevent the
American consumer from overmedicating himself, while at the
same time giving him free access to "over-the-counter" (OTC)
products that will or are alleged to relieve transient
ailments of a relatively trivial nature?

Such problems are not exclusive to the United States, but
solutions which have worked for other countries are not
necessarily practical here.  In Great Britain, for example,
drug manufacturers need prove only safety, not efficacy, for
government clearance to market a new product.  Under the
British National Health Service, prescribed drugs are,
however, available at nominal cost.

Drug advertising to British physicians has traditionally
been muted - the local penchant for understatement, perhaps.
Another difference:  Television programing tends to begin in
the late afternoon and ends at midnight, and television
advertising of products of any kind is quite limited.  This
means that housewives are not constantly exhorted to medicate
themselves and their families.

Britain is comparatively a small country and it was a
relatively simple matter when, for example, prescribing of
amphetamines rose to alarming heights, to run

filled-prescription forms through a computer and identify the very few practitioners who were responsible for writing the majority of amphetamine prescriptions. These doctors received a personal visit from a government physician-consultant, and together they went over the conditions for which amphetamine might rationally be prescribed, and the conditions for which the drug was not therapeutically desirable. Amphetamine prescribing then dropped sharply.

The United States solution to drug problems, however, tends to focus on the legislative approach. American physicians are so peer oriented that most are reluctant to testify against a brother M.D. even in malpractice cases, and local medical societies seldom find cause to chastise a member of their group.

American physicians and the Federal Government have been at odds since the advent of social security coverage, which most doctors denounced at the time. In general, most government steps toward greater protection of citizens in health matters have been denounced by M.D.'s as "socialized medicine," and physicians continue to jealously guard their right to prescribe any manufactured drug as they see fit. The British example of a practicing M.D. and a government man in a cozy chat about the proper use of a drug is quite unthinkable here.

Moreover, the cost of medical attention in the United States is sufficiently high that prospective patients prefer to choose from an array of OTC products in search of relief, while promising themselves that "if it doesn't go away in a week, I'll see the doctor."

Under such conditions, the American consumer has turned to federal legislation in an attempt to secure drug safety and drug efficacy, as no other practical options seem available.

Legislative History

Wiley Act Of 1906 In 1906, the country's first Pure Food and Drug Act was passed by the Congress. The Act was meant to prevent the manufacture, sale, and transportation of adulterated, misbranded, and deleterious foods, drugs, and chemicals. The key word here is "transportation." Transportation was included in the terms of the 1906 Act because the Congress could not constitutionally prohibit the manufacture of adulterated products within the 48 states, but it could, and did, prohibit their shipment in interstate commerce.

Six years later, in 1912, the Act was amended to prevent false statement of curative or therapeutic activity on drug

labels.  Except for minor amendments, federal authority
continued unchanged until the mid-1930s, when a bill to
tighten it up was introduced by Sen. Royal S. Copeland
(D.-N.Y.).

Although the measure passed the Senate and the House,
during the Senate-House conference there was disagreement as
to whether administrative authority should be vested in the
Food and Drug Administration (FDA) or in the Federal Trade
Commission (FTC).  The bill died, but was revived and passed
in the following Congress.

Copeland Act Of 1938 Passage of the 1938 Food, Drug and
Cosmetic Act (21 U.S.C. 301-392) is, in part, attributable to
the disaster involving Elixir of Sulfanilamide, which killed
107 persons.  They died because a chemist dissolved the
relatively insoluble drug in a toxic solvent.

This scenario of drug disaster followed by reactive and
presumably corrective legislation was to be repeated in the
"modern era," which began in the 1960s as a direct consequence
of the Kefauver hearings and the thalidomide disaster.

The Copeland Act of 1938 contained a number of provisions
dealing with drug labeling.  Perhaps the most interesting was
the provision which

"Prohibits traffic in new drugs unless such drugs have been
adequately tested to show that they are safe for use under the
conditions of use prescribed in their labeling..."

With its demand for safety - echoing the Hippocratic
injunction to physicians, "Primum non nocere" (first, do no
harm) - the 1938 Act rested.  Dormancy continued until the
stir caused by Sen. Kefauver in the 1959 to 1962 period.

The 1962 Kefauver-Harris Amendments In January 1962, the
Department of Health, Education and Welfare (DHEW) announced
that it needed some changes in the Food, Drug and Cosmetic Act
and asked the help of President Kennedy in getting the changes
through the Congress as amendments to the existing law (1).
President Kennedy, in his State of the Union message said he,
too, would "recommend improvement in the food and drug laws."
(1)

However, neither DHEW nor the President dealt in specifics
at this stage.  In March 1962, the President's 10-point health
message to the Congress contained no mention of proposals to
amend the Food, Drug and Cosmetic Act.

Sen. Kefauver had just wound up hearings before his

Subcommittee on Antitrust and Monopoly on his antitrust bill,
S. 1552 (87th Congress).  Washington-watchers nevertheless
expected it to die because of its controversial patent
provisions, designed to lower drug prices.  The bill provided
that a drug manufacturer's period of patent exclusivity be
limited to three years, followed by extension of compulsory
licensing to other manufacturers.  The U.S. Patent Office,
before fuling on a patent for a drug modification or a drug
combination, would have been required to obtain a statement
from DHEW that the modification or combination was
therapeutically superior to the parent drug and the single
ingredients of the combination.  Sen. Kefauver wanted to
eliminate what he considered minor molecular modifications of
a chemical ("me-too drugs") that would enable its owner-
manufacturer to qualify for another 17-year exclusive patent.

Other provisions of S. 1552 required a label statement of
drug efficacy, printing of a drug's generic name in type as
large as that carrying the proprietary name, and registration
of drug manufacturers with the FDA.

The patent provisions of the bill came under strong fire in
the Congress, from Republicans and Democrats alike.  The bill
was referred to the Senate Judiciary Committee, which assigned
it to the Subcommittee on Patents, Trademarks, and Copyrights,
then and now chaired by Sen. John L. McClellan (D.-Ark.).

Early in April, 1962, President Kennedy came out in favor
of the Kefauver bill minus its patent provisions.  His
approval was in the form of a letter to Sen. James O. Eastland
(D.-Miss.), chairman of the Senate Judiciary Committee (2).
Then, a few weeks later, the President decided he wanted:  (a)
provision for drug manufacturers to report to DHEW adverse
effects of a new pharmaceutical; (b) empowerment of DHEW to
withdraw approval of a new drug on the basis of safety or lack
of efficacy; (c) machinery to prevent channeling of habit-
forming drugs into illicit uses; and (d) in-house quality
control measures on both prescription (Rx) and OTC drugs (3).

President Kennedy's proposals were introduced in the House
of Representatives in May 1962 by Rep. Oren Harris (D.-Ark.),
along with several new wrinkles:  premarket proof of drug
efficacy; and, if DHEW had not established a name for a drug,
the U.S. Pharmacopeia name was to be employed.  Otherwise, the
common name was to be superior in prominence to the
proprietary name (4).  Rep. Harris's bill, H.R. 11581, also
asked that biologicals be placed under control of the FDA.
This move was not made until 1971, following hearings before
the Senate Government Operations Subcommittee on Executive
Reorganization, when Sen. Abraham Ribicoff (D.-Conn.), the

Subcommittee's chairman, charged that the Division of
Biological Standards (DBS) was incompetent, played favorites
among manufacturers, and released defective lots of vaccine.
The DBS was formally cleared of the charges; nevertheless the
Division was shifted to FDA.

In the spring of 1962, Sen. Kefauver's bill (S. 1552) was
rated as having a possibility of Senate passage, but little
change of getting through the House.  Then a veteran
Washington journalist, Stephens Rippey, reported that the

"strongest push ever given to food and drug legislation by the
White House is greatly enhancing the possibility of getting a
law enacted this year." (3)

In an August 1962 news conference, President Kennedy urged
support for Rep. Harris's bill over Sen. Kefauver's bill
because, he said, the Harris bill would prevent another
thalidomide episode from ever happening in the United States.
One of the most extraordinary features at the time was the
favorable publicity given the FDA for its handling of the New
Drug Application (NDA) data submitted on behalf of
thalidomide.  Articles in the daily newspapers and high-
circulation magazines saluted Dr. Frances O. Kelsey, a staff
scientists of the FDA, as being personally responsible for
holding up a thalidomide NDA sponsored by the Wm. S. Merrell
Co.  Uneasy about the drug, but with few specific areas of
complaint, Dr. Kelsey delayed approval of the NDA for 14
months.  At about the time she was running out of delaying
tactics, European physicians discovered a cause-and-effect
relationship between ingestion of thalidomide during pregnancy
and production of a hitherto rare birth defect - phocomelia.
The Wm. S. Merrell Co. then withdrew its NDA for thalidomide.
Americans were horrified by photographs of babies with
vestigial arms and legs.  The emotional impact of phocomelia
was so strong that in 1972 a British court forbade newspapers
in Great Britain to discuss the subject for the duration of
litigation between parents of phocomelic children and the
British manufacturer of thalidomide.  The court feared lest
publicity and photographs of the children prejudice the case -
a suit over the amount of damages to be paid.
For her role in the thalidomide affair, Dr. Kelsey was
acclaimed a heroine and given the Distinguished Service Medal -
the highest federal civilian award - by President Kennedy.
Some in industry, however, looked upon the medal as a reward
for the traditional bureaucratic ploy of when-in-doubt-do-
nothing.

The thalidomide disaster had no little effect in building
sentiment for passage of strong federal authority for the
control of drugs.  It was pointed out by many that FDA
regulations then in effect could not have ensured protection
against a similar disaster in the United States.

It is now, in part, accepted that current statute still
provides no absolute guarantee against a thalidomide-type
disaster in this country.  It took Dr. Charles Delahunt, of
Pfizer Laboratories, two years of laboratory investigation
before he succeeded in producing thalidomide-affected infant
monkeys (5).  And Dr. Delahunt knew what he was looking for.
The timing of thalidomide administration proved to be crucial
to the production of abnormalities.

Late in 1962, Sen. Kefauver's bill passed the Senate and
Rep. Harris' bill passed the House, and the Kefauver-Harris
bill was signed into law (P.L. 87-871).  Most of the
provisions were intended to take effect in May 1963.

The new law was remarkably broad in scope.  It required -
for the first time - that drug manufacturers prove their new
products effective.  In turn, NDA's could be withdrawn by the
FDA if drugs were shown not to be effective or to constitute
an "imminent hazard" to public health; the provision by which
drugs were automatically approved unless the FDA objected
within 60 days after NDA filing was dropped; antibiotics were
required to be certified by the FDA, and procedures were set
up for decertification; generic names were to appear one-half
the size of brand names on labels; drug ads must give such
negative data as the product's side effects and
contraindications; good manufacturing practices were to be
employed in drug plants, and the FDA was given the right to
examine the manufacturing plants.

Implementation The favorable publicity enjoyed by the FDA at
the time of the thalidomide affair was the agency's last real
experience with praise.

Before 1962 had ended, the now-familiar cry of "laxity" was
being raised by Sen. Hubert H. Humphrey (D.-Minn.) (5).  The
1962 drug amendments clearly pointed up the deficits of the
past, and Sen. Humphrey professed shock that the FDA had
never, on its own, thought of requiring premarket clearance of
drugs and tighter control of toxic drugs.

In the spring of 1963, Sen. Humphrey's Government
Operations Subcommittee on Reorganization and International
Organization began to probe FDA operations.  Among its
witnesses was an FDA pediatric cardiologist, Dr. John O.
Nester, who complained that his superiors, some of them

non-M.D.'s, tended to overrule medical decisions.  Dr. Nester,
generally known to industry as "the man who failed to approve
one drug in 10 years at FDA," complained also that FDA did not
move fast enough on removing dangerous drugs from the market.
Dr. Nester specified MER/29 which, he said, should never have
been approved because evidence of safety was inadequate (7).
This drug was belatedly withdrawn from the market in 1961,
after 18 months' availability, because of toxicity.

The FDA in 1962 said it was mulling over the desirability
of ending its policy of secrecy on NDA's and might consider
making public the names of drugs it approved, the names of
manufacturers, and such drug information as the therapeutic
use, side effects, and contraindications, all of which
information was then considered privileged by the FDA.

When, a year later, Sen. Humphrey found the lack of further
information "intolerable," the FDA timidly commented that it
was considering opening its files and revealing all
information but that specifically designated as trade secret -
defined as information dealing with a manufacturing method or
process (8).  It didn't then and still hasn't now in 1974,
although manufacturer's summaries of toxicological data have
recently been made available.

Dr. Kelsey, the heroine of 1962, found herself on the other
side of the fence when testifying before the House Government
Operations Subcommittee on Intergovernmental Relations,
chaired by Rep. L. H. Fountain (D.-N.C.).  Chairman Fountain
deplored the lack of routine memoranda which would show just
how decisions had been arrived at in her department.  Dr.
Kelsey could not recollect or explain the rationale for
certain actions on Investigational New Drugs (IND's) and there
was nothing on paper.  Rep. Rountain remarked that such FDA
procedures were "sloppy." (9)

The FDA, which in August 1963 had announced it was
considering dropping its habit of secrecy, was still
considering this move in August 1967.  Dr. James Goddard, then
FDA Commissioner, stated that he wanted to make the data
available, but he wasn't sure it could be done legally under
existing law (10).

"You're talking nonsense," was the friendly response of
Sen. Gaylord Nelson (D.-Wis.), who, as chairman of the
Monopoly Subcommittee of the Senate Select Committee on Small
Business, was to become a constant critic of industry and an
occasional chider of the FDA (10).  Sen. Nelson, anxious to
see generic drugs more widely used, wanted the FDA to release
confidential NDA data so that the small drug manufacturers,
who did no original research, could gain the know-how to

compete with the brand-name producers in the manufacture of the most widely prescribed drugs.

The latter half of 1968 ushered in for the FDA a new period of low morale, largely due to an Executive Branch which could not make up its mind how the FDA should be run. A Consumer Protection and Environmental Health Service (CPEHS) was organized within the DHEW and the FDA was shifted to the new agency as a subordinate unit - at least according to the table of organization. The agency still basically ran itself, however.

By December, 1968, the outgoing DHEW Secretary Wilbur Cohen was debating whether the FDA's actual operating responsibilities should be turned over to CPEHS. Secretary Cohen decided to make the shift, and the FDA lost its semiautonomous status.

Three months later the new (Republican) DHEW Secretary, Robert H. Finch, publicly rethought the former Secretary's move and decided that the FDA should continue under CPEHS. Six months later, Secretary Finch again publicly brooded about whether the FDA should be cut loose from CPEHS and made the direct responsibility of an assistant DHEW Secretary. A few months later, the CPEHS was abolished; thoroughly demoralized, the FDA regained its independence.

Continuing congressional dissatisfaction with the agency's status and performance led, in the 92nd Congress (1972), to several proposals. Although Rep. Paul G. Rogers (D.-Fla.) tried to strengthen the FDA within DHEW, he failed. Legislation to create an independent Consumer Protection Agency, including the functions of the FDA, was sponsored by Sen. Warren G. Magnuson (D.-Wash.), chairman of the Senate Commerce Committee, and by Sen. Frank E. Moss (D.-Utah); however it was opposed by the Nixon Administration and the Pharmaceutical Manufacturers Association (PMA).

At the time, the PMA's president, C. Joseph Stetler, was careful to explain that the Association's opposition to the bill marked no change in its adversary position towards the FDA. Mindful of the intense political pressure exerted on the FDA, Stetler felt that the superagency proposed by Senators Magnuson and Moss would become a huge bureaucratic tangle in which staffers could survive only by saying "no" to everything and everyone.

When finally enacted in 1972, the Senate-House compromise on the Consumer Product Safety Act (P.L. 92-573) set up an independent regulatory agency, the Consumer Product Safety Commission, with authority over almost everything but food, drugs, and cosmetics. Thus, the FDA retained its regulatory hold on these three categories.

Pushed by its critics, at the year's end the FDA finally
published a proposal, to implement the Freedom of Information
Act, which would open its drug files to allow examination of
all drug data except that designated "trade secret."  FDA
would make the decision on what was a legitimate trade secret
and the burden would be on the manufacturer to show due cause
why certain data pertaining to his products should not be
revealed.  The FDA proposal was still pending in September
1973 but may yet be superseded by a proposal of DHEW's that
would provide for confidentiality of trade secrets and
financial data, but would allow the FDA to make its approve-
or-deny rulings without the red tape of first checking with
DHEW.

## Proving The Efficacy Of Marketed Drugs

With enactment of the 1962 Kefauver-Harris Amendments (P.L.
87-871), the FDA was required to demand proof of efficacy as
a prerequisite for clearance of new drugs.  But what of
pharmaceuticals marketed before the 1962 amendments were
passed?  The FDA's eventual interpretation was that the
pre-1962 drugs were covered, and that so-called grandfather
exemptions of the older drugs simply did not exist (11).

The FFDC Act defines "new drug" [Sec. 201(p)] as

"(1) Any drug (except a new animal drug or an animal feed
bearing or containing a new animal drug), the composition of
which is such that such drug is not generally recognized,
among experts qualified by scientific training and experience
to evaluate the safety and effectiveness of drugs, as safe and
effective for use under the conditions prescribed,
recommended, or suggested in the labeling thereof, except that
such drug not so recognized shall not be deemed to be a 'new
drug' if at any time prior to the enactment of this Act if was
subject to the Food and Drugs Act of June 30, 1906, as
amended, and if at such time its labeling contained the same
representations concerning the conditions of its use; or

(2) Any drug (except a new animal drug or an animal feed
bearing or containing a new animal drug) the composition of
which is such that such drug, as a result of investigations to
determine its safety and effectiveness for use under such
conditions, has become so recognized, but which has not,
otherwise than in such investigations, been used to a material
extent or for a material time under such conditions."

However, the Food, Drug and Cosmetic Act also refers

[Sec. 505] to new drugs and provides a procedure by which manufacturers may submit NDA's.  This provision carries a footnote defining the enactment date of the 1962 new drug provisions (12).  In part this footnote says,

"In the case of any drug which, on the day immediately preceding the enactment date, (A) was commercially used or sold in the United States, (B) was not a new drug as defined by Sec. 201(p) of the basic Act as then in force, and (C) was not covered by an effective application under section 505 of that Act, the amendments to Sec. 201(p) made by this Act shall not apply to such drug when intended solely for use under conditions prescribed, recommended, or suggested in labeling with respect to such drug on that day."

That is, drugs marketed before the 1962 Kefauver-Harris amendments were enacted may continue without being considered new drugs and are not subject to NDA provisions unless their labeling is changed.  It would seem, then, that the intent of the Congress was for such drugs to have "grandfather" protection.

With FDA's decision to examine the labeling of pre-1962 drugs the agency began a hotly contested battle with industry, which took the view that the Congress had meant drugs existing before the 1962 laws to be exempt (12).

What particularly offended industry was that only the holder of the original drug application would be asked to prove label claims.  Subsequent manufacturers of the same drug, the so-called me-too's, were under no obligation to submit substantiation of labeling unless the original holder declined to do so and ceased marketing the drug.

The tenure of FDA Commissioner James Goddard was tumultuous.  His most memorable decision, and the one to have the greatest effect on industry, involved the pre-1962 drugs.  Commissioner Goddard contracted with the National Academy of Sciences-National Research Council (NAS-NRC) to investigate the efficacy of the pre-1962 drugs (13).  The NAS-NRC findings were then to be reviewed by the FDA, which could accept, reject, or modify the findings.

The procedure was to set up a number of specialist panels to review the evidence and report back to the FDA by December 1967.

The FDA's estimate was that virtually every drug - both OTC and Rx - marketed between 1938 and 1962 would be affected.  Because advertising claims of OTC products are handled by the Federal Trade Commission (FTC), the FDA and the FTC agreed

that the FTC would follow through on the NAS-NRC findings and
implement them.

Drugs were to be rated "effective," "probably effective,"
"possibly effective," and "ineffective." Those judged
ineffective would have their drug applications withdrawn by
the FDA.

In its review, the NAS-NRC found a number of fixed-
combination antibiotics to be ineffective. They expressed the
opinion that patients should receive the single antibiotic
effective against their particular infective organism, and
that combined antibiotics were therefore unnecessary.

The FDA, in perfect agreement, moved to decertify these
drugs on grounds of ineffectiveness (14). The new FDA
commissioner, Dr. Herbert Ley, Jr., speaking at a February
1969 meeting of the Pharmaceutical Advertising Club, told
manufacturers that the FDA would accept "substantial evidence"
of combination efficacy if the manufacturers chose to submit
such data; however, he was confident that no such data existed
because efficacy of the combinations couldn't be proven (15).

The combination drugs were ordered off the market. The
Upjohn Co., manufacturer of Panalba, one of the top 200-most-
frequently-prescribed items, however, asked for a stay on the
ground that the FDA's own rules required holding a hearing
before revocation of an antibiotic's certification. The
Upjohn Co. went to court on this issue (16) and got a stay
(17).

The FDA answered that no hearing was required because
Upjohn had not submitted a "statement of reasonable grounds
for a hearing." Such a statement, according to the FDA, must
"identify the claimed errors in the NAS-NRC evaluation and
identify any adequate and well-controlled investigation" to
support the manufacturer's claim of safety and efficacy (18).
Upjohn went back to court.

A Delaware district court, ruling on a PMA suit, held FDA's
"substantial evidence" order to be invalid (19), but two
months later the Cincinnati district court, ruling on the
Panalba case, decided that FDA had the right to remove the
combination without an evidentiary hearing (20). The court
agreed with the FDA that no hearing was necessary unless the
manufacturer was prepared with "substantial evidence" of
safety and efficacy. The Upjohn Co., who might have carried
the matter to the Supreme Court, decided instead to terminate
sale of Panalba (21).

The FDA then revised its "substantial evidence"
requirement, giving manufacturers an exemption from the
requirement for controlled clinical studies if they had an

acceptable alternative (22).

The FDA then revoked the certification of Pfizer's antibiotic Signemycin, again denying the manufacturer a hearing. The Second Court of Appeals also upheld the FDA's right to deny an evidentiary hearing, saying that the clinical experience of physicians who had used the drug - which was what Pfizer supplied - was not the equivalent of "adequate and well-controlled studies."

Commenting on these cases, in 1971, James R. Phelps, attorney with Burditt and Calkins, a Chicago law firm, said that

"It seems clear that FDA will be able to proceed with its implementation of the NAS-NRC efficacy review without granting a single hearing. Through its definition of 'adequate and well-controlled investigations,' FDA has been permitted to create and apply to all antibiotics and 'new drugs' a standard which, as a practical matter, can be met only if FDA says it has been met. And, of course, if FDA thinks that standard has been met, then FDA will agree with the conclusion and there will be no need for a hearing. Naturally, without a right to establish a record at a hearing, an appeal from FDA's orders, except on the issue of whether there are adequate and well-controlled studies, will be virtually impossible." (23)

Phelps went on to say that

"In spite of the court's rulings, there are legitimate differences of medical opinion, even though they cannot be backed by the 'adequate and well-controlled' test... . FDA and everyone involved in regulating the practice of medicine should be required to listen to those legitimate differences, and to provide for their resolution in a proper forum. The best forum, of course, would be a hearing. This would be consistent with the legislative history of the 1962 amendments, which says that a medical view need not even be the preponderant view, so long as it is a responsible view. The decisions of this past year will not encourage FDA to listen to all responsible opinion; for example, the opinions of the practitioners which, courts' opinions notwithstanding, do have validity. If FDA does not listen to all responsible opinions, inevitably they will hurt the public they are trying to protect."

The FDA, having reviewed the first 900 drugs considered by NAS-NRC, reported 40 percent of them to be ineffective (24).

Meanwhile, the American Public Health Association (APHA) and the National Council of Senior Citizens filed suit against the FDA for foot-dragging on removal of these ineffective drugs from the market. Their point was that drugs which had been declared ineffective were still being prescribed and sold to the detriment of the citizenry.

In 1972, U.S. District Court Judge William B. Bryant upheld the complaint against the FDA and ruled that the agency must complete implementation of the NAS-NRC findings within four years. Judge Bryant further stated that all NAS-NRC reports had to be released, together with FDA's evaluation of them, and that drugs ruled ineffective were to be dealt with first, within one year's time (25).

The FDA, undecided about how to apply effectiveness findings, decided, late in 1972, that

"an identical, similar or related drug product is covered by the NDA for the basic product and thus is directly affected by a drug efficacy notice." (26)

So much for the "me-too drugs."

But this flew in the face of a court ruling that grandfather drugs, those which had never been covered by an NDA, could not be subjected to the NDA requirements of the 1962 law.

However, when this point was put to the FDA counsel, it was explained that the identical, similar, or related would be liable to charges of misbranding (false or misleading labeling) under the provisions of the 1938 drug amendments if manufacturers failed to comply.

Several manufacturers challenged the FDA's handling of ineffective drugs, the viability of the grandfather clause, and the right of the FDA to "arbitrarily" call a product a new drug. The cases were accepted for review by the Supreme Court.

In June 1973 the Court ruled in favor of the FDA, agreeing that the agency has primary jurisdiction over what is a new drug; that drugs subject to an NDA between 1938 and 1962 do not have grandfather protection; that me-too drugs identical or similar to a product covered by an ineffective NDA are subject to drug efficacy requirements; and that, during NDA withdrawal proceedings, the FDA need not grant a formal hearing to manufacturers who fail to supply data from "adequate and well-controlled investigations."

Regulation Of Over-The-Counter Drug Products
In its efforts to ensure safety of prescription medicines, the
FDA largely ignored efficacy of OTC products.  Over the years,
however, both the FDA and the FTC have indicated displeasure
with labeling and advertising claims of OTC drugs.

When the FDA did spare a thought for OTC's, the agency
underwent criticism.  In 1964, for example, the FDA decided to
relabel phenacetin-containing drugs to include a warning of
possible kidney damage from high doses and/or usage over long
periods.  The American Medical Association, resentful of
government meddling with drug prescribing, tore itself away
from criticizing the FDA's procedures on prescription drugs to
argue that the phenacetin warning was "not indicated by the
best available evidence." (27)

Basically, however, both the FDA and the FTC floundered in
efforts to control OTC products.  In 1965, both agencies
agreed that they wanted to act against what they considered
exaggerated claims for cold remedies but didn't know how to
proceed because they had no data on which to make a move (28).
Their difficulty was compounded by the shared responsibility:
the FDA has authority for everything on OTC drugs except
advertising - which is in the hands of the FTC.

Neither agency had the funds to carry out large-scale drug
trials, and there were no volunteers from the academic world.
Reluctant to take on both the drug manufacturers - many of
whom had some clinical data tucked away in the files against
just such an eventuality - and the practicing physicians - who
continued to resent federal interference - both agencies
dropped the issue.

There were sporadic complaints against industry practices;
However, when, for example, FDA Commissioner Goddard told the
Proprietary Association that its 1966 voluntary ad code was
ineffective, the tone was one of sorrow and anger - but the
commissioner wasn't prepared to fight (29).

In 1971, at the Senate Select Committee on Small Business
Monopoly hearings on advertising and promotion of OTC drugs,
the Chairman, Sen. Gaylord Nelson, was compelled to comment
that perhaps the FDA, not the FTC, should control OTC
advertising.  An FTC aide, Robert Pitofsky, claimed that since
OTC ads were of the soaps/cereal class, not the prescription
class, they, therefore, belonged with soaps and cereals under
FTC jurisdiction.

Eventually, the FDA found the remedy it had sought.  The
agency decided on a review of safety and efficacy of all OTC
products (30).  In addition, the FDA, not sure how many OTC
drugs were on the market, decided to group the products by

category and have each category reviewed by a panel of experts
who would examine evidence supplied by manufacturers.  The
review would culminate in monographs detailing the standard
for each category.  Whether the monographs would constitute
substantive regulations in themselves - in which case any
product not in conformance with the monograph was ipso facto
breaking the law - was unclear.

In December 1972, when Washington was empty because of the
Presidential election and Christmas holiday, the Senate Small
Business Monopoly Subcommittee again was holding hearings on
OTC's.

Dr. Henry Simmons, the then director of the FDA's Bureau of
Drugs, explained the procedure followed by the agency for OTC
drug efficacy reviews.  At the time, he observed that the
monograph procedure was chosen because

"the agency must prove OTC's misbranded or unsafe or
ineffective.  The burden of proof falls heavily on the
agency." (31)

Senator Nelson was surprised to find that OTC drugs are
regulated under the 1938, not the 1962 amendments, and that,
therefore, manufacturers were not required to document safety
and efficacy - instead, it is up to the FDA to prove the
products unsafe.

The record shows Sen. Nelson, addressing no one in
particular, saying,

"...would somebody explain to me why the FDA has not come to
the Congress and asked for legislation that would make the
burden of proof the same for all drugs?"

FDA counsel Eugene M. Pfeifer baldly stated the obvious:

"The over-the-counter drug market has, because of the agency's
attention to the prescription drug area, been unregulated for
many years."

The OTC efficacy review, he said

"is our first real attempt to get to the problem existing in
the over-the-counter drug market."

Counsel Pfeifer commented that Sen. Nelson's proposed
measure (S. 3296, 92nd Congress) to repeal the grandfather
clause and to give the FDA authority on OTC drug advertising

would be helpful; however, he also felt that the monograph
approach is still the only means of handling OTC efficacy.
Sen. Nelson's bill was pending before the Subcommittee on
Health of the Senate Committee on Labor and Public Welfare.

The attorney frankly anticipated that industry would
challenge if the FDA took the position that the monographs are
substantive.  Dr. Simmons said that if the monograph approach
doesn't work,

"we will be back to the Congress and say 'if you want this job
done you must pass other authority'."

In opening December 1972 hearings on OTC's, Sen. Nelson
complained that

"The massive promotion of drugs for self medication is nothing
short of scandalous.  In 1969, the public spent the incredible
sum of $900 million for cough and cold remedies, including
over $200 million for cold tablets and capsules, nasal drugs,
and nasal sprays.  Many of these products are at best mostly
useless, while many are harmful, and some are even dangerous."
(32)

Sen. Nelson also commented, however, that "the public
itself must share the blame for the fact that we have become a
nation of pill poppers."

The weapon of ridicule was brought into play by his
Monopoly Subcommittee's staff economist, Benjamin Gordon, who
was widely quoted in the consumer press for his comment that
Mrs. Gordon's chicken soup seemed to be a more effective cold
preventive than vitamin C.  Some witnesses testifying before
the subcommittee agreed.

Americans doubtless laughed at the chicken soup line but,
as an FDA survey has shown, the public is still quite trustful
of OTC drugs and OTC drug ad claims.  Then-FDA Commissioner
Charles Edwards, detailing a survey of almost 3,000 persons,
found that while Americans are suspicious of their physicians,
they are full of confidence in OTC agents, and naive about the
functioning of the human body (32).

According to Commissioner Edwards, the survey bears out
what he already knew; namely that his agency, rather than the
FTC, should control OTC drug advertising, "since Congress has
already given us the job of insuring that such drugs are safe
and effective."

The FDA may not need authority over OTC drug ads to tighten
its hold on OTC products.  The Supreme Court's June 1973

decision, while not specifically addressed to OTC's, seems to
say that the monograph system is valid and that monographs
constitute substantive law.

## Regulation Of Drug Advertising
Efforts at controlling prescription drug advertising began
early in the 1960s, but the first steps were tentative.

The 1962 Kefauver hearings, in the windup stage, were
examining drug advertising to physicians.  Senator Kefauver
concluded that prescription drug ads were misleading and
lacking in full description of possible side effects (33).

The FDA decided to set up "full disclosure" regulations for
Rx products.  However, it was soon revealed that "full
disclosure" did not mean full disclosure.

The regulations, a member of the FDA's Bureau of
Enforcement explained, specifically excluded journal
advertising to physicians from its provisions.  Under existing
law [Sec. 502(f) of the 1938 drug amendments], the requirement
applied only to labeling; in turn, "labeling" meant the
package label, brochures, booklets, and mailing pieces sent to
the physician separately from the drug.

Full disclosure, then, definitely did not encompass medical
journal advertising.  The FDA's proposed regulations would
require adequate directions for use; indications; effects;
dosage; routes, methods, frequency, and duration of
administration; and any relevant hazards, contraindications,
side effects, and precautions.

Veterinary drugs and therapeutic devices were subject to
the requirements, but new drugs, antibiotics, and insulin were
to be exempt if their uses and hazards were "commonly known,"
and if the ads gave quantitative formulae and contained no
misrepresentation of facts.

Rep. John D. Dingell (D.-Mich.) then introduced legislation
that would have compelled full disclosure in all prescription-
drug ads (35).  The final legislation, incorporated in the
1962 drug amendments (P.L. 87-871), required that ads give
such negative data as side effects and contraindications.

Under agreements reached by the FDA and industry attorneys
late in 1963, drug advertising to physicians was to contain a
"fair balance" between claims and negative effects (36).

In 1965, the FDA threw shock waves throughout the drug
industry by instituting criminal proceedings against a "Pree
MT" ad appearing in the Journal of the American Medical
Association (JAMA) (37).  According to the FDA, the ad lacked
the legally required brief summary of side effects; moreover,
it falsely stated that the drug had no contraindications when,

in fact, it had two.

By 1966, the FDA was saying that even rarely-occurring side effects must appear in labeling. The cited drugs were long-acting sulfonilamides, which carried a rare hazard of inducing the Stevens-Johnson syndrome.

In 1966, FDA Commissioner Goddard seized "Peritrate SA" on the grounds of false advertising. Interestingly, although the ad ran in a number of medical journals, the FDA citation for false advertising specified only the JAMA. Commissioner Goddard denied that he was sending the AMA a covert message to look to its advertising practices.

The 1966 seizure by the FDA of the antibiotic "Lincocin," because its ad lacked fair balance (again, a JAMA ad), so infuriated the manufacturer that it cancelled about $300,000 worth of medical journal advertising; other drug companies threatened to follow suit. The Upjohn Co., maker of Lincocin, was particularly disturbed that it had no prior notice of the seizure, even though the ad had been running in journals for a number of months.

Fair balance also must appear in promotional material, the FDA announced. The PMA objected on the grounds that ads were not meant to be "permanent reference monographs."

Later the FDA's guidelines spelled it out: Ads should have no extension of claims over what was an FDA-approved use; contain no quote that could mislead the reader into thinking statements were based on a large clinical study; the ad could not wax fulsome in quoting favorable results from poor-quality studies while ignoring unfavorable results from good-quality research; no quotations out of context; no pitting of one medical authority against another; no citations of clinical trials that reported an absence of side effects while failing to mention clinical work that revealed unwanted effects; no omission of potential danger to health; and no misleading references to a drug's value in terms of the total available armamentarium (38).

When, in January 1967 Sen. Nelson took over as chairman of the Monopoly Subcommittee of the Select Committee on Small Business, the attack on drug advertising was stepped up. On the basis of Subcommittee hearings, Sen. Nelson concluded that physicians have "misplaced confidence in ads." (39) The Senator took on the AMA, calling it "grossly derelict" in notifying physicians about improper advertising claims.

He also was critical of the promotional activities and "black bag" expenditures pharmaceutical companies directed toward medical students.

The black bag hearings focused on testimony from medical

students who decided to return pharmaceutical company gifts.
Sen. Nelson, in pursuing the effect such gifts have on student
physicians, quoted Dr. Harold Upjohn, vice president of the
Upjohn Co., who had told a group of students:

"You know why they give them [gifts].  No question about it.
They want doctors to be interested in prescribing their
brands."

   The Senator was particularly unhappy with the AMA's role in
handling drug advertising.  Although, for example, editorial
material appeared in JAMA warning against prescribing of
chloramphenicol for trivial pruposes, the journal continued to
carry a Parke-Davis ad for its chloramphenicol that stated
merely "Chloramphenicol when it counts," accompanied by
graphics indicating that the drug was recommended for upper
respiratory infections.
   Sen. Nelson commented that he knew of instances where the
drug was prescribed for truly trivial conditions, such as acne
and hangnail, although it was never advertised for these
purposes.  Chloramphenicol, because it induces such serious
side effects as depression of bone marrow production and
potentially fatal anemias, is meant to be reserved for
serious, chloramphenicol-sensitive infections, such as typhoid
and typhus.
   Sen. Nelson's Monopoly Subcommittee also was critical of
the AMA's stance - or lack of it - on the use of fixed
combination antibiotic drugs (40).  The issue of fixed
combinations dated back to 1963, when the FDA had been advised
by expert physicians that antibiotics were not to be used in
combination with other drugs for the treatment of the common
cold.  The expert group was headed by Dr. Harry Dowling,
chairman of the AMA's Council on Drugs.
   The agency's use of physicians in academia was protested by
practicing M.D.'s - who doubted "Ivory Tower" expertise - and
by the PMA - which said that the FDA had exceeded its
statutory authority.
   Sen. Nelson wondered why the JAMA failed to accept its own
experts' recommendations, since the Journal had an advertising
council that presumably accepted ads only for substantiated
drug claims.  Moreover, the NAS-NRC effectiveness ratings on
antibiotic combinations, which were unfavorable, had been
released although not yet been published in JAMA.
   When FDA Commissioner Ley appeared before a monopoly
subcommittee hearing, he observed that chloramphenicol use was
perhaps waranted in about 10 percent of the estimated 1.5 to 2

million patients receiving it.  Dr. Ley revealed that the FDA
was considering a suggestion of Sen. Nelson's that ads carry a
statement saying that "this is no longer the drug of choice
for any disease in this country." (41)

The Nelson Monopoly Subcommittee pointed out that
chloramphenicol prescribing rose and fell sharply according to
the attention paid to it.  When in 1952 warnings about
chloramphenicol-associated blood dyscrasias were published,
use of the drug dropped for a few years, then rose again.
When in 1960 to 1961 stronger warning labels were required,
the 54 million grams of certified drugs in 1960 dropped to
nearly 27 million grams in 1961.  By 1968, however, the
certified drug output was up to 47.5 million grams.  When the
Senate Small Business Monopoly Subcommittee had finished
hammering away at chloramphenicol, the certified output had
fallen from about 42.5 million grams to about 17.5 million
grams.

Witnesses before the Monopoly Subcommittee had no
difficulty in explaining the chloramphenicol experience.
According to the Library of Congress analysis of the hearings,
the chloramphenicol incident

"constitutes dramatic evidence of how the successful promotion
of a drug minimizes the impact of new and perhaps adverse drug
information on the prescribing choice of physicians.
Chloramphenicol had been introduced amid much fanfare in the
medical community about the 'broad spectrum' concept in
antibiotic therapy.  Great prominence was given in the
advertising and promotion of the drug to its effectiveness in
a wide range of therapeutic circumstances.  The product's
limitations or hazards failed to receive anywhere near the
same emphasis.  The effect...created attitudes on the part of
some prescribers toward the uses of certain drugs, which over
time and in the light of changing developments in the drug
area, were no longer valid.  The result - wholesale
misprescribing of certain products in circumstances where
these drugs were no longer indicated." (41)

In 1967, the Task Force on Prescription Drugs, set up by
DHEW Secretary John Gardner, noted the "high esteem" in which
some promotional activities of major drug companies were held
by the medical profession (42).  Support of medical
conferences and provision of educational material, and
scholarships and fellowships are highly regarded, it pointed
out.

On the other hand, the task force cited the estimate of

$3,000 per physician spent annually by the major drug
companies on advertising. The task force observed that the
incidence of biased and inaccurate drug advertising had been
reduced by the FDA's strong enforcement campaign begun in
1967. But, it also noted that

"The overall value of such advertising volume continues to be
seriously questioned. Similarly, the potential impact of
these large advertising expenditures on the editorial policies
of the journals which are supported in large part by drug
advertisements appears to deserve careful study." (42)

Although Sen. Nelson has continued his interest in
antibiotics in general and in chloramphenicol in particular,
his attention was caught by ads for mental drugs.
Under his scrutiny, a particular species of ad died. This
was the tranquilizer ad that recommended various drugs for
"the everyday anxieties of childhood," for the "excessive
anxiety resulting from unavoidable day-to-day pressures," and
for "the anxiety that comes from not fitting in." As
witnesses observed, at one time or another such descriptions
can be applied to the entire populace.
In testifying on "mood" drugs, FDA Commissioner Charles
Edwards said,

"The advertising industry took advantage of two factors, the
increasing complexity of our society and the discovery of the
mood drugs, to promote and advertise these drugs in such a way
as to actually create a climate of need."

According to the Commissioner,

"A casual examination of the medical journals indicates that
prescription mood drugs are being promoted at such rates and
with such themes as to create an unrealistic demand for these
drugs."

Unlike many situations in the drug industry, ones that
continue to be wrangled over for years, mood drug advertising
of this kind simply disappeared from the medical journals.
Another attack on mood advertising was carried by Rep. Paul
G. Rogers (D.-Fla.), who asked manufacturers and TV networks
to voluntarily restrict OTC mood drug ads on television or he
would introduce legislation to outlaw them (43). Included
were aspirin ads that promised mood alterations. Rep. Rogers
fretted that Americans were becoming an over-medicated

society, and that such ads contributed to drug abuse.

Shortly thereafter, Rep. Fountain's Government Operations Subcommittee on Intergovernmental Relations issued a report, "Regulations of Prescription Drug Advertising," that said physicians were still exposed to false advertising (44).  The report recommended that the FDA set up guidelines for remedial action on ad violations and that ads be required to show the drug's NAS-NRC rating.  Later, the FDA decided that the ratings, after they have been reviewed by the agency, will indeed be part of the labeling.

Sen. Nelson, perhaps wary of voluntary ad guidelines, introduced legislation in the 93rd Congress, S. 956, for the control of advertising.  He would require that

"The Secretary of HEW shall approve all advertising in advance that appears in either the electronic media, or in any publication or advertising circular, for any drug.  The Secretary will approve only advertising which does not mislead or misrepresent the product, either in text or layout."

Under present law, pre-approval of drug advertising is required only in extraordinary circumstances.

Another piece of legislation proposed by Sen. Nelson deals with a drug manufacturer's detail men, who would be required to give physicians an FDA-approved document on a drug before beginning their detailing talk.  Such legislation might prove as difficult to enforce as that regulating private sexual acts between consenting adults.  For, certainly, the physician can be led to drug information, but he cannot be forced to read it it.

The 1967 DHEW Task Force on Prescription Drugs also mentioned detail men, but wasn't sure whether to classify their activities as

"primarily promotional [or] primarily educational.  It is doubtful, however, that physicians can expect such detail men to give invariably unprejudiced and objective advice." (42)

The AMA commissioned a study of physician responses to the drug advertising process.  One purpose of the 1950 study was to determine why the AMA's own journal had lost advertising pages to two competitor's magazines: Medical Economics and Modern Medicine.  The study was in two parts:  a 1953 survey from the advertiser's viewpoint, and a 1956 study of physicians.

The survey was carried out in Fond du Lac, Wisconsin, and

measured local physician responses to the typical drug
marketing process as applied to five different drug products
(45).  The survey was limited to M.D.'s in the Fond du Lac
area and is not projectable to the nation.

Of some 55 physicians surveyed, 20 felt that detail men
were their most important means of learning about drugs.  Four
physicians cited ads in medical journals, four cited direct
mail from drug firms.  Nineteen mentioned papers and/or
articles in journals, two specified national medical
conventions, two listed county medical meetings, two said
hospital staff meetings, one said reference books, and one
cited postgraduate courses.

When the question was limited to commerical sources only,
31 of the 55 physicians cited detailing as the one "most
worthwhile for learning about new products."  Seven answered
drug company periodicals, five responded to medical journal
advertising, and five picked direct mail.  Asked their opinion
of detail men, there were such physician comments as

"The detail man is an excellent source on indications and
contraindications, dosages, and comparisons between products."

Another, however, said,

"We don't have time to go through the professional literature
and the detail man can provide us everything we need.  Of
course, his word is likely to be biased..."

Another, who preferred to learn about new drugs through
detailing, commended,

"The other media are too uncertain and leave it up to the
doctor to sort it out.  The detail man, on the other hand, is
quite careful about what he tells the doctor because of
possible repercussions later."

Sometimes it is not a question of advertising practices;
rather, it is a physician's desire to try something new -
though he may not wish to spend the time, or may not have the
expertise, to use some of the newer, powerful drugs.

Methotrexate, a potent antineoplastic agent, never has been
advertised for use in psoriasis.  It has been used
successfully in hospitalized patients for a very severe type
of the disease (psoriasis arthopathica).  However, when
reports began to appear in the literature indicating that
methotrexate was of value in serious cases of psoriasis, a

condition notoriously difficult to treat, physicians lacking
experience with modern chemotherapeutic agents began to
prescribe the drug on an outpatient basis in general practice,
even for relatively trivial cases of this disease.

Methotrexate labeling now carries a warning that psoriasis
patients have died under treatment with the drug, and that

"In the treatment of psoriasis, methotrexate should be
restricted to severe, recalcitrant, disabling psoriasis which
is not adequately responsive to other forms of therapy, but
only when the diagnosis has been established, as by biopsy
and/or after dermatologic consultation."

## Who Uses Drugs?

In its second interim report, in 1967, the DHEW Task Force on
Prescription Drugs, which studied all facets of drug
operations, found that aged citizens constitute only about 10
percent of the U.S. population; however, they account for
about 23 percent of all prescription drug expenditures (42).

The Task Force's examination of health expenditures showed
that outpatient expenditures for drugs between 1950 and 1966
rose from $1 billion to $3.2 billion, while total national
expenditures for hospital costs, M.D. fees, and drug costs,
rose from $11.9 billion to $41.8 billion.

According to the Task Force, Medicare has increased the
ability of many of the aged to pay doctor/hospital bills,

"not entirely but in large part.  Expenditures for out-of-
hospital prescription drugs, however, are not covered by the
present medicare law, and it has been necessary for elderly
patients to utilize other sources."

At the request of the DHEW Task Force, the USPHS developed
a Master Drug List of the products most frequently prescribed
for the elderly in 1966, and that made up about four-fifths of
their drug usage.

The list contained the 409 most prescribed products,
accounting for $174.7 million, or 88 percent of all community
pharmacy prescriptions dispensed.  The value of the drugs was
$682.3 million at the retail level.

Of the 409 products, some 379 were dispensed by brand name;
87 of them had chemical equivalents available, "often but not
always at lower cost," and could have been prescribed
generically.  Thirty of the drugs were dispensed generically.

The average cost of the drugs was $3.91; for the 379
dispensed by brand name, it was $4.11; for the 30 generics, it

was $2.02.

Another variable in prescription drug costs is the
sometimes arbitrary price charged by the retailer.  A survey
in Money showed a price range of from $2.37 to $4.75 charged
by retailers for the same number of Darvon capsules (46).   In
a middle-income suburb of Los Angeles the price charged for 50
Polycillin tablets was $10 and $20.  The survey revealed that
(36):

"When it comes to determining whether a drug price is fair,
most buyers are in the dark, and the pharmacists seem
determined to keep them there,"

said Money, which observed that manufacturers

"are beginning to be embarrassed about the way their products
are marketed at retail....  Many price discrepancies seem to
reflect nothing more than the chaotic state of the
pharmaceutical market, but our survey did suggest some
patterns."

Among them, stores in wealthy suburbs and those in ghettos may
charge more than drugstores in middle-class areas, and the
name "discount store" is no assurance of lower prices.

Money favors prescription-price posting laws, so that
consumers can shop around for the best price.  It advised
readers to discuss the cost of a prescription with the
physician and to urge the M.D. to prescribe generically:

"There may sometimes be good reasons why he wants you to have
a brand-name drug rather than its unbranded chemical
equivalent, but not always." (36)

## Will Generic Prescribing Reduce Drug Prices?

Sen. Kefauver proposed to cut drug prices by limiting the term
of patent protection to drug manufacturers.  They would have
been required to cross-license other distributors, thus
reducing prices (47).

In 1962, however, it was a tenet of faith that generic
drugs were therapeutically equivalent, and that allowing
small, but reliable, drug houses to manufacture the most-
prescribed drugs would inevitably lower prices.

The long fight to compel generic prescribing began in 1963,
when the PMA went to court to void an FDA regulation that the
generic name of a product had to appear each time the brand
name was shown on the label.  The courts eventually came down

on the side of PMA, saying that the Congress's intent only was that the generic name appear "prominently." (48)

In its appeal of the verdict, the FDA ingenuously remarked that the generic-every-time principle was designed to encourage generic prescribing.

The generic-every-time provision was finally decided in 1967, when the Supreme Court ruled against the FDA (49).

In 1966, a policy statement from DHEW urged generic-drug purchases whenever practical (50). The policy was applied to several USPHS hospitals.

Shortly thereafter, Senators Paul H. Douglas (D.-Ill.), and Russell B. Long (D.-La.), tried a different tack (51). Sen. Douglas introduced legislation that would have allowed reimbursement of prescribed drugs under Medicare. On the other hand, Sen. Long wanted generic drugs to be mandatory in Medicare and welfare programs funded by federal money. Sen. Douglas's bill, when approved in 1966 by the Senate Finance Committee, provided for payment to the patient, but limited it to the lowest generic price plus the pharmacist's fee. The measure was killed during a Senate-House conference. This was attributed to an unfamiliarity with the bill, rather than any distaste for its provisions, which were to surface again.

Within only a few months, President Johnson asked for a study that would estimate the cost of providing generic drugs under Medicare (52).

Sen. Philip A. Hart (D.-Mich.) also came out in favor of governmental promotion of generic drugs, but only if such drugs were safe (53).

A 1967 DHEW report found that

"Doctors often prescribe costly brand-name products when equivalent drugs could be made available to the patient at lower cost under the generic name. Requiring generic prescribing, under Government programs, however, will not be possible until doubts are resolved about whether certain drugs with the generic name are actually equivalent in therapeutic trials." (54)

The report continued,

"Moreover, even if the doctor prescribes a drug by its generic name, the patient may not be offered the least generic-cost drug by his pharmacist. Pharmacists have no incentive to give the consumer the cheapest drug since they receive a mark-up on cost."

And it is right here, perhaps, that Dr. Richard Burack made
his greatest impact on the medical-pharmacy habits of
Americans.  Before the advent of Dr. Burack's popular Handbook
of Prescription Drugs, asking one's physician what drug he was
prescribing was borderline gentility.  Moreover, shopping
around for the best Rx price was lower-middle-class at best
and sometimes downright humiliating.

Dr. Burack, a pharmacologist at Harvard Medical School,
changed that.  His advocacy of generic-drug shopping made it
seem smart, if not chic.  His Handbook told patients that the
doctor's obligation was to prescribe the best drug for the
least money (55).

In addition, he suggested that generic drugs, because they
were older and "have stood the test of time," may be more
safely prescribed than newer drugs, whose long-term toxicity
is still in doubt (56).  Thus, patients were encouraged to
make sure prescribing physicians marked the Rx form "label."
In turn, patients were advised to check that the pharmacist,
in fact, did put the drug's name on the label - for safety's
sake.

The Handbook contained a list of basic drugs; a
prescription drug list of the most commonly used
pharmaceuticals; a price list culled from manufacturers'
catalogs; and a price catalog for pharmacists from the Drug
Topics Red Book; a list of the then top 200 drugs; the names
of generic-drug distributors; and a very strong plea for use
of generic drugs, buttressed by some highly unfavorable
comments about the brand-name pharmaceutical industry.  For,
as Dr. Burack testified before Senator Nelson's Small Business
Monopoly Subcommittee in 1967,

"There's no doubt about it - there's no difference [between
performance of brands and generics]." (57)

However, the Task Force on Prescription Drugs set up a
program to study equivalency of some chemically equivalent
drugs which found that such drugs were not biologically
equivalent.  The Task Force recommended that DHEW continue
studying biological equivalency of "important chemical
equivalents." (58)

Meanwhile, other aspects of price schedules were drawing
congressional attention and fire.  In April 1967, the
Subcommittee on Activities of Regulatory Agencies Relating to
Small Business of the House Select Committee on Small
Business, chaired by Rep. John D. Dingell (D.-Mich.), heard
witnesses tell of quantity discounts given to hospitals and

physicians, with preferential drug prices to institutional
buyers (59).

Later, Sen. Nelson's Small Business Monopoly Subcommittee
heard testimony that Schering Corp. had charged two different
rates to hospitals and government purchasers and to druggists.
Asked to justify the practice, Henry Conzen, president of
Schering, explained that

"Government agencies purchase pharmaceutical products in large
quantities on the basis of competitive bids.  Such orders may
be highly attractive and many companies are convinced that
these orders should be sought even at prices which would be
unprofitable if normal accounting practices were followed."
(60)

The prices, he explained, ignore the cost of business
operations, such as manufacturing and overhead.  Prices are
based only on the cost of the raw materials and the direct
labor costs required to product the drug at the bid price.

Some witnesses before the Sen. Nelson's Subcommittee
observed that, under the two-price system, and in the absence
of real competition within the pharmaceutical industry,
undesirable or unnecessary expenditures can be passed along
to the patient at the retail level.

Industry witnesses defended the two-tier level on the
premise that the industry is made up of two kinds of drug
companies:  first, those that carry out primary research, and,
second, those nonresearch-oriented companies that market
popular drugs whose patents have expired.  It was noted that
research-oriented members of industry have to price their
drugs at levels which include both the cost of research and
the risk involved in developing new pharmaceuticals.

One industry witness argued that a drug price is reasonable
if it provides what no other use of the same sum of money will
give.

"If a $4 prescription, or six of them, will keep a patient
from losing a couple of day's pay or spending a night in a
hospital, the price is reasonable." (61)

This view of the situation was criticized by George Squibb,
former member of the Squibb drug house, who noted that

"Exploitation of the value of medicines used in life-
preserving or life-saving situations by setting prices far
above the cost is what must be deliberately and

conscientiously avoided, no matter what justification or
economic temptation is felt by the manufacturer." (62)

At about the same time as Sen. Nelson's Monopoly
Subcommittee hearings were taking place, the Task Force on
Prescription Drugs was finding (63) that the kind of
competition that exists in the pharmaceutical (among other)
industries brings

"an intensive competition between companies, with the promise
of a greater share of a relatively limited market and richer
profits for the successful competitor - but...these activities
have little to do with normal price competition in the retail
marketplace [and with] the promise of eventual price savings
to the consumer."

The Task Force also addressed itself to the trend of drug
prices, which, according to the Consumer Price Index of the
Bureau of Labor Statistics,

"have been decreasing steadily since 1958. [From three
independent surveys] it is equally obvious that these prices
have been increasing during the same period." (64)

The problem is that the surveys have been measuring
different things. The Bureau of Labor Statistics have been
measuring about a dozen selected drugs whose average price has
decreased. The items chosen by the Bureau, however, do not
reflect the most widely used drugs; moreover,

"they do not reflect the changes in consumer expenditures
which constantly occur when new and more costly products are
introduced on the market and replace less costly products. On
the other hand, the independent surveys are not concerned with
the price changes of any individual drug products, but instead
are aimed at determining the average price of the
prescriptions which people do purchase."

In its quiet way, the Task Force also observed that drug
prices at the manufacturer's level are marked by research and
development costs that are high in comparison with those of
other industries,

"and which include a substantial degree of effort yielding
only duplicative or 'me-too' drugs and combination products
that contribute little to the improvement of health care."

The prices also reflect high promotional efforts and a high
degree of competition based only on quality and innovation,
"rather that the normal competition based on quality,
innovation, and price." (64)
    The Task Force concluded that

"the exceptionally high rate of profit which generally marks
the drug industry is not accompanied by any peculiar degree of
risk, or by any unique difficulties in obtaining growth
capital, and that industry profits have not been significantly
reduced by new governmental regulations concerning drug
safety, drug efficacy, or drug advertising." (64)

    While the Sen. Nelson's Monopoly Subcommittee and the Task
Force were examining pricing, the question of whether generic
drugs were clinically equivalent was raised.  Toward the end
of 1967, Parke-David showed that generic chloramphenicol
approved by the FDA's antibiotic certification program was
substandard.  Later independent tests proved the Parke-Davis
claim that competitive brands failed to meet the standard of
Parke-Davis chloromycetin (65).  Then, the FDA decided that
Parke-Davis chloromycetin would be treated as a reference
standard and that competitive drugs must meet it.
    Meanwhile, whether in line with the Senate Monopoly
Subcommittee's hearings or purely fortuitously, Merck, Sharp &
Dohme decided to set uniform drug prices for all their buyer
categories.  The firm's drug line was promptly dropped by two
wholesale companies, who complained that wholesalers were
being discriminated against by being asked to pay the same
prices as everyone else.
    Over the years, many congressmen have recognized that one
way to change industry's price structure is to amend the
patent laws.  Their success has been no better than that of
Sen. Kefauver whose 1962 patent provisions were the first to
be dropped.
    The latest attempt at eliminating "pricing excesses" was
made by Sen. Nelson, who proposed the Public Health Price
Protection Act, that would license competitive manufacturers
to produce patented drugs "for a reasonable royalty" under
specific circumstances.
    The licensing provision only would apply if the Surgeon
General of the USPHS and the FTC found that:  (a) the average
price of an important patented drug is more than five times
the manufacturer's direct cost of materials and labor, or
higher than the average price of the drug to a patient in a
foreign country; (b) that annual sales of the drug topped $1

million for three or more years; and (c) that the exclusivity
of a patent in itself substantially contributed to the drug's
high price.

One of the last acts of the 92nd Congress was to drop the
coverage of certain "maintenance" prescription drugs for
outpatients from the social security reform bill that became
law.

The amendment, which passed the Senate Finance Committee,
was linked to a federal formulary designed to reduce the cost
of drugs. The formulary plan, patterned along lines suggested
by Senators Joseph M. Montoya (D.-N.M.) and Vance Hartke
(D.-Ind.), made it as far as the Senate-House conference, but
it was deleted becasue of cost - $709 million estimated for
the first year.

The FDA by the end of 1972 had decided that generic drugs
are not therapeutically equivalence and that exact equivalence
among drug products cannot be expected (66). Therefore, the
FDA proposed that certain prescription drugs undergo
bioavailability testing. A priority has been set, "with
primary attention directed toward those in which a defect in
bioavailability would be most detrimental to patient care."

## Drug Testing

FDA Requirements The regulations set up under the 1962 drug
amendments defined a "new drug" as one that is not generally
recognized by qualified experts as being safe and effective
for the use proposed. Under the definition, an old drug
proposed for a new use would be considered a "new drug"; the
FDA's own example was: "If aspirin tablets were labeled or
promoted as a seasickness remedy, they would be considered a
'new drug'." (67)

Even an accepted remedy, used for years, if manufactured in
a new form, such as a timed-release capsule, is considered to
be a new drug requiring evaluation by the FDA (67).

The procedure falls into several steps: the sponsor of a
drug must supply the FDA an IND form, which contains, first,
complete information on drug composition and source; second,
manufacturing information to show that appropriate standards
exist to insure safety; and, third, preclinical studies,
including those performed on animals.

The overall intent of the IND is to demonstrate no
unreasonable hazard in studies on humans. The FDA's general
minimum requirements are acute toxicity determinations in two
species of animals, and the effects of longer-term
administration - two to four weeks in at least two species,

using the same route of administration that will be used in humans.

The IND also must describe the investigations that will be undertaken and give background on the training and experience of the investigators. The form provides an agreement that the drug sponsor will notify the FDA and participating investigators if adverse reactions are seen; certification that informed consent will be obtained from all humans given the drug; and agreement to submit annual progress reports.

If the drug eventually reaches clinical investigation, it first undergoes two steps called Phase 1 and Phase 2, both described as "clinical pharmacology."

In Phase 1, the drug is permitted to be given to healthy volunteers to determine toxicity, metabolism, absorption, and elimination, other pharmacologic actions, the preferred route of administration, and the dosage range.

When Phase 1 is satisfactorily completed, the sponsor can proceed to Phase 2, which allows initial trials in humans - treatment or prevention of disease for which the drug is intended. At this point, the sponsor is looking for evidence of safety and efficacy in the sick. To support safety the drug sponsor may be required to do further animal work as well.

Phase 3 studies - extensive clinical trials - permit not just experienced investigators but others, including practicing physicians, to administer the drug under careful monitoring.

When the drug laws were written there was no Phase 4 category. Phase 4 was developed to handle drugs like L-dopa, an old material proposed for use in Parkinson's disease - a condition for which there is no accepted treatment. L-dopa is not without side effects; it is not effective in every patient; and it doesn't provide dramatic relief of Parkinson's in many patients. Weighing the risks and benefits, the FDA set up the Phase 4 category, under which there is post-marketing surveillance of a drug.

A sponsor who files an IND is permitted to go directly into clinical pharmacology unless the FDA has a specific objection. There are three exceptions to this rule. FDA approval is required, first, before initiating work on hallucinogenic drugs; second, on materials so toxic that their use may be justified only under special conditions; and, third, on reinstitution of drug studies that had been terminated by the FDA commissioner.

Once the three required phase of clinical testing are complete, the sponsor can submit an NDA to the FDA containing

all the supporting data to show safety and efficacy, and
copies of the proposed drug labeling.

Under its own rules, the agency is required to act on the
NDA within 180 days. On review of the NDA, the FDA may find
it complete and approve the application so that the sponsor
can market the drug. If the NDA is considered incomplete in
certain areas, the sponsor is told to supply the missing data.

A drug sponsor who disagrees with the conclusions made on
his NDA by members of the Bureau of Medicine can request
conferences to discuss the data that have been labeled
deficient. If the conferences do not result in FDA approval,
the sponsor can either go back and do the work requested,
which is what now happens in practice, or he may ask for the
administrative hearing to which he is entitled. A negative
ruling in an administrative hearing may be appealed to the
courts.

Who Shall Carry Out Testing Of Drugs? In 1962, a year-old FDA
report turned up (68). The report was sent to Sen. Humphrey
for use in an investigation being carried out by the
Subcommittee on Reorganization and Internal Organization.
In reality, the FDA report was the text of a speech prepared
by William Weiss, an FDA statistician, who had delivered it
for Shelby T. Grey, director, Bureau of Planning and Approval,
before the annual conference of FDA bureau and district
chiefs. It stated that the department had seen

"apparent fraudulent reporting of the results of therapy by
doctors in private practice who have been commissioned by a
company to evaluate a drug. From the reporting of the same
drug by other doctors similarly commissioned, it can be
easily demonstrated that the former have either succeeded in
repealing the natural law relating to the variability of data,
or else have discovered a new research technique so precise as
to completely overshadow in importance the drug under test.
Flagrant frauds occur infrequently and can be detected readily
.... The greatest hazard, in my view, lies not with the
possibily few outright frauds, but with the demonstrably large
number of investigators subject to unconscious bias, derived,
as it has been said, from the infinite capacity of the human
mind for self-deception.... Another major weakness we find in
many clinical studies submitted with NDA's is that their
designs are such that they are incapable of making an
adequately sound scientific demonstration." (56)

Citation was made to a massive document submitted in

support of a cholesterol-lowering chemical.  The clinical data
on this drug had been obtained on selected patients by
practitioners in private practice.  According to the FDA
report, patients had been excluded from the study when they
showed no response to the drug.  Thus, a strong bias was set
up for favorable conclusions on the test drug, as all the
non-responders would be eliminated.  Another faulty design
aspect cited was that many of the patients were concomitantly
receiving several types of therapy designed to lower cholester
cholesterol levels, and results of the test drug could not be
distinguished from the other treatments.

Moreover, the subjects selected to be controls (those not
receiving the test drug) were inmates of a home for the aged -
and the very old tend naturally to have very low cholesterol
levels.  The active patients, of course, all had high
cholesterol levels, so that no true comparison was being made.

The FDA cited the typical pitfall of a small study with few
patients.  Results indicated no significant statistical
difference between active and control groups, which is
interpreted to mean that no difference exists:

"The fallacy is that the company, with which the burden of
proof of safety lies, has turned the tables so that the
Government is saddled with the burden of proof of hazard."
(68)

The FDA report also raised questions about licensing of
physician-drug evaluators.  In turn, FDA Assistant
Commissioner Winton B. Rankin firmly stated that the FDA would
not license clinical investigators or set up investigatory
guidelines because such was the responsibility of the drug
companies (69).

Six months later, however, it was revealed that a Maryland
physician, in private practice, had filed false test data on
the drugs of five different manufacturers.  Sen. Humphrey
commented that while drug companies are "extraordinarily
careful" in choosing clinical investigators, sometimes they
get stuck with poor investigators because of the shortage of
good ones.

The physician was indicated by a federal grand jury on
charges of fictitious tests that had caused the five
manufacturers to file false case studies in support of their
NDA's (70).

The investigator shortage was pointed up by an apparent
conflict of interest at FDA.  FDA Commissioner George Larrick,
observing that the best people were already consulting for

industry, made a remarkable statement:

"It is self-evident that in this field we will have to appoint
people who either are under contract to industry or who have
performed services to industry, perhaps on the very products
on which we will consult them."

Within a few months 19 physician-investigators were under
an FDA cloud.  Two of the M.D.'s had supplied data to 30 drug
companies.  The suspicion was that the men had supplied "paper
reports" - the term for data that exist only in someone's
imagination (71).

Sen. Humphrey, prepared to commiserate with industry over
the manpower shortage, became irked when more than 15 drug
companies refused to tell how much they paid their drug
testers (71).

In March 1964, in the first action of its kind, a federal
grand jury indicted the Richardson-Merrell drug company and
three of its researchers for falsifying data on MER/29, a
cholesterol-lowering drug.  Named in the indictment were the
company, the vice president in charge of research, and two
others.

The indictment said that the company had "willfully and
knowingly" filed false statements with the government, and
that those indicted "concealed and covered up relevant
clinical data."

The "false, fictitious and fraudulent" information was
given to the FDA in an NDA, in correspondence, and through
personal contact with agency staff.

In one claim against the company, it was charged with
failing to reveal certain animal toxicity, such as unwanted
ovarian changes in a monkey.  Also falsified, according to the
indictment, were toxicity results on the rate of conception,
litter size, and viability of offspring of test animals (72).

Richardson-Merrell, while claiming that it was not guilty
of the charges, surprisingly pleaded nolo contendere (no
contest) to the government's indictment (73).  The company
attorney and the individual defendants understood that a plea
of nolo contendere was tantamount to a plea of guilty.
Explaining the reasons for the plea, Richardson-Merrell sent a
letter to their stockholders which claimed that contesting the
government case would have been prejudicial because

"the question of law and fact involved would be novel,
difficult, and complicated.  Some of the questions would
involve the appraisal of highly technical matters of

scientific judgment in the evaluation of complex animal experimentation." (61)

The company also said that litigation would

"divert the company's efforts away from defending the civil suits, and at the same time, would complicate our defense against these suits." [Several hundred civil suits were pending.]

More significant, though, was the company's statement that, at the time the NDA was filed,

"the food and drug laws did not require the submission of literally all data which might have come to the attention of company scientists.... Rather, it was the general understanding that scientists could properly exercise professional judgment in determining which test reports and results were sufficiently significant and material to require reporting. It is believed that the Government, in consenting to a plea of nolo contendere, recognized that this was a gray area where there is a legitimate difference of opinion in respect to the interpretation of the law on this point as it existed at the time."

Two years later, FDA Commissioner James Goddard, before a PMA meeting, referred to the kind of data appearing in NDA's, stating he was

"shocked at the clear attempt to slip something by us. I have been shocked at the quality of many submissions to our investigational new-drug staff. The hand of the amateur is evident too often for my comfort. The so-called research and so-called studies are submitted by the cartonful and our medical officers are supposed to take all this very seriously." (74)

The next damning comment on the quality of drug test data came in 1969, from the NAS-NRC drug efficacy and labeling study of the 1938 to 1962 drugs. Their review panels called the quality of data supporting the drugs "poor." (75)

The NAS-NRC group recommended that the FDA use expert consultants on a continuing basis for drug evaluation, rather than just calling them in for specific situations. The opinion was expressed by the NAS-NRC group that the agency cannot be expected to be expert in all fields, thus making a

value judgment both on the drug company data submitted and on
the FDA staffers who accepted the data.

The following month (August 1969), Sen. Nelson proposed the
establishment of a National Drug Testing and Evaluation Center
within the FDA (76), commenting that

"The danger involved in the dependence on drug firms to
perform, direct, or arrange for the marketing of drugs in
which they have a financial interest is obvious....  It is
also unavoidable in many cases that at least some of the
scientists the drug firms employ for their testing are also
anxious to secure future contracts for drug testing and are
reluctant to reject a drug."

The center proposed by Sen. Nelson would carry out some
work on its own and subcontract work out to others, including
medical schools, the Veterans Administration, and so on.  The
drug companies would pay testing expenses and carry a share of
the center's overhead.  This proposal is still pending.

In an effort to simplify and tighten up the testing
process, Rep. Paul G. Rogers proposed that clinical
investigators on IND's be chosen by the FDA and report
directly to the agency (77).  Rep. Rogers's suggestion was
turned down by Commissioner Ley, who was of the opinion that
the FDA was not empowered to make judgements on investigators.

On Whom Shall Drugs Be Tested?  The first groping toward
informed consent came in 1962 when Senators Jacob K. Javits
(R.-N.Y.) and John A. Carroll (D.-Colo.) suggested that the
Kefauver-Harris amendments include a provision to authorize
the FDA to require that humans given experimental drugs be
told that the agents had, or had not, been proven safe in man.
These Senators' proposal was not reflected in the final
statute, which made the vague statement that "the interests of
patients" should be taken into consideration.

By 1966, the FDA's position was that physicians must have
written consent for human use of investigational drugs -
except in cases where it was either not feasible or contrary
to the patient's welfare.  These broad exceptions virtually
negated the written consent requirement.  This was pointed up
by a 1966 study showing that patients in a drug trial don't
perceive it to be "research." (78)  In fact, the report showed
that patients are so naive about what constitutes "treatment"
that they can be taken advantage of by a physician.

When the FDA's final rule on consent was published, it
represented a compromise.  The physician was allowed to use

his own judgment in deciding on oral or written consent for
Phase 3 studies; however, Phases 1 and 2 definitely required
written consent (79).

By 1969, FDA Commissioner Ley had proposed peer review of
clinical NDA work carried out in institutions.  It was
believed that the review by a panel of one's peers would
assure that studies were adequately supervised and the rights
of subjects safeguarded.  Such peer review did not become
mandatory until April, 1971.

Commissioner Ley's recommendations followed on the heels of
a scandal involving a physician who was said to have
supervised 25 to 50 percent of initial drug tests in the
United States.  This work was performed on southern convicts;
it also was reported that some of the projects had resulted
in deaths (80).  A review of the files showed that the
physician had been involved in 1,939 IND's and 36 NDA's.  The
bigger blow:  His physical setup had been previously inspected
by the FDA and had passed their review.

Dr. Henry K. Beecher, anesthesia professor at Harvard, who
has long seen a need for more ethical behavior in drug and
medical testing, argued that the FDA's peer review proposal
was not adequate to deal with "sometimes amateurish, sometimes
dishonest and sometimes unethical testing." (81)  He also
proposed that the FDA develop comparable supervision methods
for tests conducted outside of institutions.

Government, presumed to be one stronghold of ethical
behavior, fell into further disgrace when it was revealed in
1972 that the USPHS had been conducting a long-term study of
syphilis in which control subjects received no treatment
whatsoever.  The study, begun in 1932, was being performed on
poor blacks in Alabama; however, the patients were denied the
undoubted benefits of penicillin, which became available in
the 1940s, despite expert medical knowledge on the disability
and early death in store for untreated syphilitics.  The
subjects apparently never were told that they would not
receive treatment.

Even more interesting, however, was the DHEW's astounding
revelation that:

"a technical and medical advisory panel convened in 1969 by
the U.S. Public Health Service is reported to have
recommended, with some ambiguity, that the [syphilis study]
participants surviving at that time should not be treated."
(82)

What Test Procedures Should Be Employed?  It is generally

accepted that the animal studies required during the
preclinical investigation of a drug cannot eliminate all risk
to the eventual human user.

The FDA's general guidelines on animal toxicity testing are
based on the route and duration of administration proposed for
humans.  On oral and parenteral drugs, for example, duration
of subacute or chronic animal toxicity tests depends on
whether the human will receive the drug for several days, up
to 2 weeks, up to 3 months, or from 6 months to an unlimited
period (70).

When the drug will be employed for several days, 2 weeks of
toxicity testing in two species of animals are required.  When
the drug may be administered for an unlimited period, chronic
toxicity testing for 18 months in a rodent and 12 months in a
nonrodent species are required.  The subacute or chronic
studies are always performed by the route to be used
clinically.

For a drug intended to be applied to the skin, the toxicity
testing time ranges from a single, 24-hour exposure followed
by two-week observation for a drug meant to be given in one
application to man, to a 6-month intact skin study for a drug
that will receive unlimited clinical application.

"The duration of chronic toxicity studies has become, in
the past few years, a subject of considerable controversy
among toxicologists.  Some consider 3 to 6 months adequate for
studies to support the use of a drug in humans for indefinite
periods.  They contend that the potential of any drug for
organ damage, carcinogenesis excepted, can be estimated
through well-designed studies of this scope.... In view of
evidence to the contrary, we feel that routine reliance on
studies of such short duration is inherently risky." (83)

According to the FDA's Dr. Goldenthal (83), his agency has
seen toxicity between the sixth and 12th months of treatment:
eye changes with some mental drugs, and endocrine changes with
some anticonvulsants:

"As an alternative to an 18-month study in rats, we would
accept a 12-month chronic rat study, provided a 2-year mouse
carcinogenesis study is also performed."

Carcinogenicity testing now is not required by the
regulations.  In practice, however, it is routinely performed
on new materials because the FDA's Bureau of Medicine
routinely "requests" it.  Such a request is, in effect, an

order, as the FDA can deem an NDA incomplete without a
carcinogenesis study.

The FDA's view is that while short-term toxicity is
adequate for many drugs, others require a long period of
testing to uncover problems.

Since the agency may request what it likes, its
requirements for oral contraceptives are not those of the
general recommendations, for instance.  The FDA requires, as a
minimum, a one-year toxicity study in a rodent and the dog
before the drug is given to women for the typical three-cycle
study.  The agency also has recommended a concurrent chronic
study in the monkey, along with other standard requirements of
Phase 2.  However, when an oral contraceptive reaches Phase 3,
all general guidelines go out the window.  Before the large-
scale trials of Phase 3 begin, the FDA insists on a dog study
of up to 7 years duration, and a monkey study of up to 10
years.  The FDA requires that:

"The results of studies of 2 years' duration in the rat, dog,
and monkey should be submitted in consideration for approval
of an oral contraceptive for marketing." (83)

A Vexing Current Issue - Genetic Hazards  Now being debated is
the value of several recently developed tests to determine a
drug's mutation-causing potential.  In November 1970 a group
of geneticists and other experts spent a day publicly
wrangling over the predictive ability of tests to predict a
drug's mutagenic effects (84).

Mutagenicity conferences are held regularly, but still
participants have not reached a consensus.  Many claim that
while tests have not yet been absolutely perfected, there is
no need to delay further for improved, second-generation
procedures, which are still under research.  This lends weight
to the prudent concept that it is clearly better to use the
existing methods than to use none at all.

The FDA does not agree.  Apparently unconvinced of the
existing tests' value, the agency has tended to resist their
incorporation into testing guidelines.  Industry, equally
fearful of false negative and false positive results, also had
resisted their codification.

Dr. Marvin Legator (a proponent of mutagenicity testing and
developer of the host-mediated assay mutagen test while he was
chief of the Cell Biology Branch, Bureau of Food, Pesticides,
and Product Safety, FDA) put the matter into the form of an
unanswerable question (84).  Suppose thalidomide had not been
a teratogenic drug but a mutagenic drug?  And, suppose it had

not produced the spectacular (and rare) effect of armless and legless children, but the unspectacular effect of mental retardation? For mental retardation exists and it doubtless has numerous causes. Therefore, drug-induced mental retardation would probably go unnoticed for years.

So if thalidomide had been a mutagen, not a teratogen, its effects would (a) have taken years to uncover, (b) might never have been attributed to the drug but to some other cause, and (c) the drug would probably still be on the market as a highly respected sedative. Dr. Legator expressed the view that mutagen testing begun now, might prevent such a calamity.

The FDA may have been unwilling to make the procedures mandatory and suffer the risk of having been proved hasty. The agency, in cooperation with PMA experts, plans to develop guidelines for mutagenicity (and carcinogenicity) testing. Latest enunciation of this plan was in July 1973. Such plans and claims, however, have frequently been aired before, and still nothing has been done. A possible reason is infighting among FDA staff, who would prefer not to spell out guidelines - any guidelines. Their argument, presumably, is that setting up guidelines is an invitation to industry to follow the guidelines implicitly - and go no further. Guidelines have a way of becoming the lowest common denominator - rather than being the minimum testing effort put forth, guidelines tend to represent the maximum that will be performed.

## Narcotics And Dangerous Drugs

In 1964, Sen. Thomas J. Dodd (D.-Conn.), proposed a bill (S.2628) to control the manufacture and distribution of amphetamines, barbiturates, and other dangerous drugs. A similar bill was introduced in the House (H.R. 10409) by Rep. James J. Delaney (D.-N.Y.). The Dodd-Delaney proposals were an acknowledgement that the problems of abuse and addiction in the general population were now of greater magnitude than the problems associated with physicians' unsafe handling of drugs.

The Senate passed Sen. Dodd's bill, but the measure died in the 88th Congress. In the 89th Congress, Rep. Oren Harris (D.-Ark.) introduced H.R. 2, an anti-abuse measure. Sen. Dodd agreed to Rep. Harris's measure with only minor changes, and in July 1965 the bill was signed into law.

In December 1969 Sen. Dodd again proposed tighter drug controls (85). A particular problem was the amphetamines, then so widely prescribed for treatment of obesity - a therapeutic indication on which experts disagreed.

Rep. Paul G. Rogers asked FDA to lay the foundation for

"eliminating amphetamines by conducting studies to show that they are necessary and effective in only very limited medical situations." (86)

The agency decided to relabel amphetamines, permitting such indications as narcolepsy, hyperkinesis in children, and short-term use in obesity (amphetamine products lose their appetite-suppressant ability after a few weeks of administration) (87).

The Department of Justice, traditionally responsible for the actual enforcement of federal drug policies, revealed that in 1969 it couldn't account for as much as 38 percent of domestic production of the amphetamines and asked manufacturers to curb unnecessary production.

A tighter measure, the Comprehensive Drug Abuse Prevention and Control Act of 1970 (P.L. 91-13) was enacted and the Bureau of Narcotics and Dangerous Drugs (BNDD) of the Department of Justice, came up with new ideas for its implementation.

The statute set up five categories of controlled drugs: Schedule I, drugs with no accepted medical use which have a high potential for abuse [including heroin, d-lysergic acid (LSD)]; Schedule II, drugs with medical uses but with high potential for abuse (opiates, methadone, etc); Schedule III, drugs with approved medical uses but with lower abuse potential than preparations in Schedules I and II (barbiturates and some narcotics); Schedule IV, drugs with medical uses and low abuse potential (the minor tranquilizers, meprobamate, phenobarbitone, etc.); and Schedule V, drugs with low abuse potential and limited dependence, such as the so-called class X narcotics.

Under the new law, drugs in Schedule I could not be refilled on the same prescription, while prescriptions for Schedule III and IV drugs were limited to five refills for a period not longer than 6 months after the prescription was issued.

In March 1971 the proposed regulations implementing the new laws were published (89). Later regulations required the manufacturer to keep records on controlled substances to show the quantity of finished substance and the disposition of damaged quantities (89).

In July 1971 BNDD decided to move amphetamine and methamphetamine to Schedule II, but permitted five combination amphetamine drugs to remain in Schedule II (90).

In testimony before the Subcommittee to Investigate Juvenile Deliquency of the Senate Judiciary Committee, several

manufacturers testified against proposed new legislation that
would have moved such stimulants as methylphenidate
hydrochloride and phenmetrazine into Schedule II.  Both
Senators Birch Bayh (D.-Ind.) and Thomas F. Eagleton (D.-Mo.)
were irritated to find the FDA opposed to them in this matter.
These Senators were even more irritated to find that the
deputy director of BNDD, John Finlator, preferred to use
regular BNDD procedures for schedule changes, rather than to
achieve them through legislation.

Late in 1971 the BNDD decided to sharply curb the amount of
amphetamine available, and set the amphetamine-methamphetamine
production quota at 40 percent of the 1971 production total.

In 1972 the FDA also decided to relabel obesity drugs to
show their limited-term effect in appetite suppression.

In December 1972, at hearings before Sen. Nelson's Small
Business Monopoly Subcommittee on antiobesity agents, Dr.
Henry Simmons, director of the FDA's Bureau of Drugs,
displayed graphs to demonstrate that legislative measures were
effectively reducing the abuse potential of amphetamine-based
drugs (91).

He explained that in May, 1971, amphetamines were being
prescribed at a rate of 2 million a month.  When drug labeling
claims were limited, the prescription rate went down to 1.6
million a month, and when the drugs were reclassified into
Schedule II, the rate dropped to 673,000 prescriptions a
month.

The FDA made one further move on antiobesity agents.  It
issued a proposal to take amphetamine combinations off the
market on the grounds that such combinations as amphetamine,
to depress appetite, and amylobarbital, to prevent the patient
from becoming overstimulated, added nothing to the drug's
efficacy.

Trends For The Future
The Supreme Court's June 1973 decisions upholding the FDA's
regulatory authority under the 1962 drug amendments were
couched in such broadly approving language that this authority
is now unchallengeable.  The Court lauded the FDA's across-
the-board rulemaking, and clearly said that the agency can
issue substantive regulations and is not limited to authority
spelled out in the 1962 amendments.  Thus the FDA has been
given a great deal of maneuvering room; however, it also
increases the pressure on the FDA.

Traditionally, the FDA has tried to show that it can be
tough and responsive to consumer demands while not pushing so
hard that it invites congressional friends of industry to clip

its claws.  Its new added power will increase the squeeze on
the FDA to go out and do good works.

Industry, still trying to achieve its end, continues to
attack the FDA's position, but in a muted way, lest industry
gains rouse the fury of consumer groups who will again push to
have the FDA removed from DHEW and incorporated in a consumer
protection agency.  Should this happen, as industry sees it, a
completely unmanageable bureaucracy would be created,
responsive only to its own life-survival force.

A review of the FDA's procedures, and of the Food, Drug and
Cosmetic Act, requested by both the PMA and by a committee of
physicians in academia, now has no chance of taking place.
The Congress is caught in a cleft stick.  It cannot well
afford to take a stance that could be interpreted as pro-
industry during a period of consumer militancy.  Any
congressman who might have been tempted to open the issue now
may have had second thoughts as a result of the March 1973
hearings conducted by Sen. Nelson's Small Business Monopoly
Subcommittee.  Such witnesses as former FDA Commissioner
Edwards (now Assistant DHEW Secretary for health and science),
and Dr. Henry Simmons (former director of the Bureau of Drugs
and now an assistant to Edwards), expressed their opinion
that the only drugs available to the consumer in the United
States were those that were either unsafe or non-efficacious.
As Sen. Nelson squelched any clamor for a review, the High
Court's rulings will have a further chilling effect.

An equally dim future may be in store for two amendments to
the drug law that the PMA would like to have introduced and
passed through the Congress.  The PMA would like the FDA to
take into account "clinical experience" with a product as well
as "adequate and well-controlled studies."  Unfortunately,
clinical experience means clinicians - and the Congress is not
in a particularly pro-physician mood.

It was probably inopportune, therefore, for the AMA to pass
a resolution at its June 1973 annual convention protesting the
FDA's regulatory activities,

"which have the effect of restricting the use of prescription
drugs to approved labeling recommendations or which threaten
to interfere with the exercise of a physician's professional
prerogatives in selecting the drug of choice for a patient."

The PMA may have more luck with the second of its two
desired changes:  the right to ask for a review by an expert
committee - outside government - on questions involved in
clearance or withdrawal of an NDA or antibiotic monograph.

The very fact that the FDA was given more power by the Supreme Court may make the agency even more sensitive to scientific advisory group participation.

Drug abuse will continue to be a thorny problem. At the close of 1972, BNDD submitted a proposed quota system for controlled substances that would have moved the United States closer to the British method of dealing with physician prescribing of controlled drugs.

Under BNDD's proposal, DHEW would determine domestic medical needs for the drugs, and the production quota would be set near that figure. Under the present method, the industry manufacturing quota is determined by consumption.

PMA's anti-proposal letter to BNDD got in just under the wire. The Bureau was abolished on June 30, and a new, super-size Drug Enforcement Administration, combining the functions of BNDD and other federal drug abuse departments, was set up within the Justice Department. The need to prove its worth may act as an incentive to the new department, created under a reorganization plan of President Nixon's, to just such heroic measures as the BNDD quota scheme.

The drug program provisions of H.R. 1, designed to cover hospital outpatient drug costs, failed to pass the 92nd Congress, but they'll be back. Because of the cost involved in such a program, congressional passage of a similar bill may be delayed for several years; however, a modified bill, in which the patient picks up a portion of the drug tab, may be enacted. The White House already has been asked for its recommendations on outpatient Rx drug coverage under medicare; the request came from the Senate.

Meanwhile, the Nixon Administration, which was facing a get-tough Congress even before Watergate, may not be in shape to fight the Health Maintenance Organization bill submitted by Sen. Edward M. Kennedy (D.-Mass.).

Hearings held by Sen. Kennedy's Subcommittee on Health of the Committee on Labor and Public Welfare have led - or pushed - DHEW into studying ways of improving procedures under which medical research on humans is conducted.

However, Sen. Kennedy also has introduced a few bills on his own: one calls for establishment of a human-experimentation commission within DHEW, with authority over DHEW-funded projects. It may be possible for the Congress and the Executive Branch to work out some suitable legislation between themselves - as long as the Senate experimentation hearings dwell on the use of prisoners as research subjects, the populace-at-large won't have any strong urge to intervene.

Sen. Nelson has reintroduced his omnibus drug bill, S. 966.

but its patent provisions will doubtless prove as unpalatable this year - and next year - as last year - and ten years ago. The Congress, with the exception of a few Democratic members, is deeply reluctant to alter the fundamentals of patent protection.

Further efforts will probably be made at pushing the generic prescription of drugs, but enthusiastic supporters of generics tend to forget that the dispensing pharmacist is legally liable for his choice when he picks the drug with which to fill a generic prescription. On the other hand, the physician is legally responsible for the consequences when he writes a prescription for a brand-name drug.

Therefore, there is little doubt that his liability will restrict the pharmacist's enthusiasm for generic prescribing. One manufacturer has recognized the pharmacist's dilemma and acted accordingly. E. R. Squibb and Sons has offered to provide any necessary legal defense for a pharmacist who fills a generic prescription with a Squibb product.

Should other major manufacturers follow suit, but the little firms don't, and all other factors remain the same, it is easy to perceive that generic prescriptions will be filled wtih big-name products.

There will be further attempts to force physicians to prescribe through use of drug compendia. Such attempts ignore the physician's response, which is one of boredom. The physician, in the plainest way possible, has been grumbling that he wants fast, accurate information on drugs. He also wants information obtainable in a way that doesn't tax him or interfere with his prerogatives. In other words, he definitely doesn't want a compendium under Federal Government sponsorship.

Nevertheless, the trend toward regulation of the practice of medicine generally and of the pharmaceutical industry in particular will not stop - it may not even slow down!

Acknowledgment In rereading 10 years' worth of Drug Trade News (DTN) as a refresher for this chapter, I recognize the debt owed to Stephens Rippey and Catherine M. Cooper, one-time Washington editors of DTN, who consistently made sense of the often baroque drug happenings in Washington. However, any opinions which have crept into this chapter are not theirs, or the editors', but mine alone.

References

1.  Drug Trade News (hereafter referred to as DTN) Jan. 22, 1962, p. 1.

2.  Ibid. April 16, 1962, p. 1.

3.  Ibid. April 30, 1962, p. 1.

4.  Ibid. May 14, 1962, p. 1.

5.  Science Dec. 4, 1964.

6.  DTN Oct. 15, 1962, p. 1.

7.  DTN April 1, 1963, p. 1.

8.  Ibid. Aug. 5, 1963, p. 6.

9.  Ibid. July 6, 1964, p. 1.

10.  Ibid. Aug. 28, 1967, p. 2.

11.  Federal Food, Drug, and Cosmetic Act As Amended, Food and Drug Administration, Feb. 1969.

12.  DTN June 8, 1964, p. 1.

13.  Ibid. May 9, 1966, p. 1.

14.  Ibid. Jan. 13, 1969, p. 1.

15.  Ibid. Feb. 24, 1969, p. 1.

16.  Ibid. June 2, 1969, p. 2.

17.  Ibid. July 28, 1969, p. 2.

18.  Ibid. June 2, 1969, p. 2.

19.  Ibid. Jan. 26, 1970, p. 1.

20.  Ibid. March 9, 1970, p. 1.

21.  Ibid. March 23, 1970, p. 1.

22. Ibid. May 18, 1970, p. 1.

23. Food Drug Cosmetic Law Journal April 1971, p. 192.

24. DTN Oct. 5, 1970, p. 2.

25. Product Management Oct. 1972, p. 9.

26. DTN July 24, 1972, p. 28.

27. Ibid. Oct. 26, 1964, p. 1.

28. Ibid. July 5, 1965, p. 2.

29. Ibid. May 22, 1967, p. 2.

30. Ibid. Nov. 1, 1971, p. 1.

31. Unofficial transcript by the Proprietary Association

32. Product Management Nov. 1972, p. 11.

33. DTN Feb. 5, 1962, p. 1.

34. Ibid. Feb. 19, 1962, p. 6.

35. Ibid. Feb. 5, 1962, p. 2.

36. Ibid. Oct. 14, 1963, p. 1.

37. Ibid. Nov. 21, 1966, p. 1.

38. Ibid. June 5, 1967, p. 1.

39. Ibid. Oct. 7, 1960, p. 1.

40. Ibid. April 7, 1969, p. 1; May 19, 1969, p. 1.

41. Competitive Problems in the Drug Industry. Summary and Analysis prepared by the Congressional Research Service, Library of Congress, U.S. Government Printing Office, Washington, D.C., 1972, pp. 61 - 62.

42. Task Force on Prescription Drugs, Report and Recommendations, U.S. Government Printing Office, Washington, D.C., Aug. 30, 1968, p. 14.

43.   DTN April 20, 1970, p. 2.

44.   Ibid. Dec. 28, 1970, p. 1.

45.   Competitive Problems in the Drug Industry, Hearings before the Subcommittee on Monopoly, 91st Congress, Part 14, pp. 5839-5841.

46.   Money Oct. 1972, pp. 31 - 34.

47.   DTN Feb. 19, 1962, p. 1.

48.   Ibid. May 11, 1964, p. 1.

49.   Ibid. June 5, 1967, p. 1.

50.   Ibid. Jan. 17, 1966, p. 1.

51.   Ibid. Aug. 1, 1966, p. 1.

52.   Ibid. March 13, 1967, p. 1.

53.   Ibid. Feb. 13, 1967, p. 1.

54.   Ibid. March 13, 1967, p. 1.

55.   New Handbook of Prescription Drugs.  Pantheon Books, New York, 1970, p. 10.

56.   Ibid. p. 14.

57.   DTN June 19, 1967, p. 74.

58.   Supra 42, p. 30.

59.   DTN April 10, 1967, p. 2.

60.   Supra 45, Part 2, p. 642.

61.   Ibid. Part 5, p. 1743.

62.   Ibid. p. 1579.

63.   Supra 42, p. 13.

64.   Ibid. p. 15.

65.  DTN Jan. 1, 1968, p. 1.

66.  Product Management Dec. 1972, p.

67.  FDA Papers March 1967.

68.  DTN Dec. 24, 1962, p. 1.

69.  Ibid. March 4, 1963, p. 16.

70.  Ibid. Oct. 14, 1963, p. 1.

71.  Ibid. April 13, 1964, p. 6.

72.  Ibid. March 30, 1964, p. 1.

73.  Ibid. April 13, 1964, p. 1.

74.  Ibid. April 11, 1966, p. 1.

75.  Ibid. July 14, 1969, p. 1.

76.  Ibid. Aug. 11, 1969, p. 1.

77.  Ibid. Sept. 22, 1967, p. 1.

78.  Journal of Nervous and Mental Disease 143:199, 1966.

79.  DTN July 3, 1967, p. 4.

80.  New York Times Aug. 20, 1969.

81.  DTN Oct. 20, 1969, p. 2.

82.  Initial Recommendations of the Tuskegee Syphilis Study,
Ad Hoc Advisory Panel, Office of the Secretary of HEW, Oct.
25, 1972.

83.  FDA Papers May 1968.

84.  DTN Nov. 16, 1970, p. 35.

85.  Ibid. Dec. 15, 1969, p. 14.

86.  Ibid. Aug. 15, 1970, p. 24.

87.  Ibid. Aug. 24, 1970, p. 1.

88.  Federal Register March 13, 1971.

89.  DTN June 14, 1971, p. 13.

90.  Ibid. July 12, 1971, p. 5.

91.  Unofficial Transcript by the Proprietary Association.

# 4

PESTICIDES:  REGULATION OF AN EVOLVING TECHNOLOGY

John E. Blodgett

CONTENTS

## Introduction

The Federal Government has engaged in three major activities
regarding pesticides: (a) research and development; (b) pest
control; and (c) regulation. This chapter reviews the
regulatory activities, which have developed along the
following four lines:

Agricultural - to protect the farmer from adulterated or
ineffectual pesticides;
Health-oriented - to protect the consumer from unnecessary or
excessive exposure to hazardous residues of pesticides;
Environmental - to protect fish and wildlife, in particular,
and the quality of the environment in general; and
Farmworker - to protect the farmworker from field residues of
pesticides.

Responsibilities for each of these functions were lodged in
separate departments of the Federal Government until 1970,
when the Environmental Protection Agency (EPA) was created.
How each concern became institutionalized and the consequences
of federal regulation are the subject of this chapter. An
understanding of the historical development will clarify the
current situation and contribute to the resolution of the
problems which continue to arise about the use of many
pesticides, particularly such persistent ones as DDT, Aldrin
and Dieldrin.

## Technology Of Pesticides

The technologies of pesticides - the dominant types and uses -
have significant interrelationships with regulation. There
has been a tendency for technological developments or
innovations to proceed faster than statutory authority for
regulation, leading to potentially hazardous situations.
Pesticide technologies have evolved through three stages (1)
(excluding purely cultural methods for which no regulatory
issues arise), as follows.

First was the era of inorganic and natural organic
pesticide formulations. Arsenicals, sulfur, copper sulfate,
oils, and plant derived products (such as pyrethrums)
dominated the scene until the late 1940s. The organic
chemicals in these pesticides tend to be short-lived and
minimally toxic to mammals. Arsenic is known to be acutely
toxic and is persistent, but its environmental mobility is
small.

The second major pesticide era is that of synthetic organic
pesticides. These compounds, first produced in the early
1940s, have dominated pest control technology since about

1950.  These synthetic organic compounds have introduced new concerns into regulatory policies.  Several, particularly the organochlorines, are persistent, environmentally mobile, and tend to accumulate and concentrate in the food chain.  Others are acutely toxic.  Little was known, however, of the chronic effects of any of these pesticides.

The early successes of these new chemical pesticides led to their widespread use, and as they were relatively inexpensive in comparison to the potential value of crops, they often were applied prophylactically, by the calendar, without actual evaluation of the threat of pest damage at the time.

The third era of pesticide technology is just beginning (2).  The use of synthetic organic chemicals has begun to level off, partly because of their decreasing effectiveness due to growing pest resistance, partly because of their suspected long-term lack of efficacy and partly because of restrictions necessitated by adverse health and environmental effects, and partly because of more sophisticated knowledge on when and how to apply them most effectively (3).  The emerging era of pest control technology is based on "integrated pest management," a system blending for maximum efficiency chemical, biological, and cultural controls and designed to manage pests below the level at which they cause economic harm.

Table 1 presents data on pesticide use in the United States.  The trend for lead and calcium arsenate represents the first generation inorganic pesticides, the use of which peaked in the early 1940s, then dropped quickly.  In the second generation, use of the organochlorine pesticides rose very rapidly through 1960, after which their use leveled off somewhat, while use of parathions (organophosphates) continued to rise rapidly until 1965.  The use of synthetic organic herbicides, along with other second generation techniques, also grew rapidly through the mid 1960s, in part because of military demands; the drop in 1969 may have resulted largely from reduced military use.  No satisfactory measures exist of the increasing use being made of third generation pest management techniques.

The bulk of this chapter is focused on the evolution of regulations to deal with synthetic organic pesticides.  These pesticides are highly diverse, and their different characteristics raise particular issues.  By 1965, there were some 400 active chemicals formulated in over 60,000 registered products, of which some 35,000 were for agricultural application.  By 1973, however, the number of registered products was 33,000, incorporating nearly 900 different

Table 1  Trends in Use of Selected Pesticides, United States (a)

| Pesticide | Millions of Pounds | | | | | | | | |
|---|---|---|---|---|---|---|---|---|---|
| | 1917 | 1942 | 1950 | 1955 | 1960 | 1965 | 1967 | 1969 | 1971 |
| Copper Sulfate (b) | NA | NA | 124.6 | 78.0 | 80.3 | 92.2 | 85.3 | 99.8 | 70.2 |
| 2,4-D (acid basis) | 0 | 0 | 17.6 | 28.0 | 31.2 | 50.5 | 67.0 | 49.5 | 32.2 |
| 2,4,5-T (acid basis) | 0 | 0 | 1.3 | 2.5 | 5.9 | 7.2 | 15.4 | 3.2 | 1.4 |
| Aldrin-Toxaphene group (c) | 0 | 0 | NA | 54.4 | 75.8 | 80.6 | 86.3 | 89.7 | 85.0 |
| DDT | 0 | 0 | 57.6 | 61.8 | 70.1 | 53.0 | 40.3 | 30.3 | 18.2 |
| Calcium Arsenate | NA | 84 (D) | 38.8 | 3.9 | 7.3 | 3.5 | 2.3 | 2.1 | 2.5 |
| Lead Arsenate | 5 (e) | 91 (f) | 27.5 | 13.3 | 11.2 | 8.1 | 6.2 | 7.7 | 4.1 |
| Parathions (e) | 0 | 0 | NA | 5.2 | 19.2 | 45.7 | 44.7 | 50.6 | NA |
| Botanicals (imports) (e) | NA | NA | 18.3 | 18.6 | 14.8 | 12.6 | 14.6 | 14.9 | NA |

(a) Unless otherwise indicated, figures are for "domestic disappearance," defined as: beginning of year inventory + production + imports - exports - end of year inventory; includes military shipments abroad. Most computations are on a crop year basis.
(b) Includes industrial use; use as pesticides is substantially less than above indicated data.
(c) Includes aldrin, heptachlor, toxaphene, dieldrin, endrin, strobane, and chlordane.
(d) Figure for production, peak year.
(e) Figures for production.
(f) Figure for 1944 production, peak year.
Sources: ref. 4, p. 13; ref. 5, pp. 27, 31; ref. 6.

chemicals, although 20 substances amount to 75 percent of U.S.
production.  In terms of use, these were directed at insect
pests (insecticides), weeds and foilage (herbicides), fungi
(fungicides), and rodents (rodenticides).  Minor uses were as
plant regulators and desiccants.  Insecticide uses grew the
quickest, but have since leveled off.  They are of three basic
chemical types:  organochlorines, which have low acute human
toxicity, are generally persistent, environmentally mobile,
and concentrate in organisms; organophosphates, which often
have high acute toxicity, but are generally short-lived; and
carbamates, which are highly variable in effects, though less
acutely toxic than most organophosphates and less persistent
than the organochlorines.  Environmental contamination by
several organochlorines has led to the cancellation of most
registered uses of DDT, the first and best known, and
reduction in use of others; the production of organophosphates
has increased in part to replace these uses.

Pesticides are usually thought of in terms of agricultural
uses, but, in fact, governmental, industrial, and home users
apply substantial quantities (4, p. 10; 7), as shown in Table
2.  Estimates based on dollar value of the proportions of
pesticides used in agriculture range from 55 to 61 percent,
and the estimates of home use range from 15 to 19.3 percent;
but, as the price of home use pesticides tends to be high, the
actual quantity of home-applied chemicals is proportionately
less, perhaps 5 percent (5, p. 41).  Home use is important,
however, because applications tend to be heavy and people are
likely to come into close contact with the chemicals.

Industrial uses include both sanitation of factories and of
products such as mothproofed fabrics, and various other uses
such as powerline and right-of-way clearing.  Governmental
uses include various eradication or control programs directed
at particular pests, including mosquitoes, road right-of-way
maintenance, and brush and pest control on public lands.
Also, the Department of Defense uses considerable quantities
to control various pests - e.g., the malaria-carrying
anopheles mosquito in tropical areas where servicemen are
stationed - and, during the Vietnam war, to defoliate forests
and roadsides, apart from crop-growing lands of the enemy.

The Rise Of Diverse Interests

Agriculture The story of agricultural chemical pesticides
begins about 1867 when paris green (copper arsenate) was used
to control the Colorado Potato Beetle (8, 9).  The success of
this agricultural technique and the ever-increasing need for

pest control - a need largely brought about by the change to a
monocultural agriculture - led to an increasing use of
pesticides and to related research.  The Federal Government
supported considerable research on pests and on pest control
techniques; this research was carried out within the U.S.
Department of Agriculture (USDA), particularly by the Bureau
of Entomology.

This initial agricultural orientation was revealed clearly
in the complaint of an entomologist in the Entomology Bureau,
who defined "economic entomology" as "the science of
entomology as applied or related to human welfare," and noted
that the Adams Act of 1907 (34 Stat. 63), which established
research grants in agricultural economic entomology:

"provides that it shall be applied only to paying the
necessary expenses of conducting original researches or
experiments bearing on the agricultural industry of the United
States..." (10)

This provision led to specialization and precluded research
into such areas as health, although the entomological aspects
of several diseases were known.

The farmer's interest in pesticides was perfectly clear;
pesticides increased profits.  A USDA Farmer's Bulletin of
1901 concluded that

Table 2  Domestic Use of Pesticides, United States Average,
1968-70

| Use | Value of sales, in percent |
|---|---|
| Farm | 55 |
| Urban-suburban | 15 |
| Industry | 20 |
| Federal, State, and local government | 10 |
| Total | 100 |

Note:  Estimated by Econ. Res. Serv. based on published
reports and discussions with pesticide specialists in
government and industry.
Source:  ref. 4, p. 10.

"The overwhelming experience of the past dozen years makes it almost unnecessary to urge, on the basis of pecuniary returns, the adoption of the measures recommended...against insects." (11)

Despite the benefits of using pesticides, however, farmers were adopting them slowly at the turn of the century, partly because of inertia, partly because of inadequate information, and partly because of the disrepute of pesticides - a disrepute resulting from adulterated chemicals and from charlatans hawking various ineffectual compounds, much as others sold quack medicines (9).  To prevent farmers from being bilked, USDA publications during this period typically recommended that the farmer make his own pesticides and included directions on how to test commercial chemicals to see that they were effective and not adulterated (11, 12).

Interest in and concern with pesticides expanded in the opening decade of the 20th century.  Large scale commercial production of pesticides got underway, although industry by and large depended on government and university research.  As mentioned, the Adams Act (34 Stat. 63), establishing research grants in agricultural economic entomology, passed in 1907. The Journal of Economic Entomology was founded in 1908.  In the same period, the doctrine of "caveat emptor" - "Let the buyer beware" - was being undermined as new scientific and technological capabilities increasingly meant that the consumer no longer had the knowledge or equipment to test the quality or efficacy of products.  Scientists like Dr. Harvey W. Wiley of the USDA's Bureau of Chemistry and muckrakers like Upton Sinclair urged that the public be protected from unscrupulous manufacturers.  A number of consumer protection acts passed during the first decade, including the Pure Food and Drug Act in 1906 (34 Stat. 768).  With the farmer fearing ineffectual pesticides and the manufacturers fearing unbridled competition, the decade concluded with the Federal Insecticide Act of 1910 (36 Stat. 331):

"an act for preventing the manufacture, sale, or transportation of adulterated or misbranded paris greens, lead arsenates, and other insecticides, and also fungicides, and for regulating traffic therein..." (13).

The Act provided that the USDA could seize as contraband any adulterated or misbranded product covered by the Act. Basically, it guaranteed the farmer that the pesticide he bought consisted of and did what the label said.  This Act gave statutory basis for the USDA to regulate pesticides, adding that function to its research programs and to its pest control activities.

Thus, the first dominating interests in pesticides were agricultural. At the federal level, these interests were institutionalized in the USDA, which had unilateral authority to regulate pesticides in commerce until 1970, and, in Congress, in the House and Senate Committees on Agriculture, which until 1972 held sole jurisdiction over the basic federal legislation for regulating pesticides.

Health During the 1920s, however, it was becoming apparent that the consumer and the user was being adversely affected by pesticides. Chemical residues on produce were being noted. In 1925,

"England placed an embargo on all apples from the United States that contained more than 0.01 grain of arsenious oxide per pound." (14)

To counter this threat to a major export, the Bureau of Entomology performed research and developed a washing technique to remove the toxic residues. In 1927 the Food, Drug, and Insecticide Administration (FDIA) was established within the USDA to take over enforcement of the Food and Drug Act from the USDA's Bureau of Chemistry. However, it did not include in its domain the Federal Insecticide Act which protected the farmer. Instead, the FDIA's concern was for the consumer. This reorganization marked the separation of regulatory activities directed at protecting the farmer from those concerned with the consumer. To protect the consumer, the FDIA set tolerances on arsenic; and in 1934 a tolerance on fluorine and in 1935 on lead. These actions led to further research by the Bureau of Entomology (14, 15).

The 1930s saw the first statutory protection of the public health from pesticides. In the first half of the decade a spate of books appeared proclaiming the danger to the public of unhealthy foods and drugs. Then, "in the wake of public health scandals," the Food, Drug, and Cosmetic Act (FDCA) (52 Stat. 1045) passed in 1938 (16). This Act forbade

"interstate commerce in any food or drug and in any cosmetic that was adulterated or misbranded; [a food was considered adulterated if it] was poisonous or harmful to health, decayed, filthy or putrid, or some harmful chemical or other dangerous substance, for example, the residue of a pesticide spray..." (16)

The Act provided authority to set tolerances for pesticide residues, but the process of setting tolerances was very difficult and could be undertaken only after the product was marketed.  The Act was enforced by the renamed Food and Drug Administration (FDA), which in 1938 was still located in the USDA, but which in 1940 was transferred to the Federal Security Agency.  Enforcement consisted of spot checks of processing plants and shipments of products, but the manufacturer remained free to market any product he wished. The FDA could prevent sale of a product only by proving after the fact that a marketed product was poisonous or dangerous. With regard to labels, too, the FDA had the burden of discovering and proving that a label was untruthful, misleading, or inadequate.

At this point World War II intervened.  It accentuated the need for pesticides:

"Malaria, the greatest single factor reducing the effectiveness of South Pacific Troops, caused five times as many casualties as enemy action in the South Pacific." (18)

This led to considerable research.  During World War II, the usefulness of DDT for pest control was dramatically proved, and by 1945 this first of the synthetic organic pesticides was being recommended for civilian uses.  Very shortly after the war, the first synthetic organic herbicide, 2,4-D, also appeared.

The war marked significant changes in the pesticide industry, in pesticide technology, and in the role of the Federal Government.  Geared to wartime production, the chemical manufacturers found a large domestic market available to exploit with the new pesticides, which became an integral part of the scientific agricultural revolution that had been delayed by depression and war.  The chemical manufacturers expanded research on chemical pesticides, and took the research lead away from government and university scientists. As interest in chemical pesticides grew, research in other pest control measures, especially biological controls, dropped proportionally (18, 19).  The era of synthetic organic pesticides was at hand.

In the face of the multitude of new pesticides being marketed and the inability of users to assess their safety and efficacy, the Congress in 1947 repealed the 1910 Federal Insecticide Act and passed the Federal Insecticide, Fungicide,

and Rodenticide Act (FIFRA) (61 Stat. 163).  In the process,
the Congress made several fundamental changes in the
principles of regulation.

First, it provided that new chemical pesticides should be
automatically submitted to USDA for registration of the labels
before they were marketed.  The USDA could refuse to register
a pesticide if it were found to be mislabeled, if it lacked
suitable warnings and directions for use, or if it was
injurious to beneficial organisms.  Second, the manufacturer
had the burden of proving the safety and efficacy of the
pesticide.  If the USDA denied registration, however, the
manufacturer could still market his product under "protest
registration," without any indication of its unregistered
status; for FIFRA expressly prohibited the label from
indicating that it had been registered.  To force an
unregistered product off the market, the USDA had to prove in
court that it was unsafe or mislabeled.

In hindsight, FIFRA had a number of serious shortcomings.
Fundamentally it was intended to serve the same basic function
as the 1910 Act - to protect the farmer from adulterated,
ineffectual, or unsafe products.  The Act was not intended to
provide direction and authority for dealing with health and
environmental problems; nor did it recognize the need to
protect farmers from damages to beneficial insects or the
potential of insects to develop resistance.  These failures,
which became evident in the late 1950s and irresistible in the
late 1960s, probably resulted largely from ignorance of the
potential problems (20).

A major cause of this deficiency in FIFRA was a failure to
recognize the new characteristics of the second generation of
pesticides, the synthetic organic chemicals.  Among first
generation pesticides, problems of persistence combined with
biomagnification were not significant.[*]  But in the second
generation pesticides, problems of chronic effects were
largely overlooked:  environmental burdens, mobility, and
concentration; effects on crop ecosystems; and the development
of pest resistance were not addressed.  Sen. Abraham Ribicoff
(D.-Conn.), who chaired a Senate subcommittee investigating
the environmental and health hazards of pesticides in 1963-64
(21), commented that FIFRA had been passed on the premise that

---------------------------------------------------------------

[*]Arsenic was, of course, persistent and in some orchards
reached levels toxic to plants; however, it tended to stay in
the area sprayed and concentration in food chains was not a
significant problem.

pesticides stayed where they had been applied, a premise made
false by the new synthetic organic chemicals which moved
through the ecosystem and became concentrated in organisms
(13, pp. 3-4).

In the years following World War II, concern also grew for
the effects of pesticides on human health.  In 1950, the House
adopted a resolution creating a Select Committee to
Investigate the Use of Chemicals in Food.  It was headed by
Rep. James J. Delaney (D.-N.Y.), who was to be active in this
area for many years.  The tolerance-setting mechanisms of the
Food, Drug and Cosmetic Act having proved totally unworkable,
the Select Committee in 1952 and 1953 recommended that
additives in food be subjected to prior testing for safety, so
that tolerances could be set before a product was marketed.
In 1954, this recommendation was implemented with regard to
pesticides by the Miller Amendment to the FDCA (68 Stat. 511).

The Miller Amendment provided that the USDA would not
register under the provisions of FIFRA any pesticide which
would leave a residue on a raw agricultural product until the
Food and Drug Administration - now moved to the Department of
Health, Education, and Welfare (DHEW), created in 1953 - set a
tolerance indicating how much residue might be present.  The
manufacturer had the burden of proving that a requested
tolerance would be safe.  If FDA denied a tolerance,
registration by USDA was denied for any use that would produce
a residue; if a tolerance was set, then USDA registered only
uses which would leave residues smaller than the tolerance.
However, a manufacturer could still sell his product under
protest registration if the registration were denied.

While the Miller Amendment afforded the consumer protection
through the setting of tolerances on residues of pesticides in
raw agricultural products so that the USDA could not register
a use on a food crop which would leave a residue in excess of
the tolerance, the USDA retained complete authority to
register pesticides.  Moreover, the USDA alone had authority
to regulate many pesticide uses which came into direct contact
with people, such as household insecticides, mothproofing
chemicals, and disinfectants.  In addition, there was no way
the FDA or the U.S. Public Health Service (USPHS) could
directly affect non-food crop uses, even if these uses
resulted in environmental contamination and subsequently
resulted in residues in foods.

The last years of the 1950s saw several amendments to
FIFRA and FDCA.  FIFRA was extended in 1959 to cover several
new chemical uses - nematocides, plant regulators, defoliants,
and desiccants (73 Stat. 286).  The FDCA's prior-testing-for-

safety of pesticides was generally extended to food additives
and drugs in 1958.  As a part of this 1958 Food Additives
Amendment, a clause inserted by Rep. Delaney provided that

"no additive shall be deemed safe if it is found to induce
cancer when ingested by man or animal." (22)

This ban, which applied even if supposedly safe tolerances
could be established, meant the FDA has to set "zero
tolerance" or "no residue" limits on any deliberate food
additive which was carcinogenic.  Although the wording of the
part of the FDCA amended by the Delaney Clause appears to
exclude its application to accidental food additives such as
pesticides, many people have nevertheless argued its
relevance; and it was cited as the basis for regulatory action
which led to the 1959 "cranberry scare," which is discussed
later.  Thus, though of questionable applicability to
pesticides, the Delaney Clause has become associated with the
set of regulatory authorities affecting pesticides.

Environment Also in 1958, a third federal agency, the U.S.
Department of the Interior (USDI), was given a legislative
mandate on pesticides, but only to conduct research.  Large-
scale pest control programs of the USDA, especially the Fire
Ant Eradication Program, begun in 1957, were suspected of
killing and injuring wildlife, but evidence and research were
scant.  In 1958, the Congress passed legislation (P.L. 85-582)
directing the Department of the Interior, which had some pest
control programs of its own,

"to undertake continuing studies of the effects of
insecticides, herbicides, and fungicides upon fish and
wildlife resources of the United States."

The sum of $280,000 was provided annually for this research.
The next year, Congress amended the authorization to provide
$2,565,000 annually.  No regulatory powers were granted the
USDI.

Early Efforts at Coordination With the emergence of these
three points of view - the USDA and agriculture, DHEW and
public health, and USDI and wildlife - it is not surprising
that problems resulting from a lack of agency coordination and
a failure to cooperate appeared.  Various interest groups and
lobbyists contended, as pesticides affected the farmer, the
manufacturer, the consumer, the sportsman, and the

conservationist.  The vertical organization of the federal
administration hampered coordination, although informal
liaisons helped.  Administrative agreements were made, and in
some cases statutes required coordination, as between the USDA
and FDA in registration.  The committee structure of Congress
contributed to problems of coordination.

Only at the Cabinet level do USDA, DHEW, and USDI come
naturally together, and coordination at this level is a seldom
achieved ideal, with conflict not unusual (23).  The lack of
coordination concerning pesticides regulation was driven home
in 1959 when Arthur S. Flemming, Secretary of the DHEW,
without notifying the USDA, announced that cranberries had
been contaminated by a "cancer-causing" herbicide
aminotriazole.  This famous "cranberry scare" revealed the
problems and the need for integrating regulatory activities
which affect diverse, sometimes contradictory, interests.

In 1957, some farmers sprayed their cranberry bogs with
aminotriazole, but they voluntarily withheld the berries from
the market because they would have been subject to seizure, as
the pesticide was not then registered.  In 1958, the USDA
registered aminotriazole for use on cranberry bogs a few days
after harvest, for if used then, no residues on the next
year's crop resulted.  Nevertheless, the FDA was asked to set
a tolerance so that aminotriazole could be registered for
spraying at other times, when a residue might occur.  During
1958, the manufacturers conducted toxicity studies in attempts
to find a "safe tolerance," but in 1959 the FDA rejected any
tolerance, citing the Delaney Clause.  Some cranberry bogs had
meanwhile been sprayed at the wrong time, however, and the
resulting residues meant that the product was "contaminated."

Then, on November 9, 1959, DHEW Secretary Flemming, without
advising the USDA of his action, issued a statement beginning
as follows:

"The Food and Drug Administration today urged that no further
sales be made of cranberries and cranberry products produced
in Washington and Oregon in 1958 and 1959 because of possible
contamination by a chemical weed killer, aminotriazole, which
causes cancer in the thyroid of rats when it is contained in
their diet, until the cranberry industry has submitted a
workable plan to separate the contaminated berries from those
that are not contaminated." (24, p. 45)

While the contaminated berries represented only a part of the
crop and the consumer had nothing to fear from marketed
berries, the spectre of cancer dropped the bottom out of the

cranberry market.  The USDA, not warned, was understandably
upset; and it had to get authorization from Congress for
$10,000,000 to indemnify those growers who had not misused the
pesticide, but who nevertheless could not sell their crop.
The working out of the aftermath of the cranberry scare came
through cabinet level conferences in the White House.

A second incident occurred a month after the cranberry
scare and involved the use of the synthetic hormone
Diethylstilbestrol (DES) in poultry fattening.  Although DES
is not a pesticide, analogous problems arose.  In this case,
the use of the chemical had been legal, but new testing
techniques revealed residues which had hitherto been
undetected, and the residues were subject to the Delaney
Clause.  This time, some consultation between the Departments
was evident in Secretary Flemming's announcement, coming on
December 19, 1959, which explained in a very matter-of-fact
and reassuring way - in contrast to the statement on
cranberries - that there was no danger and that everyone was
cooperating:

"Mr. Flemming indicated that he was confident of cooperation
[with the USDA] and simultaneously released a copy of a letter
from Acting Secretary of Agriculture, True D. Morse, also
under date of December 10..." (24, p. 63)

The Morse statement began, "We have appreciated having been
advised in advance..." (24, p. 65)

But the problem of coordination had not been solved.  No
formal mechanism existed to ensure cooperation.  Despite the
statutory linking of USDA and FDA in registration,
coordination still depended on informal liaison.  A year after
the cranberry scare, a Congressman asked Dr. Clarkson of the
USDA's Agricultural Research Services, which includes the
Pesticides Regulating Division,

"if there has been any understanding with Mr. Flemming that
hereafter he will make every effort to handle this problem [of
condemning contaminated foods] without unnecessarily inflaming
the public?
    [Clarkson replied:] 'That has been discussed very intensely
and there is a proposal now under consideration for a
mechanism between the two departments to consider matters of
mutual concern'." (24, p. 15)

But efforts at formal coordination were not taken until 1961
when a formal interdepartmental agreement led to the

establishment of the Federal Pest Control Review Board
(FPCRB), which included representatives of USDA, DHEW, USDI,
and DOD.  However, it functioned only to coordinate pest
control programs and did not coordinate registration.
Nevertheless, the FPCRB gave the USDI, for the first time, a
formal voice in pesticides policy.  Previously, the USDI had
largely been ignored when it objected to certain pesticides
usages, as the original Fire Ant Program (25); but in fact the
USDI suffered from a debilitating handicap in affecting policy
on pest control usages or registration:  it lacked good, hard
information to back up its point of view.  In 1960, the USDI
admitted that it had "been unable, due to lack of research
information, to make a specific recommendation for modifying
the [Fire Ant] Program." (26)
      Thus in 1960 the situation was that the USDA had control
over the preponderance of pesticides policy.  It had sole
authority to register pesticides, although the FDA had
authority to set tolerances on residues in raw agricultural
products, so the USDA could only register food crop uses
which did not leave pesticide residues exceeding the
tolerances.  The USDI's authority was limited primarily to
research on the effects of pesticides on fish and wildlife.

Rachel Carson and the USDA's Preponderance of Authority
In 1962, there occurred the first of a series of events which
were to culminate in 1970 with the creation of the
Environmental Protection Agency (EPA) and the complete
restructuring of federal pesticides regulation.  This initial
event was the appearance of Rachel Carson's Silent Spring
(27).

Silent Spring Carson's famous book contended that pesticides
were being used excessively and without proper regard for
their possible harmful effects on fish and wildlife or for
humans.  She did not say, as her critics often allege,
pesticides should be eliminated or banned.  She said
ignorance of possible consequences should not be a license for
promiscuous use and that more research and understanding was
needed about the effects of pesticides before they could be
used as permitted and advocated by USDA and FDA (21, p. 229;
27, pp. 12-13).
      The main problem was the determination of the chronic
effects of pesticides.  Originally, tests on pesticides
required before registration mainly concerned their acute
toxicological effects, but carcinogenic effects of chemicals
had come into prominence with the passage of the Delaney

Amendment of 1958 and the cranberry scare of 1959.  In 1962,
the thalidomide affair tragically directed attention to the
teratogenic effects of chemicals.  But most pesticidal
chemicals in use had been registered before substantial
testing for carcinogenic and teratogenic effects were required
by the Federal Government.

The responses to Silent Spring were sharply polarized.  One
group, primarily composed of persons directly and indirectly
associated with agricultural and agrichemical interests and
also their academic consultants, argued that the book was
unscientific and biased, contained unsubstantiated
conclusions, and represented an anti-progress, defeatist
philosophy.

When Rachel Carson accused many scientists dealing with
pesticides of paying more heed to the interests of their
employers than to objective study, I. L. Baldwin, Chairman of
the National Academy of Sciences-National Research Council
(NAS-NRC) Committee on Pest Control and Wildlife Relationships
and a former USDA employee, objected strongly in his review of
Silent Spring for Science.  While he praised her concern, he
condemned her one-sidedness, implied that she wanted to ban
pesticides, and called for a book as well written on the
benefits of pesticides (28).  Other scientists prominently
identified with industrial interests, also in positions of
evaluating pesticides policy, went much further than Baldwin
in identifying themselves with vested interests and in
condemning Silent Spring.  George C. Decker, Chairman of the
NAS-NRC Subcommittee on Evaluation of Pesticide-Wildlife
Relationships, reviewed the book for Chemical World News,
where he called it "science fiction." (29)  William J. Darby
of NAS-NRC and a past Chairman of its Food Protection
Committee, and now a leading member of the so-called
"citizens" commission on hunger law and the food supply (a
commission in which no citizen or consumer groups appear to be
represented), reviewed it for Chemical & Engineering News,
where he said:

"This book should be ignored, [but] the responsible scientist
should read this book to understand the ignorance of those
writing on the subject..." (30)

What is most noticeable about these reviews is the extent
to which the reviewers attacked Carson's values rather than
her data.  Darby was most explicit:

"Her thesis is revealed by the dedicatory quotations:  'Man

has lost the capacity to foresee and to forestall.  He will
end by destroying the earth.'  (Albert Schweitzer)  'Our
approach to nature is to beat it into submission.  We would
stand a better chance of survival if we accommodated ourselves
to this planet and viewed it appreciatively instead of
skeptically and dictatorially.' (E. B. White)

Such a passive attitude as the latter, coupled with such
pessimistic (and to this reviewer, unacceptable) philosophy as
the former, means the end of all human progress, reversion to
a passive social state devoid of technology, scientific
medicine, agriculture, sanitation, or education.  It means
disease, epidemics, starvation, misery, and suffering
incomparable and intolerable to modern man.  Indeed, social,
educational, and scientific development is prefaced on the
conviction that man's lot will be and is being improved by a
greater understanding of and thereby increased ability to
control or mold those forces responsible for man's suffering,
misery, and deprivation." (30)

Since Rachel Carson admitted her interests and acknowledged
that she was telling only one side of the story, perhaps one
ought not be concerned about attacks on her values.  But these
attacks raise several questions, the two most important being:
did Rachel Carson suggest that man revert to barbarism as
Darby implies? And, Carson's values aside, what of her
assessment of pesticides policy - were the critics attacking
her values because they couldn't attack her data effectively?

In contrast, another group, including independent
scientists and those persons most closely allied to
conservationist and environmental concerns, praised the book
as a timely warning (31).  In retrospect, Miss Carson's
occasional errors and conclusions and the exaggeration of the
parable of the "silent spring" were irrelevant.  Most of her
most impassioned critics and some of her ardent supporters
missed her point.  She was not condemning chemical pesticides
out of hand.  She was condemning the inadequacies of
regulation which permitted chemicals to be widely used without
careful testing of their hazards, particularly of chronic
health and environmental effects.

In testimony before the Senate Committee on Government
Operations Subcommittee on Reorganization and International
Organizations, which held extensive hearings (the "Ribicoff
hearings") on pesticides in 1963 and 1964, Miss Carson noted
that the unequal bargaining strengths of the diverse interests
was a basic cause of pesticides misuse, and she recommended
DHEW and USDI should have voices in regulating pesticides

(21, p. 224).

PSAC, Use of Pesticides Two important results of Silent Spring
were that it served as a symbol of resistance to the
irresponsible promotion and use of a technology, and that it
led to the decision by President Kennedy and his Science
Advisor Jerome Wiesner to ask the President's Science Advisory
Committee (PSAC) to prepare a report on the use of pesticides.
    The PSAC report appeared in 1963 (32). Science news editor
Daniel S. Greenberg said its evaluation of pesticides policy
was "temperate" and added up to "a fairly thorough-going
vindication of Rachel Carson's Silent Spring." (33) The focus
of the report was on the inadequacy of regulation. It
concluded that while data on the benefits of pesticides are
fairly well, though not critically, established, data on
hazards are not. The report recommended reviews of several
specific pesticides, including

"heptachlor, methoxychlor, dieldrin, aldrin, chlordane,
lindane, and parathion, because their tolerances were
originally based upon data which are in particular need of
review."

Looking at the problems of regulation, the report recommended
the Secretaries of USDA, USDI, and DHEW

"review and define their roles in the registration of
pesticides that are not present in food, but that may impinge
on fish and wildlife or come into intimate contact with the
public."

    Noting the potential dangers from residues of persistent
pesticides, the report recommended that "the accretion of
residues in the environment be controlled by orderly reduction
in the use of persistent pesticides."

Efforts to Redress the Balance The PSAC Report Use of
Pesticides had several effects. President Kennedy endorsed it
in his covering letter and directed the relevant departments
and agencies to implement its recommendations. At least some
action was in fact taken to implement virtually all of them
(21, part 1, app. IV), although these actions were in several
cases ineffectual.
Administrative Efforts The PSAC Report gave added support to
those interests seeking to redress the balance of authority
among USDA, DHEW, and USDI in the setting and carrying out of

pesticides policy.  For the most part, these changes occurred
administratively.  In 1964, the Departments acted to meet
PSAC's recommendations for coordination of research, pest
control, and regulation.  The FPCRB was reconstituted as the
Federal Committee on Pest Control (FCPC) with responsibilities
for coordinating both research and pest control.  "To give
effect to the pertinent recommendations" of PSAC concerning
coordination of registration, the USDA, DHEW, and USDI
entered into a formal agreement for the

"coordination of activities of the three Departments
pertaining to pesticides with special reference to
registration and the setting of tolerances." (34)

By signing the agreement, which was drawn up by the USDA,
the USDI finally achieved some formal access to registration
policy, and each department had a mechanism for informing the
others of actions, hopefully to prevent such debacles as the
cranberry scare.  The agreement set out the following
responsibilities for each department (34):

Department of the Interior
Fish and Wildlife Services:  Conserving beneficial wild birds,
mammals, fish, and their food organisms and habitat, with
regard to pesticides.

Department of Health, Education, and Welfare
U.S. Public Health Service:  Protecting and improving the
health of man in regard to pesticides.
Food and Drug Administration:  Establishing tolerances for
pesticides in or on raw agricultural commodities and processed
foods.

Department of Agriculture
Agriculture Research Service:  Providing for the safe and
effective use of pesticides, including the registration
thereof.

In order to implement and coordinate these
responsibilities, the 1964 Agreement set forth the following
activities:

(a) The sharing of information, including specifically that
the USDA

"undertake to furnish to the other two Departments on a weekly
basis a listing of all proposals affecting registration and
reregistration (and HEW do likewise on) all proposals
affecting tolerances."

(b) The establishing of a series of procedures for effecting
coordination, including a provision that if scientists
designated by the respective departments cannot resolve a
matter, it shall be referred to Department Secretaries for
final action.

(c) Providing that

"at least once a year the Departmental representatives will
arrange a general conference (to discuss research and policy
matters) including public information relating to pesticides."

(d) Providing that the FCPC

"may be asked from time to time to consider broad questions on
policies..."

Administrative Action in Place of Legislation:  A legislative
recommendation of the PSAC report suggested revising the
wording of FIFRA to state explicitly that the consideration of
harmful effects on "useful vertebrates and invertebrates" in
registration included protection of fish and wildlife.  At the
Ribicoff hearings in 1963, Secretary of the Interior Stewart
Udall complained that the USDA personnel responsible for
registration interpreted the term narrowly, to refer only to
domestic animals.  Udall contended fish and wildlife were
included in the sense of the term.  Secretary of Agriculture
Orville Freeman concurred that fish and wildlife were
included, but apparently agreement at the cabinet level was
not sufficient to ensure implementation at the bureaucratic
level.

The issue was resolved administratively, not legislatively.
Sen. Ribicoff insisted that Freeman have his USDA General
Counsel meet with the USDI General Counsel to "work this out
administratively."  In about two months the USDA reported to
Sen. Ribicoff that the wording of appropriate regulations had
been changed to state clearly that useful vertebrates and
invertebrates "protected by FIFRA included fish and
wildlife."* (21, pp. 115-117)

A series of legislative attempts were made to give the USDI
a statutory voice in pesticide registration.  During each
Congress of the 1960s, legislation was introduced to give the

----------------------------------------------------------------

*It should be noted that the Ribicoff hearings were
"oversight," examining the implementation of the law.
Legislative authority concerning FIFRA rested with the
Agriculture Committees.

USDI authority to provide information to be included on
labels. In 1964, a bill passed the House which would have
(a) expanded USDI research, (b) directed the USDI to transmit
information to the USDA Secretary who would require the
information to appear on labels, and (c) authorized the USDI
to distribute to interested persons information "about the
effects of pesticides." The Senate, however, deleted all but
part (a) before passing the bill. Attempts at compromise
proved fruitless. The Congressional Quarterly commented:

"The reasons why further compromise attempts were not made
never became entirely clear, but opposition to the legislative
provisions expressed during floor debates provided clues.
Members objected that the bill would limit the Agriculture
Department's authority over pesticides and that the
requirement for dissemination of information might cause
unnecessary "scares" and increase the cost of federal farm
programs." (35)

Thus, the agriculture-pesticides policy-makers composed of
Congressmen, bureaucrats, and clientele successfully defended
the USDA's preponderance of authority in the regulation of
pesticides. To this group, the advantage of administrative
solutions and the disadvantage of legislative solutions was
that administrative agreements provided more flexibility and
did not detract from the USDA's statutory position of ultimate
authority. For example, the creators of the interdepartmental
FPCRB consciously acted administratively to preclude
legislated requirements for coordination. The minutes of the
meeting at which creation of the FPCRB was proposed state:

"Dr. Popham [of USDA] mentioned that...Congressman Dingell had
expressed a great deal of interest in the possibility that
this committee might be formed.... At this point, it was
admitted that the prime purpose of the committee idea involved
the pending H.R. 4668, introduced by Congressman Dingell....
Mr. Paul [of USDI]...believes Congressman Dingell would not
press for this bill if he could be assured that there was a
clear-cut understanding by the group in the Executive Branch
which would meet the objectives he seeks. It was apparent
that no one in the room was at all in favor of the bill..."
(36)

Similarly, from an agricultural viewpoint, Rep. Paul C. Jones,
Chairman of the Subcommittee on Departmental Oversight of the
House Committee on Agriculture, said of a jurisdictional

dispute involving the USDA,

"I hope that the USDA and HEW can get together and not leave
it to this committee to settle, because we are like anyone
else, we would like to have it resolved before it comes to
us." (37)

And as legislation impacting on FIFRA and the USDA's
authorities fell under the Agriculture Committee's
jurisdictions, they could forestall attempts to lesson the
USDA's authority.  Moreover, the Congressional Quarterly
asserted that the USDA and agricultural interests caused

"The administration...[to enter] the pesticide controversy
cautiously and not [to] call for some administrative reforms
suggested by the (President's) Science Advisory Committee."
(35, p. 139)

Legislation:  In 1964, legislation (78 Stat. 190-193) was
enacted to revise a limited portion of the registration
process.  These revisions corrected several deficiencies noted
in the PSAC study, but did not affect or in any way lessen the
authority of the USDA vis-a-vis the DHEW or USDI.
     The major provision of the enactment eliminated protest
registration.  No longer would manufacturers be able to
produce and sell pesticides in interstate commerce if the USDA
refused to register the product.  Actually, this loophole
had not been very significant; from 1947 to 1964 only 17
products had been registered under "protest."  But the change
symbolized the continuing trend toward making the manufacturer
prove the safety of a product before it could be marketed,
thus placing the burden of proof of safety on the manufacturer
rather than placing the burden of proof of hazard on the
regulator.  Registration of a product was made evident, too,
as the new law permitted labels to bear the registration
number.
     Protest registration had been the mechanism by which
manufacturers could challenge USDA regulatory decisions.  In
its place, the new bill provided an appeal mechanism for the
manufacturer who disagreed with a Pesticides Regulation
Division decision not to register, or to cancel or to suspend,
a pesticide.  In appealing, the manufacturer could request a
hearing and/or the creation of a science advisory committee,
the committee being analogous to ones provided for the Miller
Amendment of 1954 authorizing FDA to set tolerances.
     Finally, the Act included wording permitting "any person

who will be adversely affected" to challenge in the courts the
decisions made under the Act.

Regulatory Changes

Zero Tolerance:  During 1964-1965, another major problem
involving pesticides regulation was addressed - the problem of
"zero tolerance," or "no residues," as set by the FDA.  A
"zero tolerance" registration meant that "no residue" of the
pesticide was permitted.  The FDA set "zero tolerances" on one
of two bases.

Frequently, "zero tolerances" were set as a matter of
convenience.  If a petition asked the FDA to set a tolerance
for a pesticide on a food crop, and if tests did not reveal
any residues, the FDA often set a "zero tolerance" based on
the "no residue" finding.  Legally, this meant that no residue
at all was permitted, but technically it meant that no residue
could be detected with existing analytic techniques.

Besides these "zero tolerances" set by administrative
convenience, the Delaney Amendment forbade any residue of any
chemical which proved carcinogenic, and specified that such
chemicals have a zero tolerance.

In the early 1960s the technologies for measuring residues
improved by several orders of magnitude (38).  Cases where
zero tolerances had been registered because no residues could
be detected suddenly became cases where finite residues could
be detected by the new measuring technologies - meaning that
the food was legally contaminated and subject to seizure.  The
existence of the residue had not changed; rather, the analytic
capability had - but the zero tolerance was tied not to the
capabilities of measurement but to the assumption of no
residue.  FDA seizures followed, and the USDA, which had
registered the pesticides on the basis of the FDA-set zero
tolerances had to establish a fund for indemnifying farmers
whose crops were seized even though they had been sprayed as
directed.

The PSAC report recommended this problem be studied by a
NAS-NRC ad hoc Pesticides Residues Committee, which was
created in 1964.  The NAS-NRC Committee argued that
registration and enforcement should be tied to measuring
capabilities.  But the committee was the scene of heated
discussions over the question of how to measure the effects of
low levels of residues.  One member, in particular, contended
the committee must address the question of what testing
protocols should be required to determine the effects of
residues.  Ultimately, the NAS-NRC Committee recommended that
"zero tolerance" and "no residue" concepts be phased out and
that they be replaced by finite tolerances for "negligible

residues"; but the committee did not say how to determine when
a residue was negligible.  Nor did the committee explicitly
address the question of the statutory requirements for zero
tolerance as required by the Delaney Amendment (39).

The USDA endorsed the report, one recommendation of which
urged that the existing concentration in USDA of registration
authorities be continued.  In fact, the "Statement of
Implementation" of the Committee's recommendations in the
Federal Register (40) appeared under the USDA's rubric,
although the FDA had actually contracted the NAS study.  In
implementing the recommendation, pesticides registered on the
basis of "zero tolerance" would, by 1970, be re-registered
with finite tolerances (41).  Contrary to what some
registrants expected and hoped, however, the FDA required data
on the effects of "negligible residues" to be as thorough as
for more substantial residues.

Persistent Pesticides:  The most controversial PSAC
recommendation was to phase out persistent pesticides, such as
DDT and Dieldrin.  Most representatives of agricultural
interests argued that persistent, broad spectrum pesticides
were ideal because few applications were needed to control
many pests.  These persons generally casually dismissed
concerns on chronic toxic effects of pesticides on health and
the environment, such as those raised by Rachel Carson.  In
1965, another PSAC report, Restoring the Quality of Our
Environment, reiterated the recommendation that use of
persistent pesticides be curtailed (42).

The persistent pesticides were attacked for several
reasons.  They tended to kill beneficial predacious insects,
so that when the toxic properties of the chemical wore off,
the pest populations upsurged, for populations of plant
feeders are usually more resilient than those of predacious
insects.  They tended to kill predators of mites, but did not
themselves kill mites, resulting in mite damage that had to be
controlled by other sprays.  In addition, insect resistance to
these chemicals was increasing.  But the main attack on
persistent pesticides was based on their persistence and
mobility in the environment.  Being fat soluble, they tended
to concentrate in organisms, particularly at the top of food
chains, and several species of fish and wildlife suffered
reproduction failures as a result (43).

While the USDA said that it was acting to implement the
recommendations of these two PSAC reports, in fact, it did not
make persistence of pesticides an explicit criterion for
registration until 1969, when it cancelled some uses of DDT on
the basis of persistence and unnecessary hazard.  (21, part 1,

app. V; 44).

A critical action, implementing another of PSAC's
recommendations was the DHEW's contracting in 1964, through
the National Cancer Institute, of a long-range study of the
chronic effects of numerous pesticides.  This study, conducted
by the Bionetics Laboratory, produced results which
significantly contributed to reconsiderations of pesticides
policy in the late 1960s.

In addition to this long-range Bionetics Study, the results
of which became available in 1969 and 1970, the FDA, at PSAC's
urging, focused on several pesticides for intensive immediate
review, the PSAC committee having found their tolerances based
on very poor data.  So, in 1964 and 1965, the FDA convened a
series of ad hoc committees to review new data pertaining to
tolerances of several pesticides, including aldrin and
dieldrin, endrin, and chlordane.  Thus, the FDA, in general,
responded positively to the PSAC report and moved to upgrade
its procedures.

Summary The history of pesticides policy through the mid 1960s
reveals an evolutionary pattern.  The USDA, the earliest
policy-maker, achieved a position of preponderance of
authority.  Later, health and environmental interests found
institutionalization in DHEW and USDI respectively, but with
limited authorities.  Three trends led to the disposition of
authority in the 1960s:  changing technology, changing
conceptions of government responsibilities, and changing
patterns of policy-making in the government.

As pesticide technology changed, so too did conceptions of
the roles of industry and government for the protection of the
public interest.  Pesticide formulations and chemistry became
so sophisticated that farmers couldn't make their own.
Increased use of pesticides on food crops raised the issue of
public health.  Following World War II, the rapid increase in
pesticide use, coupled with fundamental changes in their
chemicals properties, led to heightened concern about health
and environmental contamination.  As the public became more
exposed to pesticides and less able to comprehend or to
control their effects, the concept of regulation replaced that
of caveat emptor.  At first, regulation implied governmental
responsibility to condemn dangerous products on the market,
but later regulation preceded marketing, so that the burden of
proving the safety of a product shifted from the government to
the manufacturer.

Moreover, as the technology changed and affected new
interests, these new interests joined the policy-making

process.  When in 1928 it was said of the latest pesticide
regulation that "it affords a large measure of protection to
the consumers" (15), the consumers referred to were farmers.
Soon, however, public health also became a concern, a new set
of interests coalesced, and in 1938 they received statutory
recognition in the FDCA.  Although in 1947 the first response
to the new synthetic organic pesticides was increased
protection of the farmer, in 1951 a writer observed the
propriety of dual protection:

"When we consider that the use of pesticides is essential to
the successful production of many crops and that at the same
time foods must be protected from excessive or harmful
contamination, it would appear that Congress acted wisely in
establishing a dual system of control by the Food and Drug
Administration and the Department of Agriculture....  In this
way all interests are more nearly assured proper and adequate
consideration and the probability of unjustifiable arbitrary
action is greatly reduced." (45)

Yet, within a few years it appeared that a significant danger
was being overlooked, and support for the protection of the
environment in general and of fish and wildlife in particular
was growing.  As a spokesman for the National Audubon Society
complained in 1965,

"One kind [of regulation] is directed mainly at aiding the
industry of agriculture, the producing of crops and other
things that farmers do; the other kind of regulation is aimed
at protecting people.  The effects on fish and wildlife
resources and on the general ecology were overlooked, and we
are now trying to bring that phase of it up to date and get it
corrected.  It has been quite a struggle." (46)

   In 1970, a fourth viewpoint, protection of farmworkers,
emerged and was institutionalized in the Department of Labor.
The emergence of this viewpoint into a separate agency shows
again how new perspectives are added to policy-making.  This
development is discussed at greater length later.
   The disregard of earlier writers for viewpoints later found
important does not necessarily indicate unreasonable bias.
Each of these men was reflecting the nature of the technology,
the state of available information, and the conception of the
role of the government at the time he was writing; but even as
he wrote, the technology, the information and the role of
government were changing.  Excessive resistance to change,

however, could be called unreasonable and while the historical
evidence shows that new viewpoints have joined the policy-
making process, the joining has occurred only with difficulty
and potentially serious delays.

After the criticisms of Silent Spring, the USDA made some
administrative changes, giving DHEW and USDI advisory roles in
registering pesticides, but no statutory realignments of
authority occurred.  The pattern of the late 1960s is one of
increasingly strong and more sophisticated attacks on the
position of the USDA as the preponderant maker of pesticides
policy.

The major events in the evolution of pesticides policy are
summarized in Figure 1.  It also shows how the new interests
have been institutionalized, including the issue of
farmworkers and re-entry standards, under the Department of
Labor (DOL).  The major policy-makers for the 1960 to 1969
period are shown in Figure 2, which can be compared to Figure
3, showing major policy-makers of the period since 1969.

## Pesticides, the Government, and the Law:  Strains on the Pesticides Policy-Making Structure

Although Silent Spring had an immediate impact, it and the
other events of the early 1960s also had delayed effects which
combined to raise questions about pesticides regulation.  A
crucial development throughout the decade was heightening
sensitivity concerning chronic health and environmental
effects.  The accumulation of forces, including improved data,
congressional oversight, commission studies, and lawsuits,
finally led to complete revision of pesticides policy and
regulation.

New Scientific Data Lack of adequate data was recognized as a
major part of the controversy in the early 1960s, and several
actions to develop improved information occurred during the
mid-1960s.  The PSAC Use of Pesticides panel found data on
effects and efficacy poor, and data on pesticides usage and
their dissemination in the environment and chronic public
health implications virtually nonexistent.  In the most
obvious measure of the recognition of the need for better
information, research monies on pesticides increased
dramatically - almost doubling from Fiscal Year 1964 to Fiscal
Year 1965 (see Table 3).
New Information Systems The USDA established in 1965 the
Pesticides Information Center in its National Agriculture
Library.  It puts out a bi-weekly Pesticides Documentary
Bulletin.  For the years 1964 and 1966 the Economic Research

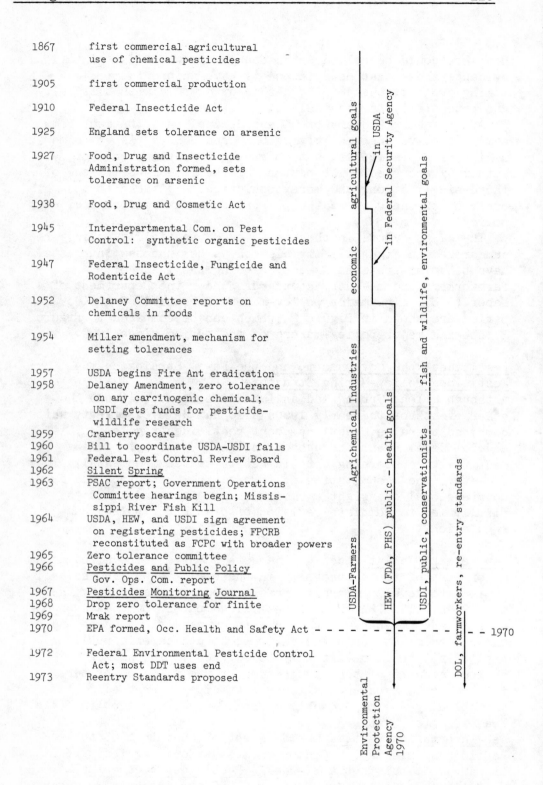

1867    first commercial agricultural
        use of chemical pesticides

1905    first commercial production

1910    Federal Insecticide Act

1925    England sets tolerance on arsenic

1927    Food, Drug and Insecticide
        Administration formed, sets
        tolerance on arsenic

1938    Food, Drug and Cosmetic Act

1945    Interdepartmental Com. on Pest
        Control: synthetic organic pesticides

1947    Federal Insecticide, Fungicide and
        Rodenticide Act

1952    Delaney Committee reports on
        chemicals in foods

1954    Miller amendment, mechanism for
        setting tolerances

1957    USDA begins Fire Ant eradication
1958    Delaney Amendment, zero tolerance
          on any carcinogenic chemical;
          USDI gets funds for pesticide-
          wildlife research
1959    Cranberry scare
1960    Bill to coordinate USDA-USDI fails
1961    Federal Pest Control Review Board
1962    Silent Spring
1963    PSAC report; Government Operations
          Committee hearings begin; Missis-
          sippi River Fish Kill
1964    USDA, HEW, and USDI sign agreement
          on registering pesticides; FPCRB
          reconstituted as FCPC with broader powers
1965    Zero tolerance committee
1966    Pesticides and Public Policy
          Gov. Ops. Com. report
1967    Pesticides Monitoring Journal
1968    Drop zero tolerance for finite
1969    Mrak report
1970    EPA formed, Occ. Health and Safety Act - - - - - - - - - - - - - - - 1970

1972    Federal Environmental Pesticide Control
          Act; most DDT uses end
1973    Reentry Standards proposed

Figure 1   Major events in pesticides policy or regulation.

| Executive | Administrative | Legislative and/or Appropriations (selected) | Interest groups |
|---|---|---|---|
| USDA | ARS (research; pest control) PRD (regulation) | Com. on Agriculture (HR) Subcom. on Ag. Approp. (HR) Com. on Agri. and Forestry (S) | Agriculture, chemical |
| HEW | FDA (regulation) PHS (research, pest control) | Com. on Interstate and For. Commerce (HR) Com. on Labor and Public Welfare (S) | Health, consumer |
| USDI | FWS (advisory; research, pest control) | Com. on Merchant Marine and Fisheries (HR) Com. on Commerce (S) | Conservation, sportsmen |

President

PSAC-OST

1964 Interdepartmental Agreement

Figure 2  Major federal policy makers in pesticides regulation 1960-1969.

| Executive | Administrative | Legislative and/or Appropriations (selected) | Interest groups |
|---|---|---|---|
| President | | | |
| USDA, HEW, USDI | advisory | Com. on Agriculture (HR), Subcom. on Ag. Approp. (HR), Com. on Ag. and Forestry (S), Com. on Commerce (S) | Ag. and chemical ind., health, sportsmen |
| CEQ — EPA | Categorical Program Pesticides (regulation) | Subcom. on Ag. Appropriations | Environment, health |
| DOL | OSHA (Reentry standards) | Com. on Education and Labor (HR), Com. on Labor and Pub. Welfare (S) | Farmworkers |

Federal Working Group on Pest Management

HR = House of Representatives
S = Senate

Figure 3  Major federal policy-makers in pesticides regulation 1970–1973.

Table 3  USDA Expenditures for Pesticides Research, FYs 1964-1972, in $1,000

| Research On | 1964 | 1965 | 1966 | 1967 | 1968 | 1969 | 1970 | 1971 | 1972 |
|---|---|---|---|---|---|---|---|---|---|
| Non-chemical pesticides | 12,328 | 22,666 | 23,493 | 24,394 | 23,569 | 23,891 | 25,493 | 28,953 | 34,045 |
| Chemical Control | 8,612 | 16,146 | 16,713 | 17,246 | 18,296 | 19,285 | 20,116 | 23,212 | 27,504 |
| TOTAL | 20,940 | 38,812 | 40,206 | 41,641 | 41,865 | 43,176 | 45,549 | 52,165 | 61,549 |

Source: USDA.

Service of USDA prepared a series of reports on quantities of
pesticides used by farmers.  The PHS established a Pesticides
Intelligence System for collecting and dissemination
information on pesticide residues.

To monitor environmental levels of pesticides residues, a
Pesticides Monitoring Journal was established in 1967,
published by the Federal Committee on Pest Control, which
coordinated USDA, DHEW, and USDI and was funded by
administrative agreement.  The divergent interests of the
sponsors of the Pesticides Monitoring Journal made it
impossible for them to agree on interpretations, however, and
so it generally reproduced raw data.  The preface to the first
issue noted that

"it will be the intent of this Journal to publish the data in
a form that will permit each reader to interpret the results
for himself." (47)

Chronic Effects A major finding of Rachel Carson and the PSAC
Panel was that data on chronic effects of pesticides was
totally inadequate.  Several actions were taken to improve the
amount and quality of this information.  Requirement for
testing chronic effects before pesticides could be registered
or tolerances given were re-evaluated.  Degradation studies
were required in 1965.  Nevertheless, it was not until 1970
that several tests for environmental effects were required
(48).

The NCI-contracted Bionetics study of the chronic effects
of numerous chemicals, as recommended by the 1963 PSAC study,
began to produce results in late 1966.  Because of problems in
testing protocols and questions of interpretation, however,
the results were in most cases not absolutely certain; but
they provided, often for the first time, data on the potential
safety or hazards of the chemicals.  Of the study's specific
findings, the most critical was one stating that 2,4,5-T and
its esters, a herbicide in very wide use, were highly
teratogenic, although it was subsequently found that part of
the teratogenicity activity resulted from contamination with
dioxins during manufacturing, which had later been
significantly reduced, although high yields of dioxins are
produced from combustion of these herbicides.  Questions are
still being raised, however, about the toxicity of dioxins
even at these lower levels, and of the safety of 2,4,5-T
itself (49, 50, 51).

The Bionetics study, a key pioneering effort in
investigating chronic effects of toxic chemicals, played a

significant role in evaluating many pesticides in the late
1960s and was a prime factor leading to the "Mrak Commission."
This Commission, created by the Secretary of the DHEW, Robert
Finch, together with four panels, undertook a comprehensive
survey of "Pesticides and Their Relationship to Environmental
Health." (52)  (The report is discussed in more detail below.)
As a coalescer and analyzer the state of knowledge as of 1969,
the panel reports are unsurpassed.  The expert panels examined
carcinogenicity, teratogenicity, mutagenicity, and chemical
interactions.

The implications of these chronic health effects problems
have been widely discussed (52, 53).  Major points to consider
are that because of the vast number of chemicals and their
potential effects, information is never complete; that the
relevance of animal tests to human effects are strongly
presumptive; and that low level effects posing significant
hazards may not be statistically demonstrable in laboratory
tests, using small numbers of animals, unless compensated by
testing at high doses.  Hence, all decisions on regulation
have to be judgements (52, p. 3; 54; 55), reflecting a wise
balancing of risks (often long range, imprecise possibilities)
and benefits (often immediate and tangible).

The same problems of identifying human health effects that
may be delayed and of low order make difficult the evaluation
of environmental effects.  The best data on environmental
effects of pesticides have been summarized in a report of the
Office of Science and Technology, Ecological Effects of
Pesticides on Non-Target Species (43).

Most scientists agree that certain pesticides have
adversely affected the reproductive capabilities of several
species of birds; in particular, DDT is believed to have
caused Bald Eagles, Ospreys, Peregrine Falcons, and Brown
Pelicans to lay thin-shelled eggs, which are less likely to
hatch successfully.  Subsequent investigations suggested that
DDT was interfering with calcium metabolism in the birds.
Although the data were inferential, they provided bases for
challenging the continued registration of persistent
pesticides.  Controlled laboratory experiments carried out
during the late 1960s demonstrated the egg-shell thinning
effects of DDT (53, pp. 16-19).  The significance of this
finding was that residues, concentrating in food chains, could
reach levels inhibiting reproduction, thus threatening the
species with extinction.  This contrasts to incidents in which
birds may be killed by coming in contact with spray, killing
individuals but not threatening the population.  Most
scientists believe that acute effects are less serious, in

that birds which have been killed can be replaced as long as
chronic effects do not inhibit reproductive capabilities.
Alternatives Also during the 1960s information developed on
the effectiveness of pesticides use (3, 56).  Numerous studies
suggested that chemical pesticides are significantly over-used
on some crops; and that improved application procedures,
including use of field scouts to eliminate prophylactic
treatments, can reduce the use of pesticides by up to 50
percent on cotton, the crop using the most chemical
pesticides.  The development of integrated pest management
systems (3, 57, 58, 59) promises reduced dependence on
chemicals, which would extend their effectiveness through
reducing the onset of pest resistance.
Problems Despite the efforts to improve data on which
pesticides policy is based, serious deficiencies remain.  In
1972 the Stanford Research Institute (SRI) completed for the
Council on Environmental Quality a study of Environmental
Indicators for Pesticides (5).  It reviewed data on the
production and use of pesticides and on their environmental
diffusion and monitoring, and examined appropriate additional
information.  It found that data concerning virtually every
stage of pesticides use, from production and application to
environmental and public health effects, are grossly
inadequate and in many cases missing or, if some data are
available, inaccurate.

    With respect to production and use figures, the main
problem is restriction on the publication of data which can
reveal figures for any one firm.  As a result, there are
available production figures for only about 10 percent of
pesticides in use.  Few attempts have been made to compute the
amounts of pesticides actually applied.  The USDA has prepared
reports on 1964 and 1966 (60), and is preparing one for 1971,
but the SRI suggests that the figures may be erroneous by as
much as 50 percent.  The lack of production data means there
is no way to double-check the figures on use.  Because of the
lack of data on use, it is difficult to evaluate how policies
affect the economics of crop production and environmental
burdens.

Congressional Oversight of Regulation In late 1968 and early
1969, the Government Accounting Office (GAO), an investigatory
arm of Congress, reported to Congress on investigations into
the USDA's Pesticide Regulatory Division's (PRD) general
administrative practices and also into its handling of a
particular pesticide product, Lindane Pesticide Pellets (37).
The GAO sharply criticized the PRD's actions in protecting the

public from misbranded, adulterated, or unregistered products.
The GAO found the USDA did not obtain shipping data to see if
all shipments of illegal materials were removed from the
markets.  It did not report violations to the Justice
Department for prosecution, even in cases of repeated
violations or when shippers did not correct violations.  In a
separate report, the GAO found that the PRD continued the
registration of Lindane Pellets for use in continuously
vaporizing devices in commercial and industrial establishments
even though FDA, USPHS, and federal, state, and private
organizations had long opposed the use.

These two GAO reports served as the background for an
oversight hearing on "Deficiencies in Administration of FIFRA"
by a subcommittee of the House Government Operations Committee
(the "Fountain hearings") (61).  These hearings revealed that
while the USDA had submitted registration applications to USDI
and DHEW, as required by the 1964 Interagency Agreement, it
had unilaterally ignored every objection of USDI and DHEW in
registering the pesticides.  The USDA's PRD had never withheld
a pesticide objected to nor followed the procedures for
resolving disagreements as set forth in the 1964 Interagency
Agreement.

A main point of contention at these hearings was the
USPHS's insistence that once a pesticide was registered,
questions of safety were not sufficient to require the PRD to
take action toward restricting or cancelling the product; the
PRD maintained that once a product was registered, critics of
the registration had to offer scientific proof of harm.  The
PRD interpreted the evidence, however, and not once accepted
any FDA or USPHS objections as "proof" (61, pp. 66-69).

The following colloquoy between Mr. Naughton, the
Subcommittee's counsel, and Dr. Irving, Administrator of the
USDA's Agriculture Research Service, typifies the controversy:

"Mr. Naughton.  The interagency agreement has been in
effect since 1964, hasn't it approximately?
Dr. Irving.  1964.
Mr. Naughton.  Doesn't it require that if there are
unresolved questions, for instance between two agencies such
as ARS and the Public Health Service, as to the safety of
these compounds, that the questions are to be resolved within
2 weeks and if they are not resolved within 2 weeks, that they
shall then go to the Secretary of the Department concerned?
Dr. Irving.  I believe that's the language; yes, sir.
Mr. Naughton.  Now, we just heard testimony there were 252
products in 1 year's time alone to which PHS objected.  Did

the Public Health Service withdraw its objections to those 252
products?

    Dr. Hays.  Mr. Naughton, again I would repeat that of the
252 products involving the six or eight chemicals, at no time
have we received any scientific data in support of the
objection.

    Mr. Naughton.  But you received the objections.

    Dr. Hays.  Just the objections.

    Mr. Rosenthal.  The answer is they didn't withdraw their
objections.

    Dr. Hays.  No, sir.

    Mr. Rosenthal.  It was in a form unsatisfactory to you?

    Dr. Hays.  That's correct.

    Mr. Naughton.  Were any one of these 252 products to which
there were unresolved objections referred to the Secretary of
Agriculture as required by the agreement?

    Dr. Irving.  No, sir.  I believe the record is that we have
referred nothing to the Secretary of Agriculture.

    Mr. Naughton.  So in effect you have not been following the
agreement?

    Dr. Irving.  We have resolved the issue - we feel we have
resolved the issue by taking action.

    Mr. Naughton.  In other words, you went ahead and put it on
the Market?

    Dr. Irving.  Yes, sir.

    Mr. Naughton.  Without calling it to the attention of the
Secretary of Agriculture as required by the agreement?

    Dr. Irving.  The agreement requires if we didn't resolve
that we take it to the Secretary of Agriculture.  Our
contention is we have resolved it.

    Mr. Rosenthal.  You unilaterally tore up the agreement.
That's what you did.  Why waste everybody's time?  Tell them
to take the agreement and forget about it.

    Dr. Irving.  I don't want to get into bickering of this
either, but I would say, if we said we don't know what to do
because of this objection, then we would have reason to send
it to the Secretary of Agriculture.  We knew what to do,
because we registered it." (61, p. 66)

    In the case of Lindane used in continuously vaporizing
devices, the USDA had maintained its registration of these
devices since 1952 despite objections by federal, state, and
local health authorities.  In 1965 a USPHS ad hoc committee
unanimously recommended that the registration be terminated,
but the USDA ignored the finding.  In 1968, the GAO prepared
its report criticizing the USDA's action.  At the Fountain

hearings, the USDA contended that there were no data to prove the devices were harmful.  Data were lacking on whether residues would appear on food in rooms where the devices were operating, and on the effects of the chemical when inhaled. At these hearings, the subcommittee pressed USDA witnesses strongly, and finally Dr. Irving, said the PRD would act to require Shell Chemical Co. to relabel certain uses of the devices (61, p. 87).

The significance of the hearings lay in their exposure of the breakdown of administrative methods for bringing DHEW viewpoints to bear effectively on the registration process. While it is probable that not all the USPHS objections were valid, the USDA's unilateral ignoring of everyone of them showed that the 1964 Interagency Agreement was ineffectual. The House Committee on Government Operations prepared a very highly critical report of the USDA's actions and procedures (62).

Mrak Commission  On March 27, 1969 the FDA seized some Coho salmon caught in Lake Michigan because of DDT residues.  The costs of the seizures, the question of who was responsible for the contamination and the lack of information on hazards - as the FDA set an arbitrary limit on DDT residues - created considerable publicity.  At this same time, the Bionetics report was nearing completion, the two GAO reports had just appeared, Ralph Nader's "raiders" were preparing for a complete study of the FDA, and evidence was emerging that DDT was a carcinogen.  DHEW Secretary Robert Finch announced the creation of a Commission on Pesticides and Their Relationship to Environmental Health, chaired by Dr. Emil Mrak.  Secretary Finch charged the committee to review the problem and in particular to make recommendations on DDT and on the Delaney Amendment.  Some persons argued that DDT is a carcinogen and food contaminated with it is subject to the Delaney Amendment; DDT residues being widespread in the environment, many foods of animal origin contain DDT residues.

The "Mrak Report," completed by the end of the year, is the most comprehensive document ever prepared on the hazards of pesticides, man's health, and his environment (52).  The Commission made 14 unanimous recommendations, including ones to revise the 1964 Interdepartmental Agreement, to end all non-essential uses of DDT and other chlorinated hydrocarbons in two years and to upgrade the DHEW's capabilities for evaluating pesticides hazards.

Not everyone was happy with the report, some thinking it too critical of pesticides, others finding it too uncritical.

William H. Rodgers, Jr., in an article criticizing the report
(63), highlighted the difficult problems of assessing
Congressional-Administrative actions.  Rodgers strongly
objected to the Commission's recommendation to revise the 1964
Interagency Agreement and called for legislation

"wresting exclusive control over the process of registering
chemical pesticides from the USDA.  [He argued that] the Mrak
Commission's view that a new Interagency Agreement would be
sufficient to strengthen cooperative action among the
Departments ignores inevitable deficiencies in the
administration of interagency agreements and overlooks legal
and political realities.  To accomplish reform in the
registration process and the other statutory obligations,
FIFRA should be amended specifically to assure participation
by HEW and USDA." (63, p. 571)

But this assertion itself ignores legal and political
realities:  legislation to amend FIFRA would necessarily be
referred to the House and Senate Agricultural Committees,
where it would not be viewed very sympathetically if it
curtailed the USDA's authority.  What the Mrak Commission did
was make the strongest possible recommendation consistent with
these.  And the USDA, in the spring of 1970, did accede to a
new agreement significantly strengthening the voice of DHEW
and USLI, and agreed to let DHEW in effect register certain
pesticides for non-agricultural uses (44, pp. 12-14).  Also,
the Commission's recommendations on DDT marked a crucial
advance; Rodgers felt it merely repeated recommendations of
earlier panels.  The Mrak Commission said:

"Eliminate within two years all uses of DDT and DDD in the
United States excepting those uses essential to the
preservation of human health or welfare and approved
unanimously by the Secretaries of the Departments of Health,
Education, and Welfare, Agriculture, and Interior."

Unlike statements of earlier panels, this was the first
recommendation by a group of such high standing to set a
deadline for ending uses of DDT and to define an operational
criterion for determining what uses might be continued.  This
criterion of unanimous agreement among USDA, DHEW, and USDI in
effect meant the last two would have veto power over USDA
decisions; this would have represented a major realignment of
authorities.  In addition, the Mrak Commission made a similar
recommendation to require USDA, DHEW, and USDI agreement on

uses of aldrin, dieldrin, endrin, heptachlor, chlordane, benezene hexachloride, lindane, and compounds containing a arsenic, lead, or mercury - all chemicals which are persistent and can cause contamination of the environment.

Besides its recommendations the Mrak Report included another major contribution to pesticides policy.  Four panels created by the Commission prepared reports on pesticides' carcinogenicity, mutagenicity, teratogenicity, and interactions with other chemicals.  Each panel reviewed the relevant tests on effects of individual pesticidal chemicals, evaluated their finds and categorized the chemicals as to whether they were proven carcinogenic, mutagenic, or teratogenic, suspected or apparently free of these effects; or needed further investigation.  A number of commonly used pesticides were found to be hazardous, including 2,4,5-T, aldrin, dieldrin, DDT, and Mirex.  The panels prepared lists giving priorities for further testing.

Congressional Oversight of Environmental Hazards After the FDA seized the Coho salmon, the Senate Commerce Committee held hearings on The Effects of Pesticides on Sport and Commercial Fisheries (64).  These hearings investigated the extent of environmental contamination by DDT and other persistent pesticides, and questioned the USDA's policies on regulating them.  The USDA submitted for the record a long list of cancellations of persistent pesticide uses; however, examination of the list reveals that the cancellations were based not on persistence or environmental hazards, but on other reasons, usually the occurrence of residues on food products.

In 1970, the same Senate Commerce Subcommittee again held hearings, this time on The Effects of 2,4,5-T on Man and the Environment.  These hearings brought out that while 2,4,5-T tested in the Bionetics study had been contaminated by a highly teratogenic chemical, dioxin, pure 2,4,5-T itself showed teratogenic activity in various test animals (48).

Also, the Migratory Labor Subcommittee of the Senate Labor and Public Welfare Committee, as a part of hearings on Migrant and Seasonal Farmworker Powerlessness, investigated the effects of pesticides on farmworkers (65).  This event marked the belated emergence of a new set of interests achieving institutionalization:  the farmworker, interested in protection from exposure to pesticides.  This new force, finding congressional support in the Senate Labor and Public Welfare Committee, was to achieve statutory protection under the Occupational Safety and Health Act of 1970 (29 U.S.C.

655), as will be discussed later.

These oversight hearings of the Senate Committees, as well as those of the House Government Operations Committee on regulation, brought to public light for analysis the processes, rationales, and decisions of registration.  With respect to pesticides, the 91st Congress (1969-1970) was one of information gathering and analysis.

## Challenge Of Law

National Environmental Policy Act of 1969 The growth of knowledge on environmental pollution and rising public concern led to a key action of the 91st Congress - passage of the National Environmental Policy Act of 1969 (NEPA).  NEPA established the quality of the environment as an issue of high national priority, and its Sec. 102(2)(c) requirements that agencies prepare "environmental impact statements" of major actions provided a basis for extending information requirements.  For while the NEPA did not provide a statutory basis for challenging federal decisions because of their possible adverse environmental effects, it did provide a basis for challenging them because of inadequate impact statements. NEPA has led to numerous legal efforts by environmentalists to delay and improve such potentially harmful actions as building the Alaska Pipeline and the Calvert Cliffs nuclear generating plant.  The Imported Fire Ant Eradication Program has also been challenged.

Suits on Pesticides Regulation In the atmosphere of increasing concern for the environment, and in possession of improved data, in 1969 the Environmental Defense Fund (EDF) sued the USDA and DHEW to force them to end registration of DDT.  The EDF was created in 1967 to combine the methods of law and the knowledge of science in defense of the environment (66).  The EDF consists of a core of lawyers and scientists who draw on a large number of scientists who have made themselves available for service as expert witnesses.

The basis of the EDF suit against the USDA was that DDT was an environmental hazard and, as such, mislabeled in the meaning of FIFRA, so its registration should be ended.  The USDA, in its response, challenged the standing of the EDF to sue, but the decision in Environmental Defense Fund vs. Hardin, 428 F.2d 1093 [D.C. Cir. (1970)], accorded standing to "private interest" groups to seek judicial review.  The basis of the suit against DHEW was that DDT is a carcinogen, and that therefore no tolerance for residues should be permitted. As an environmental contaminant, DDT occurs in many foods.

The EDF did not maintain all such foods be banned, but that
DDT's registrations should be ended to minimize residues.
     These lawsuits provided another avenue by which scientists
who felt that information on potential hazards was not being
given proper attention could bring their data to the fore, and
challenge those claiming harmlessness of pesticides (66).  As
of February 1974 cancellation hearings on three pesticides,
dieldrin, mirex, and 2,4,5-T, involving EPA, EDF, and multiple
parties, were being held before an administrative law judge
appointed by the civil service commission.

Summary Up through the mid 1960s, the USDA maintained its
predominance in pesticides policy.  The criticisms of Rachel
Carson and PSAC were a blow; but while they led to significant
improvements in the FDA's setting of tolerances, they had
little immediate effect in curbing the USDA's authority.  Most
of the changes the USDA made were administrative and actually
represented little effective change.  The DHEW and USDI still
had very limited effects on regulation, and the USDA could,
and did, ignore many of their recommendations.
     But the forces of the late 1960s began to tell.  The
congressional investigations of environmental contamination,
potential health effects, and regulatory inadequacies; the
findings of the Mrak Commission; the increasing data on
pesticides residues and their potential effects; and the legal
challenges of the EDF and other public interest groups - all
these pressures were becoming irresistible by the end of the
decade.  The USDA cancelled certain DDT use registrations in
1969.  It concurred in a revision of the 1964
Interdepartmental Agreement concerning regulation and it
agreed to the DHEW having the authority to regulate a number
of non-agricultural pesticides uses.

The Creation Of The Environmental Protection Agency

New Directions Soon after his inauguration, President Nixon
appointed Roy Ash of Litton Industries to study government
organization.  One of the outcomes of this study was
Reorganization Plan No. 3 of 1970 creating the EPA.  Included
within this new agency were a wide range of anti-pollution
programs:  water, air, solid wastes, certain radiation and
noise standards - and pesticides regulation.  The Pesticides
Regulation Division of USDA, the tolerance setting offices of
FDA, and certain research authorities of USDI were transferred

to EPA[*] (see Table 4).

It will be noted that this reorganization occurred not from new legislation, but from Executive initiative. Reorganization plans go into effect unless specifically rejected by Congress within 60 days. Although some objections were made to the creation of EPA - and in particular to transferring pesticides regulations to it - the plan was not disapproved by Congress. Some environmentalists were not happy, however, in that in the House of Representatives, the Subcommittee on Agriculture of the Committee on Appropriations received jurisdiction over the EPA, for the chairman of the Subcommittee had written a rebuttal of Silent Spring (67).

The new orientation of pesticides legislation was made explicit by EPA's Administrator, William D. Ruckelshaus. He said,

"EPA is an independent agency. It has no obligation to promote agriculture or commerce, only the critical obligation to protect and enhance the environment." (68, p. 736)

At 1971 House Agriculture Committee hearings on revising pesticides regulation, Rep. George A. Goodling (R.-Pa.) asked Administrator Ruckelshaus if he had in fact made the statement. He responded, "I did," at which time the following exchange occurred:

"Mr. Goodling. You have absolutely no obligation to help promote agriculture?

Mr. Ruckelshaus. No statutory obligation. What I was doing was defining the statutory obligation I inherited with the creation of this Agency.

Mr. Goodling. Who is going to look after agriculture in the use of pesticides?

Mr. Ruckelshaus. Mr. Goodling, I think you have been doing a pretty good job here this morning. yourself.

This statement to which you refer, Mr. Goodling, was a statement in a speech that I made about 6 weeks ago, and the context in which I made this statement was an explanation of what I think was a very important trust to this Agency, which

-----------------------------------------------------------------

[*] Not included in the new EPA, however, was the just emerging problem of re-entry standards which could be promulgated under the Occupational Safety and Health Act of 1970 (P.L. 91-596) (see Figure 1). This regulatory activity is discussed later.

Table 4   Pesticides Transferred to EPA by Reorganization Plan 3, 1970

| Program | Transferred from | Functions |
|---------|------------------|-----------|
| Pesticides | DHEW | The FDA's pesticides program consists of setting and enforcing standards which limit pesticide residues in food.  EPA will have authority to set pesticide standards and to monitor compliance with them, and to conduct related research.  FDA retains authority to identify and remove from the market food with excess pesticide residue |
| Pesticides | Interior | Authority for research on effects of pesticides on fish and wildlife is transferred from Interior.  This is specialized research authority under the 1958 pesticides act.  Interior retains research on all factors affecting fish and wildlife.  The transfer involves only one laboratory, Gulf Breeze of the Bureau of Commercial Fisheries.  EPA will work closely with Bureau of Sport Fisheries and Wildlife laboratories. |
| Pesticides registration | Agriculture (Agricultural Research Service) | Agriculture's pesticides registration and monitoring function is transferred to EPA, to be merged with pesticides programs from HEW and Interior.  Agriculture will continue research on effectiveness of pesticides, furnishing this information to EPA.  EPA |

Table 4 (cont.)

| Program | Transferred from | Functions |
|---|---|---|
| Pesticides registration (cont.) | | will handle pesticides' licensing after consideration of environmental and health effects. EPA will use Agriculture's expertise, as in evaluating efficacy of various pesticides as related to other pest control methods and effects of pesticides on non-target plants, livestock, and poultry. Agriculture's educational program on pesticide use will continue to be carried out through its extension service. |

is, as I believe has come out here this morning and has
probably come out in previous hearings, that there is a good
deal of public misunderstanding about many of the problems
that exist in the environment, and I think some of this
misunderstanding has arisen because the agencies within the
Government who were charged with the responsibility of
protecting the environment also had other charges.  They
seemed to be at one time both the regulator and promoter, and
this gave arise to many, many feelings that they were paying
more attention to promotional responsibility than regulatory
responsibility.  I do not think that necessarily was true, but
I think that is what a lot of people felt, and I believe it is
important for people concerned with the environment, not only
with the question of pesticides but radiation, air, and water
pollution, all of our responsibilities, to feel confident that
there is one agency in the U.S. Government whose primary
responsibility is to see that the environment is protected,
and that responsibility is our No. 1 priority.  It does not
mean that we simply ignore every other problem that exists in
society and that we do not pay any attention to the impact of
what we are doing on the other facets of society.  But our
primary mission is protection of the environment." (68, pp.
736-737)

Thus EPA Administrator Ruckelshaus pointed up the problem:
the distribution of authorities among the mission-oriented
distribution of authorities among the mission-oriented
agencies.  The EPA is an institution created to remove
potential conflicts of interest, the pressures of particular
interests, and to establish the supremacy of an overriding
environmental viewpoint.

The EPA, nevertheless, immediately had a "legitimacy"
problem with respect to pesticides.  Those who were oriented
to the agricultural uses of pesticides feared the EPA might
overweigh environmental factors, while ignoring pesticide
needs for the production of food and fiber.  On the other
hand, as the EPA's pesticides regulation office was basically
the USDA's PRD and its then existing personnel transferred to
a new office, and as the Agricultural Subcommittee of the
House Committee on Appropriations held the EPA's purse
strings, many environmentalists feared that the EPA might
still overweigh the agriculturalist's preferences.

The EPA has acted in many ways to justify its activities
both to industry and environmentalists.  With respect to
industry concerns, an important action of EPA was to speed up
greatly the handling of applications for registering
pesticides (49, p. 250).  Also, the EPA refused to suspend the

registration of DDT, so its use could continue while
cancellation proceedings continued.

On the other hand, consistent with its responsibilities to
protect health and the environment, EPA has undertaken many
enforcement actions.  The GAO had strongly criticized the USDA
on its record on citing violations.  Indeed, in 1968 GAO
reported that in 13 years the USDA's ARS had taken no actions
to report violators of the law to the Department of Justice
for prosecution (61, p. 143).  In contrast, in 1973 the EPA
issued 1,500 violation notices and initiated 75 produce
seizures and 300 criminal prosecutions.  In 1974 the EPA hopes
to issue 1,500 violation notices and to initiate 200 stop
sales and 500 criminal prosecutions (48, pp. 607-608).

In other actions supporting the environmental-health
viewpoints, the EPA added requirements for additional testing
on prospective pesticides for teratogenicity and various
mobility and residue studies (48, pp. 549-555); additionally
EPA has proposed guidelines on mutagenicity testing.  The
evolution of the testing requirements for pesticides
registration and tolerance setting are shown in Tables 5-8.
It can clearly be seen that since 1970 requirements have been
significantly expanded to include more environmental and
health parameters.  Many of these had originally been
recommended by the 1963 PSAC Use of Pesticides panel.  Finally
Finally, in addition to these actions, the EPA cancelled all
uses of DDT and initiated reviews of several other
organochlorines.

Regulatory Decisions The EPA had little opportunity for a
grace period.  Among the pesticides registration
responsibilities transferred to the new agency were
cancellation proceedings against numerous pesticides uses,
including DDT and 2,4,5-T.

On January 7, 1971 the U.S. Court of Appeals for the
District of Columbia handed down two decisions.  In EDF vs.
Ruckelshaus, F2d (D.C. Cir., January 7, 1971), the Court ruled
that the EPA must commence cancellation proceedings against
all DDT uses and to consider whether DDT uses should be
suspended (immediately halted).  And in Wellford vs.
Ruckelshaus, the Court ruled that the EPA must review the
government's decisions in relation to 2,4,5-T and to
articulate its findings.  In addition, on December 2, 1970,
the EDF filed a petition requesting cancellation and
suspension of all uses of aldrin and dieldrin, some uses of
which had been cancelled earlier as the result of an
administrative review.  On March 18, 1971, the EPA presented a

report, Reasons Underlying the Registration Decisions
concerning Products Containing DDT,2,4,5-T, Aldrin and
Dieldrin (69).  This document is the EPA's articulation of the
factors affecting its registration policies, and a more formal
review of the several factors - statutory, economic, health,
and environmental - affectings its DDT, aldrin and dieldrin,
and 2,4,5-T actions.  The study found that each pesticide use
must be viewed individually, as "The range of variables in the
chemical formulation, pattern of use, risk and benefit is too
broad to permit responsible general criteria."

Even though it said each regulatory action was unique, the
EPA's actions on these pesticides would significantly affect
the Agency's future.  The outcome would indicate which of its
potential clientele - including agriculturalists,
environmentalists, medical persons, and the public - were to
feel most propitiated and which most ignored; and if its
decisions ended many uses of these pesticides, significant
changes would follow in farming practices for several crops,
and also in the position of some pesticide manufacturers.

During its first year, the EPA's action tended toward
middle ground.  On the one hand it cancelled all uses of DDT;
on the other, it refused to suspend them, despite suits by the
EDF requesting it to do so.

The first major break in normal bureaucratic procedure came
when the 2,4,5-T advisory committee, convened by EPA
Administrator Ruckelshaus after the January 7, 1971, decision
on Wellford vs. Ruckelshaus, issued its report of May 7, 1971
(70).  The 10-member committee split.  A nine-member-majority
concluded 2,4,5-T could be used around the home, on water, and
food crops, without posing a threat to man.  They recommended
rescinding suspensions imposed in 1970.  One member, Dr. T.
Sterling, dissented, saying that data were not adequate to say
2,4,5-T is safe.  In keeping with usual practices, the report
was not made public, pending Ruckelshaus' decision.  However,
on July 14, 1971, it was leaked, and at an ad hoc press
conference a number of independent scientists, headed by Dr.
Samuel S. Epstein, and public interest representatives sharply
challenged the majority conclusion of the report.

These challenges to the report were based on several
grounds, but primarily that this risk/benefit decision should
not be based on an assumption that further tests would prove
safety, but should be based on restrictive action until
further tests proved lack of hazard.  At issue were the
inability of the manufacturers to eliminate the highly toxic
dioxin contaminant, the fact that dioxins could be produced in
significant quantities by combustion of the herbicide, the

Table 5  Basic Tests Required for Pesticides Registration
(48, p. 550)

| Tests | Date Established | Cost (estimated dollars) | Time Implication |
|---|---|---|---|
| 1. Chemical and Physical Properties (Such as solubility, vapor pressure, flash point) | 1947 | 5,000-15,000 | |
| 2. Degradation Studies | | | |
| Persistence (soil) | 1965 | | 6-24 months |
| Persistence (water and sediment) | 1970 | | Less than 1 year |
| Photochemical | 1970 | | 2-6 months |
| 3. Mobility Studies | | | |
| Runoff | 1970 | | Less than 6 months |
| Leaching | 1970 | | Less than 3 months |
| 4. Residue Studies | | | |
| Fish | 1970 | | 2-6 months |
| Birds | 1970 | | 2-6 months |
| Mammals | 1970 | | 2-6 months |
| Lower trophic levels of food chains | 1972 | | 6-9 months |
| 5. Microbiological Studies | 1970 | | Less than 3 months |

A rough estimate of these requirements in their entirety would range between $100,000 and $250,000.

It should be noted that much of the data generated by these tests is utilized in studies of human, fish, and wildlife safety.

Table 6   Tests for Tolerances (48, p. 554).

| Tests | Date Established | Cost (estimated dollars) | Time Implication (months) |
|---|---|---|---|
| 1.  Toxicology | | | |
| Acute (rat and non-rodent) | 1954 | 5,000 | 1 |
| Subacute (rat and dog) | 1954 | 50,000 | 6 |
| Chronic, 2 year (rat and dog | 1954 | 160,000 | 28 |
| 2.  Reproduction (rat) | 1960 | 35,000 | 20 |
| 3.  Teratogenesis | 1970 | 10,000 | 2 |
| 4.  Mutagenesis | 1972 | 10,000 | 2 |
| 5.  Metabolism | | | |
| Plant | 1954 | 50,000 | 6 |
| Animal | Before 1960 | 25,000 | 3 |
| 6.  Analytical Methodology | 1954 | 100,000 | 4-6 |
| Crops, Meat, Milk, Poultry, Eggs | 1965 (Poultry) | | |
| 7.  Field Residue Data | | 100,000 | 12 |
| Drop, Feed, Meat, Milk, Poultry, | | 100,000 | 6 |
| Eggs | Before 1960 1965 (Poultry) | | |

Table 7　Human Safety Evaluation; Minimum Registration Requirements (48, p. 557)

| 1950 | 1960 | 1970 | 1971-80(?) | Mean Average Cost (a) 1970 |
|---|---|---|---|---|
| Acute toxicity | Acute toxicity | Acute toxicity | Acute toxicity | $18,405 |
| | | Subacute dermal | Subacute dermal | 6,940 |
| | | Subacute inhalation | Subacute inhalation | 6,120 |
| 30-90 day, rat | 90 day, rat | 90 day, rat | 90 day, rat | 12,765 |
| | 90 day, dog | 90 day, dog | 90 day, dog | 17,381 |
| | 2 year, rat | 2 year, rat | 2 year, rat | 30,000 |
| | 1 year, dog | 2 year, dog | | |
| | | Reproduction, 3 gen., rat | Reproduction, 3 gen., rat | 35,410 |
| | | Teratogenesis, rodent | Teratogenesis, rodent | 10,420 |
| | | | Mutagenesis | 8,170 |

(a) Cost figures taken from Statement of R. E. Naegele, Manager, Agricultural Department, The Dow Chemical Company, before The House Committee on Agriculture, March 8, 1971.

Table 8  Fish and Wildlife Safety Review (48, p. 549)

| Criterion | Date Established 1947-62 | 63-70 | 71-73 | Cost (estimated dollars) | Time Implication |
|---|---|---|---|---|---|
| 1. Fish (2 species), Acute $LD_{50}$ | | X | | 600-800 | Less than 1 month |
| 2. Birds (2 species), Acute Oral $LD_{50}$ | | X | | 600-800 | " |
| 3. Crustacean, Acute | | X | | 1000 | " |
| 4. Mollusc, Acute | | X | | 1000 | " |
| 5. Simulated Field Testing, Birds and Mammals | | X | | Highly variable - More than 6,000 | " |
| 6. Bird (2 species), Subacute Feeding | | | X | 800-1200 | " |

Table 8 (cont.)

| Criterion | Date Established | | | Cost (estimated dollars) | Time Implication |
|---|---|---|---|---|---|
| | 1947-62 | 63-70 | 71-73 | | |
| 7. Special Testing | | | | | |
| (a) Field monitoring of effects on wildlife populations | X | | | Highly variable | Less than 1 year |
| (b) Aquatic ecosystems (laboratory) | | | X | Highly variable | 3-9 months |
| (c) Aquatic invertebrates (laboratory) | | | X | Highly variable | 1-12 months |
| (d) Other | | | X | Highly variable | Less than 1 year |
| 8. Reproduction Studies, Fish, Birds, Mammals | | | X | Greater than 10,000 | 6-12 months |
| 9. Residue, Fish, Birds, Mammals | X | | | Unknown | Less than 6 months |

determination of "no-effect" teratogenic levels of dioxins and
of purified 2,4,5-T, and the safety factor which must be
assumed in transferring results on other animals to man.  Many
critics of the advisory committee contended it was obviously
"biased," and that it ignored certain critical data on
2,4,5-T's effects.  The ultimate importance of this episode of
the 2,4,5-T committee lies neither in any critic's attacks on
the committee or on its scientific validity, nor really on the
findings of further scientific research - its importance lies
in forcing the issue to the public arena, where the values of
risk/benefit could be debated.

As a result of the controversy over the 2,4,5-T report, EPA
Administrator Ruckelshaus took two unprecedented steps:
first, with respect to 2,4,5-T, he refused to accept the
recommendations of his advisory committee and called for
public "hearings"; second, with respect to regulation, he
issued a set of rules to ensure that regulatory procedures
would be more open to public scrutiny, and ordered that
reports of advisory committees be made available for public
comment for a period of 60 to 90 days prior to their formal
consideration by the agency (71).

In fact, due to prolonged legal maneuvering and the
problems in obtaining new research results, the public
hearings on 2,4,5-T, have yet to be held, although
cancellation hearings, involving EPA, EDF and multiple
parties, are being held as of February 1974.  The suspensions
opposed by agriculturalists remain in force, while some uses
opposed by environmentalists continue.

On the other hand, after years of controversy, legal
maneuvers, and studies, the decision on DDT seems final.  As
required by the January 7, 1971, D.C. District Court ruling,
the EPA cancelled all DDT registrations.  Appeals led to the
creation of a science advisory committee and to a public
hearing.  The committee recommended a continued phasing out of
DDT uses, but did not set a time schedule.  It did not
recommend immediate suspension.  The hearings were long and
involved.  Controversies arose over the rules of evidence set
by the hearing examiner, Mr. Sweeney.  After 7 months and
thousands of pages of testimony by over 300 witnesses, Mr.
Sweeney ruled for the appealing manufacturers.  He said the
evidence did not prove DDT was mislabeled as defined by FIFRA,
and that the propositions that DDT was a health risk and
damaging to fish and wildlife not convincing (72).

On June 14, 1972, EPA Administrator Ruckelshaus ruled that
except for health and quarantine uses and three limited
agricultural uses, all DDT registrations should be cancelled.

He said,

"The Agency and EDF have established that DDT is toxic to
non-target insects and animals, persistent, mobile and
transferable and that it builds up in the food chain.  No
label directions for use can completely prevent these
hazards - [He concluded that] these facts alone constitute
risks that are unjustified where apparently safer alternatives
exist to achieve the same benefit." (73)

The trade-off, as expressed by Mr. Ruckelshaus, was that no
controls on DDT could ensure protection against the chronic
hazards posed by the persistence and environmental mobility of
DDT, while training of applicators could minimize the acute
toxicity dangers associated with organophosphate substitutes,
which tend to degrade rapidly and thus do not pose a
significant risk of chronic hazard.

Problems The delays and controversies in assessing regulations
for 2,4,5-T and DDT were the final proof, if proof were
needed, of the necessity for revising FIFRA.  When FIFRA was
written in 1947, the environmental ahd health implications of
pesticides were barely recognized and had virtually no impact
on the deliberations over the legislation.  By 1970, FIFRA was
obviously inadequate in several ways.
        Basically, the conceptual basis of FIFRA was to regulate by
labeling requirements, so as to protect farmers from
ineffective, harmful, and adulterated products and to protect
manufacturers from unscrupulous competitors.  It made no
provisions for standards based on such environmental hazards
as persistence.  Interpretation of the Act as protecting fish
and wildlife came only after Sen. Ribicoff directed the USDA
and USDI to work out a solution, as discussed previously.
        Because FIFRA regulated only labels, controls on how
pesticides were actually used were indirect.  Penalties for
misusing a pesticide were either the expense of the chemical
or the possibility of having a crop seized because of illegal
residues.  Neither penalty was necessarily effective.  The
costs of many pesticides were so low (particularly true of
DDT) that many farmers felt that the "insurance" value of
overuse or calendar use was well worth the added costs of the
chemical.  Indeed, agrichemical companies encouraged calendar
spray programs, based not on need, but on sequences of dates
which would protect crops whether pests were present or not.
And the danger of producing crops with illegal residues, while
real, was largely conterbalanced by the unlikelihood of the

crop being checked by inspectors.  Thus, while regulation
depended on users following meticulously the directions on the
label, no research was performed to determine just how well
users were in fact following the label, though some studies
showed that many users did not understand terms on labels and
that some labels were contradictory (74; 75, part 1, p. 164).

Also, evidence indicates that persons of lower socio-
economic groups accumulate more residues in their bodies.
This may result from their living in substandard housing with
more pests, and from misuse of pesticides because of ignorance
or inability or failure to read and follow directions (52,
p. 323).

Indeed, the result of misuse or overuse of pesticides was
often such that the farmer had to use even more chemicals
(58, 59).  Entomologists are finding more and more examples
where chemical pesticides have created more problems than they
solved; for example when spraying for one pest has resulted in
the suppression of beneficial insects controlling another
pest, for which new sprays must be made.  In an often
publicized case in California, a pesticide (Azodrin) was
vigorously marketed for control of the cotton pest bollworm.
Calendar applications were recommended by the producers; state
experts recommended against Azodrin's use.  But the timing of
treatment was so critical that calendar applications often
resulted in more damage by bollworms rather than less.

The problem with the 1947 FIFRA was that its regulatory
concept was too narrow.  Based only on labeling and focused on
agricultural uses of a pesticide, it did not provide for
systematic consideration of a pesticide's effects on the full
context of environmental factors - including not only effects
on fish, wildlife, and man, but also on the interdependencies
of an ecosystem linking crops, pests, beneficial insects,
hedgerows, etc. together (77).

Experiences with 2,4,5-T and DDT were graphic proof that
the procedures for cancelling or suspending pesticides were
too clumsy and time-consuming.  A potentially dangerous
product could remain on the market for years while various
appeals were made.  The procedures did not provide for a way
of determining what information was needed for resolving the
question of safety or whether the pesticide should be
withdrawn from markets pending the accumulation of the
information.

Proposed Legislation Recognition of these problems was not
new.  But the creation of EPA was a new impetus to reform.
Early in 1971 the Administration proposed a Federal

Environmental Pesticides Control Act.  President Nixon called
for passage of pesticides legislation in his environmental
message, and the Council on Environmental Quality identified
revision of FIFRA as one of the top five environmental
priorities of the year (along with ocean dumping, national
land use, toxic substances, and water pollution).  The
proposed Act completely rewrote FIFRA.  The new proposal made
protection of the environment an explicit criteria in
registering pesticides.  It streamlined cancellation and
suspension procedures, including the elimination of the
scientific advisory committee.  It provided for inspection of
manufacturing establishments.  And it established three
categories by which pesticides might be registered to
greater control over use:  "General use" pesticides would be
regulated as under FIFRA, by registering the label.  The
"restricted use" category would be pesticides usually highly
toxic and would be applied only by certified pesticide
applicators.  In this way accidents to applicators could be
minimized.  And the "use by permit only" category would
include pesticides which were persistent and environmentally
hazardous.  By requiring permits, the Administrator could
control the amounts used and the places sprayed, and he could
require specific determinations of need.  These categories of
use were derived from a recommendation of the Mrak Commission.

Federal Environmental Pesticides Control Act of 1972
Whereas the 90th and 91st Congresses had been ones of
oversight of pesticides issues, the 92nd was one of
legislation.  Four hearings were held on legislation to revise
FIFRA.  But whereas in the 90th and 91st Congresses the House
Committee on Government Operations and the Senate Committees
on Commerce and on Labor and Public Welfare had held the
oversight hearings - largely critical of existing USDA
policies - in the 92nd Congress the legislative process moved
first to the House and Senate Agriculture Committees, which
historically had had sole jurisdiction over pesticides
regulation legislation, except tolerances (under the Food,
Drug, and Cosmetic Act), USDI research, and labor and
farmworker issues (see Figure 2).

What became the Federal Environmental Pesticide Control Act
of 1972 (P.L. 92-516) evolved through six major stages:  The
Nixon administration's proposal and hearings; the "clean" bill
(H.R. 10729) reported and passed (with an amendment) by the
House; hearings and amendments of the Senate Commerce
Committee; the Senate passed version; and the bill as reported
from conference and signed into law.

The development of the bill as it progressed through these
stages was determined by several factors, most importantly by
the balance of competing interests and the natural iterative
improvement of ideas.   Underlying the interests and affecting
the decisions made were conflicting views of the adverse
health and environmental effects of pesticides on the one hand
and the need for pesticides on the other.   Critical to these
conflicts were difficulties in selecting and interpreting
technical information and relating it to policy.   These
conflicts were easily apparent in the hearings (78).

Development Of The Legislation

Public Input:   Hearings Both the House and Senate Agriculture
Committees held early hearings on pesticides legislation,
including the administration's bills (79).   These hearings
raised many general questions about pesticides regulation –
whether new legislation was necessary, the potential effects
of regulating use, and how a permit program for using certain
pesticides could be administered.   The committees heard
testimony representing the entire spectrum of opinion – from
sharp critics of FIFRA and persons asserting serious dangers
to the environment, to staunch supporters of existing
regulations and persons rejecting most claims of environmental
and health hazards.

Most witnesses accepted the need for new legislation,
although the National Cotton Council of America felt that
FIFRA had proved workable in protecting health and the
environment so that retaining FIFRA was "far preferable to
charting a new course" and EPA "should be given an opportunity
to work with the present law before drastically changing it."
(68, p. 434)  But, instead of objecting to substantive new
legislation, nearly all witnesses focused on points in the
proposed bills that they wanted changed.

The agrichemical and agricultural industries zeroed in
especially on the proposed "use by permit only" classification
of pesticides and said this would be too burdensome.
Representatives of industry suggested dropping the use by
permit only (68, pp. 340-341), adding an indemnity provision
(68, p. 332), prohibiting "essentiality" as a registration
criterion (68, pp. 387-388), and retaining advisory committees
(68, pp. 341-342).

Environmentalists proposed various amendments to strengthen
the bill.   Sen. Nelson testified - and later proposed, along
with Sen. Philip A. Hart (D.-Mich.) - a series of amendments
involving the definition of environmental harm, the
registration process, objectivity of advisory committees,
farmworker protection, and authorizing use of "essentiality"

as a criterion (75, pp. 140-150 and part II, pp. 66-80, 362-364).

Thus the need for legislation was recognized, and the debate and controversies mainly focused on just what regulatory authorities were necessary and how they should be established. The balancing of points of view depended largely on the persuasiveness of arguments concerning the extent to which regulations would protect health and the environment and how regulations would affect production and innovation of necessary farm chemicals.

Effects of Pesticides and the Resolution of Technical Uncertainties Most of the testimony at these hearings either described adverse effects of pesticides as proving the need for stricter regulations, or presented arguments that hazards were minimal and less strict regulations sufficient. The effects of DDT - against which cancellation proceedings were then pending - became a focal point. Testimony was presented that DDT caused eggshell thinning in certain birds, and testimony was presented that it did not (68, pp. 575-590, 680-706).

For the scientist, the hearing room is a difficult place to resolve conflicts of interpretation of scientific issues. Hearings are designed to get points of view on record. On his remarks when opening the House Agriculture Committee Hearings on pesticides legislation, Chariman W. R. Poage (D.-Tex.) commented,

"We...hope that all groups throughout the country who have an interest - and that includes those who have fixed conviction as well as those who are seeking light - will have an opportunity to put their views on record." (68, p. 3).

Once testimony is presented, questions are framed by committee members or their staff. Experts can seldom address directly other witnesses to challenge their data or interpretations, although this may be done in supplementary statements. As a result, when witnesses at a congressional hearing present conflicting testimony, it is often difficult to be certain which side, if either, is correct. Critical questions about the quality of data, assumptions made, and parameters used may be missing. Sometimes one or another witness may be wrong through an error of calculation or a false assumption; at other times adversaries may both be partially right, if their assumptions are explicated. It is these points of difficulty that have led the EDF to promote court challenges where rules of evidence and cross-examination are set. Consider, for

example, the following exchange from the Senate Agriculture
Committee's hearings on the pesticide bill:

"Mr. Sherman.  Thank you, Senator Allen, for sitting this
out.  I hope Dr. Hickey will remain while I comment on some
something he had just said.
"I have here an article from Nature, the Instructional Journal
of Science, for December 14, 1968.  It is entitled
'Polychlorinated Biphenyls in the Global Ecosystem.'  And I
would like to read about the peregrine falcon on which has
just been commented:
  'In both Great Britain and North American it was a decline
  of the peregrine falcon which initiated concern about the
  extent of the harmful effects of environmental
  contamination.  Breeding peregrines persist in
  approximately normal numbers in British Columbia and the
  Arctic.  In 1967 we collected an unhatched abandoned egg of
  a peregrine falcon in southwestern North American, where a
  small remnant population remains.  The analysis of this egg
  showed that it contained about 5 milligrams of DDT.
  Unknown peaks present in the chromatograms of the egg
  extract were unidentified until polychlorinated biphenyls
  (PCB) were detected in European wildlife.  Positive
  confirmation of their identification was accomplished by
  mass spectrometry in Sweden.  The retention times of the
  unknown peaks in the peregrine extract proved to be
  identical with those of several PCB compounds.'
And I have other information about ospreys, and the other
birds that are mentioned most prominently in the supposedly
endangered species.
  Senator Allen.  Thank you, Mr. Sherman, for your testimony.
I am sure the committee will give it serious consideration.
  Mr. Sherman.  PCB is something that Dr. Hickey did not take
into consideration.
  Mr. Hickey.  I would be glad to reply, Mr. Chairman.
  Mr. Sherman.  It was not mentioned in the testimony.  The
whole area he has glossed over and ignored is PCB.
  Senator Allen.  Dr. Hickey, you may have 3 minutes to
reply.
  Mr. Hickey.  The speaker's "mass of data" hardly included
even a single volume like this [indicating volume on the
peregrine falcon].  He neglected to mention in the paper by
Mulhern, et al., that about 10 percent of the bald eagles now
being found dead in the United States appear to have died from
dieldrin.
  PCB's indeed are interfering compounds with DDT and DDD.

We routinely check this out. This is part of the phenomenon
of studying the environment. And we find that the compound
that is present after we have allowed for PCB's is DDE. The
ratio of DDE to PCB runs about 1 to 1 in San Francisco Bay and
in Lake Michigan. In the sea birds of the North Atlantic the
ratio is 0.2, 0.3, and 0.4 to 1. So we are finding DDE in
substantial amounts in our ecosystems after allowing for this
interfering chemical.

With respect to the soil samples that were found to have
chlorinated hydrocarbons, insecticides, although they had been
collected before 1916, I should report that this study was
done at my university by the department of soil science at my
instigation. I had already run for these compounds fish
collected in 1926, and robins collected in 1938.

What they found, Mr. Chairman, in the soil study was that
indeed there were chemicals that looked like these compounds
at a part per billion basis.

Now, this is not anything like what we are reporting when
we look at our birds. Here is a rednecked grebe which we ran
in Wisconsin last summer, 647 parts per million of DDE on a
lipid basis. We are not talking about parts per billion.

It seems to me, therefore, that the pro-pesticide people
are violently exaggerating the intellectual traps which I
think we have successfully gotten around.

Mr. Sherman. Might I read just two sentences from this?

Senator Allen. Very well.

Mr. Sherman. 'The relatively small amounts of chlorinated
hydrcarbons required to produce this effect (of thin eggshell)
have made irrelevant much of the parts-per-million approach to
pollutant ecology based on toxic data alone.'

In other words, if you have either DDT of PCB, no matter
how much or how little, it still has this effect.

Mr. Hickey. You say, PCBs were reported at the lab last
year -

Senator Allen. Thank you, gentlemen. You may discuss it
to your heart's content, but let us leave it off the record.

We will place in the record at this point Mr. Sherman's
prepared statement, which will appear...as though read by
him." (75, pp. 404-405)

These observations do not mean congressional hearings are
ineffectual or poorly designed; they mean that these hearings
are not an ideal forum for scientific analysis, nor are they
intended to be. Legislating takes into account much more than
scientific variables - legislating subsumes economics,
politics, social forces, science, as well as the personal

predilections, hopes, and expectations of the law-makers.  For
policy-makers, then, the problem is one of trying to interpret
the contentions of scientists with differing viewpoints, and
how to relate them to other social, economic, and political
forces.

Two major controversies revolving around technical
conclusions arose at these hearings, but were never settled.
The members of the House Committee on Agriculture heard
several hundred pages of testimony on DDT and its
environmental effects.  Yet, when the Chairman Poage
introduced the committee's "clean" bill on the floor of the
House, he said:

"The witnesses who came before the committee included the
very top authorities throughout the country in the fields of
science, agriculture and conservation - the last group
including ecologists and environmentalists.  I might point out
that among these recognized experts there often were sharp
difference of opinion.  We had some testify that pesticides
had caused the loss of birds and fish in particular instances,
but we had equally authoritative witnesses emphatically
testify that there was no positive proof that pesticides had
caused these deaths.  We on the committee do not claim to
know." (80)

And indeed, as noted above, the hearing record does include
testimony as vigorously rejecting the hypothesis of DDT's egg
shell thinning effect as other testimony supports the
hypothesis.

On another important effect of pesticides, conflicting
assertions about tests on effects of pesticide exposure of
farmworkers re-entering fields were never resolved.
Representatives of farm labor organizations testified before
the Senate Committees on Agriculture and Forestry and on
Commerce that certain tests on farm laborers who re-entered
fields after they had been sprayed had revealed harmful
effects, and that the experiments themselves were unethical
and improperly done.  Rebuttals to these charges were
submitted to the record, but the actual situation and
implications of the tests were never made clear (75, part II,
pp. 317-348).

As the hearings did not provide a satisfactory resolution
of the controversies concerning the chronic effects of DDT nor
of the circumstances surrounding the farmworker tests, the
Congress used criteria other than the scientific method for
evaluating the issues.

Political scientists have observed that when Congressmen face conflicting technical testimony, they tend to resolve the different views not by scientific criteria, but by the application of common sense based on personal experience and by the economic test of the free marketplace. In one of the most famous cases, the so-called AD-X2 battery additive affair, several congressional committees became embroiled in the question of whether the additive actually rejuvenated batteries. Although National Bureau of Standards tests showed it did not, several Congressmen felt that the fact people bought the additive, used it, and bought more, proved the additive's worth (20, 81).

At the hearings on pesticides this tendency of laymen to rely on experience and the marketplace to answer highly technical questions was several times manifested. Listening to a witness assert the adverse effects of pesticides on birds, one Congressman, an orchardist, described an orchard frequently sprayed in which quail and cottontails abounded, and said that they "seem to have survived pretty well in this pesticide-infested ground." (68, pp. 226-227) At another point, he said he had sprayed "tons and tons of insecticides that you are demeaning today," and yet "I have lived reasonably long and I think I am reasonably healthy." (68, p. 110) Another Congressman based his argument on the apparent safety of 2,4,5-T on the grounds that economic forces require pesticides to be used safely; He said:

"...always the greatest test has been the economic test. If any of those ranchers felt there was any danger to those cattle, they sure wouldn't leave them on those pastures and spray them with 2,4,5-T; but they all do it, and there has been no known loss to livestock whatsoever that I have ever heard of." (68, p. 595, also p. 2; 82)

While Congressmen will naturally and necessarily consider non-scientific criteria in their decisions, the conflicting testimony also means that representatives of one or more interpretations of the data may feel that the legislators' decision does not adequately reflect their interpretation of the data.

Pesticides Innovation and Regulation The impact of the proposed legislation on the agrichemical industry also received attention at the hearings, especially the question of innovation. Most industry spokesmen contended that increasing testing costs diminished the attractiveness to industry of investing in pesticides research and development (R&D) at the

very time pest management experts need more specific
pesticidal chemicals that cause less environmental damage.

Mr. Naegele of Dow Chemical Co., at the House Agriculture
Committee hearings, developed this thesis most fully.  He
said that from 1956 to 1969, pesticide R&D costs increased 340
percent.  He noted the increasing numbers of required safety
evaluation requirements (68, p. 299).  He also observed that
requirements for testing meant that R&D funds often were
diverted to re-testing existing chemicals rather than used for
developing new pesticides.

In conclusion, Mr. Naegele named 12 companies which he
understood to have quit pesticide R&D and 5 others (including
Dow) which had cut back significantly.

Industry figures do indicate that pesticide R&D leveled off
in the late 1960s.  However, this reduction in R&D effort was
not limited to pesticides, but extended across to many of the
chemical industry programs (84), and thus the decline may
reflect a general chemical industry pattern and not
necessarily be related to regulation of this class of
chemicals.

Telling critique of these claims of diminishing returns on
pesticide R&D comes from an industry spokesman, Dr. George L.
Sutherland, Director of R&D for American Cyanamide's
Agricultural Division.  He stated in a talk before the
National Association of Farm Broadcasters that he

"emphatically [takes issue with the line of reasoning that]
escalating regulatory demands have made the cost of research
and development prohibitive, thus drying up any incentive to
go develop new agricultural chemicals...

...In the first place, [argues Dr. Sutherland,] new
regulations imposed since the creating of EPA affording better
protection to fish and wildlife were overdue.  More important
is the changing aspect of the marketplace, particularly in the
pesticide area.  Growers now have available to them many
first-rate products...many of these are quite inexpensive.
What the chemical people are really telling you is that while
research costs continue to rise, to come up with still better
compounds costing no more money than what's already being sold
is a tough proposition...the companies with weak research
organization, a shakey financial position, are dropping out.
They would rather have FDA and EPA take the rap rather than
acknowledge the overall problem." (85)

In any event, information in 1973 suggests that the
profitability of pesticides and their development is again

rising (47, pp. 251-252).

Alternatives To Pesticides Several alternatives to the use of
chemical pesticides, especially the persistent organochlorine
ones, were discussed at the hearings.  Mr. Roland Clement of
the Audubon Society proposed the use of more degradable
pesticides and the cultivation of more land as alternatives to
DDT (68, pp. 215-240).  Many alternative chemicals to DDT,
however, are more acutely toxic.  Dr. Crosby of the National
Canners Association pointed out that first class agricultural
land is limited and that production on poorer lands required
more expensive care.  Dr. Crosby also considered and rejected
the arguments that consumers would accept products with
greater insect damage (68, p. 538).

The development of biological controls was discussed, but
it was pointed out that continued use of chemicals was still
necessary (68, p. 141).  At the Senate hearings, however, the
need to develop integrated pest management systems was
emphasized by Sen. Nelson, Dr. van den Bosch, Chairman of the
Division of Biological Control, Department of Entomology and
Parisitology, University of California (Berkeley), and Mr.
Dietrick, who ran an integrated pest management firm.  They
contended that integrated pest management systems could reduce
chemical pesticide usage, increase farm profits, and extend
the length of time that chemicals would be effective when
needed (75).

What was not clearly addressed at the hearings, however,
was the extent to which the proposed legislation would both
facilitate the innovation of integrated pest management and
control adequately new types of pest control agents, such as
viruses and hormones.  In short, the hearings tended to focus
on the basic problems of second generation pesticides -
persistence and chronic effects and development of chemical
pesticides - and tended not to look forward to possible
problems emerging from the development and use of third
generation pesticides.

H.R. 10729 The House Agriculture Committee reported a "clean"
bill (H.R. 10729) (86).  It was based on the administration
proposals, but deleted the "use by permit only" category of
registration, so that use of pesticides posing health of
environmental hazards would be regulated through their
registration in the "restricted use" category, to be applied
by or under the direction of a certified applicator.  Also,
H.R. 10729 introduced a provision to indemnify persons owning
pesticides which were suspended; it expressly forbade use of
the criterion of essentiality in registration; and it
redefined who could seek judicial review.

Environmentalists felt the bill inadequate and supported a package of six amendments proposed by Rep. John G. Dow (D.-N.Y.).  These amendments were to make the bill more responsive to environmental problems.  Of the six, one amendment was adopted, to allow States to regulate "general use" pesticides, an authority pre-empted by H.R. 10729 as reported.  Five amendments were defeated:  to eliminate the section for indemnities when a pesticide was suspended; to retain FIFRA's wording that "any person who will be adversely affected" could file suit; to increase the input of environmental data in registration; to allow the administrator to refer to data concerning one application for registration in considering another application; to establish essentiality as a criterion; and to eliminate advisory committees.

These were to be major points of debate in subsequent hearings and amendments to H.R. 10729, which passed the House of Representatives on November 9, 1971 (87).

Following House passage of H.R. 10729, the revised Federal Environmental Pesticides Control Act of 1971, the Senate Agriculture and Forestry Committee's Subcommittee on General Research and Legislation re-opened its hearings.  Whereas the earlier hearings had gotten general views on the record, these new hearings focused on the House passed bill.  Witnesses addressed specific points, proposed deletions, amendments, and retentions.  After the hearings, the subcommittee drew up a list of every proposed amendment - 56 typewritten pages.  The Senate Committee made some 50 amendments to the House-passed bill.  Among these were the redefinition of essentiality, a revision of the suspension process, deletion of the indemnities provision, and a revision of the registration process.

After the Senate Agriculture and Forestry Committee reported H.R. 10729 (88), it was re-referred to the Commerce Committee.  This re-referral is a critical juncture in the development of pesticides policy, for it indicated that a new set of views, those represented on the Commerce Committee, had achieved legislative access to pesticides regulation.  The Subcommittee on the Environment had previously held hearings on the effects of pesticides on fish and on the effects of 2,4,5-T on man and the environment - a perspective generally viewed as pro-environment.  Now that subcommittee held hearings on H.R. 10729 and had an opportunity to amend the bill (89).

As indicating new forces having new effects of pesticides policy, the importance of this re-referral can hardly be over-emphasized.  The situation illustrates the problem of

conflicts of jurisdiction of congressional committees, and
shows how long it took for the environmental perspective to
achieve congressionally instituted input to regulatory
authority under FIFRA[*].

The re-referal was not simply a matter of the Commerce
Committee's desire and saying it had partial jurisdiction over
pesticides because of its environmental concerns.
Jurisdiction is a critical power of a committee.  According to
an article in the Washington Post (90) the re-referral
represented part of a trade (91, pp. 67-69).

The new input of the Senate Commerce Committee resulted in
improved access to the legislation of environmental and farm
labor groups.  The Commerce Committee reported H.R. 10729 with
numerous amendments (92), many of them based on the Nelson-
Hart proposals, including ones redefining adverse
environmental effects, protecting farm laborers, authorizing
citizen civil suits, and permitting local government control
of pesticides.  The Senate Agriculture and Forestry Committee
objected to many of the Commerce Committee amendments, and
prepared a supplemental report rebutting them (91).  In
subsequent negotiations between the two Senate Committees, a
compromise was worked out in which the redefinition of adverse
environmental effects was basically retained, but the
authorization for record-keeping by private applicators, local
regulation of pesticides, and specific reference to
farmworkers were deleted; other differences were compromised
(91, pp. 69-73; 93).  This compromise version unanimously
passed the Senate.

Then the bill went to a joint House-Senate conference in
which the differences between the House and Senate passed
versions were ironed out (94).  Generally, the final form of
the bill includes most of the Senate amendments, important
exceptions being the re-institution of indemnity payments, and
the deletion of citizen civil suits.  Other deletions included
a specific requirement that the administrator request all test
data, provisions providing more liberal disclosure of trade
secrets, and a prohibition against export of pesticides which
would cause unreasonable harm to the environment of the United
States.  The bill finally passed both House and Senate in the
last days of the 92nd Congress and was signed by President
Nixon on October 21, 1972 (P.L. 92-516).

--------------------------------------------------------------------

[*]It will be noted that in the House, the Agriculture Committee
maintained sole jurisdiction.

Federal Environmental Pesticide Control Act Of 1972 - P.L.
92-516 The Act which emerged from two years of concentrated
legislative activity, including hearings, debates, votes, and
conferences, was a collection of compromises among
agricultural, health, and environmental proponents.  Depending
on his point of view, a person can hear contentions that any
one side predominated.  The key provisions of P.L. 92-516 are
as follows (78):
Environment It explicitly provides for environmental
protection by prohibiting the registration of pesticides that
cause

"unreasonable adverse effects on the environment, [defined as]
any reasonable risk to man or the environment, taking into
account the economic, social, and environmental costs and
benefits of the use of any pesticide."

Registration It revises the process of registration in several
key ways.  Pesticides shipped intrastate are subject to the
Act.  Most important - one of the most critical innovations of
the Act - it provides for the registration of pesticides in
one (or both) of two categories:  for "general use" and
"restricted use."  "General use" pesticides are regulated much
as under previous law:  the label sets forth the uses, levels
of application, and appropriate warnings.  "Restricted use"
pesticides, however, can only be used by or under the direct
supervision of a certified applicator; or, in the case of
possible environmental harm, other restrictions as deemed
necessary by the Administrator of EPA.  Certification is to be
done through State programs under federal guidelines.  Unlike
FIFRA, the new Act makes illegal any use of a pesticide not in
accordance with the label - another critical innovation.
    Major issues in the development of FEPCA were the kinds of
data manufacturers had to provide for registration and its
public availability, and the extent to which it would be
proprietary.  The Act authorizes the Administrator of the EPA
to determine the data he wants.  Although the Commerce
Committee had provided that these data would be publically
available before registration, as desired by most
environmentalists, the Act provides that the EPA Administrator
must make the data (except proprietary information) available
within 30 days of registration.  And the Act provides a
mechanism by which the EPA Administrator can use test data
submitted for one registration in evaluating the registration
of another.  By this mechanism, if the Administrator uses the
data of one registrant in evaluating an application, the

manufacturer making application must pay a fee to the
registrant for the use of his data.  This provision means that
each applicant need not repeat tests of another, and is
designed to help protect a firm's investments in research and
development.

Another issue regarding registration was "essentiality."
Environmentalists have generally contended that pesticides
should be used only if essential.  Industry had generally
argued that if a pesticide met regulatory requirements, it
should be registered regardless of essentiality.  The problem
with essentiality as a criterion for registration is that it
does not account clearly for such factors as cost, nor for
action when several pesticides do the same job similarly.  The
House bill prohibited the EPA Administrator from considering
essentiality.  The Senate Agriculture and Forestry Committee
replaced the prohibition with a clause saying the
Administrator should not in preference register one pesticide
equal to another; the Senate Commerce Committee authorized the
word "essentiality" as a criterion.  The final bill includes
both the prohibition and the clause on not registering in
preference one of two equal pesticides, thereby implying this
as the sense of the prohibition.

The relationship of FEPCA to the States was the subject of
a House amendment, the only one to pass.  FEPCA applies to all
pesticides, including for the first time those shipped only
intrastate.  H.R. 10729, reported to the House, provided for
almost complete federal preemption of State regulation.  The
amendment that passed authorized State regulations if not less
strict than the federal ones.  The Senate Commerce Committee
proposed allowing local regulations too, but this was
defeated.  However, the final bill provides that states can
register pesticides for certain local needs if approved by
EPA.

Cancellation and Suspension Under prior law, actions to cancel
registrations often led to appeals that took many years to
resolve (e.g., DDT).  The new Act streamlines the process,
mainly by having the public hearing and the scientific
advisory committee occur simultaneously.  The hearing
examiner, if requested, can have scientific questions referred
to the advisory committee, which then prepares its report as
other questions are debated at the hearing.

One of the most hotly contested questions was the provision
for paying indemnities to owners of stocks of a pesticide for
which registration was suspended and cancelled.  The House
Agriculture Committee introduced this provision which was
proposed and supported by industry as a method of protecting

research and development investments.  An amendment to strike
this provision was defeated in the floor of the House.  The
Nixon Administration objected to the provision in the second
set of Senate Agriculture and Forestry Committee hearings.

That Senate Committee removed the indemnities and provided
added safeguards for industry in the process of suspension by
providing for an expedited hearing.  But the provision for
indemnities was re-inserted in the bill in conference,
although with a clause excluding a manufacturer who withheld
information.  Critics of the provision have argued that
indemnities lessen the manufacturer's responsibilities for
ensuring the safety of their products, and some have charged
that this provision will lead manufacturers to rush pesticides
into production without adequate testing, and that EPA, which
must pay the indemnities, will be hesitant to suspend them
because of the cost.  On the other hand, industry cannot
rush a product onto the market faster than EPA provides in its
requirements for data before registering it.  And its having
to pay indemnities might make it even more careful about
registering pesticides than otherwise.[*]

Inspection And Records FEPCA requires pesticides manufacturing
establishments to be registered with EPA, and authorizes EPA
to require certain records be kept and to enter establishments
to take samples and examine records.  This authority is new.
Citizen Action The rights of citizens in overseeing and
contesting actions concerning pesticide regulation have been a
major issue, though perhaps slightly less critically so since
EPA replaced USDA as the registering authority.  FIFRA, as
amended in 1964, authorized "any person who will be adversely
affected" to obtain judicial review.  H.R. 10729 as passed by
the House, changed the wording to "party at interest" - a
change of unknown implication.  Environmentalists wanted the
original wording; in the final bill, procedures for any
interested person to appeal are made clear.
Research And Monitoring FEPCA authorizes the EPA to conduct
research on pesticides, with a focus on integrated pest
management.  Also, EPA is directed to set up and conduct a
national monitoring program - a need long recognized but
inadequately met.
Funding And Implementation The Act spells out the process of

-----------------------------------------------------------------

[*] Sec. 15 of P.L. 92-516, which provides for indemnities, would
be repealed by a bill pending before the Senate of the 93rd
Congress [S. 426, Sec. 7(f)].

implementation. It will be completely in effect four years
after enactment. The authorization authority expires after
Fiscal Year 1975, so further legislation will be necessary at
that time.

One other provision, benefiting the registrant, appeared in
the conference report. Earlier forms of the bill included a
provision forbidding the EPA to require fees, except
appropriate registration fees. The bill as reported from
conference deleted all mention of fees and the conference
report said the conferees intended no fees whatsoever should
be charged, even for registration. EPA has complied with this
directive.*

## Recent Events
Farmworkers and Re-Entry Standards The formation of EPA and
the inclusion in it of the regulatory authorities for
pesticides from USDA and DHEW, as well as certain activities
formerly under USDI, seemed to tidy up management of
pesticides regulation. But just as EPA was being created, a
new interest was being institutionalized - farmworkers'
safety. It will be recalled that the Senate Committee on
Labor and Public Welfare held hearings on pesticides and
farmworkers. Under the authority of the Occupational Safety
and Health Act of 1970 (29 U.S.C. 655), reported by this
Committee, the Secretary of Labor can set standards for
exposure of farmworkers to pesticides. The Senate report on
the bill said that pesticides pose an "unmistakable danger"
and that "no effective controls presently exist over their
safe use and no effective protections against toxic exposure
of farmworkers or others in the rural populace (95). In his
environmental message of 1972, President Nixon said he was
directing the Secretary of Labor, in cooperation with DHEW, to
develop standards to protect farmworkers.

To develop re-entry standards, an advisory committee was
constituted under the Federal Working Group on Pest
Management; the DOL, EPA, USDA, and Council on Environmental
Quality (CEQ) were represented. After delays in getting
standards, in September 1972 the migrant Legal Action Program,
Inc., filed a petition with the Occupational Safety and Health
Administration requesting the promulgation of emergency

---------------------------------------------------------------

* However, EPA still charges fees for setting tolerances, as
this is required by the Food, Drug, and Cosmetic Act, and is
unaffected by FIFRA (48, pp. 595-596).

standards.

On May 1, 1973, the Occupational Safety and Health Administration (OSHA) published emergency temporary standards for exposure to organophosphate pesticides (96).  These were based on recommendations of an interdepartmental task force set up under the Federal Working Group on Integrated Pest Management, under the CEQ.  In terms of policy, while EPA coalesced the three major elements of pesticides regulations in 1970, a fourth had now emerged (see Figure 1), and had to be coordinated.

The new OSHA standards were vigorously attacked by many industrial representatives, mainly on the basis that costs would be prohibitive and that there was no emergency.  In an illustration of the inadequacies of data, the original Senate Report on OSHA gave figures of 800 killed and 80,000 injured by pesticides.  The validity of these figures has been strongly attacked, however.  A frequently cited alternative figure is 200 to 300 fatalities per year, based on the assumption that the known pesticide poisonings in the U.S. (collected by the Poison Control Center) represent perhaps 10 percent of all pesticides fatalities.  It is uncertain how accurate and complete occupational disease resulting from agricultural chemicals is diagnosed and reported.  Currently over 70 percent of all reported deaths resulting from agricultural chemicals result from accidental ingestion by children under 10, indicating the problem of household use of pesticides.  California has the best existing reports on pesticides poisonings; in that state between 1951 and 1969, 163 accidental deaths occurred, of which 35 were occupational occupationally incurred.  The EPA is planning to begin a comprehensive collection of data on pesticides poisonings. For a good review of the available data, from which the above figures were drawn, see SRI's analysis (5, pp. 95-104).

Numerous Congressmen objected to the re-entry standards, and the Senate amended its farm bill (S. 1888) to delay the effective date of the regulations until public hearings had been held and the results submitted to Congress (97).  In the House, the Agriculture Committee reported its farm bill (H.R. 8860) with a provision moving the authority for setting re-entry standards to USDA, a move obviously consistent with its jurisdiction; however, this provision was deleted on the floor.

OSHA suspended its proposed standards on June 15, 1973, saying the numerous petitions had been received and that "some modifications and clarifications of the provisions of the published standard seem to be necessary." (98)

What re-entry standards will utlimately be established
remains uncertain.  On June 21, 1973, the DOL promulgated
revised standards, reducing the number of pesticides affected
and, in several cases, the number of days for re-entry.
However, even these standards have been set aside by the Fifth
Circuit Court of Appeals.  But certainly a critical question
is going to be the relationship of this regulatory activity to
the regulatory actions of EPA.  It would seem rational to make
re-entry standards part of the requirements in registering a
pesticide, but the separation of legislative and statutory
authorities makes this difficult, unless an administrative
sponsored reorganization occurs, such as the one originally
creating EPA.

Implementation Of FEPCA

Rules And Regulations The EPA has laid out a plan (99) for
developing regulations to implement FEPCA.  These regulations
are critical to the impact of legislation.  Considering the
evolution of pesticides regulation under USDA, in which
actions were typically covert,* an important aspect of this
plan is its openness.  Numerous public meetings or hearings
are being held.

The author attended a public meeting on implementation of
legislation procedures on April 25, 1973, in Washington, D.C.
While 50 or 60 persons attended the meeting, only 5 made
public statements for the record.  As far as could be
ascertained, no federal agency other than EPA was represented,
and no environmentalists, conservationists, public interest
group representatives, or non-industry scientists attended.
There were representatives from three states and numerous
pesticide related trade organizations and firms.  For the most
part, the statements and questions were very general.

This meeting raised the question of which diverse interests
are really concerned about voicing their views on alternative
ways of implementing FEPCA.

Budget The Fiscal Year 1974 EPA budget reveals substantial
increases for "Abatement and Control" and for "Enforcement."
(See Table 9)  Much of these funds are to increase
registration personnel to meet the requirements for
re-registration and to register intra-state products, and to
increase personnel for field work, checking products and

---

* For example, in 1965 the USDA convened an ad hoc advisory
committee to review registration procedures and policy; the
committee and its report were not made public (61, pp. 248-
300, esp. p. 249).

Table 9   EPA Budget Authority for Pesticides (in $1,000) (101)

| Research and Development | | Abatement Control | | Enforcement | | Totals | |
|---|---|---|---|---|---|---|---|
| 1973 | 1974 | 1973 | 1974 | 1973 | 1974 | 1973 | 1974 |
| 5,252 | 5,441 | 14,112 | 17,224 | 1,626 | 2,808 | 20,990 | 25,473 |

taking samples.  The other main outlays will be for state
assistance in setting up certification programs and for
instituting a data system which will computerize registration
data and human health poisoning and accident data.  Funds for
pesticides research increase slightly.  This budget shows that
EPA's efforts will be increasingly devoted to regulation and
enforcement, proportionately less to research.

## Summary And Conclusions
Congress Where has Congress fitted into this evolution of
pesticides policy?  Two facts have clearly dominated.  First,
the jurisdiction of the Senate and House Agriculture
Committees had helped to keep the agricultural viewpoint
dominant in the face of mounting criticisms of pesticides
policy in the 1960s.  As legislation affecting FIFRA was
referred to the Agricultural Committees, they were in a
position to select what they would act upon.  Many proposals
for more stringently regulating pesticides* or for giving USDI
or DHEW a greater voice died in these committees.

Second, largely because the Senate and House Agriculture
Committees controlled legislation, the impact of other
viewpoints, insofar as it was expressed by Congress, tended to
come from oversight hearings.  Specific instances where over
oversight hearings led to USDA adjustment of policy can be
cited, for example in the cases discussed above - whether
wildlife are protected in the sense of FIFRA and in reviewing
the registration of lindane - but these are infrequent.
Nevertheless, these oversight hearings provided a forum for
other viewpoints, produced important compilations of data, and
exposed the way decisions were being made in a relatively

-----------------------------------------------------------------
*
 An example not previously mentioned is that in the 88th,
89th, and 90th Congresses the USDA proposed legislation
providing for registration of pesticide-producing
establishments; no committee action was taken.

closed policy-making process.

The 1970 creation of EPA, and the 1972 assertion of shared
jurisdiction over pesticides legislation by the Senate
Commerce Committee, indicate new patterns are emerging in the
old structure which evolved with the agricultural interests in
a commanding position.

But a more basic characteristic remains.  The combining
under one agency of the pesticides regulatory decisions
regarding health, environment, and agriculture occurred
administratively.  These three viewpoints had evolved
separately - in large part because of divergent committee
jurisdictions.  The institutionalization of the health and
environmental interests in the different committees and
agencies was a way of reducing the USDA's preponderance of
authority.  But the administrative re-organization creating
the EPA occurred without any concomitant change in the
committee jurisdictions.  H.R. 10729 added new criteria for
preventing chronic health and environmental hazards to FIFRA,
but it still fell under the Agriculture Committee's
jurisdiction.  H.R. 10729 did not amend the basic Act
regulating the health aspects of pesticides in foods (the
Food, Drug, and Cosmetic Act).  This separation of legislative
jurisdictions is now leading to a new regulatory focus.  The
issue of farmworker safety and of re-entry standards has
primarily become the responsibility of the committees with
labor jurisdictions; regulations are authorized under OSHA,
and they are administered by the Department of Labor.
Meanwhile, the mention of farmworkers in H.R. 10729 was
deleted.

Thus, the process of separate development of new interests
continues.  Pressures can now be expected to build for
coordination of the EPA's authorities and those of OSHA; but
the past shows how difficult it is to achieve centralized,
coordinated policies.  Justifying separation is the argument
(whether or not correct) that EPA is not sufficiently
concerned about farmworkers, while justifying centralization
is efficiency and making re-entry standards part of the
registration process.

While the new legislation in its revisions of FIFRA
reflects the growing, effective strength of the health and
environmental viewpoints, it leaves unanswered some basic
questions about regulation and about Congress' role.
Hearings The discussion of the hearings on FEPCA illustrate
the difficulties which can arise for congressmen when
"experts" present conflicting testimony on controversial
technical issues.  The difficulties are particularly acute

when clear-cut answers have significant policy implications - in the case of pesticides, the stringency of the legislation would be significantly affected by the certainty with which damage to the environment or to the public health could be identified.  But the committee members heard conflicting testimony, and lacking personal scientific competence to evaluate the contentions, they tended to interpret much of the information in the light of their personal experiences and of economic trade-offs.

While many science-policy observers have felt the Congress has not been able to handle highly technical information as well as would be desirable, suggestions for improvement have not been consistent or very effective (20, 54, 55, 81).

Dr. Alvin M. Weinberg, a scientist and administrator at Oak Ridge National Laboratories, has described how many "scientific" questions about chronic effects of low level environmental contaminants - such as pesticide residues - cannot be scientifically measured because tests cannot be large enough to give statistically significant answers. Therefore, other than scientific findings and values will be required to reach decisions.  Weinberg concludes that adversarial processes may be the solution in resolving these "trans-science" problems (54).

In discussing the problems of measuring the effects of 2,4,5-T, which has proved scientifically difficult (51), Weinberg explains the impediments to decision-making and proposes an adversarial procedure as follows:

"[the question] What is the effect on human health of very low levels of physical insult?  can be stated in scientific terms; it can, so to speak, be asked of science, yet it cannot be answered by science.  I have...proposed the name trans-scientific for such questions...

Let me use as an example of a trans-scientific question the problem of low-level radiation dose...  One may well ask, assuming the does-response curve to be linear down to zero dose, how large an experiment would be required to demonstrate empirically that 170 millirems...would increase the mutation rate by the 0.5 percent predicted by the linear dose-response theory.  The answer is that around $8 \times 10^9$ mice would be required to demonstrate a 0.5 percent level at the 95 percent confidence level.  So large an experiment is beyond practical comprehension.  The original question as stated is therefore, in my terminology, trans-scientific.

...Where low level effects are concerned, there will always be a trans-scientific residue.  To decide on standards when

science can say neither yea nor nay requires some procedure
other than the one usually used by scientists...Some version
of an adversarial procedure, whether formal...or informal...
probably is the best we now have the resolving the trans-
scientific questions that underly so many of the conflicts
between science and technology and society." (83)

Another scientist, Eugene Rabinowitch, who has been a close
observer of the policy-making process, contends however, that
serious problems arise when science is injected into
adversarial proceedings (55):

"In adversary proceedings in which science or one of its
applications (such as technology, medicine or psychiatry) are
involved, both sides enlist the cooperation of experts -
scientists for the prosecution and scientists for the defense,
scientists for the government and scientists for the
opposition.  This procedure makes a mockery of science; in
fact, it often comes dangerously close to its prostitution.
     Juries, parliaments and electorates, when called upon to
judge between contesting claims, often are unable to judge the
arguments of their scientific experts rationally, and often
rely on the impression the competing experts make on them, on
their formal credentials, and on the forensic quality and
vigor of their presentation."

But Rabinowitch's only solution to resolving disputed
scientific findings is an idealized unanimity which is not
necessarily consistent either with the personalities of all
scientists nor the processes - such as the congressional
hearing - of policy-making:

"Scientists, psychiatrists, physicians and technologists
should be asked to analyze a problem and to render their
conclusions, without advance presumption as to what point of
view they are to defend.  If, at a certain point, their
conclusions begin to be affected by extra-scientific reasons,
they must have sufficient intellectual honesty to state:  'Up
to this point, I spoke as a scientist; from here on, I will
speak also as a politically, ethically or ideologically
committed citizen.'
     A group of scientific experts, drawn from different
political, economic, ideological or religious backgrounds, can
be required to come up with a unanimous statement of the
scientific facts, followed by an agreed summary of different
opinions and suggestions derived from these facts with

differences explicitly attributed either to different
scientific assumptions or to different extra-scientific
commitments." (55)

Obviously, congressmen and their staffs could pose their
questions in wasy that would facilitate scientific debate.
Likewise, scientists could often be more explicit in setting
forth their technical findings and their policy conclusions
derived from them.  But the political interactions occurring
at the usual congressional committee hearing mean that
scientists who wish successfully to interject their findings
and conclusions into policy, need to respond to the whole
system to discover what channels - which committees and
agencies, or the courts - provide the best access to policy-
making.
Regulation FEPCA provides a general mandate for the regulation
of pesticides (Sec. 3(c)(5)), based on the definition of
"unreasonable adverse effects on the environment."  The
administrator is required to establish testing protocols and
to set standards for measuring when the use of pesticides may
cause "unreasonable adverse effects."  Given present
conditions, Congress is not capable of generating more
specific guidelines.  The legislative process is not equipped
to determine specific scientific issues.  Moreover, the
consequences of competing jurisdictions tends to result either
in one viewpoint dominating, or in long delays in balancing
the interests.
The Delaney Amendment does specify one criterion for
evaluating food additives - any chemical, used as an
intentional food additive, which in appropriate tests on man
or animal cuases cancers shall have a "zero tolerance."
Questions have been raised over the suitability of this
statutory requirement.  One view, often alleged by industrial
toxicologists and industrial consultants, is that "zero
tolerance" is an unscientific and impossible concept because
it is not related to the capabilities of measuring
technologies, and that most chemicals are carcinogenic if
large enough doses are given.  A contrary view held by the
overwhelming majority of independent professional cancer-
research workers and also by national cancer institute
scientists is that only a small proportion of chemicals are in
fact carcinogenic and that, for these, levels of residues
below which "no effects' occur cannot be determined.
Proposals have been made by industrial spokesmen to repeal the
Delaney Amendment, to retain it as is, and to extend it to
mutagens and teratogens (52, 102, 103, 104).  In the

legislative development of FEPCA, promulgating such standards
for regulation did not become an issue.  As legislation
affecting the Delaney Amendment would not fall under the
jurisdiction of the Senate and House Agriculture Committees,
no consideration was made of amending it.  But the controversy
over the clause illustrates the legislative problems.

However, Congressional actions on pesticides regulation
will significantly affect how standards are made.  First, by
authorizing regulation of use, FEPCA greatly expands the EPA's
means of controlling environmental residues.  Hitherto, only
by banning a pesticide could the administrator control the
dispersal of pesticides.  Now he can impose controls on use.
Second, the legislation authorizes more public input to
registration.  The USDA's years of successful unilateral
ignoring of challenges from the DHEW to its registration
decisions proved the need for better oversight.  The issue of
2,4,5-T specifically exemplified the need for truly
independent "outside" experts to be able to assess policies,
and the concomitant need for open policy-making in the agency.
The EPA's new rules, and now REPCA, will ensure that
registration will not be the domain of the closed group.

Pesticides Policy Pesticides policy has been continually
evolving.  The rise of the diverse interests and their
relative authorities are explicable in terms of the historical
development of institutionalization and access to policy.  In
hindsight, it is clear that evolution of the institutions and
their authorities did not keep pace with changes in
agriculture, social needs, and especially the technology of
pesticides – particularly the new factors of persistence,
environmental mobility, and potential chronic toxicity
introduced by the synthetic organic pesticides following World
War II.  By 1960, the balance of decision-making in pesticides
policy did not accurately reflect the full scope and weight of
the diverse interests.  If one takes the 1962 appearance of
Silent Spring as the identification of the problem, it took
exactly 10 years for comprehensive new legislation to be
enacted.  Depending on the information base and the viability
of alternative actions, 10 years may be a reasonable period
for significant social legislation.  But from another point of
view, it took 25 years to amend the 1947 Act so as to make it
fit the needs of the new synthetic organic pesticides.

The diversity of interests and the fragmented jurisdiction
of congressional committees also means that the EPA has a

problem maintaining the legitimacy of its decisions (3, p. 730).  Whether it cancelled the uses of DDT or retained them, EPA would be criticized.  Probably every action EPA takes in regulating pesticides will be criticized by someone:  its task will be in careful justification of each action.

The Future Although each diverse interest sees some shortcomings in the Federal Environmental Pesticide Control Act of 1972, the Act does provide a basis for regulating the second generation synthetic orgnaic chemicals.  But as integrated pest management techniques are developing to supplement and to replace in some cases chemical controls with cultural and biological controls, the question arises whether FEPCA provides adequately for this new generation of pesticide technologies.

Several new techniques of pest management utilizing viruses, bacteria, sterilants, insect hormones, and other materials are now in various stages of development.  Many tests for the health and environmental implications of chemicals are inappropriate for the biological and biological-chemical controls.  What tests are appropriate to deal with many of them are not yet well understood.  So the first question about FEPCA and third generation technologies of pest management is whether it provides adequate regulation to prevent undesired effects, just as FIFRA, as passed in 1947, provided inadequate regulations to deal with the new synthetic organic chemicals.

The second question follows from the first.  Most biological control techniques are not profitable for industry to develop, so the costs of developing, testing, registering, proving, and, in many cases, producing them must be borne by governmental agencies.  As FEPCA tends to be oriented towards providing a procedure for registering chemical pesticides produced as a part of commercial development and is less clear on procedures for dealing with biological controls produced in a non-profit setting, it may inhibit the development of the latter.  For where no clear procedures exist, delays seem inevitable while protocols are proposed and developed.  For the scientist who discovers a useful biological control techniques, registration delays would be demoralizing.  FEPCA does provide for experimental use permits and for research focused on integrated pest controls, but as integrated pest management techniques become more and more important and sophisticated, the way FEPCA is applied in registering

biological control agents will become critical.[*]  However,
with the EPA conducting registration under the Act,
implementation in the face of evolving pest control
technologies may be more flexible than in the past.


------------------------------------------------------------------

[*]
 EPA has recently acted to facilitate the introduction of the
first "viral pesticide":  upon a determination that "any
residues of the nuclear polyhedrosis virus which kills several
major insect pests of the cotton will not harm consumers...the
Agency has granted a petition filed by the International
Minerals and Chemical Corporation...exempting its Viron/H
product from the requirements for establishment of a residue
tolerance on cottonseed."  This was the first ruling on a
tolerance petition for a virus insecticide announced by the
Federal Government (105).

References

1.   Williams, C. M., "Third Generation Pesticides."
Scientific American 217:1, 13-17 (July, 1967).

2.   Newson, L. D., "The End of an Era and Future prospects
for Insect Control." Proceedings, Tall Timbers Conference on
Ecological Animal Control by Habitat Management, No. 2
(Tallahassee, Florida:  26-28, February, 1970), 117-136.

3.   Blodgett, J. E., and Musgrove, C. A., "Pesticides Use:
Trends and Problems," in U. S. Congress, House of
Representatives, Committee on Appropriations, Agriculture-
Environmental and Consumer Protection Appropriations for 1974.
93rd Congress, 1st Session, GPO, 1973, Part 5, pp. 995-1060.

4.   Environmental Protection Agency, Office of Water
Programs, "Patterns of Pesticide Use and Reduction in Use
Related to Social and Economic Factors." Washington, D.C.,
Nov. 1972.

5.   Stanford Research Institute, Environmental Indicators for
Pesticides.  Prepared for Council on Environmental Quality,
Washington, D. C., 1972.

6.   Department of Agriculture, Pesticide Review 1972 p. 24.

7.   Environmental Protection Agency, Office of Water
Programs, "The Use of Pesticides in Suburban Homes and Gardens
and Their Impact on the Aquatic Environment." Washington,
D.C., May, 1972.

8.   Davis, John J., A. Contribution to the History of
Commercial Pest Control.  Lafayette Ind., Purdue University,
1961, pp. 70, 82.

9.   Howard, L. O., A History of Applied Entomology.
Washington, D.C., Smithsonian Institution, November 29, 1930,
p. 64.

10.  Sanderson, R. D., "What Research in Economic Entomology
Is Legitimate under the Adams Act?" U.S. Department of
Agriculture, Entomology Bureau, Bulletin 67:77-78 (1907).

11.  Marlott, C. E., "Important Insecticides." U.S. Department
of Agriculture, Farmer's Bulletin No. 127, p. 40 (1901).

12.  Haywood, J. K., "Insecticides and Fungicides." U.S. Department of Agriculture, Farmer's Bulletin No. 146 (1901).

13.  Senate Committee on Government Operations, Pesticides and Public Policy, Report No. 1379, 89th Congress, 2nd Session, GPO, 1966, p. 69.  This document includes a "Legislative History of Federal Laws Regulating Economic Poison, 1910-1964, 1964," pp. 69-86.

14.  Department of Agriculture, Bureau of Entomology and Plant Quarantine, The Work of the Division of Insecticide Investigations, 1927-1939 p. 24 (November 1940).

15.  Weber, Gustavus A., The Food, Drug, and Insecticide Administration.  Baltimore, The Johns Hopkins Press, 1928, p. 54.

16.  Congressional Quarterly Service, Congress and the Nation. Washington, D.C., Congressional Quarterly Service, 1965, pp. 1160-1161.

17.  Quoted in E. C. Cushing, History of Entomology in World War II.  Washington, D.C.:  Smithsonian Institution, 1957, p. 42.

18.  American Chemical Society, Cleaning our Environment:  The Chemical Basis for Action, Washington, D. C.:  American Chemical Society, 1969, p. 195.

19.  Mitchell, L. E., "Pesticides:  Properties and Prognosis," in Organic Pesticides in the Environment, A. A. Rosen, and H. F. Kraybill, eds., Washington, D. C., American Chemical Society, 1966, p. 7.

20.  Library of Congress, Congressional Research Service, Technical Information for Congress, Report to the Subcommittee on Science, Research, and Development of the House Committee on Science and Astronautics, 91st Congress, 1st Session, GPO, April 25, 1969.  Committee Print. Chapter 15.

21.  Senate Committee on Government Operations, Subcommittee on Reorganization and International Organizations, Hearings on Environmental Hazards Coordination (Pesticides), 88th Congress, 2nd Session, GPO).

22.  21 USC 348(c)(A) (1970 edition).

23.  Fenno, Richard F., Jr., The President's Cabinet.  New York, Random House (Vintage Books), 1959, pp. 141-154.

24.  House Committee on Appropriations, Subcommittee on Agriculture Hearings on Department of Agriculture for 1961, 86th Congress, 2nd Session, GPO, 1961, part 5.

25.  House Committee on Merchant Marine and Fisheries, Subcommittee on Fisheries and Wildlife, Hearings on Pesticide Controls, 88th Congress, 1st Session, GPO, 1963, p. 69.

26.  House Committee on Merchant Marine and Fisheries, Subcommittee on Fisheries and Wildlife, Hearings on Coordination of Pesticide Programs, 86th Congress, 2nd Session, GPO, 1960, p. 56.

27.  Carson, Rachel, Silent Spring.  Boston, Houghton Mifflin, 1962.

28.  Baldwin, I. L., "Chemicals and Pests."  Science 137:1042-1043 (September 28, 1962).

29.  Cited in Frank Graham, Since Silent Spring.  Boston, Houghton Mifflin, 1970, p. 39.

30.  Darby, William J., "Silence, Miss Carson."  Chemical & Engineering News 40:60-63 (Oct. 1, 1962).

31.  Supra 29.

32.  President's Science Advisory Committee, "Use of Pesticides."  Washington, D. C., The White House, April 15, 1963.

33.  Greenberg, D. S., "Pesticides:  White House Advisory Body Issues Report Recommending Steps to Reduce Hazards to the Public."  Science 140:878 (May 24, 1963).

34.  House Committee on Agriculture, Hearings on Administration of Pesticides Laws and Regulations, 88th Congress, 2nd Session, GPO, 1964, pp. 8-9.

35.  Congressional Quarterly Service, Congressional Quarterly Almanac.  Washington, D. C.:  Congressional Quarterly Service, 1964, vol. XX, p. 142.

36.  Anon., "Memorandum of Conference, 26 April 1961," Files of Federal Committee on Pest Control, FCC (Interdepartmental Pesticide Agreement, vol. I. 1945-1964.

37.  House Committee on Agriculture, Hearings on Registration of Economic Poisons, 88th Congress, 1st Session, GPO, 1963, p. 35.

38.  Gunther, Francis A., "Advances in Analytical Detection of Pesticides," in Scientific Aspects of Pest Control, Washington, D. C., NAS-NRC, 1966, pp. 276-302.

39.  National Academy of Sciences - National Research Council, Pesticides Residues Committee, Report, Washington, D. C., NAS-NRC, 1965.

40.  Federal Register, 31:5723-5724 (April 3, 1966).

41.  House Committee on Appropriations, Hearings on Department of Agriculture and Related Agencies Appropriations for 1968, part 2, pp. 321-329, and ibid., Agricultural - Environmental and Consumer Protection Appropriations for 1974, part 2, pp. 466-473.

42.  President's Science Advisory Committee, Task Force on Environmental Pollution, "Restoring the Quality of Our Environment," Washington, D. C., The White House, 1965.

43.  Pimentel, David, "Ecological Effects of Pesticides on Non-Target Species." Washington, D. C., Office of Science and Technology, June, 1971.

44.  House Committee on Appropriations, Subcommittee on Agriculture, Hearings on Department of Agriculture Appropriations for 1971, 91st Congress, 2nd Session, GPO, 1970 1970, part 2, p. 283.

45.  Decker, George C., "Pesticide Lack Means an Inadequate Food Supply." Agricultural Chemicals vol. VI, p. 40 (June 1951).

46.  House Committee on Merchant Marine and Fisheries, Hearings on Miscellaneous Fisheries and Wildlife Legislation - 1965, 89th Congress, 1st Session, GPO, 1965, p. 99.

47. Bennett, Ivan, preface, Pesticides Monitoring Journal vol. 1, no. 1 (June, 1967).

48. House Committee on Appropriations, Hearings on Agricultural-Environmental and Consumer Protection Appropriation for 1974 (Supra 3), pp. 547-554.

49. Senate Committee on Commerce, Subcommittee on Environment, Hearings on the Effects of 2,4,5-T on Man and the Environment, 91st Congress, 2nd Session, GPO, 1970, parts I and II.

50. Helling, C. S., et al., "Chlorodioxins in Pesticides, Soils, and Plants." Journal of Environmental Quality 2:2, 173-178 (1973).

51. Sterling, T. D., "Difficulties of Evaluating the Toxicity and Teratogenicity of 2,4,5-T from Existing Animal Experiments." Science 174:1355-1359 (Dec. 24, 1971).

52. Department of Health, Education, and Welfare, Secretary's Report on Pesticides and Their Relationship to Environmental Health, GPO, Dec. 1969.

53. Epstein, S. S., "Environmental Pathology." The American Journal of Pathology 66:353-373 (Feb. 1972).

54. Weinberg, Alvin, "Science and Trans-Science." Minerva 5:208-222 (April 1972).

55. Rabinowitch, Eugene, "Back into the Bottle." Science and Public Affairs April 1973, 19-23.

56. Pimentel, David, "Realities of a Pesticide Ban." Environment 15:18-20, 25-31 (March 1973).

57. Council on Environmental Quality, Integrated Pest Management, Washington, D. C. (1972).

58. Smith, R. F., and van der Bosch, R., "Integrated Control," in Pest Control, by W. Kilgore and R. Doutt, eds., New York, Academic Press (1971).

59. Doutt, R. L. and Smith, R. F., "The Pesticide Syndrome-Diagnosis and Suggested Prophylaxis," in Biological Control, C. B. Huffaker, ed., New York, Plenum Press (1971).

60.  Department of Agriculture, Economic Research Service, _Quantities of Pesticides Used by Farmers in 1966_.

61.  House Committee on Government Operations, Subcommittee on Intergovernmental Relations, _Hearings on Deficiencies in Administration of Federal Insecticide, Fungicide, and Ro Rodenticide Act_, 91st Congress, 1st Session, GPO, 1969, pp. 141-217.

62.  House Committee on Government Operations, _Deficiencies in Administration of Federal Insecticide, Fungicide, and Rodenticide Act_, 91st Congress, 1st Session, House Report No. 91-637.

63.  Rodgers, William H., Jr., "The Persistent Problem of Persistent Pesticides:  A Lesson in Environmental Law." _Columbia Law Review_ 70:567ff.(April 1970).

64.  Senate Committee on Commerce, Subcommittee on Energy, Natural Resources, and the Environment, _Hearings on the Effects of Pesticides on Sport and Commercial Fisheries_, 91st Congress, 1st Session, GPO, 1966, part I and II.

65.  Senate Committee on Labor and Public Welfare, Subcommittee on Migratory Labor, _Hearings on Migrant and Seasonal Farmworker Powerlessness_, 91st Congress, 1st and 2nd Sessions, GPO, 1969, part 6, "Pesticides and the Farmworker."

66.  Carter, Luther J., "Environmental Law." _Science_ 179: 1205-1209, 1310, 1312, 1350 (March 23 and 30, 1973).

67.  Whitten, Jamie L., _That We May Live_.  Princeton, M. J., Van Nostrand (1966).

68.  House Committee on Agriculture, _Hearings on Federal Environmental Pesticide Control Act of 1971_, 92nd Congress, 1st Session, GPO, 1971.

69.  Environmental Protection Agency, "Reasons Underlying the Registration Decision concerning Products Containing DDT, 2,4,5-T, Aldrin and Dieldrin" (March 13, 1971), mimeo.

70.  ----- , 2,4,5-T Committee _Report_ (Washington, D. C.: 1971).

71.  <u>Federal Register</u> 36:9476 (May 11, 1972), amended in <u>ibid</u>. 38:8670 (April 5, 1972).

72.  Sweeney, Edmund S., <u>Consolidated DDT Hearings:  Hearing Examiner's Recommended Findings Conclusions, and Orders</u>. Washington, D. C., EPA, 1972.

73.  Administrator, EPA, <u>Consolidated DDT Hearings-Opinion</u> of the Administrator, Washington, D. C., 1972, p. 28.

74.  Rodolfo, N. Salcedo et al., <u>Improving the Communication Adequacy of Pesticide Labels, Phase 1 Summary Report</u>, Agricultural Communication Research Report 25, University of Illinois, Urbana-Champaign, January 1971.

75.  House Committee on Agriculture and Forestry, Subcommittee on Agricultural Research and General Legislation, <u>Hearing on Federal Environmental Pesticide Control Act</u>, 92nd Congress, 1st and 2nd Session, GPO, 1972, part I and II.

76.  Wellford, Harrison, <u>Sowing the Wind</u>.  New York, Grossman (1972), pp. 244-245.

77.  See, for example, R. W. Stark and R. F. Smith, "System Analysis and Pest Management," in <u>Biological Control</u>, supra 59.

78.  For a review of these hearings and the resulting legislation, see John E. Blodgett and Connie A. Musgrove, "Pesticides," in U. S. Congress Committee on Interior and Insular Affairs, <u>Congress and the Nation's Environment</u>, 93rd Congress, 1st Session, committee print, pp. 703-736.

79.  H.R. 4152, S. 745, of the 92nd Congress.

80.  <u>Congressional Record</u> 117:168 H10675 (Nov. 8, 1971, daily ed.

81.  Lamson, Robert, <u>Scientists and Congressmen</u>.  University of Chicago, Ph.D. Thesis, 1960.

82.  For other examples in the pesticides policy area in which a Congressman resolved differing "scientific" contentions on the basis of common sense, see:  U. S. Congress, Committee on Agriculture, Hearings on Administration of Pesticide Laws and Regulations, 88th Congress, 2nd Session, GPO, 1964, pp. 32-33.

Also see Congressional Record, 119:S10748 (June 8, 1973, daily edition).

83.  Weinberg, Alvin M., "Letters," Science 174:546-547 (Nov. 5, 1971).

84.  -----, Chemical & Engineering News, June 5, 1972, pp. 45-46.

85.  Sutherland, G. L., "Agriculture Is Our Best Bargaining Tool." Farm Chemicals 135:44 (Sept. 1972).

86.  House Committee on Agriculture, Federal Environmental Pesticide Control Act of 1971.  Report to accompany H.R. 10729 (Sept. 25, 1971), 92nd Congress, 1st Session, House Report No. 92-511.

87.  Congressional Record, 117:H10674-H10680, H10726-H10774 (Nov. 8 and 9, 1971, daily ed.).

88.  Senate Committee on Agriculture and Forestry, Pesticide Control.  Report to accompany H.R. 10729, June 7, 1972, 92nd Congress, 2nd Session:  Senate Report No. 92-838.

89.  Senate Committee on Commerce, Subcommittee on Environment, Hearings on Federal Environmental Pesticide Control Act of 1971, 92nd Congress, 1st Session, GPO, 1972.

90.  Cohn, Victor, "2 Senators Yield on Meat, Pest Bills." The Washington Post (June 7, 1972.

91.  Senate Committee on Agriculture and Forestry, Protection of Man and the Environment.  Supplemental Report on H.R. 10729, Oct. 3, 1972, 92nd Congress, 2nd Session:  Senate Report No. 92-838, part II.

92.  Senate Committee on Commerce, Federal Environmental Pesticide Control Act of 1972.  Report to accompany H.R. 10729, 92nd Congress, 2nd Session:  Senate Report No. 92-970.

93.  For comments by Leonard Bickwitt, staff counsel of the Commerce Committee's Subcommittee on the Environment, concerning the pressures he was under, see Congressional Quarterly, Weekly Report, vol. XXX (October 14, 1972), pp. 2637-2638.

94.  House Committee of Conference, Federal Environmental
Pesticide Control Act.  Report to accompany H.R. 10729, (Oct.
5, 1972, 92nd Congress, 2nd Session:  House Report No. 92-
1540.

95.  Senate Committee on Labor and Public Welfare, Report
(1970), 91st Congress, 2nd Session:  Senate Report No. 91-
1282.

96.  Federal Register 38:10715-10720 (May 1973).

97.  Congressional Record 117:S10747-S10748 (June 8, 1973,
daily edition).

98.  Federal Register vol. 38 (June 15, 1973).

99.  Environmental Protection Agency, "Implementation Plan,
Pesticide Control Act."  Federal Register, 38:1142-1145
(January 9, 1973).

100.  ------, "Pesticide Control Act Implementation Plan."
Federal Register 38:3002-3003 (January 31, 1973).

101.  -----, Environmental News (January 29, 1973).

102.  Stokinger, H. E., "Sanity in Research and Evaluation of
Environmental Health."  Science 174:664 (Nov. 12, 1971).

103.  Culliton, B. J., "Delaney Clause:  Defended against an
Uncertain Threat of Change."  Science 179:666-667 (February
16, 1973).

104.  Epstein, S. S., "The Scientific Basis of the Delaney
Amendment."  New York Academy of Sciences (Jan. 15, 16, 1973),
mimeo.

# 5

## PRINCIPLES OF FOOD ADDITIVE REGULATION

James Turner

CONTENTS

Introduction
The White House Conference on Food Nutrition and Health, held
in December of 1969, focused some attention on the safety of
chemicals added to food.  The Food Safety Panel of the
conference correctly pointed out that

"it is not possible to determine with absolute certainty the
safety of the ever-increasing number of chemicals added to or
present in our foods." (1)

Critics of the increasing use of chemicals added to food,
as well as defenders of this practice, agree that proof of
"absolute" safety of food chemicals is beyond the capability
of reasonable scientific methods.  The debate between
defenders and critics of food additive use revolves around how
this fact is viewed by the various affected interests.
Critics tend to view the limitations on the proof of safety
as a warning against too readily adding chemicals to food.
They argue that if chemicals turn out to be unsafe after they
have been widely used, the damage they cause by increasing the
amount of cancer, the number of birth defects, or the
prevalence of genetic damage can never be undone.
Defenders of current food additive policies of the Federal
Government and the food industry aruge that since absolute
safety cannot be proved, every additive is suspect.  They
argue from the extreme position that if strict safety
standards urged by critics are followed then nearly all food
additives will eventually be banned.  The issues revolve
around the opposite conclusions drawn by two opposing sets of
advocates from the fact that safety is an illusory concept.
The problem is thus to develop a mechanism to adjudicate the
various food chemical controversies in a way that will
minimize their attendant risks to the public while not
unreasonably restricting those beneficial uses that food
chemicals can sometimes serve.
During the deliberations of the Food Safety Panel, between
July and December 1969, the Secretary of Health, Education and
Welfare banned the artificial sweetener cyclamate.  In
November 1969, less than a month after the cyclamate ban, the
manufacturers of baby foods voluntarily agreed to remove
monosodium glutamate from their products.  Early in 1970, the
Food and Drug Administration (FDA) removed brominated
vegetable oil from the list of food chemicals "generally
recognized as safe" (GRAS).
Since then, food additive controversies have been regular
occurrences.  Scientists announced that nitrite could combine

with other chemicals in the body to form nitrosamines, a potent class of cancer-causing agents (2). The food color FD&C Red No. 2 also caused fetal deaths in experimental animals. Both these findings led to heated debates which still continue today. The FDA later banned Violet No. 1, a color used in candy and easter egg dye and to mark meats as prime or choice. Animals tested on sacharrin developed cancer, causing the FDA to seek the advice of the National Academy of Sciences (NAS) as to whether it also should be banned.

In 1972 Sen. Gaylord Nelson (D.-Wis.) introduced a proposed new food additives bill. His concern was based on indications that the food additive industry would massively expand in the next 10 years. Citing papers presented at the 161st American Chemical Society meeting in 1971, the Senator pointed out that the food additive industry was expected to grow from $500 million in 1972 to $756 million by 1980.

A break down of the projected figures suggested a growth trend in the use of food additives (both old and new additives) between 1971 and 1980 as follows: flavoring materials, 50 percent; stabilizers, 50 percent; surfactants, 40 percent; flavor enhancers or potentiators, 100 percent; acidulatants, 60 percent; synthetic sweeteners and bitter agents, 60 percent; antioxidants, 100 percent; and preservatives, 67 percent. With such projections, it seems likely that the controversy over food additives will also continue to grow.

The American battle for control over additives to food began in the 1880s with the introduction of several pure food bills. Dr. Harvey W. Wiley, Chief of the Bureau of Chemistry in the United States Department of Agriculture (USDA), led the agitation for a food protection law. In 1906, after more than twenty years of struggle, Dr. Wiley succeeded in getting the Congress to enact the Pure Food and Drug Act of 1906. Important legislative and organizational steps affecting food additive regulation for the next half-century came in the following order:

1906
Passage of the Pure Food and Drug Act of 1906 assigning regulatory authority directly to the Bureau of Chemistry in USDA.
1912
Dr. Wiley left the Bureau of Chemistry, categorizing it as ineffective because of the policies of the Roosevelt and Taft Administrations.

1927
Bureau reorganized with regulatory function assigned to a new
Food, Drug and Insecticide Administration of USDA
1931
The food regulating arm of USDA renamed Food and Drug
Administration.
1938
Food, Drug and Cosmetic Act of 1938 passed by the Congress and
Pure Food and Drug Act of 1906 repealed.
1941
FDA transferred to the Federal Security Administration
1950-53
Hearings of the House Select Committee to Investigate the Use
of Chemicals in Food Products, Chaired by Congressman James
Delaney of New York (3).
1954
FDA became part of the newly created Department of Health,
Education and Welfare, which took over most of the major
functions of the Federal Security Administration.
1954
The Congress passed the Pesticide Amendments of 1954.
1958
The Congress passed the Food Additive Amendments of 1958.
1960
The Congress passed the Color Additive Amendments of 1960.

The FDA also has been given wide authority to regulate
animal drugs - drugs used in animal feeds, as well as in
direct application to animals to enhance growth and control
disease - which often find their way into finished animal food
products.  The amount of legislative and regulatory action on
food and drug regulation over the past 70 years suggests a
widespread public concern about the need for a safe food
supply.  Sorting out the details of this concern and the
resulting legal efforts can help provide guidelines for new
efforts to control food additives.

Food Additive Laws
On three separate occasions within the past seventy years the
Congress has attempted to establish a national policy
concerning the addition of chemicals to food.  As mentioned,
in 1906 the Congress enacted the first Pure Food Act (4).
Subsequently, in 1938 it enacted the Food, Drug and Cosmetic
Act (5) and between 1954 and 1960 three amendments to the 1938
Act were enacted, designed to control the addition of
chemicals to the food supply.

The first of these, the Pesticide Amendments of 1954 (6), established the authority to set limits on the amount of pesticide residue allowed in food.  The second, the Food Additive Amendments of 1958 (7), established procedures for the addition to foods of chemicals other than colors.  The third, the Color Additive Amendments of 1960 (8), established similar procedures for color additives.

The pesticide, food additive, and color additive amendments to the 1938 Food, Drug and Cosmetic Act each became the responsibility of the Department of Health, Education, and Welfare (DHEW) and, in turn, the Food and Drug Administration (FDA).  All these amendments resulted from a series of hearings held by the House of Representatives Temporary Select Committee to Investigate the Use of Chemicals in Food Products (3).  Rep. James J. Delaney (D.-N.Y.), currently (1973) a member of the House Rules Committee, chaired that committee.

Each of these congressional efforts to set statutory food additive policy turned out to be less than effective, requiring subsequent amendments.  Currently, the Congress once again has under consideration an effort to revise national food additive policy.*  Understanding how past efforts have failed can aid evaluation of present proposals.

The Pure Food Act of 1906 (4) The 1906 Act developed an apparently straightforward approach to the food additive problem.  It defined as "adulterated" any food that "contained any added poisonous or other deleterious ingredient which could render such article injurious to health." (4)  The Act also barred any adulterated food from interstate commerce (4). But this simple provision presented several difficult regulatory problems.

First, the law contained no provision for establishing safe quantities of added poisonous[†] or deleterious ingredients. The Congress assumed that ingredients added to food fell into

---

* The author of this article worked with the staff of Senator Nelson in the preparation of these bills.  They are S. 76 and 3163 (1972) and were the subject of Hearings by the Select Committee on Nutrition and Human Needs in October of 1972.

[†] Webster's New International Dictionary (2nd ed. 1957) defines "poisonous" as "having the properties or effects of poison"; i.e., "any agent which, introduced...into an organism, may chemically produce an injurious or deadly effect."  It defines "deleterious" as "hurtful," "noxious," i.e., "unwholesome."

the easily identified categories: "safe" or "unsafe."  The
Act required law enforcement officials to remove from
interstate commerce any food that contained any intentionally
added poisonous or deleterious substance - no matter how small
the amount and no matter the reason for its addition.

Second, the Act did not allow regulatory action against a
food merely because it contained an added poisonous or
deleterious substance.  The food itself - combined with the
substance - had to be proven injurious to health.

Third, the Act required the agency to ignore the
accumulated presence of any unintentionally added poisonous or
deleterious substance occurring the food supply.  If a food
containing such substance did not injure health, the agency
could take no action against it, even if so many foods
contained the same chemical that their accumulated intake
posed a serious hazard.

Therefore, the Act failed in its effort to protect the food
supply from unwanted chemicals.  It forced the agency
enforcing it to make a chemical-by-chemical, food-by-food
determination of safety.  This task was impossible.  In its
1933 Annual Report the FDA, by then responsible for
enforcement, explained, why the food additive provisions could
not be enforced:

"A complete elimination of all poisonous substances in foods
is in some instances impossible.  Where the presence of
poisons is unavoidable their quantities must be kept so low
that by no possibility will the food be harmful to the user.
Where they may be dangerous in any quantity they should be
absolutely prohibited.  The present statute contains no
provision authorizing either the complete prohibition of
traces of poison in foods or the establishment of tolerances
for poisons.  On the contrary, it imposes upon the government
the obligation of showing affirmatively in every instance
that a food containing an added poisonous ingredient may be
harmful to health under the conditions of use.  The problem
of establishing possible poisonous effects as a result of the
consumption of minute quantities of poisonous ingredients in
foods presents extreme difficulties.  Without such proof a
food containing an added poison cannot be condemned as
adulterated.  The government is not permitted in establishing
its case under the terms of the present statute to take into
consideration similar poisons in other items of the diet,
although these may contribute to the total intake of the
poison and be an important factor in determining the relative
harmfulness of the adulterant." (9)

The Congress had based the 1906 Act on the concept, agreed by all parties to the debate, that the safety of ingredients added to foods could be scientifically established. As a result, the Act allowed the addition to the food supply of any substance not shown to be unsafe. It also allowed the addition of chemicals, even when shown to be unsafe, provided such addition did not make the food product itself unsafe. It required the Federal Government to demonstrate, on a case by case method, that a food containing an unsafe substance was safe itself, before taking action to restrict its sale. In every case, the agency bore the burden of proof. On the other hand, the food industry objected to the 1906 Act because the government could not set tolerances for chemicals used in the "proper" manufacture of foods which subsequently wound up in the finished product.

Soon after passage of the 1906 Act, the various difficulties with its enforcement led President Roosevelt to appoint two committees to oversee the work of Dr. Wiley and the USDA's Bureau of Chemistry. One committee, the Referee Board of Consulting Scientific Experts, was chaired by Ira Remsen, President of Johns Hopkins University and the discoverer of saccharin. On the other hand, Dr. Wiley believed that the use of saccharin should be restricted because its use misled the public into excess prices for products sweetened with a cheap chemical.

The second committee, the Board of Food and Drug Inspection, was chaired by Dr. Wiley. This Board, however, had three members, two of whom generally opposed Dr. Wiley's regulatory decisions. They were the Solicitor of the USDA and Dr. Wiley's Associate Director of the USDA's Bureau of Chemistry. Both these individuals organized a bureaucratic campaign to take over Dr. Wiley's job. Thus, Dr. Wiley was faced with two committees controlled by his avowed adversaries.

Technically, the 1906 Act conferred its authority directly to the Bureau of Chemistry for the seizure of unsafe food containing added poisonous or deleterious substances shipped in interstate commerce. Dr. Wiley vigorously, almost religiously, pursued this mandate. However, the two committees appointed by the President to oversee administration of the 1906 Act claimed the right, although not a statutory right, to review his proposed actions.

As a consequence some two-thirds of Dr. Wiley's regulatory decisions were reversed by these committees. In 1912, he resigned from government (to found the Good Housekeeping Institute, of "Seal of Approval" fame) and condemned the 1906

Act and the Bureau of Chemistry that he had labored for more
than thirty years to build.  For the next twenty years
lethargy, reorganization, and congressional dissatisfaction
plagued the federal food protection agency.

By 1933, enforcement of the food additive section of the
1906 Act had completely broken down.  Before a food could be
barred from national markets, the Federal government had the
obligation to show affirmatively that it contained added
poisonous or deleterious substances which might be harmful
under normal conditions of use.  In 1933, the Congress
considered new legislation designed to meet the regulatory
difficulties.  In 1938, after five years of debate, the
Congress passed the Federal Food, Drug and Cosmetic (FFDC) Act
which contained new authority to regulate food additives.

The Food, Drug and Cosmetic Act of 1938 (5) The drafters of
the 1938 Act considered them as straightforward in approach as
their predecessor.  The 1938 Act attempted to deal with each
of the weaknesses of its forerunner.  An effort was made to
eliminate the impossible burden of proof placed on the FDA by
providing a definition of the term "unsafe" and by changing
basic food protection procedures.  In place of the 1906 Act's
flat prohibition of added poisonous and deleterious substances
that rendered a food injurious to health, the Congress
substituted the following process:

First, the Act [Sec. 402(a)] redefined "adulteration,"
stating

"A food shall be deemed to be adulterated...if it bears or
contains any added poisonous or added deleterious substance
which is unsafe." (5)

Second, any "unsafe substance" was defined [Sec. 406(a)] as

"Any poisonous or deleterious substance added to any food,
except where the substance is required in the production
thereof or cannot be avoided by good manufacturing practices
shall be deemed to be unsafe..." (4)

Third, within the definition of "unsafe," allowance was
made for the setting of tolerance for the addition of small
amounts found to be unavoidable in the processing of chemicals
in foods (5).

The basis of this statutory policy was to eliminate the
need to show a food injurious to health, to allow the setting
of tolerances, and to limit the use of food additives to only

those "required" in the production of food or unavoidable "by
good manufacturing practice."  Poisonous or deleterious
substances were to be severely restricted.  The FDA was to
seize any food containing them in excess of the tolerances
established.  In defining the word "safe," the Congress sought
to alleviate the problems caused the FDA by its heavy burden
of proof and the former case-by-case approach to enforcement
under the old law.

Soon, however, the administrators of the new law found that
they were no better off than they had been under the old law.
Before any of the new provisions of the 1938 Act could be used
to restrict the use of a food additive the FDA had to <u>show</u>
that the chemicals of concern were poisonous or deleterious:

"Under the law, as it was...(after 1938), the FDA could not
stop the use of a chemical simply because it was questionable
or had not been adequately tested.  It was necessary to be
able to prove in court that the chemical was poisonous or
deleterious." (10)

The difficulty of applying the Acts approach (Sec. 406) to
various chemicals arose because the drafters of the section
attempted to define an acceptable level of human risk by
using the terms "safe" and "unsafe."  The legislative history
of the 1938 Act shows that to the Congress the words
"poisonous" and "deleterious" meant unsafe.

Understood in this way, the heart of the 1938 food
protection law (Sec. 402 and 406) form a legal non sequitur.
The circular nature of the food protection device in the Act
becomes evident when the word "unsafe" is substituted for the
terms "poisonous" or "deleterious."  Then the Act reads:

"A food shall be deemed to be adulterated...if it bears or
contains any added unsafe substance which is unsafe within the
meaning of Sec. 406." [Sec. 402(a)(2)]

In turn, Section 406 would read:

"Any unsafe substance added to any food, except where such
substance is required in the production thereof or cannot be
avoided by good manufacturing practice shall be deemed to be
unsafe..."

The Congress had attempted to devise a formula for
establishing tolerances for poisonous - unsafe - ingredients
in food.  However, because the term unsafe was defined

circularly, the FDA was forced to prove, in each instance, the
poisonous or deleterious nature of a chemical.  If the FDA
could not meet this burden of proof, the tolerance provision
of the Act could not be engaged.  As a result, the FDA found
itself exactly where it had been before the 1938 effort to
correct the weaknesses of the earlier Act.  The food industry,
on the other hand, had gained an additional advantage.  Under
the 1938 Act, if a substance was proved to be poisonous or
deleterious it still might be legal to use if it could not be
avoided.

Of course, no court - let alone industry - would be likely
to openly approve the use of a chemical clearly dangerous to
humans.  However, the most hotly debated issues of food
chemical safety occur when there is scientific debate about
given chemicals or classes of chemicals.  Under the 1938 Act,
as under its predecessor, the FDA could not move to restrict a
food additive until it had established conclusively the
harmfulness of the chemicals it wished to move against.

The current argument over cancer-causing chemicals
illustrates the point.  Most independent scientists believe
that the long term effects of small traces of carcinogenic
chemicals may well cause serious public health effects;
others, particularly industrial spokesmen and consultants,
disagree.  The question faced by policy makers is how to
decide whether or not to allow traces of cancer causing
chemicals in food.  If they are allowed and do turn out to
cause damage, the damage will be irreversible and massive.
Under the 1938 Act, the FDA was unable to bar chemicals as
food additives merely because they caused cancer in animals.

In 1938, the FDA found itself right back in the middle of
the pre-1938 problems.  It could not require food
manufacturers to inform it of chemicals used in food.  It also
could not require that food additive chemicals be tested
before they were added to foods.  If a suspicious chemical was
found in food, the FDA had to identify it in their own
laboratories; show that it was poisonous or deleterious by FDA
tests; and prove that it was unnecessary or avoidable in food
manufacture.  Meanwhile, while all this activity was going on
the food additive remained in use.

The FDA could not enforce this confused law any better than
it had enforced its ineffective predecessor.  By 1950, it was
clear that the law needed to be amended again.  In that year,
Rep. Delaney's Select Committee began the hearings that led to
amendments governing pesticides, food additives, and color
additives (3).

The Amendments to the 1938 Act (6, 7, 8) By 1960 the simple
language of the Act [Sec. 402(a)] had become encumbered with a
maze of congressionally enacted bureaucratic exceptions.  It
now read:

"a food shall be deemed to be adulterated...(A) If it bears
any added poisonous or deleterious substance (other than one
which is (i) a pesticide chemical in or on a raw agricultural
commodity; (ii) a food additive; or (iii) a color additive)...
(B) If it is a raw agricultural commodity and it bears or
contains a pesticide chemical which is unsafe within the
meaning of section 409...(C) If it is, or it bears or
contains, a color additive which is unsafe within the meanings
of section 706(a)."

Each of the exceptions contained in the new laws (and
others have been added since 1960) sets up a complex
bureaucratic structure to evaluate the safety of chemicals to
be added to food on a case-by-case basis.  Establishing the
safety of the chemicals remains the purpose of the procedure.
However, the amendments enacted by the Congress shift the
burden of proof onto the company which seeks to use the
chemical.
    The food additive amendment illustrates the general
approach followed for controlling chemicals in food.  The
pesticide amendments [now largely administered by the
Environmental Protection Agency (EPA)] and the color additive
amendments follow essentially the same regulatory pattern for
determining safety.
    Because the laws covering color additives, food additives,
and pesticides contain essentially the same regulatory
procedures, it is often overlooked that the three laws
address three distinct policy issues.  Color additives are
used in food primarily for cosmetic purposes and play only the
most peripheral role in such matters as nutrition and food
preservation.
    Some food additives are also purely "cosmetic," while
others make a direct contribution to the amount and quality of
food available to the nation.  Both food and color additives
achieve their purpose by direct addition to food.  In this
feature, they both differ from pesticides, which are found in
food only as an indirect consequence of their actual use.
Likewise, pesticides are like packaging material, which give
off chemicals which contaminate foods and like animal drugs,
which are intended to protect or improve food-producing
animals, but which may become a part of the food they produce.

Unfortunately, in spite of the distinct difference between problems presented by these three classes of chemicals, a tendency persists to categorize them together.  Wrote a prominent FDA official in 1963,

"The paramount challenge of the 1960s as we see it is to insure the safe use of a multitude of chemicals permitted in production, processing and distribution of our nation's food supply:  pesticides - food additives - color additives." (emphasis in original) (11)

Earlier than this statement, Mr. Justice Brennen, writing for the Supreme Court, said that these types of chemicals could not be lumped together under one policy.  Commenting on congressional intent, he wrote that the 1938 Act

"took the view that unless coal tar colors were harmless, the considerations of the benefits of visual appeal that might be urged in favor of their uses should not prevail, in the light of the consideration of the public health.  In the case of other sorts of added poisons, though only where they were required in the production of the food concerned or could not under good manufacturing practice be avoided, a different congressional policy was expressed in the 1938 enactment.  It is the duty of the Secretary to give effect to this distinction..." (12)

The first step in insuring that no harmful additives get into the food supply is recognizing the policy differences between the color additives, food additives and pesticide amendments.  The color additives amendment address a class of food chemicals with only the smallest claim to importance other than cosmetic.  Therefore, in weighing the benefits of such a chemical versus its risk even a minor risk justifies removing such a non-efficacious chemical from food.

Unfortunately, the FDA has not been as vigorous in pursuing this standard as protection of the public health demands.  Colors such as Violet No. 1, FDC Red 2 and FDC Red 4 have been allowed in foods long after important questions about their safety have been brought to the attention of the FDA.  The FDA's recalcitrance in the color field (13 years after the Congress ordered all colors to be proven safe or removed from the market the FDA has still not acted on this) stems in large part from its failure to recognize the complete unimportance of color additives in improving the health and nutritive aspects of the food supply.

Unlike the color additive amendments, the food additive
amendments address a class of chemicals which includes both
important and unimportant additives to the food supply.  Some
food additives such as vitamins, minerals, and preservatives
improve the nutritional quality of the food supply.  Others,
such as brominated vegetable oil, serve a strictly cosmetic
function, improving the appearance of the food to which they
are added.  Yet others, like nitrite (used to preserve, but in
the process adding a red color), fall between the two
categories.  Therefore the food additives amendment must
analyze these various functions to arrive at an accurate
assessment of the risk presented by the chemicals versus the
benefits they impart.

Pesticides present an altogether different problem.  A
perfectly effective insect killer might be disastrous if it
contaminated the food supply.  On the other hand, there may be
no reason not to use it if it can be kept out of food.
Therefore, the pesticide amendments allow the use of very
dangerous pesticides if they do not get into food in a
dangerous amount.  (Other laws, for example those protecting
farm workers from pesticides, may however prohibit the use of
pesticides even if no residue gets into food.)  The same is
true of drugs used in animals and of chemicals used in
packaging materials.

Three specific regulatory cases illustrate the differences
between these areas.  The color additive FDA Red 2 has caused
fetal resorption in animal studies.  Critics of the use of
food additives argue that such evidence is enough to require
banning of this color additive.  Defenders aruge that more
evidence is necessary to justify a ban.  There has been no
claim by the supporters of the color that banning it will
cause a health hazard to develop in the food supply.

In contrast, another regulatory problem has developed
around the use of nitrite in meat (2).  It combines with other
chemicals (amines) sometimes present in cooking and in the
body, to form potent cancer-causing substances (nitrosamines).
Critics of its use argue that the FDA should consider banning
it.  The defenders of the chemical argue that it is necessary
to prevent botulism from contaminating meat.

The animal drug diethylstilbestrol (DES) illustrates the
problem of indirect additives.  The FDA, with congressional
backing, adopted the policy that the chemical could be used in
cattle as long as no traces of it reached meat products.  An
acrimonious public debate developed when new test methods
found traces of the substance in beef livers.  The FDA
attempted to devise new use rules that would eliminate the

traces.  These failed and finally the agency reluctantly
banned the use of the chemical outright, although it has
recently partially reversed this decision.

In each of these cases, the FDA used the regulatory
authority contained in the various laws it applies to come to
its policy decision.  The procedure in each law is essentially
the same.  But very different policy problems are being
addressed.

The rest of this chapter traces the development of the
procedures used in the food additive amendments.  From a legal
and regulatory standpoint they repeat the procedure in the
other regulatory areas covered by the Food and Drug Law.  It
should be remembered however that these procedures are used to
solve several different kinds of policy problems.

The Food Additive Amendments Of 1958 (7) In 1958, the FDA
found itself faced with the same burden of proof problem it
had faced under the 1906 Act.  Again, it had to be prepared to
show the courts that chemicals were poisonous or deleterious
on a chemical-by-chemical basis.  It also did not provide
authority to require food manufacturers to conduct tests of
the food chemicals they used.  The 1958 food additive
amendments made three separate attempts to shift the burden of
proof from the government.

First, it defined [Sec. 201(s)] a new class of chemicals
called food additives and distinguished it from other food
chemicals which it called Generally Recognized as Safe (GRAS).

Second, it created the Delaney (Anti-Cancer) Clause [Sec.
409(c)(3)(A)] which banned the addition to food of any
chemical which is found to induce cancer when ingested by man
or animal or which after the appropriate tests for the
evaluation of the safety of food additives is found to induce
cancer in man or animals.

Third, it allowed [Sec. 409] for an administrative
structure resulting from FDA regulations designed to evaluate
item-by-item any chemicals which were neither GRAS nor banned
by the Delaney Clause.

In other words, by means of these three approaches the
Congress attempted to block the use of substances that present
undue risk without, at the same time, placing unreasonable
restraints on chemicals that provide important benefits to the
public.  First, the 1958 Act attempted to remove from
regulatory control those chemicals, such as salt, sugar, and
vinegar, which "qualified experts" had shown to be safe
through scientific procedure, or, based on a long history of
use, were believed to be safe.  These food additives were

labeled by the Act as GRAS.  The FDA soon developed a GRAS list.

Unfortunately, the effectiveness of the GRAS list approach deteriorated.  Potentially unsafe chemicals joined the safe ones on the list.  Out of the 900 scientists who were asked by the FDA to comment on the first 189 items to be added to the list, only 350 replied.  Of these, 194 scientists either concurred with or failed to criticize the list.  The FDA ignored the majority of the complaints against the list and allowed the use of all but seven of the chemicals contained therein.  Several of these - safrole, Vitamin D, and, most notably, cyclamate - subsequently were restricted by the FDA.

The GRAS list procedure proved ineffective in discriminating between safe and unsafe substances, because the system presented the same problem of scientific choice that the earlier acts had been unable to deal with.  Earlier when the Agency had tried to choose which chemicals and which foods were safe, it had floundered trying to choose which scientists were the best judges of safety.  An FDA memorandum spelled out the guiding principle of this choice:

"In our final evaluating of the safety of a substance we have taken cognizance of the fact that all opinions are not of equal value and thus have weighed most heavily the opinions of scientifically recognized and often world-renowned experts." (13)

The Congress created the GRAS list concept because it believed industry spokesmen who claimed the food additive laws would impose an unjustified hardship on them.  Industry leaders feared that they would be required to conduct tests on chemicals which they believed had already been proven safe.  Once the 1958 Amendments requiring safety testing became effective, food manufacturers faced a minimum of an estimated two years of study (14) before gaining permission to market any new additive.  Faced with this two year delay of marketing, manufacturers sought to achieve recognition of their chemicals through the GRAS list procedure which required no testing.

Following the banning of cyclamate, President Nixon, in his 1969 consumer message to the Congress (15), called for complete review of the GRAS list.  By 1970, the list had grown to more than 700 items (16).  Another thousand (approximately) items were treated as though on the GRAS list by the FDA (17).  This FDA policy occurred as a direct result of heavy industry pressure.  Ordinarily, the FDA issues a permit to a proposed food additive that is not GRAS only after reviewing the safety tests on the chemical.  In response to a highly organized industry campaign on behalf of a large number of chemicals for which it sought GRAS status, the FDA took a different position.  The FDA promulgated a long list of untested chemicals which it did not consider GRAS, but which it would treat as safe as if testing had in fact been performed.

Under the GRAS list review instigated by the Nixon Administration (15), the FDA hoped to replace chaos with order.  For the first time, it has taken the position that only those substances it has listed as GRAS will in fact be treated as GRAS.  This determination, if upheld against likely court challenge by the food industry, could resolve a decade long controversy about the meaning of the statutory language creating the GRAS concept.  Food industry spokesmen have long argued that they met the requirements of the law if industry scientists agreed that a chemical was safe!  Critics of this position argue that if any segment of the scientific community believes that a chemical is not necessarily safe that the chemical cannot be GRAS.  This is the position that the FDA takes in determining the GRAS status of drugs.

Besides this change in interpretation about the meaning of the GRAS concept, the FDA has taken several other steps to improve the GRAS list.  First, it has contracted with the NAS-NRC for the conduct of a survey to determine from industry how much of each GRAS list chemical is used by the food industry.  Second, it has contracted with the Federation of American Societies of Experimental Biology (FASEB) for a literature review on GRAS list items.  And third, the FDA has undertaken limited testing of certain GRAS list items at their newly opened research facility at Pine Bluff, Arkansas.

The weakness of this whole program is that, except for the limited testing at Pine Bluff, the program does not require previously untested chemicals to now be routinely tested.  While the effort to improve the GRAS list is welcomed, it is long overdue and is likely to have only limited success in detecting those chemicals which will prove to be problems in the future.  The FDA effort to review the GRAS list underlines the failure of the GRAS concept to protect the public from potential hazards.

Already the weakness of the new review system has thrown the validity of its results into serious question.  It has become the FDA practice over the years to pass hard decisions to other bodies.  Its favorite receiver has been the NAS.  In particular, the Food Protection Committee of the NAS-National

Research Council has been a prime arena for the political
debates that have surrounded food additives, including sugar,
starch, monosodium glutamate, cyclamate, sacharrin, and dozens
of others, over the years.

Industry influence on this NAS-NRC committee has been so
blatant as to gain the critical attention of the Congress.  At
1972 hearings held by the Senate Select Committee on Nutrition
and Human Needs, a number of prominent independent scientists
attacked the NAS as both ignorant and biased.  Sen. Charles H.
Percy (R.-Ill.), after hearing the attacks, suggested that the
NAS was "insensitive" to conflicts of interests in its
committee procedures and membership (18).

At about the time that the NAS was falling under severe
criticism, the FDA was getting ready to pass the GRAS list
problem to some other scientific body.  It chose - by
coincidence, it is claimed - the FASEB.  Now the politics
previously so noticeable at the NAS have begun at the
Federation.  The FDA agreed that at least one scientist, in
whom food additive critics have confidence, could serve on the
seven man Federation committee reviewing the GRAS list.  The
Federation arbitrarily refused.  Instead they insisted that
they would decide all the safety issues themselves although
they were not prepared to examine problems of efficacy.
Unfortunately for their apparently well intended goal, food
industry lawyers and lobbyists began debating with the
scientists doing the research which the Federation planned to
evaluate.  So political influences continue to affect this
supposed scientific process even under the new arrangement.
At least one high ranking FDA official proposed terminating
the Federation's review because of the emerging problems of
insensitivity to consumer interests.

The procedures established for examining chemicals on an
item-by-item basis have been equally unsatisfactory.  The
entire administrative procedure - with dozens of complex rules
that often requires months, if not years, for the response to
one position in behalf of a chemical - rests on a single
provision of the amendment.  It state that

"No...regulation shall issue if a fair evaluation of the data
before the Secretary - (A) fails to establish that the
proposed use of the food additive, under the conditions of use
to be specified in the regulation, will be safe... (5)

Thus the Act [Sec. 409(c)(3)(A)] requires persons intending
to use a chemical as a food additive to get clearance prior to
doing so.  The burden of proof for the safety of a chemical is

shifted away from the FDA and onto the would-be users.  This
now is the heart, the theoretical basis, of food regulation in
the United States.  It also is here, at its heart, that food
additive regulation begins to go astray.

Since 1906, one premise has underlain all these efforts by
the Congress at food additive regulation.  Each congressional
response to the problem has operated on the assumption that
science can distinguish between safe and unsafe chemicals with
some degree of certainty.  Although food additive regulation
rests on that assumption, not all scientists share it.

The 1969 Food Safety Panel of the White House Conference on
Food Nutrition and Health stated (19):

"It is not possible to determine with absolute certainty the
safety of the ever-increasing number of chemicals added to or
present in our foods."

Yet by relying on the scientifically incorrect assumption
that food additive safety can be absolutely demonstrated, the
1958 Amendments placed the FDA in the position of having to
attempt to answer in a legal context scientific questions
which could not be answered in the laboratory.  This attempt
was not successful.

The FDA has twisted and modified its regulations trying to
cope with the statutory definition of safety since receiving
from the Congress its authority to issue safety regulations.
Initially, the FDA said (20):

"'Safe' means that there is <u>convincing evidence</u> which
establishes with a certainty tha  no harm will result from the
intended use of food additives.'* (emphasis supplied)

---

*
 Commenting on the safety provision, Charles Wesley Dunn, the
General Counsel for the Grocery Manufacturers of America,
stated:  "Such (a) requirement is basically a pretesting one
for new food additives - Whereas the FDA Act now prohibits a
food that is unsafe, this prohibition normally applies after
the food is sold and consumed, and its enforcement may be long
delayed for various reasons...moreover, in such an enforcement
proceeding the government has the burden of proving that the
food is unsafe, whereas this requirement would instead compel
the manufacturer of a food to prove in advance that it is
safe." [Hearings on H.R. 8112 Before a subcomm. of the House
Comm. on Interstate and Foreign Commerce, 85th Cong., 1st and
2nd Sess. (1957-58)].

The second definition allows untested or only partially-tested chemicals to be added to the food supply. The first definition required the party proposing the use of a chemical to provide the FDA with convincing evidence of its safety.

The new regulatory definition and the procedures that go along with it put the FDA back into the position of having to generate the evidence - at the taxpayers' expense - that shows a profitable food additive to be unsafe. This position undoes thirty years of progress in shifting the burden of proof of safety onto the food additive industry. When a product with a potential for consumer hazards is to be marketed, it should be the responsibility of its manufacturers to determine and insure that no harm will result from its use. Food additives are such a product. The food additive law is based on such a policy. There is no incentive for the promoter of a chemical to show it to be safe. If there is no available evidence on either side of the question, then his chemical can be used as a food additive. This, of course, undermines congressional intent for the entire Act.

The FDA's difficulties with defining safety also show up in its procedure for moving a chemical from the GRAS list to the regulated additive list. The FDA developed in 1970 a new "interim" regulation policy defined as follows:

"If after a responsible and substantial question of safety has been raised regarding a substance previously listed as GRAS the main weight of the scientific evidence still indicates safety (at least within certain limits), an interim food additive regulation will be proposed. This will permit further scientific investigations to define the conditions of safe use for a food additive regulation of indefinite duration." (21)

In the implementation of the Act, the FDA has struggled to promulgate additive regulations with an acceptable definition of safety. But there is no scientific agreement on just what constitutes safety. In fact, it is this same struggle with the definition of safety that made it difficult for the FDA to block marketing of unsafe foods under the 1906 Act and, again, to regulate poisonous and deleterious substances under the 1938 Act. In each case the difficulty of proving the statutory requirement of a lack of safety has thwarted implementation of legislation. The FDA's additive regulations are further thwarted by an inability to define safety within the confines of the statutory criteria.

Controversy over a chemical seldom erupts when the

scientists agree on its safety or lack of safety.  It is when
there is scientific disagreement that the FDA decision is made
difficult.  Under the Act the FDA is forced to overrule the
findings of one or the other groups of scientists when making
a determination about safety on a controversial chemical.

To date only the Delaney Clause approach has worked
effectively because it does not rest on a determination of
safety.

The Delaney Clause* As previously mentioned, the Delaney
(Anti-Cancer) Clause requires the FDA to ban those chemicals
from use in human food substances which are found to induce
cancer when ingested by man or animal or which after
appropriate safety tests are found to induce cancer in man or
animals.  There has been great controversy over this Clause.
Former FDA Commissioner Edwards stated (22) his argument
against Clause:

"My personal view and that of the FDA is that we have to put
more flexibility of interpretation or we are put into the

----------------------------------------------------------------
*
 The Delaney Clause for food additives is contained in Sec.
409(c)(3)(A) of the Food Additives Amendment of 1958, 21
U.S.C. Sec. 348(c)(3)(A) (1964).  It is also repeated in the
Color Additive Amendments of 1960, Sec. 706(b)(5)(B), 21
U.S.C. Sec. 376(b)(5)(B) (1964) that reads:  "A color additive
(i) shall be deemed unsafe, and shall not be listed for any
use which will or may result in ingestion of all or part of
such additive, if the additive is found by the Secretary to
induce cancer when ingested by man or animal, or if it is
found by the Secretary, after tests which are appropriate for
the evaluation of the safety of additives for use in food, to
induce cancer in man or animal..."
Whether the Delaney Clause applies to pesticide chemicals
is a more difficult question about which there is considerable
controversy.  The Secretary's Commission on Pesticides wrote
as if the clause could be interpreted to apply to pesticide
chemicals; however, the definition of food additives expressly
excludes "a pesticide chemical in or on a raw agricultural
commodity..."  Food Additives Amendment of 1958 Sec.
201(s)(1), 21 U.S.C. Sec. 321(S)(1) (1964).  Since there is no
anti-cancer clause in the Pesticide Amendment, it would appear
that pesticides do not fall under the prohibition of the
Delaney Clause.

position that we were with cyclamates - all or nothing.  And
it becomes a highly emotional issue at that point, allowing no
discretion on our part or anyone else's."

Such statements represent a profound misunderstanding of
both the Delaney Clause and the additive regulation section of
the Food and Drug Act.  If there were no Delaney Clause, the
Act - unless eroded by bureaucratic lethargy - would still
require the banning from food of any substance causing cancer
when fed to animals.  There is no way that such a substance
can be demonstrated or proved safe for man.  The fact that
many people argue that there is such a strong argument for
retaining and expanding the limits has the effects of limiting
the FDA's "discretion."

The Argument for discretion advanced by former FDA
Commissioner Edwards is disturbingly out of touch with
scientific reality.  In 1960 the Secretary of Health,
Education, and Welfare, Arthur S. Flemming, in making the
argument for the Delaney Clause before the House Committee on
Interstate and Foreign Commerce said (23):

"The rallying point against the anti-cancer provision is the
catch phrase that it takes away the scientist's right to
exercise judgment.  The issue this makes is a false one,
because the clause allows the exercise of all the judgment
that can safely be exercised on the basis of our present
knowledge.  The clause is grounded on the scientific fact of
life that no one, at this time, can tell us how to establish
for man a safe tolerance for a cancer-producing agent...

As I pointed out in my original testimony, the opposition
to inclusion of an anti-cancer clause arises largely out of a
misunderstanding of how the provision works.  It allows the
Department and its scientific people full discretion and
judgment in deciding whether a substance has been shown to
produce cancer when added to the diet of test animals.  But
once this decision is made, the limits of judgment have been
reached and there is no reliable basis on which discretion
could be exercised in determining a safe threshold dose for
the established carcinogen."

In 1970, DHEW Secretary Robert Finch asked a committee of
scientists (several of whom were from the National Cancer
Institute) to review the Delaney Clause.  They did; and they
concluded, after presenting the quotation from DHEW Secretary
Flemming, that

"the scientific basis on which the government's position was
established in 1960 remains valid.  The progress of knowledge
in carcinogenesis in the last decade has only strengthened the
points made in Secretary Flemming's testimony." (24)

The same committee restated the theoretical reasons for
adopting the Delaney Clause:

"While science can provide qualitative information regarding
maximum risk levels, the task of ultimately selecting socially
acceptable levels of human risk rests with society and its
political leaders." (24)

The Delaney Clause first became law as a part of the Food
Additive Amendments of 1958.  Two years later, after intense
deliberation, the Congress inserted similar provisions in the
Color Additive Amendments.  The simple question which lies at
the heart of the debate about the clause is, should the FDA
set tolerances for cancer-causing chemicals?
By their vote, the majority of Congressmen answered this
question negatively.  This was done in response to the stated
position of experts in cancer research who felt that no matter
how small the amount of a cancer-causing chemical that might
be present in food, it still might cause cancer.
Industrial spokesmen against the Delaney Clause allege that
it does not allow enough scientific discretion.  But this
confuses two issues.  In applying the Delaney Clause
scientists must first determine whether the chemical under
consideration is a carcinogen (a cancer-causing chemical)
under appropriate test conditions.  This is purely a
scientific decision, reserved solely to scientists and subject
to the professional consideration of scientists.  That is the
first issue.
The second issue concerns whether the public should or
should not be subjected to potential hazards, including
carcinogens, even in the smallest amounts, in the food supply.
This is a decision which while not purely scientific, has
evoked a response from independent qualified scientists (25).
Scientists debate the risks of including traces of
carcinogens in the food supply.  If the decision as to whether
to allow traces of a carcinogen is a matter of scientific
discretion, then the decision also would depend on which
scientists it was left to - particularly whether they were
qualified and independent or whether directly or indirectly in
the employment of the food industry (25).

The confusion between the purely scientific question as to whether a chemical is a carcinogen, and the less scientific but broader question as to how much risk the public should be subjected raises serious policy conflicts with the objectives of the food and drug law.  It also provides a place to begin remedying the failure of food additive regulation.

## The Legislative Situation

The current legislative framework of food additive regulation can be broken down as shown in Table 1.

This table sets out the current framework of regulation. The weaknesses in that framework begin with item five in the first column.  That item begins the description of the GRAS list.  As pointed out, regulatory efforts have been undertaken to correct the most glaring weaknesses in the concept.

However, Sen. Gaylord Nelson (D.-Wisc.) has proposed even more drastic measures to correct the GRAS list problem.  He has introduced legislation to abolish the concept of GRAS by deleting from the law all those items under "Any Substance" from number five on.  If Sen. Nelson's bill is adopted there will no longer be a GRAS list.

Under the exception, only item three is of specific concern.  The other exceptions, as already pointed out, concern separate acts which incorporate essentially the same procedure as the food additive amendment.  Prior sanctions are different.  In the past, if an industry decided to use a chemical but was unsure of how the FDA would treat such use, the user wrote the FDA for what amounted to an advisory opinion.  If the FDA approved the chemical's use prior to the industry's actual use of it, such permission became known as a "prior sanction."  The FDA has moved to limit to some degree reliance on these old prior sanctions, but it is unsure of how many uses still exist (between 1,000 and 10,000, agency spokesmen say) or of how widely these food additives are relied upon.  Although they should be abolished by legislation, as yet, no abolition has been proposed in the Congress.

Concerning the Delaney Clause, the table makes clear that it does allow scientific discretion.  Only if a chemical is found to induce cancer can it be banned.  Such a finding can only be made by scientists.  Indeed, the overwhelming preponderance of informed opinion has lined up behind the scientific validity of the clause.

Scientists from the National Cancer Institute and other qualified independent scientists unambiguously advised the Secretary of DHEW not to attempt to change the clause in 1970

Table 1  Food Additives

| Any Substance | Except | Delaney |
|---|---|---|
| 1. The intended use of which | 1. Pesticide chemicals | 1. No additive shall be deemed safe |
| 2. Results or may reasonably be expected to result | 2. Color additives | 2. If it is found to induce cancer |
| 3. Directly or indirectly | 3. Any substance used in accordance with a prior sanction |    a. when ingested |
| 4. In its becoming a component of food (or otherwise influencing the characteristics of food) | 4. New animal drug (1968) |    b. by man |
| 5. If such substance is not generally recognized | |    c. or by animal |
| 6. Among experts qualified by scientific training and experience | | 3. or if it is found after tests |
| 7. To evaluate its safety | |    a. which are appropriate for the evaluation of food additives |
| 8. As having been shown | | |
| 9. Through scientific procedures (pre-1958 - or experience based on common use in food) | |    b. to induce cancer in man or animal |
| 10. To be safe under the condition of intended use | | |

Note: The language in this table is taken directly from the Food, Drug and Cosmetic Act of 1938 and from the Delaney Clause. The limits are Sec. 409(c)(4) - functional effect (efficacy), Sec. 409(c)(3)(B) - deception, and Sec. 409(c)(5) - safety factors. The table was presented jointly by Mr. Eugene Lambert, Food and Drug attorney of Covington & Burling of Washington, D.C. and James S. Turner, at the January 15, 1973 Conference on the Scientific Basis of the Delaney Clause, held in New York City by the New York Academy of Sciences.

following the cyclamate ban. At a New York Academy of
Science meeting in January 1973, scientists again massively
supported the Delaney Clause. In a subsequent conference
entitled "How safe is safe," at the NAS on May 15, 1973, the
President of the Academy, Dr. Phillip Handler, called on
scientists to recognize the Delaney Clause for the commonsense
statement that it is. But the principles underlying the
Delaney Clause need to be expanded and other reforms of the
food additive law need to be accomplished.

Sen. Nelson has undertaken a major legislative effort in
the food additive area. Using the food additive
recommendations of the 1969 White House Conference on Food
Nutrition and Health as his starting point, he is attempting
to systematize and simplify various confused aspects of the
food additives regulation.

Two points in this effort are of primary importance.
First, Sen. Nelson urges extension of the Delaney Clause
principle to other diseases besides cancer. He also has
proposed that any chemical which causes birth defects or
genetic damage when ingested by animals or as a result of
appropriate food additive testing should not be allowed in
food unless such prohibition would cause greater health risks
than allowing its use.

As his second major point, Sen. Nelson urges some form of
third party testing to cut through the scientific lobbying
that has made food additive regulation so difficult. The
details of such an effort still need to be worked out, but a
general outline can be worked out. A possibility is as
follows:

A manufacturer desires to market a new additive. He
requests certification from the FDA. The FDA in turn refers
the testing of the additive to a prearranged set of private
laboratories who get their assignments in rotation. The
purpose of such an arrangement is to have the testers
communicating directly with and only with the FDA about the
safety of the additives in question. If principles of these
kind can be added to the existing legislative arrangement, the
task of sorting out food additive regulation can begin. These
concepts have been developed and extended to general
industrial practice (26).

Sen. Nelson's proposed reforms would form the framework for
the continuing discussion of food additives and their
regulations. But that discussion will continue to revolve
around the old policy questions and alternatives which have
been a part of the debate over pure food since its beginning.

Policy Questions and Alternatives The same Ad Hoc 1970
advisory committee to DHEW Secretary Finch led to two
important observations about setting food additive policy.
The Secretary stated that (24)

"While science can provide quantitative information regarding
maximum risk levels, the task of ultimately selecting socially
acceptable levels of human risk rests with society and its
political leaders,"

and the committee added,

"Chemicals should be subjected to scientific scrutiny rather
than given individual 'rights':  They must be considered
potentially guilty unless and until proven innocent."

These two observations must underlie any legislative or
regulatory efforts to establish a rational and effective food
additive policy.

The belief - made a part of the law by the 1958 Food
Additive Amendment - that a chemical must be proved safe
before being added to food, grows out of more than reasonable
prudence.  The search for the many unexplained causes of
cancer has led researchers who test food additives to the
conclusion that there is no way to prove that a chemical which
causes cancer in animals will not also cause cancer in humans
(25).  In fact, every chemical which produces cancer in man,
with the possible exception of trivalent arsenic, also
produces cancer in animals and thus could have been detected
by adequate animal tests.

For the past ten years Dr. John W. Olney, working at
Washington University, has been tracing the effect of certain
chemicals on infant animal brains.  When a number of other
scientists discovered that several of these chemicals -
including monosodium glutamate - cause lesions in animal
brains, they felt that such an effect might be related to the
large percentage of mental retardation in humans which has no
known cause.  Other scientists suggested that chemicals which
effect the genetics of animals also may effect people.

The debate over the relationship between chemicals causing
toxic effects in animals and unaccounted for problems in the
human population raises a serious policy question.  Those who
defend the use of the chemicals argue that animal studies
showing danger are not conclusive.  Just because a rat is
damaged by a chemical does not mean a man will be, they argue.

Conversely, those who see a suggested relationship between

existing damage in man and a chemical cause in animals say
that the suggestions that the chemical may cause harm is too
serious to be ignored.  The crucial question boils down to
whether the testing of chemicals should be performed
prospectively on animals or retrospectively on humans.

When a chemical widely used in humans is conclusively found
to really be harmful the discovery will <u>always</u> be too late for
a <u>substantial</u> number of individuals.  For example, hundreds of
deformed babies were caused by thalidomide before its effects
were discovered.  For cancer, genetic defects, or birth
defects, including mental retardation, the time lag between
the introduction of a chemical into the food supply and a
conclusive demonstration of its harmful effects can be decades
or even generations.  Then should the relationship be found,
if ever, to exist there may be no possibility of correcting
the genetic or carcinogenic damage already caused.  These
long-term risks must be weighed against any immediate benefit
the chemical food additive might have.  That is why when there
is animal evidence of a problem associated with a chemical
that suggestion must be taken as a serious warning against its
use in foods intended for human consumption.

One additional point about the debate should be made.  The
major scientific method for evaluating the safety of food
additives is animal testing.  When a defender of the use of
any of various chemicals presents his arguments, he always
makes reference to the animal tests which have shown the
chemical to be safe.  If tests which show safety for animals
are to be used to justify the addition of chemicals to the
food supply, then conversely tests showing danger to animals
must be used to block the addition of chemicals to the food
supply.  This is not because the animal tests give a
conclusive answer.  It is because the animal tests raise a
serious doubt about safety.

Recognizing the general potential for harm from chemicals
is the first step in designing a food additive policy that
will effectively control chemicals in food.  The second step,
as pointed out by the Ad Hoc Advisory Committee to DHEW
Secretary Finch, is to separate the fact-finding function from
the policy-setting function.  The Congress should
legislatively set the policy and the Executive Branch, the
regulatory agency, supported by the scientific community, must
find the facts to implement the policy (24).

In 1958, the Supreme Court unheld the authority of the
Secretary of the DHEW to completely ban the use of a coal tar
dye for the coloring of oranges.  In doing so, it laid out the
basic principles that underly the needed future food

protection policy outlined in this paper.

Mr. Justice Brennen delivered the Court's opinion in the case. At issue was the use by Florida and Texas orange farmers of a coal tar dye, FD&C Red 2. In 1939, the FDA had certified the dye as safe for use in oranges. In 1955, however, the FDA removed the certification after tests "cast doubt whether Red 2 was harmless," as Mr. Justice Brennen put it. From this situation, the Supreme Court outlined the basic principles which must underly any effective food protection policy.

First, the Court pointed out that no safe level for the ingestion of the chemical had been found. Second, it said that no one contends that it is impossible that someone might be injured by the use of the color additive. Finally, the Court made clear that no instance of a harmful use of the color additive had ever been discovered. Then it went on to set out the principle for upholding the ban of food additives that had not caused any damage and presented only a slight potential for harm.

The Court stated,

"In light of the overall purpose of the Act...and the specific terms here involved, it seems to us that the Congress did intend that a verdict of 'not proven' on the questions mentioned should preclude the Government from preventing the use of substances like the one in question when they were shown to have poisonous effects by themselves." (12)

It should be the policy of national food protection law that when a substantial question of safety about a food additive is raised, a verdict of not proven, to use the Court's terms, leads to a restriction on the use of the chemical. Currently the GRAS list provisions of the law allow an unproven verdict to justify the use of a chemical. The petition provisions of the law, particularly the FDA's presently used interim petition procedures, allow chemical food additives for which there are unresolved questions of substantial safety to remain in the food supply. Only the Delaney Clause provides a mechanism to overcome scientific uncertainties (25). It also provides the public with the degree of public health protection which should be national policy.

Since the general potential for harm from chemical food additives has been recognized, the Congress ought to adopt a general policy against the unnecessary introduction of chemicals in food, either intentionally or accidentally. For example, a policy could be established that no chemical may be added to the food supply, except when it is required in the production of food or cannot be avoided by good manufacturing practices, and it has not been demonstrated to cause cancer, birth defects, or genetic damage when fed to animals.  If other dangers warrant the exclusion of a chemical from food, they also should be included.  In addition, no chemical should be added to food unnecessarily, e.g., for cosmetic purposes alone.

If such a policy proved to be too restrictive, because certain added chemicals are needed to perform essential functions in the food supply, then the Congress could modify the statutory policy to allow their use.  In December 1969, the Food Safety Panel at the White House Conference on Food Nutrition and Health suggested such a policy:

"(That) no additional chemicals should be permitted in or on foods unless:  They have been shown with reasonable certainty to be safe on the basis of the best scientific procedures available for the evaluation of safety and meet one or more of the following criteria:
1.  They have been shown by appropriate test to be significantly less toxic than food additives currently employed for the same purpose.
2.  They significantly improve the quality of acceptability of the food.
3.  Their use results in a significant increase in the food supply.
4.  They improve the nutritive value of the food.
5.  Their use results in a decrease in the cost of food to the consumer." (27)

The specifics of national policy on food additives should be a subject of national debate.  However, that such a policy should be set by the Congress should not be subject to debate. The establishment of a food additive policy is not solely or peculiarly a scientific problem.

Once the policy is established, then the agency implementing it (currently the FDA), with the support of the scientific community, must collect the facts necessary for its effective implementation.  The Agency also should be required to determine whether a proposed or existing chemical's use fits with the uses prescribed by policy.  If this could not be demonstrated for a chemical, its use should not be allowed.

If the agency found the food additive to fit the definition of usefulness, then it would review the submitted data to

determine what problems the use of the chemical might
present.  In turn, the chemical food additive should be used
only when it presented no moot issues.  The agency also should
have no discretion in determining the policy of chemical use.
If the food additive presented either hazards or no
demonstrable efficacy, its use would be barred from the food
supply.  If, on the other hand, no hazard appeared in tests
and the chemical had a demonstrated positive use, the agency
could not ban it.  Such a policy would tend to relieve the
agency of the very difficult policy questions which are raised
when a food additive with a multi-million dollar market is
suspected of being a serious hazard but does not, say, cause
cancer when fed to animals.

## References

1.   Final report of the White House Conference on Food Nutrition and Health, Food Safety Panel III-3p.  (GPO, 1970).

2.   Lijinsky, W. and Epstein, S. S., Nitrosamines as Environmental Carcinogens.  Nature 225:21 (1970).

3.   For example, see Hearings on H.R. 74 before the House Select Comm. To Investigate the Use of Chemicals in Food Products, 81st Congress, 2nd Session (1951).

4.   Food and Drug Act of 1906, 34 Stat. 786 (1906).

5.   Food, Drug and Cosmetic Act of 1938, 52 Stat. 1040 (1938).

6.   Act of July 22, 1954, ch. 559, 68 Stat. 511 (now 21 USC Sec. 346a (1964)).

7.   Act of Sept. 6, 1958 (P.L. No. 85-929) 72 Stat. 397 (codified in scattered sections of 21 USC).

8.   Act of July, 1960 (P.L. No. 86-617), 74 Stat. 397 (codified in scattered sections of 21 USC).

9.   1933 FDA Ann. Rep. 14.

10.  Christopher, T., Cases and Materials on Food and Drug Law 468 (1966).

11.  Milstead, "New Challenges Ahead," Food Drug Cosmetic Law Journal 18:421-422 (1963).

12.  Flemming vs. Florida Citrus Exchange, Supreme Court of the United States 1958, 358 U.S. 153, 79 S. Ct. 160, 3 L. Ed 2nd 188, KK 58-60 at 119 see also 45 A.B.A.J. 284 (1959); 1 B. C. Ind. & Com. L. Rev. 112 (1959).

13.  FDA Div. of Pharmacology and Food Memorandum, Sept. 2, 1959.

14.  Larrick, FDA Commissioner, Hearings on H.R. 8112 Before Subcommittee of the House Committee on Interstate and Foreign Commerce, 85th Congress 1st and 2nd Sessions 60 (1957058).

15.   Richard M. Nixon, Message from the President of the United States (October 30, 1969) H.R. Doc. No. 91-188.

16.   FDA, Code of Federal Regulations 21:121.101 appended.

17.   FDA, Code of Federal Regulations 21:121; 1163, 1164, and 121.2001, appended.

18.   Gillette, Robert, "Academy Food Committees:  New Criticism of Industry Ties."  Science 177:1172-1175 (Sept. 29, 1972).

19.   Final report of the White House Conference on Food Nutrition and Health, Food Safety Panel III-3p.  (GPO, 1970).

20.   FDA, Code of.  Federal Register 21:121.1 (i) (1971).

21.   FDA, "Food Additives." Federal Register 35:18, 623-18, 624 (1970).

22.   Interview with Charles C. Edwards, Commissioner, Food and Drug Administration, in U.S. News and World Report, Apr. 19, 1971, p. 52.

23.   Flemming, Secretary Arthur S., Hearings on H.R. 7624 Before a Subcomm. of the House Comm. on Interstate and Foreign Commerce, 86th Congress, 2nd Session 501 (1960).

24.   Report to the Surgeon General, USPHS, by the Ad Hoc Committee on the Evaluation of Low Levels of Environmental Chemical Carcinogens (Apr. 22, 1970).

25.   Epstein, S. S., Testimony on "The Delaney Amendment and Mechanisms for Reducing Constraints in the Regulatory Process in General, and as Applied to Food Additives, in Particular." Hearings before the Senate Select Committee on Nutrition and Human Needs.  Sept. 20, 1972.

26.   Epstein, S. S., Testimony on "The Delaney Amendment and Mechanisms for Reducing Constraints in the Regulatory Process in General, and as Applied to Food Additives, in Particular." Hearings before the Senate Select Committee on Nutrition and Human Needs.  Sept. 20, 1972.

# 6

THE FTC'S NEW LOOK:  A CASE STUDY OF
REGULATORY REVIVAL

Harrison Wellford

CONTENTS

## Introduction

Like peasant girls in pastoral novels, independent regulatory
agencies are said to have a poignantly predictable life-cycle.
After a few good years when they look better than they ever
will again, they plunge quickly into old age.  The duration of
their bloom is the same for both - three or four years - and
so is the permanence of decline.  For most of its first sixty
years, the Federal Trade Commission (FTC) might well have been
the inspiration for this model (1) of the regulatory agency.
According to Ralph Nader, the FTC had become by 1969 a "self-
parody of bureaucracy, fat with cryonyism, torpid through
inbreeding unusual even for Washington, manipulated by the
agencts of commercial predators, impervious to governmental
and citizen monitoring." (2)

     But between 1969 and 1973, the FTC has experienced a rare
metamorphosis which, in the opinion of consumer and business
observers alike, has renewed its vigor.  The FTC's General
Counsel Ronald Dietrich noted the change when he reported to
one of the agency's former critics, the American Bar
Association, that in 1972 "the primary criticism of the
Commission today is that it's too vital, too willing to
discard old ideas about business practices and too zealous in
seizing upon new ideas."  Mary Gardiner Jones, retiring as FTC
Commissioner in October 1973, confirmed Dietrich's claims of
substantive change in the agency's attitude and performance:

"I believe today the Federal Trade Commission is far more
responsive to the public's problems in the marketplace than it
has ever been before in its history.  The real challenge which
confronts the Commission - and the public - today is whether
the changes which have taken place at the Commission will
prove only transitory or whether they portend a basic shift in
the Commissioners' perception and approach to their
responsibilities as members of what I believe is one of the
most important regulatory agencies in government." (3)

Not only FTC Commissioners and staff hold this view.  A poll
in August 1973 by this writer of 11 national consumer groups
with offices in Washington found that the FTC ranked first in
the category "most responsive to the public interest" among
all independent regulatory agencies.   In the same month, the

-------------------------------------------------------------------------

*
 The Consumer Products Safety Commission was not included
because it lacks a track record.  The term "public interest"

*Wall Street Journal* recognized the changes at the FTC with a
note of alarm:  "After decades of being viewed with some
justification as the tired old lady in the Federal Triangle, a
handmaiden to American Business, the Agency adopted a new look
early in the Nixon administration and has caught the activist
fever, always a dangerous malady when it infects bureaucrats."
(4)

    While some observers question the long-term significance of
the agency's highly publicized initiatives, the fact that the
"little old lady of Pennsylvania Avenue," as the old FTC was
derisively known, has taken off her tennis shoes and become a
swinger, is widely accepted in Washington.  That this occurred
during a Republican Administration, with an unashamedly
pro-business President, requires some explanation.  The
reasons for this change, its scope and whether, as FTC
Commissioner Jones asks, it is a "transitory" or "basic
shift," are the subject of this essay.

Historical Sketch The FTC was established by the Federal Trade
Commission Act of 1914, which with the Wheeler-Lea Amendment
of 1938, authorized it to protect the free enterprise system
from "being stifled or fettered by monopoly or corrupted by
unfair or deceptive trade practices." (5)  The FTC's primary
mission therefore is to police the marketplace for fraud and
other abuses by business.  When the abuses take the form of
non-competitive pricing or other practices which affect the
structure of business, it may invoke the antitrust laws whose
enforcement it shares with the Department of Justice.  The FTC
has responsibility for enforcement of the Clayton Act
(forbidding unlawful corporate mergers and acquisitions) and
the Robinson-Patman Act (forbidding price discrimination with
the exception of airlines, regulated by the Civil Aeronautics
Board; banks, regulated by the Federal Reserve; and trucks,
railroads, and other common carriers, regulated by the
Interstate Commerce Commission.  The FTC, as a quasi-judicial
body, has subpoena powers and other fact-finding tools not
available to the Department of Justice and may impose cease

-------------------------------------------------------------

was interpreted in both a procedural sense (openness to
consumer inquiry, scope of consumer participation in decision-
making, availability of information) and a substantive sense
(responsiveness of agency decisions and priorities to consumer
needs, as perceived by the groups).

and desist orders, divestiture orders, and other civil
remedies.  The Justice Department has exclusive criminal
jurisdiction over antitrust cases (6).
[When the abuses take the form of deceptive and unfair
practices, the FTC issues cease and desist orders to protect
the consumer.  When cease and desist orders are not obeyed,
the FTC can recommend both civil and criminal (in cases of
willful deception involving food, furs, and drugs) penalties
to the Department of Justice.] The FTC also has equity
jurisdiction to order restitution, a remedy which it rarely
applies.
[The Congress gave the FTC authority to define the deceptive
or unfair trade practice, a concept as elastic and dynamic as
the human ingenuity for fraud (7).  It includes false
advertising, misleading warranties, bogus safety or efficacy
claims on product labels, exploitive sales contracts, and a
host of other practices too diverse to be embraced in a single
statutory definition.] [One popular theory for explaining the
FTC's past failures is that the FTC's elastic jurisdiction
kept it from developing clear and precise standards (8).]
[Without predictable policy guides, the agency has lurched here
and there failing to set priorities, reacting rather than
initiating.]
The Congress gave the FTC these powers in response in part
to the public's demand for curbs on corporate power and,
paradoxically, to business demands for advance advice (and
consent) on corporate mergers and reliable data on corporate
activities (9).  While its operating statute reflected the
ambivalence of its constituencies, the FTC did enjoy a few
years after 1914 in which it partly lived up to the
expectations of its supporters (10) in the Progressive and
Democratic Parties.  But by the 1920s, with business ascendant
in a Republican Washington, the FTC had begun to decline.  In
deceptive practices and antitrust matters, its emphasis passed
from enforcement to voluntary compliance and compromise.  A
gradual shift in the orientation of its five commissioners was
climaxed by President Calvin Coolidge's appointment of William
Humphrey, who openly regarded the FTC as "an instrument of
oppression and disturbance" (11) to business.  During this
period, false advertising, rather than antitrust, became the
agency's dominant interest.  The aim of its policies more
often than not was to protect business, not consumers.  The
FTC, for example, moved against false advertising at the
behest of advertising associations which wanted the agency to

help protect their members from unfair competition (11).

In succeeding years, the FTC's failure to have any appreciable impact on false advertising or monopolistic practices had a numbing consistency little affected by changes in the White House or among the Commissioners.  The agency's tendency to identify with the interests it was supposed to regulate, its substitution of voluntarism for sanctions, and a lack of priorities reflected in its preoccupation with trivial cases became monotonous themes in a long series of critical reports on the agency over the next three decades.  In 1949, the Hoover Commission charged that the FTC had become a "passive judicial agency" which was "guilty of prosecuting trivial and technical offenses and of failing to confine these dockets to cases of public importance." (12)  In 1969, a student task force under the direction of Ralph Nader echoed these themes and also criticized the "political and regional cronyism" of the FTC, its compulsive secrecy, and its failure to develop a constituency among consumer groups to balance pressures from industry (2).

In the same year, following the furor created by the Nader Report, the American Bar Association (ABA), at the request of President Nixon, appointed a study commission under the Chairmanship of Miles W. Kirkpatrick, to evaluate the FTC. After five months of study, the ABA issued a report which, in less harsh language, confirmed the Nader group's conclusions and warned that "Further temporizing is indefensible. Notwithstanding the great porential of the FTC in the field of antitrust and consumer protection, if change does not occur, there will be no substantial purpose to be served by its continued existence." (13)

Flaws In The Regulatory Model In the press and to some degree in the Nader Report, the FTC's failures were more often attributed to individuals than to organizational structure. *
More accurately, the FTC's failures should be seen as the results of flaws in the design of the independent regulatory

------------------------------------------------------------------------------

*
The "bad apple" explanation oversimplified the FTC's problems and was unfair to many of its professional staff.  For

agency which made the FTC's responsiveness to special
interests likely, if not inevitable.  As Louis Jaffe has
noted, industry orientation in a regulatory agency "is much
less a disease of certain administrations than a condition
endemic in any agency or set of agencies which seek to perform
[a regulatory] task." (14)  The primary cause was the machine-
gun-like impact of corporate advocacy before the agency.
While the clamor of business pressure gave the appearance of
pluralism at work, consumer and other non-corporate interests
suffered from an advocacy gap (15).  The reformers' model for
the independent regulatory agency did not take this into
account.

   As conceived by the Progressives and refined by the New
Dealers, the independent regulatory agencies were monuments to
the reformers' faith in the affirmative power of the executive
government to protect the public interest against the special
interests.  The public's role in this system of regulation was
essentially passive.  The agencies, staffed by rational
experts, would act as the peoples' proxy in checking the
excesses of corporate power.  The blueprint therefore
emphasized political independence and broad Congressional
delegation of administrative discretion to experts, who, free
of the corrupting influence of politics, would define the
optimum public policy and enforce it (16).  The collegial
board of commissions, appointed by the President for

----------------------------------------------------------------

example, many of the new approaches to advertising regulation
in the 1970s had been developed by the FTC staff in the
Sixties, only to be stifled by division and bureau heads and
by Commissioners absorbed in internal quarrels.  Even at this
level there were many exceptions.  Willard F. Mueller was an
effective and vigorous chief of the Bureau of Economics in the
1960s, and Philip Elman, James Nicholson, and Mary Gardner
Jones were consumer oriented and reform minded commissioners.
Chairman Paul Rand Dixon's inability to keep peace among his
fellow commissioners in the Sixties made it difficult for the
FTC to agree on new policy departures.  Dixon was also
responsible for undistinguished appointments at the division
and bureau level.

staggered 7-year terms, was expected to pursue the public
interest in splended isolation from Congress and the
President.  So great was the reformers' faith in these
administrative philosopher-kings that their authorizing
statutes often amounted to saying, "Here is your power; find a
problem and solve it as you wish." (17)[*]  In short, as Louis
Jaffe has observed, these federal executive agencies were seen
as "an objective force which if left to itself would
inevitably produce reform." (18)  In the view of the
Progressives and New Dealers, therefore, the reformer's job
was done once an independent agency staffed by honest men was
created to regulate an industry.  There was no need for public
pressure on their agency.

From the perspective of the 1970s when Nader-type reformers
have shattered whatever liberal illusions remained about the
regulatory agencies, the faith that regulation of industry
could be left to politically insulated experts seems
intolerably naive.  In a charming reminiscence, Louis Jaffe
has described this state of innocence:

"When I served the New Deal as a young man I was prepared to
support the theory that the so-called independent agencies
could save the world.  It was somehow thought...that the well-
intentioned young men appointed to [direct the agencies] could
and would do whatever they thought to be right.  We were
misled by the fact that we were in power and were appointing
our men and that we were being given fresh and powerful
mandates by Congress.  In such circumstances an agency can get
off to a good head start before the political facts of life
catch up with it.  But how naive we were in believing that any
organization of government...can be free to do what seems
right to do!" (19)

Unfortunately the public interest in any regulatory area is
not a Platonic ideal subject to discovery by the cool
deliberation of rational men.  Instead it is the resultant of
vectors of pressures on agency officials who act, more often
than not, as arbitrators between competing interests.  Far
from being advocates of the public interest, they see

-----------------------------------------------------------------
[*]
 Regulated groups of course have often exploited the
reformers' insouciance by structuring the organic legislation
to serve their interests, particularly by weakening
enforcement powers.

themselves as umpires or mediators between organized special
interests who knock on their door.  They naturally become
sympathetic to the concerns of groups with whose problems they
are most familiar.  In most cases, this meant the businessmen
whose activities are regulated by an agency and who become
intimately and legitimately involved in its affairs.

At the same time the influence of consumer groups in
setting agency policy has been virtually nil.  While the
public interest in antitrust enforcement and honest business
practices is very large in the aggregate, it has been too
diffuse and uninformed to give birth to organized pressure
(20).  Robert Pitofsky, who directed the FTC's Bureau of
Consumer Protection from 1970 to 1973, a period when consumer
interest in the agency was high, nevertheless concluded that:

"The consumer's interest in fragmented and grossly under-
represented in ordinary agency regulatory business.  Week in
and week out at the FTC there were large numbers of
experienced and highly competent business representatives in
my office, and the offices of commissioners and other staff
members, urging views consistent with the varied interests of
their business clients...the ratio of impact by business
representatives compared to consumer representatives—taking
into account the numbers of people seen, time spent in
discussion or negotiation, experience of representatives, and
so on—is probably in the order of over 100 to 1...  In vast
areas of commission regulatory activities, no consumer input
was ever felt by any Commissioner or staff member to my
knowledge." (15)

This extraordinary imbalance of representation means that an
agency, to be fair, must not only consider the claims of
organized interests but also the claims that might be advanced
on behalf of individuals and groups not represented before
them (21).  This the FTC, with its umpire mentality, failed to
do.

Like their "public interest" orientation, the political
isolation of the agencies was also greatly exaggerated by
reformers.  The agencies often became dependent on the
congressional committees which appropriated their funds and
could expand - or shrink - their legislative authority.  The
FTC's status as an "independent agency" meant that it could
not usually invoke the protection of the President or a
cabinet official in its conflicts with powerful congressional
committee chairmen.

The President's budgetary officers, reflecting his

indifference, have generally collaborated with appropriations
subcommittees in keeping the agencies budgets small.  Many of
the FTC's failures can be attributed to the fact that until
1970 it had less than $20 million annual budget with which to
protect the consumer and competition in a $900 billion
economy.

These factors - pressures from the regulated industry, the
lact of consumer advocacy, subservience to a hostile Congress,
the indifference of the President, threadbare budgets, and a
lack of popular support - help explain why the decline of a
regulatory agency after a few aggressive years is so often
permanent.

What The Critics Overlooked These aspects of the FTC's social
and political environment have been overlooked by most
investigators of the regulatory agencies over the last four
decades.  The studies by the Brownlow Committee, the two
Hoover Commissions, James Landis, and the Ash Council
(formally known as the President's Council on Executive
Reorganization) (22) all proceeded from what might be called a
an "immaculate conception" model of the regulatory agency.
They assumed that the integrity of regulation could be
guaranteed from within government (23).  They focused on
questions of authority - how to make the agencies more
accountable to the President, how to give more power to the
chairmen - and personnel competence - "Good men," said James
Landis, "can make poor laws workable; poor men will wreak
havoc with good laws and administrative efficiency." (24)
They failed to emphasize the problem of unrepresented
interests, the absence of consumer advocacy, the impact of
bureaucratic secrecy which keeps the public from learning
about their stake in regulatory decisions, the influence of
the press, the attitudes of congressional oversight, and other
factors which determine the political and social milieu of
regulatory decisions.  As Harvard political scientist Merle
Fainsod noted in a critique of the Brownlow Report in 1940,
the effectiveness of the independent commissions goes far
beyond their relationship to the President and the smoothness
of their internal organization.  "In a more profound sense,"
he wrote, "it also involves the existence of a social and
economic environment in which regulators can function without
meeting frustration." (25)

The renaissance of the FTC between 1969 and 1973 has
occurred in part because of new leadership at the top but more
fundamentally because of changes in public opinion and in the
outside pressures on the agency which have made for a more

congenial regulatory environment and attracted aggressive
young lawyers and economists to its staff.

## Regulatory Restraint
Before examining the reasons for the changes at the FTC, the
changes themselves must be described in the context of the
FTC's traditional use of its powers.  Evidence of the FTC's
new look is found primarily in its regulation of the
advertising, content, and performance of consumer products,
rather than in its antitrust activities which have been less
vigorous and effective.[*]  Recent signs that the FTC may now be
ready to break new ground in the use of its antitrust powers -
especially with its new complaint against the major oil
companies issued in July 1973 - will be discussed
subsequently.

The FTC's Anemic Sanctions For most of its past, the FTC has
had a plausible excuse for inaction in the weakness of the
sanctions it could apply.  The Federal Trade Commission Act
[15 U.S.C. 45(a)(1)] authorizes the agency to prohibit "unfair
methods of competition, and unfair or deceptive practices in
commerce."  When the agency determined that such practices
exist, it "may issue an order...that the offender shall cease
and desist from using such method of competition."  [15 U.S.C.
45(b)]  While this seems to be a wide legal mandate on the
surface, its enforcement potential was in fact very limited.
The congressional sponsors of the Federal Trade Commission Act
in 1914 made clear that the impact of the order was to be more
educational than punitive.  Senator Newlands, floor manager of
the bill, attempted to reassure Senators who feared that the
FTC might harass legitimate business:

"The powers, of course, must be large, but the exercise of the
powers will not be against honest business but will be against
corporate and business outlaws and will be persuasive and
correctional rather than punitive, so far as well intentioned
business is concerned." (26)

The Supreme Court, interpreting congressional intent in the

---

[*]
 Research for this essay was completed in February 1973.
Subsequent major developments in both the antitrust and
consumer protection activities of the agency required an
updating of the manuscript in July 1973.

Ruberoid case in 1952, concluded that cease and desist orders
are "not intended to impose punishment or exact compensatory
damages for past acts but to prevent illegal practices in the
future." (27)

With the cease and desist order, therefore, the FTC in
effect tells the violator to go and sin no more. The orders
have only a prospective effect. No penalties, civil or
criminal, can be imposed for practices which have been found
to violate the law, no matter how flagrant and harmful they
may have been to the public. Only if the violator persists in
his wrongful action after the order has been issued can
penalties be imposed and then only after the violations has
been proved in a new, separate proceeding brought by the
Justice Department (28).

Prior to 1938, as noted above, the FTC was further
limited to issuing cease and desist orders only when an unfair
or deceptive practice could be shown to affect commerce. When
the Congress removed this restriction with the Wheeler-Lea
Trade Commission Act in 1938 which made "the consumer, who may
be injured by an unfair trade practice, of equal concern,
before the law, with the merchant of manufacturer injured by
the unfair methods of a dishonest competitor," it did not
accompany this grant of authority with an expansion of the
Commission's enforcement powers, except in the limited area of
food, drug, and cosmetic advertising. Making a distinction
between injuries to the consumer's health and assaults on his
pocketbook, the Congress added fines, criminal sanctions, and
the power to seek preliminary injunctions [Sec. 12] to be
applied only to cases of food, drug, and cosmetic promotion
where "personal injury or intent to mislead were involved."
(29)

Thus for the great majority of products and services sold
to the public, the FTC's sole enforcement weapon against
frauds and cheats has been the cease and desist order. Even
in 1938, a minority of the House Committee reporting the
Wheeler-Lea Act decried the weakness of the FTC's enforcement
powers:

"Unless the disseminator of a false advertisement knows at the
time of the dissemination that he may at some time in the
future be held accountable by a criminal or civil penalty
action for the unlawful dissemination, he will not be deterred
...It is just this...effect that is lacking when dependence
is placed upon cease-and-desist orders for enforcement." (28)

Thirty years later, the Nader Report on the FTC reached the

same conclusion:

"The only coercive legal enforcement tool generally
available to the FTC is the cease and desist order, which
imposes no retrospective sanctions but merely prohibits future
repetition of conduct against which it is aimed."

Not only does the cease and desist order do little more
than slap the hand of an offender, it also does virtually
nothing to compensate those whom the offender injures.  Even
former FTC Chairman Paul Rand Dixon, a chief target of the
Nader Report's critique, has complained that inadequate
redress for consumer grievances is a major problem:

"Administrative remedies, such as those presently provided by
the Federal Trade Commission Act, are not adequate since they
do not provide for recovery of individual losses." (30)

When the Commission does issue a "cease and desist" order,
the path to enforcement is circuitous and lengthy.  To
illustrate the complaint process, let us consider a
hypothetical case where a citizen writes a letter to the FTC
charging that "Kill-All" pesticide is decimating his
honeybees.  Kill-All, he notes, is advertised as toxic to the
boll weevil but benign to all other warm and cold blooded
creatures.  The Kill-All label, in contrast to its ads,
specifically warns, "May Be Harmful To Honeybees."  When the
FTC receives the letter the assigned staff attorney, at his
discretion, may informally check the facts and assess the
scope and significance of the alleged abuse.
    Although the Federal Trade Commission Act provides for the
formal adjudication of charges against business, an informal
enforcement procedure is followed in most cases.  An informal
agreement under this procedure may take the form of an oral or
written promise of voluntary compliance.  When informal
negotiations break down, the FTC may then initiate a formal
investigation to obtain evidence from Kill-All's manufacturer,
evaluate its defense, and consider possible remedies.  If the
Commission is satisfied, after this investigation, that the
complaint is valid and significant, it may issue a proposed
complaint.  In this case it notifies Kill-All it intends to
issue an order requiring the company to cease and desist the
exaggerated safety claims in its ads.  If Kill-All agrees to a
consent order at this stage, its terms would bind the company
just as if they resulted from an order after formal
adjudication, even though the consent agreement itself does

not constitute an admission of wrongdoing.

If a settlement cannot be negotiated with Kill-All, the FTC will then file a formal complaint. Attorneys representing the commission and the alleged violator then try the case before an FTC Administrative Law Judge introducing evidence and examining witnesses as in a courtroom trial. If this administrative judge upholds the complaint, the Kill-All lawyers may still go to the five commissioners who sit as a final court of appeals within the agency. (If the examiner finds in favor of Kill-All, the FTC attorneys may also appeal to the commissioners.) If this administrative court upholds the complaint, the defendant may finally take his case to the U.S. Court of Appeals. Using this system, the FTC took sixteen years to get the word "Liver" out of Carter's Little Liver Pills. (See Figure 1.)

While the consent order most commonly takes the form of prohibiting a deceptive practice, it can also require affirmative action from a respondent. But as the Geritol case shows, these orders also have severe limitations. In 1962, the FTC issued a complaint against the J.B. Williams Company, the manufacturer of Geritol, charging that Geritol's ads associating tiredness with "iron deficiency anemia" were deceptive. In 1965, the FTC issued a cease and desist order which required that ads for Geritol disclose the negative fact that the great majority of tired people are not suffering from an iron deficiency (31). This order was upheld by the U.S. Court of Appeals in 1967, but the offending commercials remained on the air until 1969 when the FTC finally asked the Justice Department to seek civil penalties against the company for violating its order. The FTC's victory, after over seven years of adjudication, was trivial. Geritol's ads now convey the same message as before - Geritol is a cure for tiredness - by identifying the product with zesty tableaux of vigorous middle-aged women. Since the health claim is implied, not stated, no affirmative disclosure is required.

Even when the FTC succeeds in having its order sustained, there is no guarantee that it will ultimately be obeyed. First, while there are penalties of $5,000 for disobeying its orders, the FTC cannot prosecute the offenders but must turn the case over to the Justice Department where they frequently expire from neglect. Second, in the past the FTC has often been uncertain whether its orders were being obeyed or not. The oversight and investigations staff of the House Appropriations Committee, in its 1972 report on the FTC, found the compliance effort to be "one of the weakest programs in the FTC since there is no systematic method of checking

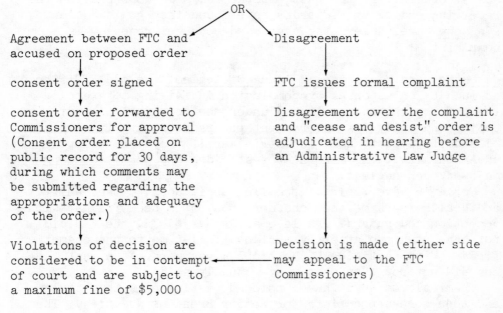

Application for complaint made by a citizen (e.g., a letter
asking the FTC to correct a deceptive practice)

Preliminary Investigation (informal check of facts
in the complaint and evaluation of the national scope
and significance of the alleged violation)

Formal Investigation (FTC formally solicits
data from affected parties, using subpoena
power and hearing if necessary)

Announcement in the Federal Register of the FTC's proposal to
issue a "cease and desist" order to stop an alleged violation

30 days allowed for negotiations between FTC and alleged violator

OR

Agreement between FTC and
accused on proposed order

consent order signed

consent order forwarded to
Commissioners for approval
(Consent order placed on
public record for 30 days,
during which comments may
be submitted regarding the
appropriations and adequacy
of the order.)

Violations of decision are
considered to be in contempt
of court and are subject to
a maximum fine of $5,000

Disagreement

FTC issues formal complaint

Disagreement over the complaint
and "cease and desist" order is
adjudicated in hearing before
an Administrative Law Judge

Decision is made (either side
may appeal to the FTC
Commissioners)

Upon disposition by the FTC
Commissioners, the accused
company may appeal to the U.S.
Court of Appeals

Figure 1   Routes for a citizen's complaint to the FTC.

outstanding orders" (32).

When a final cease and desist order is issued, the
respondent has sixty days to file a report setting forth in
detail his plans for complying with the order.  The FTC must
then make a decision whether or not the report is acceptable.
In some cases, these decisions have been absurdly overdue.
Compliance reports filed by the Mentholatum Company, Inc., and
the American Home Products Corporation in fiscal years 1962
and 1963, for example, were not accepted until May 1971 (32).
FTC officials concede that unless a report is ultimately
rejected or complaints about the company continue to come in,
compliance investigations are not normally conducted to
verify obedience to one of its orders.  In 1972, the FTC had
only one lawyer to check compliance with outstanding cease and
desist orders.  In the past, therefore, some companies on the
receiving end of an FTC order have found they could "go and
sin some more" unless the aggrieved consumer renewed his
complaint.

Cosmetics And Pesticides:  Areas Of Neglect The old FTC sinned
as much by omission as by commission in failing to exercise
the enforcement powers it had under the Act.  Not only did it
define and apply its enforcement powers narrowly, it simply
closed its eyes to some industries as if they were exempt
under the law.  The makers of pesticides and cosmetics long
enjoyed such neglect.

Cosmetic advertising, appealing as it does to the vanity
and health fears of the consumer, has often been fraught with
deception and hazard.  As late as January 1972, the FTC did
not have even one attorney assigned full-time to the cosmetics
field.  With pesticides, the problem was more often what the
ads did not say than what they actually said.

Chemical companies have promoted pesticides with a style
and tone more appropriate for Wonder Bread or Wheaties.  The
ads frequently give assurances of safety which contradict the
warnings on their labels.  Now that the organophosphate
pesticides, like parathion, which are hundreds of times more
acutely toxic than the chlorinated hydrocarbons, are replacing
DDT, Dieldrin, and other such restricted persistent
pesticides, the hazards of misuse are much greater than
before.  But the pesticide industry has refused to include
safety information in its ads (33).

In both cases, the FTC has historically deferred to other
agencies to regulate these industries.  And in both cases,
consumer frustration with the results of this regulation has
generated outside pressures from the Congress and the public

interest groups which persuaded the FTC to act.  In 1972, Rep.
Frank E. Evans (D.-Colo.), acting in response to consumer
complaints about deceptive ads for so-called "hypo-allergenic"
cosmetics, prodded FTC officials to look into this area during
hearings of the House Appropriations Subcommittee on
Agriculture, Environmental and Consumer Protection which
approves the FTC budget.  The subcommittee chairman Rep.
Jamie Whitten (D.-Miss.) also became interested.  To make sure
that the FTC got the message, he inserted an item in the
Appropriation Committee's report specifically allocating money
for ad substantiation, with special emphasis on cosmetics
(34).  A few months later, the FTC did appoint an internal
task force to investigate cosmetic advertising.  Although no
orders have yet been issued, this industry, with the House
Appropriations Subcommittee looking over its shoulder, is now
likely to get the attention it has avoided.

The FTC's action on pesticide advertising is in part a
ripple from the environmentalist tide which has swept over the
regulation of pesticides in the last three years.  In July
1972, the Center for Study of Responsive Law filed a complaint
petition with the FTC asking, among other things, that the
Commission stop Union Carbide, the maker of Sevin, and other
pesticide companies from making safety claims in their ads
which contradict the warnings on their label; that all
pesticides which bear the Skull and Crossbones symbol on their
label carry the same symbol on their ads; and that all
pesticide ads bear the affirmative disclosure, "WARNING:  This
product can be injurious to health; read the entire label
carefully and use only as directed." (33)

In the past the FTC might have ignored this petition.
There was no pressure from the Congress for the FTC to move in
this area; on the contrary, as noted above, the House
Appropriations Subcommittee which controls the FTC's budget is
chaired by Rep. Jamie Whitten (D.-Miss.), a man notoriously
protective of the pesticide industry (33, 35).  Nor were there
consumer complaints to spur the FTC on.  The victims of
pesticide misuse tend to be children, migrant workers and day-
laborers who are unlikely to know the FTC exists.

In the absence of these pressures, the causes of the FTC's
investigation of pesticides may be sought in three areas:
support by Robert Pitofsky, FTC's former consumer protection
chief; changes in the FTC's hiring practices and appeal which
allow it to attract young lawyers with experience in consumer
protection; and the presence of public interest legal groups
anxious to participate in FTC's proceedings and counter the
industry's response.  In this case, Pitofsky, after reading of

deaths of farmworkers from pesticide poisoning in the spring
of 1971, encouraged a petition from the Center for Study of
Responsive Law.  He also hired a former staff member of the
Center to work specifically on the pesticide issue.

After over a year of investigation, the FTC issued proposed
complaints on October 25, 1972, charging that three pesticide
firms, Hercules, Union Carbide, and FMC Corp., in their
advertising, misrepresented their products as safe, non-toxic,
and hazard-free; failed to disclose that they were dangerous
to health, and undermined the warnings on their labels.  For
example, the Hercules Corp. promoted its pesticide Toxaphene
with the logo, "Anyone who likes children and dogs and uses
Hercules toxaphene can't be all bad." (33)  While the ad
implied that Toxaphene was safe for children and warmblooded
animals, the Toxaphene label approved by the EPA specifically
warns that users should keep it out of reach of children, that
it may be fatal if taken internally, that it can be absorbed
through the skin in dry or liquid form, that its vapors should
not be breathed, and that it should be kept out of eyes and
off clothing.  Moreover, Hercules falsely claimed that
Toxaphene was a "soft" pesticide which did not persist or
build up in the environment.  Hercules' deceptive practices
were made more serious by the fact that Toxaphene is
frequently sold as a mixture with parathion, one of the most
acutely toxic pesticides.

With a similar blind spot for safety and fact, Union
Carbide advertised its pesticide Sevin with the following
statements (36):

"Developed at Union Carbide, Sevin carbaryl insecticide gets
rid of bugs without harming anything else.  Like birds, fish,
or people...What does all this control and convenience add up
to?  Confidence.  Confidence that you're using the most modern
insecticide you can buy.  So this season, pour it on!"

In fact, Sevin is highly toxic to honeybees (the Federal
Government compensated professional beekeepers for damage from
Sevin on numerous occasions in 1971-1972).  Its label,
approved by the EPA, states that it is harmful if inhaled,
swallowed, or allowed to come in prolonged contact with skin
and should be kept out of reach of children and animals.  The
FTC charges that despite the ads, Sevin is not relatively more
safe than many or most other pesticides on the market (36).

In its proposed order, the FTC would require that the
companies cease these deceptive ads and make two kinds of
affirmative disclosure.  All Hercules, Union Carbide, and FMC

advertising for pesticides with precautionary labeling would
have to state,

Important:  this product can be injurious to health.  Read the
entire label carefully and use only as directed.

When the pesticide label includes a Skull and Crossbones as
required for the most hazardous pesticides, the same symbol
must appear in the ads (36).
     While these proposals go far in meeting the demands of the
public interest group's petition, it falls short in one vital
respect.  The FTC failed to apply these sanctions in the form
of a rule which would apply to all advertising for pesticides.
Instead it is moving on the traditional case by case basis.
The above demands apply only to the three companies and eight
products mentioned in the complaint.  The FTC apparently hopes
that by making examples of a few pesticides, other pesticide
companies will voluntarily follow its directives.[*]

New Wine In Old Bottles
As the FTC's record on pesticide advertising indicates, its
failures as a consumer protection agency stemmed as much from
a lack of regulatory will as from a lack of legislative
authority.  The FTC's recent progressive image results not
from the exercise of new powers granted by the Congress but
from a willingness to experiment with new remedies which
expand the scope of effectiveness of its traditional powers.
Whether the FTC has exceeded its legal mandate with its
innovative orders is a subject of intense legal debate.

The "Octane" Case A major FTC weakness in the past has been
that, in protecting the consumer, it preferred to proceed case
by case, one manufacturer at a time.  By making an example of
the worst offenders, the FTC hoped that others would get the
message and mend their ways voluntarily.  In cases where a
deceptive practice is endemic to a whole industry, the case-
by-case approach leads to extraordinary delay and, in some
cases, to injustices when a firm is singled out for practices

---------------------------------------------------------------

[*]
 Roger Weil, the FTC attorney on the pesticide case,
recommended a trade rule, but at that time the FTC's
rulemaking power was stymied in the courts.  Now that the
FTC's authority has been sustained, the staff has again
recommended the trade-regulation-rule route.

common to his industry (28).

In these cases the FTC has an alternative:  It may issue a
trade regulation rule which bans an illegal practice across an
industry at a single stroke.  These rule-making procedures
amount to making laws which everyone is required to obey.  The
FTC began using the rulemaking procedure in the early 1960s in
response to complaints from various industries that case-by-
case enforcement was unduly hard on those firms selected for
enforcement.  Greater fairness would result if the FTC
formulated legally binding rules taking effect on the same
date for all firms covered by the rule.

Such rules add greatly to the thrust of the FTC's
enforcement power.  Because a rule clearly establishes the
illegality of a business practice, the FTC, in enforcing the
rule, need only prove that the respondent engaged in the
practice.  It does not have to go through the lengthy process
of proving that the practice is unfair or deceptive, for this
has already been established in the rulemaking procedure.  The
rule therefore conserves trial staff resources, always in
short supply in the FTC.

Despite these advantages, the FTC has been reluctant to use
this power for several reasons:  first, although apparently
implied by the Federal Trade Commission Act [Sec. 6(g)], it
had not been confirmed by either the Congress or the courts;
second, an industry-wide rule which disturbs the whole beehive
rather than just a few bees may generate more political
activity on Capitol Hill and the White House than politically
timid Commissioners can withstand.  In 1964, when the FTC
attempted to issue a trade regulation rule requiring health
warnings on cigarettes, the Congress intervened and passed a
law banning such action for four years.  Again in 1969, the
Congress extended the ban for another two years.

Despite then ambiguous status of its rule-making power, the
rejuvenated FTC is testing it once again in a landmark case
recently decided in its favor by the U.S. Court of Appeals.
In 1971, the Commission ruled that all gas stations had to
post octane ratings of gasoline on their gas pumps.
Christian White, an attorney in the FTC's policy planning
division, described the significance of the rule as follows:
"This ruling will put money directly into the consumer's
pocket.  If the concept of the trade regulation rule is
sustained, it will greatly increase our efficiency.  We simply
don't have the manpower to proceed case by case."  There are
approximately 135 petroleum refiners against whom the FTC
without the rule would have had to move on a case-by-case
basis to obtain octane posting.

The FTC's authority to make such rulings was overruled in 1972 by a Federal district court which found in favor of the oil industry's claim that the Congress had not given the FTC this rulemaking power.  The FTC appealed this decision and the U.S. Circuit Court of Appeals decided in its favor in July, 1973.  On another front a bill to give the FTC explicit authority to issue trade regulation rules passed the Senate in 1973 and is presently awaiting action in the House.

Ad Substantiation  In December 1969, consumer advocate Ralph Nader instructed two surprised associates to go and watch television for a couple of months.  At first, Nader must have seemed like Madison Avenue's fairy godmother, for his staff watched only commercials, turning the set off during programs. After tape-recording and describing hundreds of commercials, the staff sent letters to 58 companies asking them to substantiate the advertising claims they made on TV. Bristol-Myers, which assures viewers that "a study of hospital patients showed:  two Excedrin more effective in the relief of pain than twice as many aspirin," was asked to disclose details of its "study."  Procter & Gamble, Colgate Palmolive, and General Foods were all asked to provide their testing data showing that detergents with enzymes are safe.  In both cases, Nader's staff had previously obtained medical data which a appeared to contradict the efficacy and safety claims for these drugs and detergents.  Alarmed at the inadequacy of the companies' replies, Nader in 1970 petitioned the FTC asking, among other things, that the Commission issue a trade regulation rule stating that it is deceptive and unfair for any company to make, directly or by implication, claims for a product's safety or effectiveness which are not substantiated by competent scientific tests (37).

In July 1971, the FTC responded to the Nader petition by announcing its intention to require members of five consumer goods industries to submit data to substantiate any claims, statements, or representations regarding comparative price, safety, performance, efficacy or quality of the products advertised.  The Commission also promised to make the data public.  This ad substantiation program has two goals: education and deterrence.  It aims to help consumers to make a rational choice between competing product claims and to encourage self-regulation by advertisers who fear the embarrassment and loss of consumer confidence which might result from public scrutiny of unsupported claims.

The success of the program to date is mixed.  It has clearly shifted the burden of proof for complaints about advertising from the consumer to the manufacturer.  In the past, the skeptical consumer who doubted that Wonder Bread builds strong bodies 12 ways* had nowhere to go.  Now Wonder Bread, at the FTC's demand, has to bring in supporting charts and data for consumers to examine.  The program has been described by Sen. Frank Moss (D.-Utah), Chairman of the Senate Commerce Subcommittee on Consumer Affairs, as "successful, indeed startling, in revealing the widespread and flagrant absence of adequate substantiation." (38)  The FTC found serious inadequacies in the data sent in to support ad claims in about 30 percent of the responses (38).  One example is the case involving Black Flag Roach Killer, manufactured by the American Home Products Corporation.  The company demonstrated its product's worth in an ad comparing Black Flag with another roach killer containing Dieldrin.  The Black Flag roaches died; the Dieldrin ones survived.  When pressed, American Home Products admitted that the roaches were a specially selected strain, resistant to Dieldrin (39).

Such cases embarrass the manufacturers, but there is some skepticism as to whether they have yet done much to inform consumers.  Critics point out that very little of the product data compiled by the ad substantiation program has reached the consumer, in part because it is too technical or incomplete for the layman to comprehend.  In its preliminary analysis of the data, the FTC staff found that at least 30 percent of the substantiation material was so technical in nature that it apparently required special expertise far beyond the capacity of the average consumer to evaluate.  The Center for Auto Safety, a consumer group affiliated with Consumers Union, after analyzing data submitted by the automobile industry, concluded that it was a "mockery of the FTC" and of the principle of truth in advertising."

Robert Pitofsky, former chief of FTC's Bureau of Consumer Protection, has conceded that the ad substantiation program has not attracted great crowds of consumers to the FTC's library, but feels that it is up to public interest groups and the press to "translate all this technical jargon into

----------------------------------------------------------------

*
 FTC has lost a case before an Administrative Law Judge challenging the company's implied representations that Wonder Bread has unique nutritional qualities.  The Judge held that Wonder Bread ads did not imply this and that, in any event, no one was fooled by the advertising.  The case has been appealed to the Commissioners.

meaningful lay jargon." The program, he claims, is bringing about a fundamental change in the way ads are developed and cleared (40). The major advertising agencies have introduced new review procedures to make sure they will not be embarrassed or ridiculed for making claims they cannot support.

Corrective Advertising Although the FTC's powers are generally expressed in negative terms (e.g., to prevent deception and fraud), it has increasingly since 1969 exercised the affirmative powers in requiring respondents to disclose negative facts about their products and even to confess misrepresentations or deceptive omissions in past advertising. The courts have generally recognized the FTC's authority to require affirmative disclosure in cases where, as in the Geritol case discussed above, disclosure is necessary to prevent deception (29). Since 1969, the FTC has gone further and required companies to make negative disclosures about their products in order to counter the lingering effect of past deceptive ads on the public. For example, the Commission ordered three makers of enzyme detergents to disclose the stains their products could not remove in any ads making claims for stain removal.

Orders requiring negative disclosure do not appear to violate the FTC Act's prohibition [Section 5] against retrospective and punitive orders (29). In trying to eliminate the lingering misconceptions from past ads which would otherwise continue to influence consumer decisions in the future, they are prospective in effect. By merely requiring a truthful portrayal of the product's ingredient and performance claims, they are reasonably carrying out the purposes of the Act to prevent deceptive and unfair trade practices; their purpose is not to punish the offender for his misdeeds in the past but to prevent him from profiting from them in the future.

There is, therefore, little dispute that the FTC has authority to require a company to disclose specific information, even negative information, about his product. Exercising this power, the FTC has taken vigorous steps to supply consumers with the strategic product information they need to make rational choices among rival brands. It has required disclosure of tar and nicotine levels in cigarettes, care labeling instructions for wearing apparel, octane levels for gasoline, and phosphate content for detergents, to mention only a few of its actions. Commenting on the FTC's broad interpretation of its mandate (Sec. 5), Robert Pitofsky has

observed that "there are few important product characteristics
that consumers could and would use to assist them in the
selection process that the FTC could not mandate." (15)

Corrective advertising orders requiring confessions of past
deception are much more controversial.  In 1971, after looking
at ad substantiation data, the FTC decided that Profile bread
in claiming to have fewer calories per slice failed to reveal
that this was so only because the bread was sliced thinner.
Instead of simply stopping the deceptive ads, the FTC, for the
first time, required that future ads would have to admit
publicly the past deception.

Since then, this same corrective-ad approach has also been
used against Ocean Spray Cranberries, Inc., which had been
claiming that its cranberry juice had more food energy than
orange or tomato juice; in fact, it had more calories, but no
more vitamins or minerals.  For one year, Ocean Spray has been
ordered to spend 25 percent of its advertising budget
confessing its past deceptions.

Similarly the FTC has charged that the Chevron Oil Company
falsely claimed that its gasoline additive F-310 significantly
reduced air pollution.  The order required Chevron to reveal
in ads over a one year period that the FTC has found that its
previous ads for F-310 contained false and misleading
information and that F-310 does not in fact reduce air
pollution.

The FTC also has used this remedy against other
manufacturers, including Domino Sugar, because of its claims
that sugar consumption, before meals, may help people to lose
weight, and the makers of Wonder Bread and the analgesic
family of painkillers (e.g., Bufferin, Anacin, Bayer, and
Excedrin) because of bogus claims of uniqueness to
differentiate their products.

While the orders requiring confessions have not yet been
overturned by the courts, some legal commentators feel that
the orders contravene Section 5's interdiction against
retrospective and punitive orders.  Acheson and Tauber
conclude that

"Orders requiring confessions of offensive behavior are orders
fashioned to operate retroactively by eliciting an involuntary
declaration of responsibility for particular unlawful
practices, and therefore, their issuance is beyond the
authority of the FTC." (29)

The FTC finds support for its confessional orders in a broad
interpretations of its discretion to fashion equitable

remedies for deceptive practices, but Acheson and Tauber argue
that such implied equity power cannot overcome the specific
limits in the Act on retrospective and punitive orders (29).
The issue will probably ultimately be resolved in the courts.

Credit for the public confessional concept goes primarily
to a group of George Washington University law students,
directed by Professor John Banzhaf III. In 1969, these
students using the acronym SOUP (Students Opposing Unfair
Practices), submitted comments on a proposed FTC order
requiring the Campbell Soup Company to stop putting marbles in
the soup it advertised on television. The clear glass marbles
pushed meat and vegetables to the top, making the soup look
richer than it was. While the FTC was content with a cease
and desist order, SOUP wanted it to require Campbells to run
corrective ads confessing its deception. On May 25, 1970, by
a 3 to 2 vote of the Commissioners, the FTC turned the
students down, arguing in effect that the FTC had better
things to do than worry about marbles in soup. But while the
Commissioners decided that the cease and desist order was an
adequate remedy in this case, they did express the opinion
that the FTC had the legal right to use the corrective ad
approach when appropriate in the future.

Counter Advertising Consumer and environmental groups have
prepared advertisements to challenge the see-buy-drive pitch
of normal commercials; but local stations, supported by the
Federal Communications Commission (FCC), have resisted airing
them. Recently, the FTC has urged the FCC to allow the
counter-ads. In doing so, the FTC has implicitly sided with
groups like the Stern Community Law Fund, which has started a
crusade against "government censorship of the airwaves." The
Fund's California office has produced two counter-ads, one
against Chevrolet, and the other against the brand-name
painkillers. In the latter, Burt Lancaster looks over a
display of Bufferin and its high-priced, highly advertised
competitors, and says, "Buy the least expensive plain aspirin
you can find."

The network's reaction is less surprising than the FTC's
defense of such tactics. Not only was it trespassing on
another agency's jurisdiction, but it was waving a red flag
before a major industry with great political influence. The
FTC went so far as to suggest that TV and radio stations
regularly make available five minute blocks of prime time for
paid advertisements designed to contest advertising claims
that warrant challenge and public debate (41).

"Reasonable Basis" Doctrine In the past, complaints under the Federal Trade Commission Act [Section 5] have been primarily limited to advertising which the FTC had shown to be false and deceptive.

In the Pfizer case, decided July 11, 1972, the FTC made a statement of policy that a new violation falls within Section 5, namely, that an ad is unfair. The complaint in the Pfizer case charged that claims for the pain-relieving properties of Un-Burn gave the impression, either directly or by implication, that they had been substantiated by scientific tests conducted in advance by the manufacturer.

The Commissioners ultimately ruled that the ads did not make such representations and were not therefore false or deceptive. They concluded, however, that "the making of an affirmative product claim in advertising is unfair to consumers and therefore a violation of the Act [Section 5] unless there is a reasonable basis for making that claim." (45)

In the Un-Burn case, the only reasonable basis for the pain-relieving claims would be medical or scientific tests. If such tests did not exist, the Un-Burn claims would be unfair, even though no reference to medical or scientific substantiation was made in the ads. In the Un-Burn case, however, data to substantiate the claims was found in the medical literature, and the complaint was dismissed.

Advertising Trivia: The Skeptics' View While these remedies for deceptive advertising have been heralded by the press, many FTC insiders consider them a superficial response to fundamental economic problems. Instead of bothering with such symptoms of an oligopolistic economy, they urge the FTC to make a more basic attack on problems of competition and economic strength. As one senior staffer in the FTC's antitrust division put it in 1972:

"It's all very well to improve the moral quality of advertising by making Bayer Aspirin tell the truth, but if it does not lower prices, improve product quality, and reduce market concentration, it's an exercise in futility. There is no sign yet that corrective ads or ad substantiation is achieving any of these goals." (43)

Pitofsky's response was to argue that a primary cause of industry concentration is consumer ignorance. Secrecy kills incentives for product improvement, encourages trivial ads, and instills the assumption that the more a product costs, the better it is.*

In the past, the FTC has been criticized for avoiding major
cases which, if won, would increase competition in
concentrated industries, with maximum impact on the consumer.
The agency has been compared to a traffic cop who, in the
midst of a crime wave, hands out tickets for jaywalking at
2 a.m.  Recent cases signal a change in direction, however.

In the Octane case, as noted above, the FTC attempted to
issue a trade regulation rule for the oil industry.  A more
significant sign of change was the FTC's complaint against the
four top cereal manufacturers for illegally monopolizing their
market.  According to Michael Mann, Director of the FTC's
Bureau of Economics, the cereal case is "one of the most
exciting breakthroughs in antitrust policy in 50 years." (44)
The FTC charged that General Foods, General Mills, Kellogg,
and Quaker Oats have artifically inflated prices and reaped
excessive profits through restrictive shelf practices in
supermarkets, unfair promotion efforts, and proliferation of
brand names for virtually identical cereals.  The case is
unique in that it does not allege any conspiracy among the
firms, but instead attacks the basic market structure of the
industry.  The cereal industry, claiming that the FTC is
attacking success and bigness per se, is vigorously resisting.
While the case shows FTC's change in attitude, Mann's
description of its as a breakthrough was premature, to say the
least.  Many complaints brought forth with great fanfare die an
obscure death.

It may be too soon to assess the impact of the FTC's new
look on monopoly and deceptive practices in the business
community, but most observers agree that the potential for
basic reform is there.  In 1972, Thomas Hiura, editor of the
Antitrust Law and Economics Review, praised former FTC
Chairman Kirkpatrick for beginning to combine legal and

------------------------------------------------------------
*
 This thesis was the subject of a published theoretical
analysis by Economist Tibor Scitovsky as long ago as 1950.
See "Consumer Ignorance is a Source of Oligopoly Power,"
American Economic Review, May 1950.  The difficulty in relying
on increased information as a corrective measure, however, is
that while consumer knowledge of essential product information
may prevent the use of noninformational advertising to gain a
large share of a competitive industry, there is no indication
that an infusion of such information will, by itself,
deconcentrate an existing oligopoly.

economic analysis in major cases but concluded that the
economic benefits of his casework to date are probably slight,
if not zero.  As Mark Silbergeld, a former FTC attorney has
observed, "The dog barks and even takes a nip now and then but
will it ever learn to bite?"  Issuing complaints is the bark;
decision and enforcement is the bite.

Since that remark was made in the fall of 1972, the FTC has
issued antitrust complaints against two of the nation's most
powerful industries.  On March 6, 1973, the FTC formally
adopted a previously proposed complaint charging Xerox
Corporation with illegally monopolizing the market for office
copying machines.  On July 18, 1973, the agency's antitrust
division filed a complaint seeking "significant divesture" of
refineries and pipelines of eight major oil companies,
including Exxon, Texaco, Gulf, Mobil, Standard Oil of
California, Standard Oil of Indiana, Shell, and Atlantic
Richfield.  The complaint accused the companies of joining
together to monopolize the refining of crude oil into
petroleum products, thus forcing consumers to pay
substantially higher gasoline prices.  In this case, the FTC
appears to be reacting to the concern about the energy crisis
which is undermining, to some extent, the heretofore
impregnable power of the oil industry within the Executive
Branch and on Capitol Hill (45).

How The FTC Revived
While the FTC has still not realized its potential, its
innovative actions in the consumer protection and more
recently antitrust areas are evidence of a significant shift
in its priorities since 1969.  As noted above, the changes at
the FTC must be understood in the context of the social and
political environment outside government, not simply in terms
of its internal organization and relationships in the Federal
Executive Branch.

Change In Public Expectations Of The Agency  In 1969, the
modern consumer movement was approximately three years old, if
we date it from 1966 when President Johnson first made
consumer protection a major thrust of his legislative program,
Ralph Nader became a household word and auto safety became a
national issue.  By 1968, the Congress had passed six major
consumer bills, including Truth in Lending, the Wholesome Meat
Act, the Traffic and Motor Vehicle Safety Act, the Wholesome
Poultry Products Act, and the Natural Gas Pipeline Safety Act,
demonstrating the political muscle of consumerism.  Consumers
Union, capitalizing on the surge in consumer interest, doubled

its number of subscribers between 1964 and 1969.

These developments reflect economic and technological forces which have increased the consumer's demand for protection by government.  The concentration of corporate power which has both reduced competition and induced consumer powerlessness, the sophistication of modern advertising techniques, and the technical complexity and abundance of consumer products greatly increased the scope for deception, fraud, and injury to the consumer.  These factors, coupled with the fact that the consumer had more discretionary purchasing power than ever before, led to demands for more information, efficacy, and safety from consumer products.  As FTC Commissioner, Mary Gardiner Jones has remarked:

"Today the consumer's need for information in order to make the type of meaningful rational choices among products and services offered in the marketplace...is totally different from what it was even a decade ago." (46)

By the mid-1960s, therefore, a wide gap had opened between the purchasing skill and knowledge of the consumer and the selling skill and technological sophistication of the manufacturer. Sensing this, "consumers today," says Jones, "are seeking to experience and express some sense of conscious and knowledgeable mastery over decisions which they are called upon to make in their daily lives." 946)  The increasing number of "applications for complaint" received by the FTC in this period illustrates this increased consumer awareness:  In 1960, the FTC received 4,886 complaints, but by 1970 the number had more than doubled to 10,906 (47).

The Role Of The President The rising public expectations of the FTC came at a time when the agency's failures were mercilessly exposed by a succession of critics, including task forces sponsored by Ralph Nader and the American Bar Association.

The charges were not entirely new.  As noted above, the FTC had been studied at least seven times by Presidential commissions, congressional committees, and other bodies during its first 50 years, and all the reports were consistently unfavorable.  One of the most effective critics was FTC Commissioner Philip Elman who inveighed against the cronyism and incompetence in the Commission and even urged the Bureau of the Budget in 1969 not to increase the agency's budget because of "its manifest failures and deficiencies."  By 1969 when he retired, Commissioner Elman had gained a majority of

the Commissioners - but not the Chairman Paul Rand Dixon - for
his point of view (5).

What was new, at least in the Nader report, was the go-for-
the-throat style of criticism.  Within a few pages of the
Nader study, the FTC was unveiled as a 19th Century Southern
county courthouse, paralyzed by its inhabitants' incompetence
and senility.  Comic illustrations were provided by personnel
like the FTC staffer whom the Raiders, arriving for a
mid-morning appointment, discovered dozing the day away,
blanketed by the sports pages of the Washington Post (8).  The
charge and counter-charge, always in personal terms to pierce
the veil of ennui which usually shields regulatory agencies
from the public, kept the FTC in the news for weeks.

Because there is usually little immediate political reward
in effective regulation, Presidents traditionally show little
positive interest in regulatory agencies unless a regulatory
failure stirs widespread publicity (48).  When the American
Bar Association legitimized the Nader charges nine months
later, one of the conditions of White House interest in a
regulatory agency had been met:  the FTC had become a national
scandal (49).

Good timing also gave reform a boost.  A new President was
in the White House who could deny any responsibility for the
past errors of the Commissioners, all of whom were Democratic
appointees.*  The President had made references to consumerism
in his Inaugural Address.  Reform of the FTC was an obvious
project to demonstrate the White House's commitment to
consumer protection.

The Weinberger Regime  Nixon's first step was to appoint a new
FTC Chairman, Caspar Weinberger, to replace Paul Rand Dixon,
as chairman; however, Dixon remained as one of the five
commissioners to finish out his term.  The new Chairman
Weinberger, a former finance director for the Governor Ronald
Reagan's administration in California, began a massive house-
cleaning of personnel, a process eased by a reorganization plan
which eliminated many titled supervisory positions.  To
Chairman Weinberger's credit, the purge was relatively nonpartisan, despite the patronage demands of a Republican Party

---------------------------------------------------------------

*
 According to Mrs. Cox, in a television interview, Nixon's
interest in agency reform may have been influenced by the fact
that his daughter was soon to marry one of the Nader Report's
authors, Edward Cox.

which had been out of office for eight years.  With the help
of David Buswell, whom Commissioner Weinberger appointed as
his director of information, he began to repair the FTC's
public image.  Bright young people were brought in at the top
policy levels.

Early in his tenure, FTC Chairman Weinberger invigorated
his staff by announcing that the Commission "is receptive to
novel and imaginative provisions in orders seeking to remedy
alleged violations." (50)  This message gave the FTC staff a
hunting license to experiment with affirmative orders, such as
corrective ads and public confessionals, which in Chairman
Weinberger's words would probe the "frontiers of our
statutes." (5)

While some staff members downplayed the significance of his
reforms - "he stuck a pitchfork in a pile of manure and gave
it a flip" - Chairman Weinberger's actions greatly improved
the morale and administration of the agency.  His stay was
brief, however.  He took office in January 1970 and eight
months later "defected" to the Office of Management and
Budget.

The Kirkpatrick Regime As FTC Chairman Weinberger's
replacement, President Nixon selected Miles W. Kirkpatrick, a
conservative Republican lawyer from Philadelphia, whose
practice included an imposing array of corporate clients.
Although Kirkpatrick had directed the ABA study of the FTC, he
was greeted cautiously by the public interest bar until his
commitment to agency reform became known.  He soon became one
of the most widely respected public officials in Washington.

Kirkpatrick recruited an unusually able staff for the FTC's
top positions.  Three of his most celebrated appointments were
Dr. Michael Mann, an economist from Boston College, who became
director of the Bureau of Economics; Alan Ward, an experienced
antitrust lawyer, who became head of the Bureau of
Competition; and Robert Pitofsky, a law professor from New
York University, who became director of the Bureau of Consumer
Protection.  By the standards of the old FTC, these
appointments were notable because they were non-political
(Pitofsky, for example, is a Democrat) and because the men
chosen were recognized experts in their fields.

Under Weinberger and Kirkpatrick, the staff of the FTC was
reorganized by consolidating six disjointed and overlapping
bureaus into two - competition and consumer protection - which
corresponded to the two main areas of the agency's
responsibility.  A major change has also taken place in the
role of the FTC's Regional Offices.  Previously the offices

could not initiate their own projects.  They merely served as
a field investigating service for the Washington bureaus.  Now
the Regional Offices have been given authority to initiate
preliminary investigations, recommend complaints, try cases,
and even negotiate consent orders (40).

Another vital change was the creation of the Office of
Policy Planning and Evaluation in June 1970.  Both Nader and
the ABA Report had criticized the FTC for failing to set
priorities.  In the 1960s, while failing to combat ghetto
fraud, monitor false advertising, or check on compliance, the
Commission found time to bring a successful antitrust case
against a bubble-gum manufacturer, prevent a merger in the
gift wrapping paper business, and devote seven years to a case
against the dominant seller of toothpicks (51).  As the ABA
Report noted, the FTC, while complaining to the Congress about
lack of manpower, issued complaints "attacking the failure to
disclose on labels that 'Navy shoes' were not made by the
Navy, that flies were imported, that Indian trinkets were not
manufactured by American Indians, and that 'Havana' cigars
were not made entirely of Cuban tobacco." (13)  Before June
1970, the FTC had an Office of Program Review staffed with one
economist whose only visible output had been one memo calling
for a new commitment to planning (51).  The Office did not
even have a record on the ongoing enforcement activities of
the Commission and could therefore make no cost-benefit
assessment of the agency's programs.  The new office has
developed analytical program guides, policy planning
inventories, bench mark data systems and other tools to help
the FTC allocate its resources efficiently (51).  In 1973, the
FTC's new planning capability is seen by the FTC staff as a
major organizational reform.

One reason Chairman Kirkpatrick was able to make the FTC
respond is that, unlike most other regulatory agencies, it was
not targeted on any single industry.  Even in its worst days,
it was never a "captive" agency, in the sense that the
Interstate Commerce Commission was captured by the railroads
or the Federal Aviation Administration by the airlines.  When
Kirkpatrick came to the FTC as Chairman, he had to contend
with incompetence, passivity, low morale and other residues of
cronyism and politicization, but not with entrenched sappers
from one determined industry.

Moreover, the FTC's regulatory action in the fields of
deceptive advertising and antitrust are not so technical, so
intimately involved in the processes of a given industry that
they require much interchange of personnel between regulator
and regulatee.  This contrasts with, for example, the FDA

where the most available - and sometimes the only - source of
expertise on a drug of cosmetic issue may be the industry
itself.  The FTC's lawyers and economists, in seeking out
fraud and monopoly in American Business, are less directly
vulnerable to the deferred bribe of job offers than an FDA
toxicologist who spends his day scrutinizing drug applications
from Pfizer and Eli Lilly.

Outside Forces For Reform Other forces outside the FTC have
helped the momentum for reform:
The Press In a striking shift from its earlier boredom with
regulatory issues, the Washington press corps began to pay
attention to the FTC after 1969.  In the sixties, Commissioner
Philip Elman complained that the main trouble with the FTC was
that no one was interested in it.  This was not quite true.
The trade journals of industries regulated by the FTC were
interested and kept their clients informed about the agency.
But reports in the popular press which might have led to
counter-vailing consumer pressure were very rare.
     Between 1969 and 1970, FTC coverage began to benefit from
a general revival of interest in consumer issues.  One index
of this shift is the number of articles on consumer protection
appearing in popular magazines.  Between 1963 and 1966, there
were 33 articles, an average of about 8 per year.  Between
1967 and 1970, there were 128 articles, or 32 per year (9).
Both the Nader and the ABA reports and the public relations
work of David Buswell helped focus some of this interest on
the FTC.  Significantly, most of the press comment was very
supportive of Chairman Kirkpatrick's new initiatives.
     The difference this press support can make was revealed in
1970, in an early stage of the cereal case.  During a period
when the commissioners were vascillating about fully
developing this important antitrust case, David Vienna, a
reporter for the Washington Post, used a flood of leaks to
write a series of "Good Morning, Caspar" columns, putting
Chairman Weinberger on notice that any wavering on the cereal
case would jeopardize his progressive image.  This pressure
helped keep the case alive until Kirkpatrick's arrival.
The Congress The growing political strength of the consumer
movement and the press attention it receives have made the
Congress more sympathetic to reform in the FTC.  This has not
always been true.  Both the Nader and the ABA Reports charged
that Congressmen had undermined the FTC's competence and
integrity by patronage pressures and dissipated its energies
with trivial case-work.
     The Commission is still responsive to the interests of

ranking committee members, but these interests now have a more
consumer protective bent. The Senate Commerce Committee,
which along with the House Interstate and Foreign Commerce
Committee, drafts FTC legislation, has championed the FTC's
"new look." Michael Pertschuk, Chief counsel to the Senate
Commerce committee, states that the Democratic leadership has
made it clear, in a nonpartisan manner, that it wants and
expects reform in the Commission. Kirkpatrick "is doing some
very tough things," Pertschuk told the National Journal in
1971, "The knowledge that key committee members favor those
things has to have a supportive effect." (52) Senators Warren
G. Magnuson (D.-Wash.), Frank E. Moss (D.-Utah), and Philip A.
Hart (D.-Mich.) and Representatives John D. Dingel (D.-Mich.)
and John E. Moss (D.-Calif.) in the House have helped to spur
FTC action on ad substantiation, the relationship between
drug advertising and drug abuse, and many other of its recent
initiatives. The respective Antitrust Subcommittees of the
Judiciary Committees in the House and Senate are also in
friendly hands, with Chairmen Philip A. Hart and Peter W.
Rodino, Jr. (D.-N.J.), strong supporters of the FTC.

During the 91st, 92nd and 93rd Congresses, numerous bills
have been introduced to amend the Federal Trade Commission Act
to increase the agency's "consumer protection" powers. The
anti-regulation lobby directed by the Chamber of Commerce
remains strong enough to block most FTC legislation. In the
fall of 1973, however, a coalition of consumer, farm, and
labor organizations successfully pushed through amendments to
the Alaska Pipeline Bill which give the FTC new power to get
preliminary injunctions and to directly enforce its subpoenas
in federal court, and to obtain "line of business" information
necessary for its antitrust investigations without fear of a
veto by the Office of Management and Budget. This legislative
triumph, accomplished over the opposition of a fully mobilized
Chamber, shows the new lobbying muscle of consumer groups. In
addition, the Consumer Product Warranties and Federal Trade
Commission Improvement Act, which confirms the FTC's
rulemaking power and gives it authority to conduct its own
litigation and to set federal standards for written warranties
on all consumer products, passed the Senate in 1973 and now
awaits House action.

The FTC has also found support in the Senate and House
Appropriations Subcommittees, where Democratic liberals are
less in evidence. "Before I came to Washington," Robert
Pitofsky observed, "I had always heard that aggressive
enforcement would cause us to be cut off at the purse strings
by the Appropriations Committees. This hasn't been so. [Rep.

Jamie L.] Whitten's committee has not only held useful and
relevant hearings, but he has consistently given us all we
asked for and more." (40)

The surprise source of this congressional largesse, Rep.
Jamie L. Whitten (D.-Miss), Chairman of the House
Appropriations Subcommittee on Agriculture, Consumer
Protection and the Environment, has resisted the Office of
Management and Budget's attempts to shrink the FTC budget.
Since 1969, a period of austerity for most government agencies,
the FTC's budget has steadily increased - $16.9 million in
1969, to $19.9 million in 1970, to $22.5 million in 1971, to
$25.2 million in 1972, and to $30.0 million in 1973.  The 1973
appropriation from Rep. Whitten's subcommittee was $2 million
above the FTC request (58).  The FTC's budget therefore has
nearly doubled in less than five years, a dramatic increase
for a traditional agency.

Consumer Advocacy It is no coincidence that the growth of
consumer advocacy groups has paralleled the revival of the
FTC since 1969.  These groups have given the FTC an organized
consumer constituency for the fitst time.  Since its creation
in 1914, the FTC's staff has dealt almost exclusively with
corporate lobbyists and lawyers.  While consumer lawyers are
still outnumbered in the halls of the FTC, they have played a
major role in shifting the FTC's priorities and practices.
The FTC commissioners now regularly meet with consumer
representatives and consult them on appointments; in a huge
shift from the days when even its organization chart was
considered confidential, the FTC has adopted the most open
public information policy in government; and the agency has
allowed consumer representatives to intervene on a limited
basis in a few formal proceedings.

Robert Pitofsky concludes:

"A continuing, professional and enlightened source of consumer
advocacy will help rather than hinder the regulatory process
...Another argument I've heard from those who oppose (consumer
advocacy) is that its existence will lead to delay, confusion,
expense and general interference with existing regulatory
processes.  Experience at the FTC in recent years would
suggest, however, that these adverse effects can be
effectively controlled by the agency, and, more important,
that this is a price worth paying.  The FTC has permitted
formal intervention as a party by consumer representatives
(for example, by Students Opposed to Unfair Practices in the
Firestone advertising case) and informal participation at the
staff level (for example, by the Consumer Federation of

America and several Consumers Union affiliates in challenges
to the accuracy of supermarket price claims and by a group of
Nader associates in connection with the FTC's advertising
substantiation program).  By and large, almost no delay
occurred, confusion was controlled under the agency's ordinary
procedural rules and extra expense to the government was
slight.  On the other hand, these various groups contributed
to the ability of the FTC to reach informed and enlightened
judgments." (40)

The most important influence of consumer groups has not been
their formal intervention in the FTC's rulemaking and
adjudication.  In the Soup and Firestone cases, consumer
advocates did formally intervene, establishing important
precedents of standing, but these actions have been limited in
scope, affecting only a small fraction of the FTC's business.
According to FTC staff attorneys, the consumer groups' most
significant contribution has been in helping to restructure
incentives in FTC by first giving its staff a feeling of
scrutiny, a sense that their decisions are being watched, and
second, a feeling of support, a sense that strong action will
be applauded on the outside.  Job opportunities in consumer
groups and public interest law firms may offer additional
incentives in some cases.

The FTC's Future Chairman Kirkpatrick's leadership, morale-
building appointments, and reorganization halped to fuel the
FTC's resurgence, but by themselves they give little
assurance that the FTC has had a lasting change of direction.
Shuffling the boxes on organization charts is a well-known
reaction of agencies under fire and more often than not it can
be dismissed as a triumph of form over substance.  In the
past, the periodic reorganizations have had little impact on
the FTC's effectiveness.  Nor can the torrent of criticism
which washed over the FTC in 1968-1969 be expected to have any
lasting effect.  Indeed the evidence of many recent exposes -
of agencies like the Bureau of Veterinary Medicine, the
Interstate Commerce Commission, and the meat inspection branch
of the Department of Agriculture - is that criticism only
brings more firmly set resistance.
    As for support from the White House, there were strong
indications that the President had soured on the FTC by 1972.
Herb Klein, the President's communications director, publicly
stated that he regarded the advertising substantiation program
as "part of an increasing attack on advertising itself - an
important part of business life in America."  In July 1972,

Advertising Age, a leading trade journal, reported that
President Nixon had apologized for FTC Chairman Kirkpatrick
and the FTC's new vigor at a meeting with broadcasters and
expressed the fear that counter advertising could destroy
brand advertising in America.

The Office of Management and Budget (OMB) put additional
pressure on Kirkpatrick by freezing funds appropriated by the
Congress for the FTC.  In 1972 the OMB withheld $620,000,
forcing Chairman Kirkpatrick to abolish 72 new positions.
Before the Fiscal 1973 budget was submitted to the Congress,
the OMB had cut 208 more positions from the Agency's request,
a heavy slice for the FTC with only 1,500 staff members.
These reductions, according to a letter FTC Chairman
Kirkpatrick wrote to Senator Lee Metcalf (D.-Mont.) on May 16,
1972, forced the FTC to cancel investigations of hospital and
medical costs, the business conduct of multinational
corporations such as ITT, and patent interference and joint
ventures which result in anticompetitive practices.

FTC Chairman Kirkpatrick and most of his top staff members,
including Pitofsky, Ward, Mann, and Buswell, resigned from the
FTC in early 1973.  While Chairman Kirkpatrick gave his reason
for leaving as his desire to return to his private law
practice, he reportedly told close associates in the FTC that
he would not stay if the President did not want him.

As his replacement, President Nixon selected Lewis A.
Engman as chairman.  As a former assistant director of the
White House Domestic Council under John Erlichman, Engman's
commitment to consumer protection was suspect to many consumer
groups and Congressmen, but by the end of 1973, there was
guarded optimism about the Engman regime.  First, his
training in economics and the recent FTC antitrust complaint
against the oil companies suggest that he may give more
emphasis to a forceful antitrust policy.  Chairman Engman has
strongly endorsed congressional efforts to increase the FTC's
enforcement and investigative powers in the antitrust and
consumer protection fields.  Second, he has made some highly
distinguished appointments to the FTC's key posts.  James T.
Halverson, the new director of the Bureau of Competition;
Thomas Rosch, director of the Bureau of Consumer Protection;
and Frederic Sherer, director of an expanded Bureau of
Economics, have excellent professional qualifications and
extensive legal experience in their fields.  Staff morale,
which was sinking after Kirkpatrick's departure, is again on
the rise.  Thus, while the turnover in the FTC's principal
positions since Chairman Kirkpatrick's departure has been
virtually complete, the staff momentum behind an aggressive

enforcement policy continues to run strong.

An equally dramatic turnover has occurred among the FTC's
five commissioners, and here the outlook is more clouded.
During the Kirkpatrick regime, there was a delicate pro-
consumer balance of power.  Several key votes on the FTC's new
departures have been 3 to 2.  The line-up was normally
Chairman Kirkpatrick and Commissioner Mary Gardiner Jones
against Commissioner A. Everette MacIntyre, with either
Commissioners David Dennison or Paul Rand Dixon as the swing
votes in 3 to 2 decisions.  Commissioner Dixon, for example,
was for the cereal complaint while Dennison was against, but
Commissioner Dennison was for corrective advertising while
Dixon was against.  Now there is a whole new commission, with
Commissioner Dixon the only holdover from the Kirkpatrick era.
While the new commissioners appear more philosophically
conservative than the old, they have not yet been faced with
key decisions which would reveal their leanings.

Judging by the FTC's recent antitrust complaints, its
promises to expand greatly its rule-making functions and to
use the new enforcement powers bestowed by Congress, the FTC
is still being carried along by the reform movement launched
by Chairman Kirkpatrick.  Whether the FTC's "new look" will
survive depends on the continued support of organized consumer
groups, friendly congressional committees, and the press.  In
this effort, Chairman Engman may prove to be as effective as
Kirkpatrick.  A highly political person, with ambitions for
public office back in Michigan, he appears to want to project
a consumer-oriented image for the commission.  Moreover,
Watergate has of course dissipated whatever influence the
White House had over the new Chairman.  Engman also appears
sensitive to the need for more consumer participation in FTC
proceedings.  He won praise for his initiative in bringing
consumer and industry groups together to work out a voluntary
code for children's advertising.  The FTC is also considering
proposals to subsidize consumer intervention in formal
proceedings.

## Conclusion

In reviewing the changes at the FTC since 1969, one is forced
to conclude that previous investigations of the agency, with
their emphasis on structural reforms and internal
institutional changes, have mostly missed the point in their
attempts to make the agencies more responsive to the public
interest.  As long as the advocacy gap in the FTC's political
process remains unaffected, it matters relatively little
whether the agency is directly accountable to the President,

or quasi-independent; or whether there is one commissioner or
collegial rule; or whether rule-making or case-by-case
adjudication is dominant; or even whether the agency's
delegated missions and goals are formulated loosely or with
"strict guides, checks, and safeguards." As Roger Cramton,
former chairman of the Administrative Conference, has said:

"The cardinal fact that underlies the demand for broadened
.public participation is that governmental agencies rarely
respond to interests that are not represented in their
proceedings. And they are exposed, with rare and somewhat
insignificant exceptions, only to the view of those who have a
sufficient economic stake in a proceeding or succession of
proceedings to warrant the substantial expense of hiring
lawyers and expert witnesses to make a case for them."

Upon his departure from the FTC, Robert Pitofsky confirmed
this view in warning the Senate Commerce Committee that even
the most conscientious and public-spirited bureaucrat,
hearing day after day skilled, articulate and experienced
business representatives advancing arguments against action or
for limited action cannot help but be influenced by the
imbalance of views to which he is exposed.
To suggest, as the Ash Report has done, that the policy
bias which results from this imbalance can be cured by making
the agencies more accountable to the President is simply
naive. At best, such a fundamental restructuring will offer
marginal improvements; at worst, it creates false
expectations which are soon shattered by the next expose.
In contrast to the emphasis of the Ash Report, the FTC case
suggests that the key factor which distinguishes "citizen
responsive" agencies such as EPA, the FTC, and to some degree
the FDA, from "industry-responsive" agencies such as the Civil
Aeronautics Board, the Interstate Commerce Commission, or the
meat inspection branch of the Department of Agriculture is the
level of public participation and interest in their
activities. The curve of reform at the FTC has closely
followed the shape of the curve of public interest and
participation in its decisions. The fact that the FTC started
out on a road to reform can be attributed in the first
instance to the initiative of men like Chairman Kirkpatrick.
The fact that the FTC continues down this road after
Kirkpatrick and his staff have departed can be attributed, in
part, to the fact that public interest in the agency, focused
by consumer groups and congressional oversight, is closing
somewhat the advocacy gap at the FTC.

The new breed of consumer advocates has jettisoned the
traditional reformist model of the regulatory agency as an
aloof protector of a passive public. With its emphasis on
piecemeal reform, its steady chipping away at the blocks of
resistence to change, consumer advocacy as a model of reform
lacks the glamour of the Ash Council's grand design. But as
the FTC example modestly suggests, it is this kind of plodding
incrementalism, nurtured by an approving public and supportive
Congress, that holds the most promise for the Federal Trade
Commission's reform.

## References

1.   Marver H. Bernstein first described this model of the
agency life-cycle in Regulating Business by Independent
Commission, Princeton University Press, 1955.

2.   Cox, Fellmeth, and Schulz, The Nader Report on the
Federal Trade Commission.  Baron, New York (1969).

3.   Jones, Mary Gardiner, "The Federal Trade Commission as
Consumer Protector:  Government Can Be Responsive to Human
Needs."  Speech before the 76th Annual Convention of the U.S.
Independent Telephone Association, October 23, 1973.

4.   ----- , The Wall Street Journal.  August 10, 1973.

5.   United States Government Organization Manual, 1970-1971.
Washington, D.C. (1970), p. 440.

6.   For a critical review of the FTC's antitrust activities,
see Mark Green et al., The Closed Enterprise System.  Bantam
Books, New York (1972), pp. 319-347.

7.   The House Conference Report on the Federal Trade
Commission bill recognized the problem of definition in 1914:
"It is impossible to frame definitions which embrace all
unfair practices.  There is no limit to human inventiveness in
this field...If Congress were to adopt the method of
definition, it would undertake an endless task."  Cong. Rec.
51:1492 (1914).

8.   Friendly, Henry J., The Federal Administrative Agencies.
Harvard University Press, Cambridge (1962), pp. 19-24.

9.   ----- , Cong. Rec. 51:8842 (1914).  For a general
discussion of the thesis that regulatory agencies were more
often created to serve the needs of business than to protect
the public, see Kolko, Gabriel, The Triumph of Conservatism.
Free Press, New York (1963).

10.  Nadel, Mark, The Politics of Consumer Protection.  Bobbs-
Merrill, Indianapolis (1971), p. 26.  Richard Hofstadter
points that one prominent reformer, Louis Brandeis, was
disappointed with the FTC from the start, dismissing the first
commissioners as "a stupid administration."  The Age of
Reform, Random House, New York (1955), p. 242.  See also

Gerard Henderson, The Federal Trade Commission, Yale
University Press, New Haven (1924).

11. Ibid., p. 27.

12. U. S. Commission on Organization of the Executive Branch
of the Government, The Independent Regulatory Commission,
Washington, D. C. (1949) (better known as the first Hoover
Commission).

13. American Bar Association, Report of the ABA Commission to
Study the Federal Trade Commission. New York (1969).

14. Jaffe, Louis, "The Effective Limits of the Administrative
Process: A reevaluation." Harvard Law Review 67:1113 (1954).

15. Pitofsky, Robert, Statement on S. 707, A Bill to
Establish A Council of Consumer Advisors and an Independent
Consumer Protection Agency, and to Authorize a Program of
Grants, Committee on Commerce, United States Senate, 93rd
Congress (1973).

16. Noll, Roger G., Reforming Regulation, The Brookings
Institution, Washington, D. C. (1971), P. 34; Simon Lazarus,
"Halfway Up from Liberalism: Regulation and Corporate Power,"
in R. Nader and M. Green, editors, Corporate Power in America,
Grossman, New York (1973), p. 217.

17. Davis, Kenneth C., Administrative Law Treatise 82 (1958);
see also Discretionary Justice, Louisiana State University
Press, Baton Rouge (1969).

18. Jaffe, Louis, "Review." Yale Law Journal 65:1070 (1956).

19. -----, from unpublished manuscript quoted in S. Lazarus,
The Genteel Populists.

20. Olson, Mancur, The Logic of Collective Action. Harvard
University Press, Cambridge (1965).

21. Auerback, Carl A., "Pluralism and the Administrative
Process." Annals of the American Academy of Political and
Social Sciences 400:13 (March 1972).

22. The President's Committee on Administrative Management
(the Brownlow Committee) recommended to President Roosevelt in

1937 that the commission be abolished and their functions transferred to executive departments; U.S. Commission on Organization of the Executive Branch of the Government, The Independent Regulatory Commission, GPO, Washington, D.C. (1949), (better known as the first Hoover Commission) stressed increasing the power of the charimen, upgrading the qualifications of commissioners, and improving administrative efficiency; the second Hoover Commission:  Commission on Organization of the Executive Branch of the Government, Legal Services and Procedure, Washington, D. C. (1955), emphasized improvement of internal procedures, especially by separating judicial functions from other administrative activities; the Landis Report on Regulatory Agencies recommended to President Kennedy in 1960 the creation of an executive "czar" to oversee the regulatory agencies and gear them to Presidential directives.  The Ash Council's recommendations are discussed subsequently.

23.  Lazarus, Simon, "Halfway Up from Liberalism, Regulation and Corporate Power," in Noll, Roger G., (Supra 16) p. 229.

24.  Landis, James, Report on the Regulatory Agencies to the President-Elect, Washington D. C. (December 1960), p. 66.

25.  Fainsod, Merle, "Some Reflections on the Nature of the Regulatory Process," in C. J. Friedrich and E. S. Mason, eds. Public Policy, 1940.  Harvard University Press, Cambridge, Mass. (1940), pp. 297-323.

26.  ------, Cong. Rec., 51:376 (1914).

27.  FTC vs. Ruberoid Co., 343 U.S. 470, p. 473 (1952).

28.  U.S. Congress, Consumer Product Warranties and Federal Trade Commission Improvement Act, S. Rep. No. 92-269, (1971), p. 4-5.

29.  Acheson, E. and Tauber, M., "The Limits of FTC Power to Issue Consumer Protection Orders." George Washington Law Review 40:510 (1972).

30.  Senate Committee on Commerce, Hearings on S. 2246, S. 3092, S. 3201, before the Consumer Subcommittee, 91st Congress, 2nd Session, Ser. 48, pt. 1, p. 13 (1970).

31.  J. B. Williams Co. vs. FTC, 381 F. 2nd 884.

32. House Committee on Appropriations, Agriculture - Environmental and Consumer Protection Appropriations for 1973, 92nd Congress, 2nd Session, pp. 1059-1087.

33. Petition of Harrison Wellford and Theodore Siff on Pesticide Advertising before the FTC, July 1971.

34. Confidential interviews with congressional staff, 1972.

35. Whitten, Jaime, That We May Live. Princeton, (1966).

36. In the Matter of Union Carbide Corporation. FTC Proposed Complaint (November 1972).

37. Nader, Ralph; Adams, Aileen; et al., Petition for Trade Regulation Rule Proceeding and Issuance of Enforcement Policies.

38. Senate Committee on Commerce, Staff Report to the Federal Trade Commission on the Ad Substantiation Program, (July 31, 1972).

39. In the Matter of American Home Products Corporation and Cunningham and Walsh, Inc. FTC Complaint (May 19, 1972), p. 4.

40. Interview with Robert Pitofsky, September 1972.

41. Washington Post, January 7, 1972.

42. Dennison, David, "Modern Advertising and the FTC," remarks to Annual Meeting of the Association of National Advertisers (November 27, 1972).

43. Confidential interview.

44. National Journal July 15, 1972, p. 1155.

45. The last time the FTC developed a report charging major oil companies with illegal conspiracies to restrain trade, the three top economists who prepared the report were dismissed in an "economy" move. New York Times Sept. 3, 1953, p. 31.

46. Jones, Commissioner Mary Gardiner, Address to the Sixth Biennial World Conference of the International Organization of Consumer Unions, June 29, 1970.

47.  <u>1970</u> <u>FTC</u> <u>Annual</u> <u>Report</u>; <u>1961</u> <u>FTC</u> <u>Annual</u> <u>Report</u>.

48.  Cary, William L., <u>Politics</u> <u>and</u> <u>the</u> <u>Regulatory</u> <u>Agencies</u>,
McGraw Hill, New York (1967), p. 8.

49.  Auerback, Carl, "The Federal Trade Commission." <u>Minn</u>. <u>L</u>.
<u>Rev</u>.  48:393 (1964).

50.  FTC News Release, <u>Highlights</u> <u>of</u> <u>1970</u>, p. 2.

51.  <u>National</u> <u>Journal</u> July 15, 1972, pp. 1152-1153.

52.  ------, January 31, 1971, p. 218.

53.  Hearings, <u>Agriculture</u> - <u>Environmental</u> <u>and</u> <u>Consumer</u>
<u>Protection</u> <u>Appropriations</u> <u>for</u> <u>1974</u>.  Committee on
Appropriations, House of Representatives, 93rd Congress, 1st
Session (1973).